T0323103

# COACHING & MENTORING

Sara Miller McCune founded SAGE Publishing in 1965 to support the dissemination of usable knowledge and educate a global community. SAGE publishes more than 1000 journals and over 800 new books each year, spanning a wide range of subject areas. Our growing selection of library products includes archives, data, case studies and video. SAGE remains majority owned by our founder and after her lifetime will become owned by a charitable trust that secures the company's continued independence.

Los Angeles | London | New Delhi | Singapore | Washington DC | Melbourne

# 4TH EDITION

# COACHING & MENTORING

## THEORY AND PRACTICE

BOB GARVEY

PAUL STOKES

$SAGE

Los Angeles | London | New Delhi
Singapore | Washington DC | Melbourne

Los Angeles | London | New Delhi
Singapore | Washington DC | Melbourne

SAGE Publications Ltd
1 Oliver's Yard
55 City Road
London EC1Y 1SP

SAGE Publications Inc.
2455 Teller Road
Thousand Oaks, California 91320

SAGE Publications India Pvt Ltd
B 1/I 1 Mohan Cooperative Industrial Area
Mathura Road
New Delhi 110 044

SAGE Publications Asia-Pacific Pte Ltd
3 Church Street
#10-04 Samsung Hub
Singapore 049483

Editor: Ruth Stitt
Assistant editor: Jessica Moran
Editorial assistant, digital: Katherine Payne
Production editor: Tanya Szwarnowska
Senior project editor: Chris Marke
Copyeditor: Fern Bryant
Indexer: Melanie Gee
Marketing manager: Lucia Sweet
Cover design: Naomi Robinson
Typeset by: C&M Digitals (P) Ltd, Chennai, India
Printed in the UK

**Library of Congress Control Number: 2021934947**

**British Library Cataloguing in Publication data**

A catalogue record for this book is available from the British Library

ISBN 978-1-5297-4077-6
ISBN 978-1-5297-4076-9 (pbk)

At SAGE we take sustainability seriously. Most of our products are printed in the UK using responsibly sourced papers and boards. When we print overseas we ensure sustainable papers are used as measured by the PREPS grading system. We undertake an annual audit to monitor our sustainability.

# CONTENTS

# DETAILED CONTENTS

# LIST OF FIGURES AND TABLES

## FIGURES

## TABLES

# ABOUT THE AUTHORS

**Bob Garvey** works with a variety of people, either one-to-one or in groups. He is an internationally known keynote conference speaker, thought leader, educator and prolific writer. Bob is an honorary board member of the International Mentoring Association (IMA) and founding member of the EMCC (European Mentoring and Coaching Council). In 2014, the trade magazine *Coaching at Work* awarded him a 'Lifetime Achievement Award' for services to mentoring, and in 2018 he was 'Highly Commended' as an external coach/mentor by *Coaching at Work*. Bob is obsessed with coaching and mentoring!

**Paul Stokes** is a Principal Lecturer at Sheffield Hallam University. He is the Research Lead for the Department of Management within Sheffield Business School, as well as leading the MSc Coaching and Mentoring at the university. He is an experienced coach, mentor and supervisor as well as a designer and evaluator of many coaching and mentoring programmes within organizations, including his own. In 2016 he was awarded a PhD for his pioneering research into the skilled coachee.

# DEDICATIONS AND ACKNOWLEDGEMENTS

Bob Garvey dedicates this book to his late father, Arthur Garvey (1922–2018), and his uncle, the late Alan Garvey (1927–2006): *Thank you both for introducing me to and developing in me the capacity for argument.*

Paul Stokes thanks his family for all their support: *I would like to dedicate this version of the book to my partner, Jenny, and to my three daughters, Lowri, Savannah and Bobbie, all of whom receive a lot of unsolicited coaching and mentoring support! Thank you also to all those collaborators and students over the years who have contributed so much of the thinking here. This has been a challenging context within which to do this work, but I am proud of what we have achieved with it.*

We were both profoundly saddened to hear of the passing of our dear friend and colleague Professor David Megginson on 21 July 2021. David's original contributions to the earlier editions of this text were vital and critical to what we had to say about coaching and mentoring. His legacy in terms of the coaching and mentoring field more generally is immense and impossible to do justice to here. David was a scientist and artist, a poet, scholar, friend and thoroughly decent human being. Most of all, though, we will miss his presence and his kind, generous, quirky and very good company. Go well, David.

# ONLINE RESOURCES

Visit **https://study.sagepub.com/garvey4e** to access the following lecturer resources to support teaching:

## FOR LECTURERS

- A **Teaching Guide** providing tutor's notes and answers to key questions in the book

- **PowerPoint** slides to accompany each chapter, that can be downloaded and edited to suit your own teaching needs

# PRAISE FOR PREVIOUS EDITIONS

'A thought-provoking book which should be on the reading list for anybody studying coaching and mentoring.'

*Christopher McKechnie, Scotton Hall, HM Forces*

'It is very well researched and accessible for students who may potentially be at different stages in their studies. Educationally relevant themes are blended with practice and theory from other disciplines throughout this book which I'm sure will add further critical dimensions to students' views – this aspect I would recommend highly.'

*Christine Lewis, Professional Development, Edge Hill University*

'This is a book for those who want to think deeply about coaching and mentoring; it goes well beyond the "how-to-do-it" of many texts and challenges us to pay attention to the wider implications of what we are doing. The authors draw on many sources, always with a critical approach that invites us to think about how what has been written has been influenced by the perspectives and discourses of the time and culture.'

*Julie Hay, Nurturing Potential*

'A useful book to have to hand if you are involved in mentoring and coaching new staff and students in the workplace.'

*Stella Cosgrove, Workforce and Education Directorate, Lancashire Teaching Hospitals NHS Foundation Trust*

'Popular text up-to-date with new content and research, an ideal choice for those studying coaching and seeking an evidenced-based approach to the topic of coaching and mentoring.'

*Debra Cushen, Care and Education, University of Wales*

'For those who are already in leadership positions (and those aspiring) the links between leadership, coaching and mentoring are made clear. The case studies are varied and offer the chance for students to transfer knowledge and understanding to different work scenarios. This provides the strong synthesis of theory and practice that many professionals seek.'

*Bill Lowe, ITE CPD, Newman University*

# INTRODUCTION

This fourth edition of our book presented an interesting challenge. First, our long-time friend, colleague and co-author, David Megginson, for personal reasons was unable to work with us on this edition. The remaining authors agreed that David would still have a place in the fourth edition because he has always been such an integral part of our work and his presence in this new edition is evident. In the reviewed and updated chapters, which David originally contributed, we have tried to honour his contributions and adopted the methodologies he employed.

Second, we needed to update some data but, probably more importantly, we needed to update the previous book with new research and developments in practice. Some things inevitably remain the same but, such is the dynamic nature of coaching and mentoring, some have changed. For example, some new thoughts on the definitional issues and the hybridization of coaching and mentoring. Since the publication of the third edition, there has been and continues to be social, technological, legal, political and economic change around the world.

Thirdly, there has been the global pandemic of COVID-19. This has created more change for coaching and mentoring more quickly than any other influence. We consider the impacts and the changes brought by COVID in several chapters.

There has also been a constant push by professional associations, particularly in coaching, to influence the marketplace with policies and conditions of membership. We discuss these issues where relevant.

Every chapter has been reviewed; some have been more or less rewritten while others have had a light run over with the vacuum cleaner!

A brief word on references and case studies. We have updated the references and case studies where appropriate, but we have also retained some older references and cases because of their relevance and on the basis that good thoughts rarely age!

The full economic impact of COVID has yet to be counted but across the world there is increased economic inflation and unemployment. The ILO's 'World Employment and Social Outlook' report (2021) notes that poverty is still a major issue in the world economy; one in five of all under 25-year-olds across the globe are not in employment and these people are not developing the skills necessary to help them out of this situation. Coaching and mentoring could play an increasing role in helping people to find work, start their own business or address skills shortages. Organizations like Youth Business International (YBI) (http://www.youthbusiness.org/), which supports underserved young entrepreneurs to start, grow and sustain their businesses, reports that there are 66 million young people who are unemployed around the world. These businesses help to create jobs, build communities and change lives. Since 2014, YBI has supported and continues to support 123,114 young people to start a business in 46 different countries. These businesses are actively supported by around 14,000 volunteer mentors. Various issues relating to Youth Business International appear in Chapters 9, 10 and 16.

Coaching and mentoring activities have continued to develop, evolve and expand at a phenomenal rate in the UK (see CIPD Learning and Skills at Work: Mind the gap: Time for learning in the UK, 2020a and the CIPD Resourcing and Talent Planning Survey, 2020b). There is interest in the different forms of coaching and mentoring across all sectors of society around the globe. One change in the coaching industry is the expanded use of internal coaches. Another change is the growing awareness that the various professional bodies' competence frameworks are increasingly being questioned (see Nadeem et al., 2021).

Coaching and mentoring are used for a variety of purposes, including to:

- develop managers and leaders
- support induction and role changes
- fast-track people into senior positions
- reduce stress
- support change
- gain employment for the long-term unemployed
- reduce crime and drug-taking
- develop and foster independence
- increase school attendance and support anti-bullying policies in schools
- improve performance in whatever context in which coaching and mentoring are employed
- support talent management
- improve skills and transfer knowledge
- support equal opportunities policies and diversity
- aid social integration
- start and grow small and medium-sized enterprises (SMEs)
- support retention strategies.

The items on this list, although incomplete, have one thing in common – change and transition. This may mean changes of thinking, behaviour, attitudes or performance. Whatever the case or the context, all these applications of seemingly the same processes raise many issues and questions about how mentoring and coaching are understood and perceived by those who engage in practice.

There is still much debate about the similarities and differences between coaching and mentoring practice, and we address these in Chapter 1 by considering the concept of 'discourses' in coaching and mentoring as well as a paper from Stokes et al. (2020), which rethinks the dimensions framework we have employed since the first edition. Whatever they are called, this book is all about coaching and mentoring in a wide range of settings for a wide range of purposes.

We, the authors, are *for* coaching and mentoring but that does not mean that we are partial or partisan. This book, which draws on the literature, extensive research, our own experience as coaches, mentors, coachees, mentees, practice supervisors, scheme designers and evaluators and academics, is accessible, academic, critical and practical. It offers both challenge and support to all who are interested in mentoring and coaching. The challenge is found in our critical perspective on coaching and mentoring in theory and practice, and the support is in the theoretical underpinning and positive practical experiences we present. We have sought to write it in the spirit of coaching and mentoring by writing it in what we call the 'coaching and mentoring way'. This is our philosophical position and includes qualities of:

- mutual respect and valuing differences of viewpoint
- acknowledgement of our influences
- listening and sharing.

We hope that when we are critical, it is respectful.

Over the years of working together it is fair to say that we remain obsessed with coaching and mentoring! We engage with the processes and skills in our daily work and we help others from different sectors of society to do the same. We work with individuals, large and small businesses, the public sector and the voluntary sector, so we have experienced first-hand the power of coaching and mentoring to transform lives and working practices. We also read and write about coaching and mentoring; we believe that there is much still to learn about mentoring and coaching and, in some ways, we set an agenda here for learning about this fascinating and developing world.

## ORGANIZATION OF THE BOOK

The book has four parts; the chapters within the parts have a different emphasis on theory and practice. As academic practitioners, we believe that this blending is important and reflects the title of the book, which links the theoretical with the practical. We agree with the old adage that there is nothing as practical as a good theory. All chapters have a critical element.

## NEW PEDAGOGIC ELEMENTS

We have introduced some new pedagogic elements into the book. These include some new case studies, activities, reflective questions and an annotated 'further reading' section at the end of each chapter. All chapters end with a 'Future Direction' section. There are not case studies in every chapter because we have tried to use different approaches depending on the nature of the subject we are writing about. We are developing an accompanying set of resources with SAGE that will also be available online.

Chapters 16 and 17 are two chapters that relate to each other. In this edition we have collected case examples from the USA, Africa, Saudi Arabia, Hong Kong, Russia, Australia, South America, the Czech Republic and Sri Lanka. These commentaries, written by academic practitioners located within these places in the world, present their views of the state of play with coaching and mentoring in their location. We then discuss these by considering how far practices are converging in line with a normalizing view and how far practices are divergent, reflecting local and cultural attitudes, or how far they are 'cross-vergent' or 'glocal', i.e. hybrid pick-and-mix. We consider the question of how far professional bodies could be simply following the same patterns as the neofeudalistic tendencies of globalized business where freedom of activity is for the few and oppression through legislation and regulation is for the many. Thus we move away from the dominant discourse of psychology in coaching and mentoring towards a sociological, philosophical and economic perspective. Chapter 17 develops our original theoretical framework for coaching and mentoring found in the first and second editions and considers the political, economic, social, technical, legal and environmental issues which impact on their practice.

We have deliberately avoided including learning outcomes at the start of each chapter. As we discuss in Chapter 6, pre-specified learning outcomes are the product of a 'content' or 'linear-based' approach to learning. This, in our view, has little value in coaching and mentoring where the learning is often emergent. Further, this book is aimed at postgraduate and post-experience learners and we would not presume to predict what might be learned as a result of reading this book. We do invite readers to 'mark' their own learning as a result of the various stimuli we offer, either deliberately or inadvertently!

## THE METHODOLOGIES

Each chapter has a methodology section. At times, we use this to outline the approach taken to gathering the information needed to produce any one chapter, or we present the methodology as the way the chapter is constructed.

## PART 1: AN INTRODUCTION TO COACHING AND MENTORING

Part 1 offers an introduction to coaching and mentoring. It starts with the historical development of coaching and mentoring, moves through current issues in coaching and mentoring research, and goes on to look at the broad issue of organizational cultures which support coaching and mentoring. In Part 1, we look at the issues of scheme design and evaluation and consider the widely different models of coaching and mentoring found in today's society. Finally, we look at the power of conversational learning.

Chapter 1 is about the development of the meaning of the terms 'mentoring' and 'coaching' and is drawn from substantial historical research. It shows how coaching and mentoring have been applied in practice and demonstrates how the meaning of the terms has changed over history through practice. It helps to explain the wide discrepancies in meaning found in current practice and concludes with a way forward. Many of the themes identified in the historical research and in the sections on current practice are developed in later chapters in the book. A new addition to this chapter is based on Stokes et al. (2020) and develops the dimensions framework previously presented in other editions. This new look at dimensions to help understand the similarities and differences between mentoring and coaching is looking more like a shift towards a hybrid model of coaching and mentoring. Stelter (2019) goes further in suggesting that these are forms of facilitating dialogue.

Chapter 2 is completely rewritten. It honours previous editions and takes a critical look at research practice in coaching and mentoring. It presents some opposing but fundamental philosophical positions and links these to research practice. We raise the question of 'what is truth?' in research. The chapter suggests that there are various 'archetypes' of research practice in coaching and mentoring research. These archetypes are aimed at different audiences and have different purposes in mind. There is a cautionary note here for researchers, practitioners and scheme designers that research findings need to be understood from the 'gaze' of the writer. No one method is better than the other, but the chapter suggests that a blended approach offers the most potential to inform all users of research material.

Chapter 3 looks at creating or developing coaching and mentoring cultures and offers both theoretical and practical insights into the development of environments supportive of coaching and mentoring. The chapter introduces models of mentoring and coaching culture while outlining strategies and practices for leaders, managers and specialist coaches and mentors to widen the impact of what they do. The chapter raises some challenging questions and issues for organizations wishing to develop coaching and mentoring. There is not 'one best way' but rather many choices in specific contexts.

Chapter 4 offers insights into scheme design and evaluation. It includes a new case study. There are many resonances in this chapter with earlier chapters in the book. The chapter's focus is on practitioners and places more emphasis on the pragmatic issues of scheme design and evaluation that confront those who organize formal coaching and mentoring schemes in an organizational context. The chapter draws on the authors' work and experience and reports the work of others. We also attempt to bridge theory and practice and argue that positivistic thinking tends to dominate organizational life, and this is a further example of the notion of 'misplaced concreteness' first introduced in Chapter 1.

Chapter 5 looks at the wide variety and range of models and perspectives in coaching and mentoring. It aims to reflect the breadth and depth of the field, and to explore some of the assumptions that underpin these various approaches and models. The chapter captures the essence of each approach using selected references. It raises many challenging questions about the theory and practice of mentoring and coaching. In this fourth edition, we have also included three updated case examples. One is a new development in mentoring – self mentoring. The second reflects the increasing trend towards internal coaching schemes within organizations, and the third is an example of an inter-organizational model of coaching. We also take a slightly extended and critical look at the new emerging idea of team coaching.

Chapter 6 is about the power of one-to-one developmental dialogue. It explores the influence of the social context on learning; it discusses and compares the 'linear' view of learning with the 'non-linear' view. There are links in this chapter to the opposing views taken in research philosophy and mindset presented in Chapters 1, 2 and 4. We show that these viewpoints influence thinking and behaviour in practice. The chapter looks at the non-linear nature of coaching and mentoring conversations, presenting and analysing an example of a live conversation.

## PART 2: INFLUENCES ON COACHING AND MENTORING

In Part 2, we discuss the various influences on the form one-to-one development takes, in particular the influence of power, the development of 'learning networks', the use of technology and, finally, organizational issues such as purpose and goal orientation in coaching and mentoring. Part 2 covers a range of organizational and practice issues found in coaching and mentoring. The chapters take a critical look at the various influences on the forms coaching and mentoring take within an organizational setting.

Chapter 7 discusses the concept of power in coaching and mentoring. This is a key concept that permeates through all units of analysis in coaching and mentoring. Given that coaching and mentoring relationships are often located within organizational schemes or the wider community through various mentoring engagement schemes, it is necessary to subject them to an analysis of power. Coaching and mentoring are generally intended to enable some sort of exchange of knowledge, wisdom, and understanding between their participants, so inevitably power will be involved. Also, coaching and mentoring are often closely associated with transition, development and growth, so, again, it is inevitable that as people grow and develop (often at different rates and times), this will alter the power dynamics between them. It is therefore important to try to understand power and the extent of its impact.

Chapter 8 examines coaching and mentoring from the helpee's point of view. Up until this point in the book we have focused on the role that the helper – the mentor or coach – plays in coaching and mentoring. The analysis and fieldwork in Chapter 8 is based on Paul Stokes' PhD work. Here, we will examine the role of the coachee as described in the coaching literature and then use the field work to develop a new understanding of the coachee and the skills.

Chapter 9 considers the notion of coaching and mentoring networks. Coaching and mentoring conversations are social interactions facilitated in specific contexts and with a variety of purposes. This chapter explores the idea of multiple coaching and mentoring relationships in the context of the knowledge economy and the consequential implications for organizational structures and practices.

Chapter 10 has had a major review in light of the pandemic. It investigates the use of electronic media used to make social connections between people. This may include the use of email as well as dedicated coaching or mentoring software designed to facilitate developmental relationships. We examine the impact of these innovations on coaching and mentoring. This chapter has three new case studies – SOS Mentoring from Joerg Schoolman of YBI; Coaching in COVID by Gareth Owen from Save The Children; and Rapid Response Coaching from Auriel Majumdar, an independent coach.

Chapter 11 blends research, theory and practice. It examines some of the issues raised when introducing coaching or mentoring into organizations. It builds on the pragmatic findings of Chapter 3 on creating a coaching culture and on the theoretical considerations of Chapter 7 on power in organizations. We address some of these through the lens of 'goals'. We discuss the belief that setting goals seems to be a taken-for-granted assumption about good practice, particularly in coaching but also in mentoring. In this chapter, we look at alternative possibilities to goals and ground these in our own research as well as other perspectives that relate to our findings. Finally, we turn to the organizational implications of these issues and show how these implications illuminate a number of key organizational practices in the use of coaching and mentoring. This chapter is research-based.

## PART 3: CONTEMPORARY ISSUES IN COACHING AND MENTORING

Part 3 explores some of the contemporary debates in coaching and mentoring. This includes the concept of practice supervision, diversity issues, standards and ethics.

Although, as has been shown in Chapter 1, mentoring and coaching have long histories as professional and fully developed activities they are still nascent. This section explores some contemporary debates that are influencing the development of coaching and mentoring. These debates could be viewed as tensions within the worlds of coaching and mentoring. They involve debates that are influenced by mindset, territory, power and control. There are no straightforward 'solutions' to these issues, but we suggest that the discussion and debate should be kept alive because this will eventually lead to the main themes of Chapter 13 – tolerance, acceptance and a recognition that diversity is healthy in the context of coaching and mentoring.

Chapter 12 discusses the issue of 'supervision' in coaching and mentoring. Supervision is a relatively new term in this area. We explore the reasons for the explosion of interest in supervision as well as examining the different approaches, functions and roles that supervision can play. Some argue that contemporary demands towards the professionalization of coaching and mentoring have created this need. Others, for example paying clients, are considering issues of quality control and competence. A further driver for supervision is the training or development of coaches and mentors. The chapter takes a critical look at the arguments.

Chapter 13 is about diversity and takes a critical perspective on the issue of diversity and its relationship to coaching and mentoring. It discusses the meaning of diversity and examines current philosophies and practices found in organizations. We present a new case example from Lianne Lyne, an independent coach, and the chapter ends with an activity.

In Chapter 14 we explore the question of ethics in coaching and mentoring. In doing so, we seek to uncover some of the dilemmas, challenges and questions that ethical practice raises for practitioners, as well as examining some key conceptual frameworks for understanding and interpreting ethical practice. At the end of the chapter, we draw some conclusions for the future.

Chapter 15 looks at the debates around competencies, standards and professionalization. It raises many questions and presents a comprehensive list of arguments for and against competencies in coaching and mentoring, standards of practice and professionalization.

## PART 4: TOWARDS A THEORY OF COACHING AND MENTORING

Part 4 draws together the themes discussed in the book and moves towards a theory of coaching and mentoring. It looks at emerging issues for coaching and mentoring and presents a view of developments in the US. We conclude with extrapolated views for the future development of coaching and mentoring drawn from the current emerging trends and patterns.

Chapter 16 offers views on the state of play in coaching and mentoring practice from a variety of international perspectives. This chapter is different from previous chapters as it acts as a critical springboard into the final chapter where we refine our developing theories of coaching and mentoring.

The discussion begins with a presentation of nine case studies. All have been updated and there is a new one from Sri Lanka. To our knowledge this is the first attempt to do this and, apart from survey data (see Bresser, 2009, 2013; Sherpa Coaching, 2016; ICF, (2016) Coaching Survey) little else is published on the subject of globalization in coaching and mentoring. The cases are not presented as research or research findings but rather as illustrative examples from practitioners and academics working in various international locations. However, from a narrative research point of view, we believe that these are 'authentic' descriptions and therefore have some legitimacy.

In Chapter 17 we move towards a meta-theory of coaching and mentoring. Like Western (2017), we are not proposing this as a comprehensive theory of coaching and mentoring but a heuristic device through which the reader can explore and question current understandings of coaching and mentoring and therefore conceive of new and different ways of engaging with its theory and practice. The heuristic will inevitably be partial and derived from the particular lenses through which we understand these practices. First, we engage in a discussion about the conclusions we have drawn from the preceding chapters in this book. This is then employed to expand upon the themes identified in the chapter's introduction. Following this, we bring together those insights into a heuristic which is represented in diagrammatic form to represent the key themes. The book concludes by bringing together some key issues for the future of coaching and mentoring.

# PART 1

## AN INTRODUCTION TO
## COACHING AND MENTORING

# 1

# THE MEANING OF COACHING AND MENTORING

## CHAPTER OVERVIEW

This chapter traces the historical discourses related to mentoring and coaching and relates them to a contemporary view on coaching and mentoring discourses (Western, 2012). It argues that the meanings associated with coaching and mentoring are changing and that new hybrid versions of coaching and mentoring are emerging in practice (Stelter, 2019; Stokes et al., 2020). The research in this chapter is drawn from a substantial number of historical and contemporary sources. The chapter helps to explain the wide discrepancies in meaning found in current practice. We argue that there are many dimensions that affect our understanding of the terms coaching and mentoring. These include the intended purpose of coaching or mentoring; the nature of the relationship between coach and coachee or mentor and mentee; the timeframe available and the skills employed in the facilitated conversation (Stokes et al., 2020). It also includes contextual factors such as the learning context, economic context, temporal context and sociocultural context (Stokes et al., 2020). We develop the themes identified here in later chapters in the book.

## INTRODUCTION

There is lively debate among academics and practitioners alike as to the meaning of the terms 'mentoring' and 'coaching'. This debate is fuelled and further confused by:

- variations in the application of mentoring and coaching
- the wide range of contexts in which coaching and mentoring activities take place
- the perceptions of various stakeholders as to the purpose of these conversations
- commercial, ethical and practical considerations.

In the mentoring and coaching literature, there are many descriptions and definitions. These differences raise a key question for those interested in definition: are mentoring and coaching distinctive and separate activities or are they essentially similar in nature?

In the coaching and mentoring worlds, there are examples of distinct 'camps' and in some cases these camps are almost tribal (see Gibb and Hill, 2006) in their disdain for one another. In the book *Making Coaching Work* (2005b: 15–17), Clutterbuck and Megginson present a range of quotes listed as 'coaches on coaching', 'mentors on mentoring', 'mentors on coaching' and 'coaches on mentoring'. Each writer positions their own specific understanding of either coaching or mentoring as distinctive and different, and although this practice seems to be changing, there are still some misunderstandings between those who are *for* coaching and those who are *for* mentoring.

There is an explanation for the discrepancies and the crude positioning of different viewpoints, and this chapter seeks to develop this explanation through an examination of a range of literature on mentoring and coaching.

## METHODOLOGY

We base this chapter on extensive and rigorous literature searches and applied discourse analysis techniques to aid our interpretations. These include close scrutiny of texts by taking into account, as far as is possible, the contexts and prevailing discourses extant at the time in which the written accounts were made. We do not seek a justified or 'proved' position here but present a descriptive account of our findings from a range of discourse positions.

Overall, it seems that the meanings of both coaching and mentoring have changed in use over time. While there has been, as the comments above suggest, some positioning, branding and differentiation in both historical and more recent writings, there also appears to be both a merging of the meanings of coaching and mentoring and a polarization of the various discourses which inform the writings (Stelter, 2019; Stokes et al., 2020). In this chapter, we employ Western's (2012) analysis of coaching and mentoring discourses.

## WHAT ARE DISCOURSES?

One way to think about discourses is through the idea of narratives. Bruner (1990) argued that 'folk wisdoms' or stories play a vital role in shaping human understanding of any social phenomenon.

As a social constructivist researcher, Bruner suggests that the meanings drawn from these 'folk wisdoms' and narratives are central to human psychology: 'The central concept of human psychology is meaning and the process and transactions involved with the construction of meaning' (1990: 32–3).

Bruner states that it is the surrounding culture and external environment, not biological factors, that shape human lives and minds. People do this by imposing the patterns inherent in their culture's symbolic systems, 'its language and discourse modes, the forms of logical and narrative explication, and the patterns of mutually dependent communal life' (1990: 33). Therefore, with social phenomena such as mentoring and coaching it is necessary to interpret language, symbols and myths in the environment in which they are displayed in order to explicate meaning: 'we shall be able to interpret meanings and meaning-making in a principled manner only in the degree to which we are able to specify the structure and coherence of the larger contexts in which specific meanings are created and transmitted' (1990: 64). Bruner believes that it is through narrative that 'folk wisdom' is communicated and that 'we take meaning from our historical pasts which gave shape to our culture and we distribute meaning through interpersonal dialogue' (1990: 77). Bruner's views, we believe, relate very strongly to coaching and mentoring in that, as this chapter shows, both are social constructions subject to social communication processes and therefore both are surrounded by and shaped by stories. However, Bruner does not use the terms coaching and mentoring in his writings.

Another way to understand discourses is that they are ways of talking about human experiences. They are not just talk but, as Webster (1980: 206) puts it, 'Language is the primary motor of a culture'. Language is also tied to power positions (see Layder, 1994) and therefore the language which makes up a discourse shapes behaviour. Hatch and Cunliffe (2013) argue that power 'is exercised through practices that arise in discourse to regulate what will be perceived as normal' (p. 43). Kroger and Wood (1998) would agree when they argue that discourses are about meanings and that people organize around shared meanings; they state, 'language is taken to be not simply a tool for description and a medium of communication (the conventional view), but as a social practice, as a way of doing things' (Wood and Kroger, 2000: 4).

In relation to coaching and mentoring, Western (2012) argues that there are, currently, four main discourses. These are:

- Soul Guide
- Psy Expert
- Managerial
- Network Coaching.

Western (2012) suggests that these discourses are found in a wide range of contexts – for example, coaching and mentoring sessions, the academic and practitioner literature – and that they can be observed in websites, blogs, training courses and conferences.

## WESTERN'S (2012) DISCOURSES

### Soul Guide

According to Western, this discourse is found in a range of social and historical settings. It is about working on the 'interior aspects of the self' (2012: 132). It is concerned:

with emotions [...] spiritual concerns, identity and relationships, the unconscious, the conscience, the human spirit, values and beliefs and the human and existential concerns such as how to live with meaning, what is the good life for this individual and how to journey towards it and how to face loss and ultimately how to face death. (Western, 2012: 132)

## Psy Expert

Garvey (2011) argues that the psychology discourse is one which is found in both mentoring and coaching but treated differently in each. Psychologists are now calling themselves 'coaching psychologists', are deeply influencing practice and are the main group calling for professionalization. As Western (2012: 158) notes, 'there is a growing movement in coaching towards psychology'. He argues that the Psy Expert discourse is a product of modernity, where the scientific or objectivist mindset dominates (see below on mindsets). As Zeus and Skiffington (2002: 10) assert, 'Coaching, like therapy, is clearly a psychological process.' In making this perhaps controversial statement, Zeus and Skiffington (2002) are locating themselves firmly within the Psy Expert discourse, and with such a strong assertion they are seeking to place psychology as a dominant discourse. This approach has a focus on performance (in its many guises) and emphasizes changes in behaviour and the improvement of skills.

Within mentoring, this discourse manifests very differently. Garvey (2011) argues that psychology is employed mostly within mentoring to theory build rather than inform practice.

## Managerial

Much coaching and mentoring activity takes place within organizational settings. Garvey and Williamson (2002) argue that a dominating discourse in organizations is managerial. This is a reductionist discourse which values simplicity, practicality and objectivity. Garvey and Williamson (2002) refer to it as the 'rational pragmatic' discourse.

Western (2012) argues that this discourse is absorbed by a coach (or mentor) so that his or her 'thinking and practice of coaching become infused and underpinned by the logic of managerialism' (p. 178). He argues that this is changing as new business models develop and that managerialism, whilst bringing gains, also creates difficulties, the main one being the obsessive desire to measure. Western (2012: 187) argues that if the Soul Guide and the Psy Expert discourses work with the 'inner self and outer self', the Managerial discourse is more about the 'person-in-role' and is concerned with performance within that role.

## Network Coaching

In Chapter 8, we argue that coaching and mentoring are not necessarily one-to-one relationships any longer and that a learning and developmentally aware learner may have a network of supportive, challenging and development relationships. This idea of a network is discussed in the mentoring literature – for example, Scandura et al. (1996); Garvey and Alred (2001);

Higgins and Kram (2001); Chandler and Kram (2005); and Bozionelos and Wang (2006). Western (2012) argues that this is the new and emerging form of coaching. The network refers to the complex web of relationships and connections an individual may have within their new and emerging interconnected and interdependent world. He states that, 'Much of coaching (like much of management thinking) is in denial, repeating what we know, and looking for simplistic solutions rather than face complexity and change' (Western, 2012: 194).

This position recognizes that an individual in an organization is in a 'system', and this notion is spawning new business forms. These forms mostly employ technology, and the business focus strives to make a social contribution that is sustainable and ethical. At the time of writing, the majority of the world was in 'lockdown' due to the deadly and highly contagious virus COVID-19. One effect of this 'lockdown' was the rapid acceleration of the use of technology as a main way to continue business activity. It is likely that business activity will be changed permanently through the application of technology (see Chapter 10). Western's (2012) argument that emerging new business forms will require a new type of leadership which is distributed throughout the system is now a reality. The ways of the world are changing and changing fast! The implications for coaching and mentoring are yet to be realized, but the network coach or mentor may play a major role in helping to facilitate this new way of working to develop leadership capability across the system by helping to make and extend social connections and highlight social influence.

In the next section of this chapter, we track the history of mentoring and coaching and apply Western's (2012) discourses to our findings.

## THE HISTORICAL DISCOURSE ON MENTORING

### Homer

The first mention of mentoring in literature was about 3,000 years ago. The original mentor was a friend and adviser of Telemachus, Odysseus's son, in Homer's epic poem *The Odyssey* (see Lattimore, 1965, for a modern translation). The Indo-European root 'men' means 'to think', and in ancient Greek the word 'mentor' means adviser. So, mentor is an adviser of thought.

Within Homer, there are many confusing and contradictory events. Some writers have drawn selectively on them in order to make a point; for example, the violence of the original story is often glossed over (see Garvey and Megginson, 2004) and not incorporated into the modern interpretation; the social norms and context of the day are inadequately explored and some (Harquail and Blake, 1993; Colley, 2002) raise the confusing gender issues found in the original story. Others (see, for example, Whitmore, 2002) suggest that the Odyssey implies a directive approach to mentoring, but other interpretations (see Anderson and Lucasse Shannon, 1995 [1988]; Gibb and Megginson, 1993; Tickle, 1993; Garvey, 1994b; Brounstein, 2000; Starr, 2014) position mentoring within a developmental, almost Soul Guide discourse (Western, 2012) which emphasizes the caring, supportive, experiential learning, challenge and nondirective wisdom within the mentoring process. However, these interpretations of the ancient poem are made in the context of today to suit the modern discourse of a Soul Guide learning and development orientation. They bear little resemblance to the context of the narrative of the ancient times. Garvey (2016) refers to this way of interpreting the old poem as the 'old as the hills' argument which aims to give historical credibility to mentoring. However, taking into account the context of the times, an alternative reading of mentoring activity in Homer is perhaps less appealing to modern readers.

The story tells us that Odysseus's palace was besieged by suitors vying for Queen Penelope's attention with the intent of marriage and the acquisition of Odysseus's wealth and power. Colley (2002) interprets this as Mentor's failure. He left the royal household in chaos (Colley, 2002), and Roberts (1999: 19) suggests that Mentor was not the 'counsellor, teacher, nurturer, protector, advisor and role model' as presented in much modern literature on mentoring; in fact, he was 'little more than an old friend of King Odysseus [...] quite simply, Homer's Mentor did not mentor'.

Zeus, being concerned for the strategic importance of the kingdom of Ithaca, sent his daughter Athene to recover the situation. As goddess of wisdom and strategic warfare, she took Mentor's form to take control of the situation.

Ancient Greek society was based on the subjugation of women through dominance. It was a society riven with hierarchy, paternalism, macho violence and control, and Colley (2002) claims that Athene was born from Zeus's head and therefore she was the 'embodiment of male rationality' (Colley, 2002: 250). In the context of ancient Greece, this rationality assumed the social norms of male dominance and aggression. Certainly, Athene was not the typical ancient Greek passive woman. She performed key tasks of 'advising, role modelling, advocating, raising the young man's self-esteem' (2002: 250), devoid of the emotional attachment associated with a woman in ancient Greece, and, at the end of the story, with its violence, vengefulness and bloody aggression, she plays her part in protecting Odysseus and Telemachus from harm – not the nondirective and supportive mentor presented by Gibb and Megginson (1993).

What we have, using this alternative interpretation, is a managerial discourse at work. Zeus recognized Ithaca's strategic significance and needed it to be maintained through the leadership development of Telemachus. He sent his best asset, Athene, to do this job of work and salvage the failing situation. Athene, being goddess of wisdom (arguably, male wisdom) and strategy, was the ideal choice. While development did happen successfully in the original story, the purpose to which the development was put, i.e. the violent restoration of the kingdom and brutal murder of the suitors and the woman in the court, is, to the modern way of thinking, simply wrong. So, where is the version of Mentor that not only demonstrates successful learning and development but also has a virtuous purpose? The answer may lie in 18th-century Europe.

## EIGHTEENTH-CENTURY WRITINGS ON MENTORING

Fénelon (1651–1715), Archbishop of Cambrai and, later, tutor to Louis XIV's heir, in his seminal work *Les Aventures de Télémaque* (see Riley, 1994, for a modern translation), developed the mentoring theme of *The Odyssey*. It is a case history of human development and demonstrates that life's events are potential learning experiences. Fénelon shows us that the activity of observing others provides both positive and negative learning opportunities. He suggests that prearranged or chance happenings, if fully explored with the support and guidance of a mentor, provide opportunities for the learner to acquire a high-level understanding of 'the ways of the world' very quickly. This is perhaps the 'Soul Guide' version of mentoring that writers are seeking to find in Homer.

Eighteenth-century France viewed Fénelon's work as a political manifesto presenting an ideal political system based on the paradox of a monarchy-led republic. There was a clear focus on the development and education of leaders – something with which both mentoring and coaching are associated today. Fénelon implied that leadership could be developed through guided experience. Louis XIV saw this as a challenge to the divine right of kings and Fénelon was banished to Cambrai without financial support. However, his book became a bestseller in France and England.

*Les Aventures de Télémaque* appears again in France in Rousseau's educational treatise *Emile* (1762). Rousseau, probably the founder of the notion of 'experiential learning', was profoundly influenced by Fénelon's ideas on development. He focused on dialogue as an important element in learning and clearly stated that the ideal class size for education was one-to-one! In his book *Emile*, Telemachus becomes a model, perhaps a metaphor for learning, growth and social development. The central character, Emile, is given a copy of *Les Aventures de Télémaque* as a guide to his developmental journey.

In Fénelon we discover, through the narrative, descriptions of the benefits, characteristics and skills of mentoring. The references following these statements are taken from contemporary literature. The first reference is from the coaching literature and the second is from the mentoring literature. These serve to suggest that there are links to Fénelon's work in the current understanding of both mentoring and coaching.

These include:

- Mentors use reflective questions (Hallett, 1997; Garvey and Alred, 2000).
- Mentors support and help to remove the 'fear of failure' by building confidence (Ellinger et al., 2005; Megginson et al., 2006).
- A mentor is assertive and calm in the face of adversity (Bozionelos and Bozionelos, 2010; Wenson, 2010).
- A mentor is confident and self-aware (Nelson and Quick, 1985; Byrne, 2005).
- A mentor has charismatic leadership abilities (Godshalk and Sosik, 2000; Goldsmith, 2006).
- Role modelling goes on in mentoring (Robertson, 2005; Fracaro, 2006).
- Mentoring involves experiential learning (Kellar et al., 1995; Salimbene et al., 2005).
- A mentor is inspirational (Nankivell and Shoolbred, 1997; Vermaak and Weggeman, 1999).
- Trust is essential (Connor, 1994; Bluckert, 2005).

Further early writings on mentoring can be found in the work of Louis Antonine de Caraccioli (1723–1803). As Engstrom (2005) noted, Caraccioli wrote *Le veritable mentor ou L'education de la noblesse* in 1759 and it was translated into English in 1760 to become *The True Mentor, or an Essay on the Education of Young People in Fashion*. This work describes mentoring mainly from the perspective of the mentor. Caraccioli acknowledges the influence of Fénelon's work on his own. Caraccioli writes: 'we stand in need of academics to form the heart at the same time that they enrich the mind' (1760: vii). Caraccioli is also interested in the therapeutic effects of mentoring conversations when he says 'Melancholy, so common a complaint with the most voluptuous, has no effect on the man who possesses reflection' (vs 35, 88). This is a very interesting pre-modern psychology talking therapy observation, and perhaps it offers a hint of some Psy Expert with Soul Guide discourse (Western, 2012) entering into the mentoring world.

The term 'Mentor' was used in the English language in 1750 (*Oxford Reference Online*, 2006a) by Lord Chesterfield (published 1838) in a letter to his son (8 March 1750, letter number CVII) to describe a developmental process:

> These are resolutions which you must form, and steadily execute for yourself, whenever you lose the friendly care and assistance of your Mentor. In the meantime, make a greedy use of him; exhaust him, if you can, of all his knowledge; and get the prophet's mantle from him, before he is taken away himself.

Later, Lord Byron (1788–1824) used the term 'Mentor' in his poems *The Curse of Minerva* – 'to that Mentor bends' (Byron, 1821) and *Childe Harold's Pilgrimage* – 'Stern Mentor urg'd from high to yonder tide' (Byron, 1829), a reference to Homer where Mentor encourages Telemachus to jump from a cliff into the sea to escape his enemies, and in *The Island* Byron refers to the sea as 'the only mentor of his youth' (Byron, 1843). It is interesting to note Byron's three descriptions of mentor as 'bending', 'stern' and 'unique', as well as Chesterfield's 'friendly'.

Two volumes of the publication *The Female Mentor* appear in 1793 with a third volume in 1796. These works are recordings of conversations about topics of interest among a group of women referred to as 'the society'. The author, Honoria, identifies and describes the characteristics of the female mentor, not as the substance of the book but rather as a commentary and series of asides made throughout the volumes. The introduction to Volume 1 gives the reader the purpose of the books: 'If the following conversations should afford you some amusement, and if you should think them calculated to lead the youthful and unbiased mind in the ways of virtue, I shall feel highly gratified' (1793, Vol. 1: i). The mentor, Amanda, thanked Fénelon in the introduction for 'showing us the way'. His approach to education and life seemed to have been a model for 'the society'. The discussions in the books are broad and draw on, for example, the philosophy of ancient Egypt, Christianity, Greek civilization, comparative religion and ideas on nature. There are also discussions about famous women as positive role models, for example 'Anne Boleyn, Queen Consort of Henry Eighth', and a chapter 'On Learned Ladies'.

There are resonances here with Western's (2012) Soul Guide discourse.


## Caraccioli's mentoring model

We have linked Caraccioli's model of mentoring to modern literature using the same approach as outlined for the Fénelon contribution above. In Caraccioli, a mentor:

- expresses wisdom (Garvey et al., 1996; Bluckert, 2005)
- has self-knowledge leading to the enhanced knowledge of others (Nelson and Quick, 1985; Byrne, 2005)
- builds rapport and establishes trust (Tabbron et al., 1997; Giglio et al., 1998)
- is empathetic and inspirational (Giglio et al., 1998; Hansford and Ehrich, 2006)
- is sought out rather than seeks pupils (mentees/coachees) (Garvey and Galloway, 2002; Jones et al., 2006)
- has a sense of goodness based on deep religious values (no reference found in modern coaching literature; Lantos, 1999)
- understands the cultural climate of the pupil (coachee/mentee) (Johnson et al., 1999; Lloyd and Rosinski, 2005)

- prefers the positive and distinguishing truth from falsehood (Garvey et al., 1996; Murray, 2004)
- acts from the principle of conscience and not self-interest (no direct reference could be found in modern coaching literature to this quality of the coach – the closest is 'person centredness' found in Appelbaum et al., 1994; Bluckert, 2005)
- does not deal with trifles (Garvey et al., 1996; Giglio et al., 1998)

- draws on experiences (Kellar et al., 1995; Salimbene et al., 2005)
- helps to direct attention and assists in making decisions (Brunner, 1998; Pegg, 1999)
- encourages varied reading and discussing of literature (not mentioned in either discourse)
- develops and encourages reflection (Barnett, 1995; Ellinger and Bostrom, 1999).

Caraccioli provides a staged and progressive mentoring process model:

- observation, leading to...
- toleration, leading to...
- reprimands, leading to...

- correction, leading to...
- friendship, leading to...
- awareness.

Caraccioli's model aims to develop 'awareness' as the main outcome of mentoring and it offers four versions of mentoring within the same model: (1) Byron's 'bending mentor' who is 'tolerant'; (2) his 'stern mentor' who 'reprimands' and 'corrects'; (3) the 'friendly mentor' in Lord Chesterfield's letter to his son, who offers 'friendship'; and (4) an implied 'uniqueness' as alluded to in Byron.

Making allowances for historical changes in the meanings of words, this model also resonates with modern discourses on mentoring and coaching. For example, 'observation' can be an aspect of managerialist performance coaching and 'toleration' could be linked to a Soul Guide listening and acceptance, 'reprimand' with challenge, 'correction' with skills coaching, while 'friendship' is often discussed in mentoring literature and 'awareness' is discussed within both mentoring and coaching and may be part of the Soul Guide discourse outlined by Western (2012). And these dyadic relationships tend to be unique.

Caraccioli contributes two further concepts. The first is what we now call 'supervision'. Caraccioli's view is that a mentor needs an experienced and successful mentor as a guide. The second is a description of the phases of life:

- the torrid, which is our youth
- the temperate (the state of manhood)

- the frigid or old age where our imagination falters and our passions and desires subside.

Modern discourses on mentoring also refer to 'life cycles' and stages or phases of the relationship (see, for example, Kram, 1983; Alred et al., 1997) and these relate to elements of Western's (2012) Soul Guide discourse.

## The Honoria model of mentoring

In *The Female Mentor or Select Conversations* by Honoria (1793, 1796), we find further and similar descriptions of a female mentor, Amanda. Honoria was Amanda's daughter and she writes:

'she [Amanda] endeavoured to instil instruction into our tender minds by relating either moral or religious tales, and by entering into a course of reading, which while it inculcated a lesson, was calculated to engage our attention' (Vol. I, p. 6). *The Female Mentor* is an account of group mentoring. The group, started by Amanda, was originally for her own children, but word soon spread and the society developed to include other people's children and, later, adults. The society met fortnightly to support young women entering the world. Mentoring here is therefore associated with transition. Deep religious values underpin Amanda's work, and these volumes show that the female mentor had many of the qualities described by Fénelon and Caraccioli. The main approach for acquiring these qualities is through dialogue and role modelling. Linking to Western (2012), there are resonances here to the Soul Guide discourse.

**Table 1.1**  Historical timeline for mentoring

|  | Ancient Greece | Medieval Period | Eighteenth-Century Europe | Recent Times |
|---|---|---|---|---|
|  | Homer 1184?–1250? BC | 5th–15th century | Fénelon (1651–1715) | Levinson (1978) |
|  | The Odyssey | Knights/Squires | Rousseau (1712–1778) | Clutterbuck (1983) |
|  |  | Apprentices | Caraccioli (1723–1803) |  |
|  |  |  | Lord Chesterfield (1750) |  |
|  |  |  | Lord Byron (1788–1824) |  |
|  |  |  | Honoria (1793, 1796) |  |
| **Discourse** | Contradictions over meanings<br><br>Managerialist, Network<br><br>(see Garvey, 2017) | Managerialist, abusive/ exploitative (see Garvey, 2017) | Psy Expert, Soul Guide. | Managerialist, Psy Expert and Soul Guide<br><br>(see Garvey, 2011) |

## THE BEGINNINGS OF COACHING

In the modern coaching literature, Hughes (2003) suggests that the term coaching has its origins in ancient Greece with links to Socratic dialogue. De Haan (2008b: 1) also holds that coaching originates from ancient Greece: 'It is important to realize here that inspiring coaching conversations have been passed down from classical times.' His book has many classical images within it, as if to reinforce the link. Brunner (1998: 516) also makes this link when he asks the question: 'Would coaching thus be the modern version of the Socratic dialogue?' However, as this section demonstrates, the link to classical times is probably part of the 'old as the hills' discourse (Garvey, 2016) and is therefore associative rather than factual.

Starting with Socratic dialogue, Krohn (1998) argues that there are four indispensable components within Socratic dialogue.

## The concrete

By keeping with concrete experience, it becomes possible to gain insight by linking any statement with personal experience. In this way, the dialogue concerns the whole person.

## Full understanding between participants

This involves more than simple verbal agreement. All parties to the dialogue need to be clear about the meaning of what has just been said by testing it against their own concrete experience. Limiting beliefs need to be made conscious in order for them to be transcended.

## Adherence to a subsidiary question until it is answered

For a dialogue to achieve adherence, each participant in the dialogue needs to be committed to their work and develop self-confidence in the power of reason. This means: to be persistent in the face of challenge, and calm and humble enough to accept a different course in the dialogue in order to return to the subsidiary question. It is about honouring digressions while being persistent.

## Striving for consensus

This requires honesty, trust and faith in the examination of the thoughts of both self and others. These are the conditions of consensus and it is the striving that is important, not necessarily the consensus itself.

Clearly, there are many resonances in this explanation of Socratic dialogue with modern writings on both coaching and mentoring. However, there are no translations of Plato that we looked at that used the term 'coaching' or 'mentoring' and therefore modern writers like Brunner (1998), Hughes (2003) and de Haan (2008b) have made associative and not direct links to Socrates. Additionally, Socratic dialogue was about groups of people and not pairs as in coaching, and some (Goldman, 1984; Kimball, 1986; Stone, 1988) argue that the Socratic method is reductionist, a negative, competitive and corrosive methodology based on elimination; it creates and fosters cynicism rather than positive action. As a further challenge to Socratic dialogue, Nietzsche (1974: 206) states: 'One hears only those questions for which one is able to find answers', suggesting that the Socratic method does not account for the emotional, irrational or illogical behaviour of people.

Brunner (1998: 516), however, does offer an insightful comment on the meaning of coaching when he states: 'Coaching takes many forms, from technical counselling to the psychological domination that flirts with suggestion, for this is a domain devoid of any fixed deontology'. According to Brunner, then, coaching has multiple meanings and is subject to contextual variation. History supports this view.

*The Oxford Reference Online* (2006b) states that the earliest uses of the term 'coaching' in the English language can be traced to 1849 in Thackeray's novel *Pendennis*. This probable first use of the term is in fact a pun. Some university students are travelling back to university in a horse-drawn coach:

'I'm coaching there,' said the other, with a nod. 'What?' asked Pen, and in a tone of such wonder, that Foke burst out laughing, and said, 'He was blowed if he didn't think Pen was such a flat as not to know what coaching meant.' 'I'm come down with a coach from Oxford. A tutor, don't you see, old boy? He's coaching me, and some other men, for the little go.' (pp. 38-9)

Following this publication, the term 'coaching' seems to have been associated with supporting university students and academic attainment, for example Smedley (1866: 240–1) writes:

Besides the regular college tutor, I secured the assistance of what, in the slang of the day, we irreverently termed 'coach', which vehicle for the conveyance of heavy learning (from himself to his pupils), consisted of a gentleman, who but few years older than those whom he taught, possessed more practical knowledge, and a greater aptitude for the highest scientific research, than it had ever before been my fate to meet with combined in one individual. Under his able tuition I advanced rapidly, and reading men began to look upon me somewhat as a formidable rival.

It is not clear why the coach was regarded as irreverent; however, it is interesting that Smedley also uses and extends the pun of 'coach', but here is a direct historical link to rapid performance improvement and academic attainment through coaching which is a feature of both the Psy Expert and Managerial discourse today.

During the 19th century, the term coaching was used extensively in association with the development of boating and rowing skills as well as to enhance performance in these activities. For example, in 1867 the *Evening Standard*, on 14 February, reported on 'the crew being coached by Mr. F. Willan and Mr. G. Morrison, from the former gentleman's steamboat.' And in 1885 the *Manchester Guardian*, on 28 March, reported: 'A thoroughly clever coach was able to advise them from first to last. Under his careful tuition the crew have improved steadily.' Also associated with boating, in 1889 the *Daily News*, on 29 January, commented on the Oxford and Cambridge Boat Race: 'The President superintended the coaching from horseback.'

Additionally, another 19th-century link to sport (cricket) is in Harrison's (1887) *The Choice of Books and Other Literary Pieces*: 'To call in professional "coaches" to teach the defence of the wicket.'

Presumably referring to life skills, in 1887 Sir R.H. Roberts, in *In the Shires* (viii, 128), wrote: 'These young ladies, although ably coached by their mother...'.

There is comment in the 1866 edition of the *London Review*, on 18 August (180/1) (in *Oxford Reference Online*, 2006b), which says: 'The coach and the coachee can soothe their consciences by the reflection.' This is a very interesting reference for two reasons. First, it is probably the first recorded use of the term 'coachee' to describe the focus of the coach's activity. Second, the emphasis on reflection contrasts with the rather more didactic stance of the previous citations associated with coaching. This places this version of coaching within the Soul Guide discourse.

As far as we can discover, there are no works predating the 19th century devoted to exploring or describing the meaning and practice of coaching. We therefore conclude that coaching, relative to mentoring, is a more recent term.

**Table 1.2** Historical timeline for coaching

|  | Ancient Greece | 19th Century | Recent Times |
|---|---|---|---|
|  | Socrates 470-399 BC | Thackeray, 1849 | Gallwey, 1997a [1974] |
|  |  | Smedley, 1866 | Megginson and Boydell, 1979 |
|  |  | Evening Standard, 1867 | Whitmore, 1988 |
|  |  | Manchester Guardian, 1885 |  |
|  |  | London Review, 1866 |  |
|  |  | Harrison, 1887 |  |
|  |  | Roberts, 1887 |  |
|  |  | Daily News, 1889 |  |
| Discourses | Speculative association – Performative | Managerialist, Psy Expert, Performative, Soul Guide | Psy Expert, Managerialist, Performative |
|  | Competitive Managerialist |  | (see Garvey, 2011) |

# PULLING THE THREADS TOGETHER

 Case Study 1.1

Janet is a senior executive in a large business. She volunteered to take part in the organization's mentoring scheme and attended a one-day workshop. The workshop covered the purpose of the scheme, who it was aimed at and the basic skills necessary to facilitate a purposeful conversation. The scheme was aimed at developing leaders of the future and was part of the company's succession planning. Janet went on the company's mentoring list and a few weeks later she was approached by Gurbinder. Gurbinder was a manager in the company who had been identified through the assessment centre as having high potential. They met every six weeks for about one-and-a-half hours and discussed a range of issues – Gurbinder's ambitions, issues about his team, performance and relationship issues and his work-life balance. They got on very well.

Gurbinder said: 'We developed an excellent relationship and I felt able to discuss many things about my work and life with Janet. She was a good listener, she asked helpful questions and she helped me to find my own way to develop my leadership skills. Recently, I was confident enough to apply for a new position in the business. Janet helped me with my application and she even gave me a mock interview when I was shortlisted. While it was me that got the job, it was great to have been supported by my mentor – I learned a lot and now I feel able to lead my new team. Thanks, Janet!'

Janet said, 'Gurbinder was great to work with. He accepted my challenging questions and worked on aspects of his behaviour towards others. I am very confident that he has a great future ahead of him.'

The history of mentoring is very long. The core mentoring model, as described in the past and illustrated in Case Study 1.1, is one of a more mature and experienced individual engaging in a relationship with a younger and less experienced person. In the early accounts, the central purpose of mentoring is to assist the learner to integrate as a fully functioning person within the society they inhabit. In Case Study 1.1, Janet maintained this tradition by assisting Gurbinder to learn about himself, other people and the business. This remains one of the purposes (though not the only one) of modern mentoring. However, the mentor in current times may be a peer.

## Reflective Question

With reference to Case Study 1.1, how would you position this example in relation to Western's discourses?

In the historical writings on both coaching and mentoring, specific knowledge and skills are transferred from one to the other but with the intention of fostering independence. There is some confusion here in some of the modern literature. A typical example is in Rosinski (2003: 5), where he states:

> Although leaders can act as coaches, I have found that this role is often confused with mentoring. Coaches act as facilitators. Mentors give advice and expert recommendations. Coaches listen, ask questions, and enable coachees to discover for themselves what is right for them. Mentors talk about their own personal experience, assuming this is relevant for the mentees.

Later, he presents the issue of knowledge transfer in coaching and says:

> In my view coaches are also responsible for transferring knowledge. Coaches don't simply help resolve coachees' issues. They actually share their knowledge so that coachees can become better coaches. For example, the coach will briefly explain his frame of reference. (2003: 245)

In the first comment, 'mentor' is perhaps characterized as the 'stern mentor' giving advice or perhaps the 'reprimand' and 'corrective' model put forward by Caraccioli, with the coach represented as the 'friendly facilitator'. In the later comment, Rosinski presents the coach as a 'giver of advice' or, in his words, the 'knowledge transferer', but Rosinski reduces its significance by using the word 'briefly', almost as if 'briefly' makes the advice-giving less important. Further, it is difficult in our minds to distinguish between 'personal experience' and 'frame of reference'.

This example shows how modern writers on mentoring and coaching draw selectively on certain, albeit subliminal, dominant discourses and present them as versions of the truth. Bruner's (1990) point, made earlier in this chapter, about the importance of the social context to illuminate meaning seems to hold true. A coaching writer has a particular story to tell, as does a mentoring writer. Sadly, this is often at the expense of one over the other.

Fénelon, Caraccioli and Honoria offer similar, comprehensive and complementary descriptions of mentoring qualities, processes and skills and these attributes feature in modern writings on both mentoring and coaching. Many of the characteristics of a mentor outlined in these texts are desirable in current coaching practice.

Clearly, as shown in Case Studies 1.1 and 1.2 (below), coaching and mentoring share common skills, but it is noteworthy that the training for Janet to become a mentor was a one-day workshop, whereas David spent two years training to be a coach. Megginson et al. (2006), Klasen and Clutterbuck (2002) and Allen et al. (2006a, 2006b) state that training mentors for the role is essential; however, as Beech and Brockbank (1999) state, mentors are often senior people in organizations and they see themselves as experienced. As Garvey and Westlander (2013: 252) suggest, this can lead to a sense 'that "they know best" or are the "knowledge holders" by virtue of being senior'. Therefore, they may feel that they do not need any training. In coaching, the International Coach Federation (ICF) has an hours-based model of coach training (https:// coachingfederation.org/credentials-and-standards/acc-paths) with impressive numbers of hours advocated (see Chapter 14). The subject of training is raised again in Chapters 3, 4, 11, 12 and 13.

 — Case Study 1.2 ——————————————————————————

David is a professional executive coach. He spent two years studying for a Master's degree in coaching. One of his recent assignments was with Janet, a senior executive in a large business. Janet had recently taken on a new senior role in the business as well as the role of mentor. She asked David to assist her in understanding her new role and also took the opportunity to think through the mentoring role with David. David met with Janet around every six weeks for about one-and-a-half hours. David helped Janet think through concerns such as performance issues with her team, dealing with difficult meetings and work-life balance. They also discussed what was involved in mentoring: Janet was not only able to discuss issues with David, she was also able to observe his practice as a coach. She was struck by his ability to listen to what she had to say and then to probe and challenge her thinking. Janet read some books on coaching and mentoring but she found them to be somewhat contradictory. With the help of David, she decided to develop her own style and process and this seemed to be helpful for her mentee, Gurbinder. David and Janet established a good working relationship.

Janet said, 'David listened very well and asked challenging questions. These two activities combined helped me to develop confidence and good practical ways forward for me and my team. Coaching helped me to see a bigger picture on organizational issues, mentoring issues and it helped me set the tone for meetings.'

David said, 'Janet tells me that she is placing her team at the centre of her decision making when she is discussing performance with colleagues. By visualizing, she can then consider the impact of the decision being made. She set herself some very specific targets regarding her personal impact on others and her mentoring skills development.'

## Reflective Question

With reference to Case Study 1.2, how would you position this example in relation to Western's discourses?

---

The term coaching, when compared with the term mentoring, seems to have a more recent history in the English language. The 19th-century writings on coaching focus on performance and attainment, originally in an educational setting but also in sport and life. There is some historical evidence that coaching was also about reflection and the development of 'life skills'. Similar to the mentor, the coach is the skilled, more experienced or more knowledgeable person.

Coaching is still a dominant practice in sport, and the term is used extensively in business environments. This is either in the form of internal line manager coaches or with the use of external and paid coaches. These are often positioned as 'executive coaches'. Life coaching is almost exclusively linked to paid practice. Coaching is still associated with performance improvement of a specific kind related to a job role, but it is also increasingly linked to leadership development, transition and change and generally developing a focus for the future (see Chapter 5). We believe that coaching is adopting the historical descriptions of mentoring.

Mentoring activity is found in all sectors of society and includes both paid and voluntary activities. It is also associated with 'offline' partnerships where the mentor is not the mentee's line manager. The relationship elements are important and terms like friendship in the modern literature are generally viewed as acceptable and natural. Mentoring is more associated with 'voluntarism' than coaching, although we do accept that it would not be possible to compel anyone to be coached (see Chapter 5).

Modern concepts of coaching and mentoring also include explorations of the emotional self which resonate with Caraccioli's call, when writing about mentoring, to educate the 'mind' and the 'heart'. It is possible to detect elements of all four of Western's (2012) discourses within the variety of literature sited above.

## THE SAME AND DIFFERENT

It would seem then that, in practice, there is much common ground despite claims to the contrary found in modern writings. The Ridler reports of 2011, 2013 and 2016 provide some evidence that both coaching and mentoring are developing shared purposes. (Ridler and Co. is a senior-level executive coaching practice. Ridler and Co. regularly produces a survey-based report which analyses strategic trends in the use of coaching using data from organizational sponsors of coaching.) Ridler (2011) shows, under the heading of 'executive coaching', that coaching is employed to help people in transition and change. This chimes strongly with Levinson et al. (1978), who show that mentoring is also linked to helping people in transition. In Garvey (2012), both terms are employed within a mentoring for leadership programme. Garvey (2011) also argues that often in work settings, both are linked to learning and development and are often associated with performance improvement. Ridler (2011) also shows that coaching can be linked with talent management, as does Garvey (2012). In the *Ridler Survey* (2011), a coach may be viewed as a 'sounding board'. This function was identified for mentoring in Clutterbuck (1992). Further, the outcomes of mentoring, as articulated by Zey (1989) and Neilson and Eisenbach (2003), and coaching, as referred to in Ridler (2011) and de Haan (2008b), are dependent on the quality of the relationship, and they all suggest that personal chemistry is an important factor in determining a good-quality relationship.

Yet, despite the seemingly overlapping elements of coaching and mentoring, there persists an alternative viewpoint which seeks to differentiate them. This situation may be explained by considering the issue of 'mindset'.

The idea of 'organizational mindset' is an important one. Senge (1992) describes the concept as 'mental models' and Bettis and Prahalad (1995) call it 'the dominant logic'. They argue that mental models and dominant logic greatly influence both behaviour and thinking processes and have the potential to inhibit or enhance learning capabilities. For Senge, 'Mental models are deeply ingrained assumptions, generalizations or even pictures or images that influence how we understand the world and how we take action' (1992: 8).

According to Burrell and Morgan (1979), there are two opposing mindsets in social science – the 'objectivist' and the 'subjectivist'. The objectivist tradition favours cause and effect and positivistic methodologies and is akin to Western's (2012) Psy Expert and Managerial discourses, whereas the subjectivist tradition views social research from an anti-positivist perspective and favours a descriptive framework (see Chapter 2) which is more akin with Western's (2012) Soul Guide and Network Coach discourses.

Arguably, many decision makers, managers and funders who employ mentoring and coaching tend towards the objectivist perspective, consequently seeking cause and effect justifications to support expenditure on mentoring and coaching. This, we believe, has led to the general widespread commodification of coaching in particular as those who engage in its practice seek to demonstrate its impact in objectivist terms. Our experience shows that managers of some publicly funded schemes are also moving towards this belief (see Colley, 2003). The consequence of this shift is reflected in a change in the discourse, as we saw earlier in this chapter, in a movement away from using the language of the 'heart' towards the language of rationality or the 'brain'. Coaching and mentoring may suffer therefore from what Habermas (1974) refers to as 'misplaced concreteness'. Here, the social phenomenon is attributed with a hard, solid, rational reality as though it was a product of a factory and, in the case of mentoring and coaching, they are placed in the discourse as 'tools' of production. We also believe that either consciously or unconsciously, modern writers on coaching and mentoring make links to classical times to add credibility and substance to the coaching and mentoring phenomenon. However, there remains a core difference. Mentoring is often a voluntary activity and coaching is often a paid activity. Of course, this is not a definitive position but, as this book unfolds, voluntary versus professional is a developing theme.

Mentoring and coaching draw on different traditions of research. Coaching research, currently at least, tends to focus on outcomes and return-on-investment calculations. Mentoring research tends to look at the functional issues (see Chapter 2).

Schön offers insight into this: 'On the high ground, management problems lend themselves to solution through the application of research-based theory and technique. In the swampy lowland, messy confusing problems defy technical solution' (1987: 3).

Mentoring and coaching, in our view, despite the commodification, are quite firmly in the 'swampy lowlands' and, if there is to be enhanced understanding, we must continue to 'thickly describe' (Geertz, 1974) coaching and mentoring in as many different contexts as possible.

## DIMENSIONS

The Managerialist and Psy Expert traditions favour definition over description, but, by their very nature, definitions seek to simplify and condense. In this age of increasing complexity, simplification may have appeal. The range of contexts or domains in which mentoring and coaching are found suggests that definition alone cannot adequately reflect the complexity of meaning, and we argue that the meaning of coaching and mentoring is fundamentally determined by the social context.

A way forward is to view mentoring and coaching from a more subjectivist tradition which places the varying social conditions at the heart of any meaningful explanation of mentoring or coaching. This approach emphasizes description. The notion of 'dimensions' in mentoring was first put forward by Garvey (1994a) (see the first, second and third editions of this book) and here, Stokes et al. (2020) have employed this concept to help describe the variations of meaning found in coaching and mentoring. By looking at the dimensions of dyadic relationships in context, it is possible to consider their characteristics not as fixed positions but in relation to a moving and changing dynamic over time.

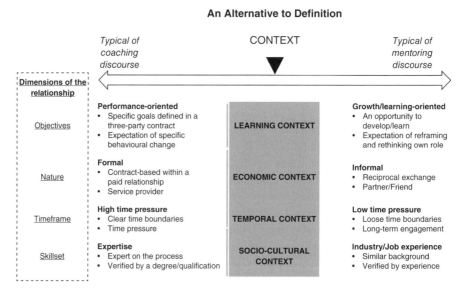

**Figure 1.1** Coaching and mentoring dimensions (Stokes et al., 2020: 2). Used with permission.

## Objectives

This dimension is a continuum between *performance orientation* and a developmental orientation (Figure 1.1).

> A performance-oriented relationship often relies on specific goals defined in a contract – typically a three-party contract in coaching with an explicit expectation of change. By contrast, a growth/learning orientation emphasizes development, both personal and professional, with objectives more broadly defined in terms of career/life goals. (Stokes et al., 2020)

It is possible to find elements of a performance orientation in the managerialist elements of the mentoring discourse (Appelbaum et al., 1994; Van Emmerik, 2008; Garvey, 2011) and elements of a development orientation within the coaching discourse (Gray, 2006; Garvey, 2011; St John-Brooks, 2013), but it is more common to link a performance-oriented relationship with the term 'coaching' and a developmental-orientation relationship with the term 'mentoring'.

Another dimension is related to the *nature* of the relationship within the dyad. Employing Garvey's (1994a) dimension of the formal and the informal, in this framework, formal relationships are generally contract based, with time boundaries. Often these relationships are paid ones. An informal relationship has looser boundaries. Here, relationships may start as a conversation between colleagues, and the nature of the relationship may be more reciprocal with both parties benefitting from the exchange. This relationship form is similar to Stelter's (2019) 'third generation of coaching', where a coach or a mentor is a facilitator of dialogue. There is evidence in both the mentoring and the coaching discourses of formal and time-bound relationships (Chao, 2009; Joo et al., 2012), but it is more likely that a paid relationship that involves the purchase of a distinctive skill set will be labelled 'coaching' and relationships that are often more informal and reciprocal without involving formal payment and contracting are labelled 'mentoring'.

A third dimension, as put forward by Stokes et al. (2020), is associated with *time*. Sometimes there may be an urgent or immediate need for the acquisition of new skills, knowledge or expertise to meet an organizational objective. This situation could be described as a *high time-pressure* environment. Some dyadic relationships may have a longer-term orientation and are therefore described as a *lower time-pressure* environment. These two points on the end of the continuum may both be described as coaching or mentoring; however, short-term interventions are often termed 'coaching' and longer-term relationships are often termed, 'mentoring' (Passmore, 2007).

The fourth dimension is about expertise versus job experience or industry knowledge. Some writers emphasize the knowledge, skill or expertise held by the coach or mentor. This may be some form of credentialing (see Chapter 15) held by the helper. Alternatively, experience in the industry or the job may be the main basis for other relationships. There are examples in both coaching and mentoring of a credentializing discourse. This is often related to the burgeoning numbers of professional bodies in the marketplace. These are much more likely to be linked to coaching and expertise that is associated with prior knowledge and industry expertise, popularly known as 'the university of life', than is more commonly associated with mentoring (Passmore, 2007).

Turning to the context in which coaching or mentoring may happen, Stokes et al. (2020) suggest four contextual dimensions. The first is the *learning* context. This is related to an assumption within an organizational context of how any learning and development activity should be conducted. This is often culturally embedded through the organizational narratives and history. This context will shape the focus taken on how relationships may be conducted and the emphasis placed on performance, objectives, goals, measurement, results or, alternatively, on growth and development.

The second contextual dimension is the *economic*. This dimension considers the internal and external financial position of the organization in relation to their impact on learning and development. This dimension contributes to the orientation within the organization towards the degree of formality or informality of the coaching or mentoring activity. If an organization is financially well resourced, it may invest heavily in learning and development activity. Within this context, there may be more opportunities for more formal contract-based relationships where skilled helpers are engaged to work with managers. In turn, this context may influence how the coach or mentor is perceived. On the one hand, they may be seen as a partner or even a friend to the organization or, on the other, they may simply be a disposable service provider.

The *temporal* context is associated with the organization's relationship with time. High time-pressure contexts are more likely to be linked to time-bounded coaching relationships, whereas a lower time-pressure context is more likely to be linked to a mentoring approach. It some cases, there may be a pressure to 'move quickly', but in other cases the organization also appreciates the need for longer-term development (see Garvey, 1995a). In this way, the *temporal* effect on coaching or mentoring may be mixed.

The final dimension outlined by Stokes et al. (2020) is the *sociocultural* context. According to Law (2013: 101), the relationship between the cultural context and coaching and mentoring is a complex one where there are:

> unique aspects of every intervention, as all behavior changes and value shifts are contextualized but not automatically transferable. Individuals always have the potential to transcend their cultural norms, however, as with the learning context dimension, the organization's sociocultural history will influence the extent to which process expertise is valued against content expertise. (Stokes et al., 2020: 9)

Where the 'university of life' concept is valued, a more traditional mentoring discourse will be selected. However, where technical expertise is valued, the discourse is more likely to be a traditional coaching discourse.

The dimensions framework presented here describes the type of coaching or mentoring within a particular setting without needing to resort to definitional positioning. It recognizes the dynamic and social nature of both coaching and mentoring.

## CONCLUSIONS

In conclusion, there can be no 'one best way' in mentoring and coaching and therefore no one definition. Practitioners draw on similar traditions of one-to-one developmental dialogue and position their particular brand according to the environment in which they operate. Both traditions draw on a similar range of skill sets and adapt them according to the nature and form of the dialogue in use within the environmental setting.

The question 'Whose agenda is it?' helps to highlight the similarities and the differences between the terms 'mentoring' and 'coaching', and we discuss this further in Chapter 7.

Another issue is the dynamic quality of the relationship between the two participants over time. The dimensions framework offers a way of agreeing on the nature and form of the relationship at the start, reviewing it over time or noticing the changes as they happen. In this way, both the similarities and the differences can be understood descriptively rather than by a positioning or tribal definition.

The meaning of coaching and mentoring is a changing dynamic, with certain elements remaining constant but with others changing (Stelter, 2019; Stokes et al., 2020), and it is this that explains the confusing array of definitions found in modern discourses and gives support to the four main discourses found in Western (2012). The debate is ongoing, and we wonder if the pursuit of definitional clarity is a 'dead end' activity!

To return, then, to the original question: are mentoring and coaching distinctive and separate activities or are they essentially similar in nature?

The above evidence suggests that although the original roots are different, both mentoring and coaching in the modern context selectively draw on a range of the same narratives or, in Bruner's (1990) term, 'folk wisdoms' to describe the activity. However, it seems that coaching and mentoring are essentially similar in nature and both draw on a humanistic philosophy (Parsloe and Leedham, 2009; Whitmore, 2009; Connor and Pokora, 2012; Western, 2012; Cox et al., 2014; Du Toit, 2014; Garvey et al., 2014).

 ## Future Direction

We acknowledge and accept that it is very unlikely that there will ever be widespread consensus as to the meaning of coaching and mentoring in any particular context. As Garvey suggests: 'in whatever the setting the terminology is used, there needs to be a common understanding of meaning within that setting' (2004: 8). This suggests that localized understanding is important, and perhaps that is the best that can be done in a social practice that has such variation of purpose, scope, contexts and applications. However, the terms 'coach mentor' and 'developmental dialogue' seem to be in use fairly commonly in the UK at least, and we wonder if this may be another way forward.

 ## Questions

- What discourse of coaching and mentoring do you relate to and how does the discourse you subscribe to influence practice?
- What evidence have you encountered that mentoring and coaching are either similar or different?
- What difference does payment make to the coaching or mentoring relationship?

**Further Reading**

For a critical account of the philosophical origins of mentoring, read: Chapter 2 in: Clutterbuck, D.A., Kochan, F.K., Lunsford, L.G., Smith, B., Dominguez, N. and Haddock-Millar, J. (eds) (2017) *The SAGE Handbook of Mentoring*. London: SAGE; also, Chapter 1 in: Gray, D.E., Garvey, B. and Lane, D.A. (2016) *A Critical Introduction to Coaching and Mentoring*. London: SAGE.

For an interesting account of the 'self-help' and therapeutic origins of coaching, read: Wildflower, L. (2013) *The Hidden History of Coaching*. Maidenhead: McGraw-Hill.

For a full account of the 'third generation' of coaching, read: Stelter, R. (2019) *The Art of Coaching Dialogue: Towards Transformative Exchange*. Abingdon, Oxon: Routledge

# 2

# RESEARCHING COACHING AND MENTORING

## CHAPTER OVERVIEW

This chapter takes a critical look at research practice in coaching and mentoring. It presents some opposing but fundamental philosophical positions and links these to research practice. We suggest that there are various 'archetypes' of research practice in coaching and mentoring research, and that these are aimed at different audiences and have different purposes in mind.

This chapter is a multi-perspective, descriptive account, which characterizes research traditions and discourses in both mentoring and coaching: we create a framework of research approaches grounded in an analysis of a range of research articles in the field. In order to illustrate those differences, we include summaries of research work, written by coaching & mentoring researchers which illllustrate some of these research discourses.

We aim to illustrate the characteristic strengths and weaknesses of each discourse, thus illustrating the preoccupations that researchers have about mentoring and coaching. We also highlight the historical differences between the two traditions in a way that throws light on the current preoccupations of those who focus on either coaching or mentoring. In the third edition of this book, we highlighted two main archetypes in coaching and mentoring research and argued that these may be changing. In this edition, we aim to examine the current terrain of coaching and mentoring research and bring to the fore some of the assumptions made by researchers when conducting and publishing such research.

We examine the context of the studies that we review and highlight how this impacts on research choices.

Finally, we offer implications and prescriptions derived from our arguments presented in this chapter that may be useful for researchers and practitioners alike.

## INTRODUCTION

As raised in Chapter 1, there are many different perspectives on the meaning of coaching and mentoring, and the research traditions similarly fall into various camps or tribes. In Chapter 1, we also raised the issue of social context and its impact on coaching and mentoring in practice. Within research, the social context also shapes the researcher's purpose and often influences the practitioner's activities as they act on a researcher's findings.

Within our framework of analysis in this chapter, we examine the gaze, the strengths and the weaknesses of each. 'Gaze' refers to the issues that various research strands privilege (by giving predominant attention to them), and an example is taken from one of our collaborative research studies to illustrate how gaze operates in shaping the perceptions of researchers and determining the findings that they uncover. This is akin to the concept of mindset raised in Chapter 1, but the difference between gaze and mindset is that gaze refers to what the researcher looks at, whereas mindset refers to what they are likely to see. We therefore see gaze as a particularly relevant intellectual tool in discussing research paradigms.

Nonetheless, there is a cautionary note here for researchers, practitioners and scheme designers that research findings need to be understood from the 'gaze' of the writer. As raised in Chapter 1, Burrell and Morgan (1979) offer some helpful insight into the gaze in the task of classifying research approaches. Morgan (1993: 276–7) comments:

> One of the main insights emerging from this work was that social scientists, like people in everyday life, tend to get trapped by their perspectives and assumptions. As a result, they construct, understand, and interpret the social world in partial ways, creating interesting sets of insights but obliterating others as ways of seeing become ways of not seeing.

Burrell and Morgan used a two-by-two matrix to describe four of these partial ways of seeing: the subjectivist versus the objectivist paradigms and the concept of radical change versus regulatory change. A widely used simplification of this model is to contrast the two approaches of positivism and phenomenology (or interpretivism). Others (e.g. Ruona and Lynham, 2004: 157) add to these two core methodologies a third – critical science. Critical science is aligned to Burrell and Morgan's concept of radical change.

To illustrate one such approach, Clutterbuck (2003) suggests that there are a dozen things wrong with most mentoring research:

1. Failures of definition: What is mentoring? Do respondents self-select?
2. Context of relationship not specified: internal or external relationships; formal or informal arrangements; inline or manager as mentor or offline for a different department section of the organization.
3. Outcomes not explored: for mentee/for mentor; sponsorship/career; some of Kram's (1985a) functions are processes, not outcomes - e.g. friendship.
4. Individual demographic variables not taken into account: for example, age, education, gender, race.
5. Quality of relationship ignored: nature of conversation; training of parties; effects of power on disclosure; effects of coercion to participate.
6. Stage of relationship: How many meetings? Duration of meetings; elapsed time since end of relationship.

7. Lack of triangulation: just mentee; just mentor; a line manager view; no 360 degree view; no scheme organizer view.
8. Over-reliance on retrospective accounts.
9. Single point samples: no attempt to track movement of the relationship by longitudinal study.
10. Direction of gaze: if you can't measure it, it doesn't exist.
11. Researcher bias not addressed: Who sees the relationship? Who asks the questions?
12. Sample size: number of respondents; representativeness is not considered.

## Reflective Question

Before reading on, how would you critique Clutterbuck's list?

It would be possible to critique mentoring and coaching research publications against such a list; however, Clutterbuck's perspective is largely a positivist one and in line with both the Psy Expert and Managerial (Western, 2012) discourses. While this is not a problem in itself and we maintain the position that no one method is better than another, we do suggest that a blended approach offers the most potential to inform all users of research material. In this chapter, we seek our own grounded methodology to analyse our selection of current research articles in mentoring and coaching.

## METHODOLOGY

To introduce the different research traditions in mentoring and coaching, we have used four different theories of truth (Darwin, 2010) to analyse the different research traditions and approaches we see in the coaching and mentoring literature. We will use accounts of research that typify these respective traditions and give a review of each. Prior to that, we offer some observations on published research in coaching and mentoring at a meta level in order to describe the terrain, which has shifted considerably since the publication of the first edition of this text in 2009.

### Mapping the terrain

A search on the Emerald Insight database using the search term 'coach*' (intended to capture all related terms, i.e. coach, coaches, coachees, coaching), conducted in July 2020, reveals that there are 14,981 articles listed. Adding research as an additional criterion reveals 12,685 articles. Of those 12,000+ articles, over half have been published in the last 10 years (7,124 articles). The same search on the term 'mentor*' revealed that over 15,000 articles had been published on mentoring with the vast majority of those being linked to mentoring research (14,255). Similarly, over half of these articles were published in the last 10 years (8,725).

Focusing specifically on the published coaching research between 2010–2020, nearly 3,000 (2,999) of the 7,000+ articles referred to coaching in the public sector; nearly 2,000 (1,996) referred to the private sector; and 2,770 referred to coaching in the third sector. The same search focused on mentoring research articles published between 2010–2020 shows that nearly 4,000 of them (3,918) referred to the public sector; over 2,600 (2,682) referred to private sector mentoring, whilst over 3,500 of the articles referred to the third sector (3,518). Pausing for a moment to consider this, it is interesting to note that, even with this crude and basic measure of research activity, several things can be observed:

- Over the last 10 years, there have been roughly equal numbers of articles published on mentoring and coaching.
- A high percentage of those articles are research based in some way.
- Of the three sectors searched, the private sector had the least amount of research articles whilst the public sector had the most, although there was a roughly even split between the three in both discourses (coaching and mentoring).

Business Source Premier, another prominent article database, suggests broadly similar findings at a macro level. A search of 'mentor*' reveals over 24,000 hits with 5,005 of these being published in academic journals and, of those, nearly 3,000 were published in the last 10 years – adding research as a limiter for the search still gives nearly 2,000 hits (1,917). A search for 'coach*' and research over the last 10 years reveals a very similar figure (2,048); according to this database, there were 20,400 articles published which mentioned coaching over the last 10 years out of over 35,000 (35,078) referring to coaching in some way, in total. Of those 35,000+ articles, 5,270 of them were classified as being published in academic journals. Interestingly, specific refinements of research criteria revealed only 26 articles were published between 2010–2020 which were coaching research based and referred to the public sector, with 13 for the private sector and only 5 for the third sector. Clearly, there is a big disparity in the number of articles between the two databases at a more microlevel. These differences might be explained, however, by the different methodologies they use to classify articles and by the differences in journals included in the searches – Business Source Premier being more general management/corporate in focus whereas Emerald focuses more on social science more broadly.

In summary, it seems reasonable to argue that there has been an increase in published research articles in coaching and mentoring. It also seems reasonable to argue that both coaching and mentoring research activity seems to span the three main sectors in the economy: public, private, and third sector. However, in order to better understand the current picture regarding coaching and mentoring research, we must delve more deeply into the nature of this activity. In previous editions of this text, we have proposed two archetypes of research: one for coaching and one for mentoring. Whilst we stand by our preceding analysis in the previous editions, we nevertheless recognize that the landscape has shifted somewhat. As Stokes et al. (2020) argue, it may be more useful to recognize a blurring of the two labels of 'coaching' and 'mentoring' in practical terms, and this has implications for how research might be conducted, going forward. Furthermore, the maturing of coaching as a research-based discourse, coupled with greater breadth of research paradigms (explored further below), has meant that making clear distinctions between coaching and mentoring discourses, in research terms, does not make as much sense as it used to. As we have argued in Chapter 1, the landscape of coaching and mentoring is changing.

We also conducted some analysis of the types of research conducted. We again used the Emerald and Business Source Premier data bases, employing Boolean logic searches to search for 'mentor*' or 'coach' against a number of common data collection approaches: mixed methods, case studies, interviews, focus groups, surveys/questionnaires and experiments. We chose to use these terms as opposed to quantitative or qualitative methods, for example, because some articles using a survey method would sometimes come under quantitative or qualitative methods. This was also the issue for case studies. The results of the searches are summarized in Table 2.1.

**Table 2.1** A summary of research methods employed in published works (figures in brackets refer to articles published in last 10 years).

| Method | Articles on Mentoring (Emerald) | Articles on Coaching (Emerald) | Articles on Mentoring (Business Source Premier) | Articles on Coaching (Business Source Premier) |
|---|---|---|---|---|
| Survey/Questionnaire Research | 8,899 (5,751) | 7,582 (4,531) | 2,136 (669) | 1,182 (811) |
| Case study | 11,813 (7,536) | 10,427 (6,082) | 318 (158) | 297 (174) |
| Mixed methods | 3,800 (2,703) | 3,410 (2,156) | 39 (38) | 34 (34) |
| Interviews | 7,573 (4,851) | 6,886 (3,914) | 501 (371) | 536 (422) |
| Focus group research | 11,996 (7,632) | 10,430 (6,125) | 66 (56) | 61 (50) |
| Experiments | 4,872 (3,147) | 4,720 (2,705) | 149 (107) | 197 (150) |

Before analysing what this table might mean, we should offer some caveats about the data in it. First, we conducted simple searches using the terms stated above. It is possible that using slightly different terms may have yielded different results. There is also the possibility that not all of the research articles counted here are strictly focused on coaching and mentoring research per se – given the volumes involved, it was not possible to check every article. We also cannot rule out the possibility of some double counting, e.g. case study articles also being included in interview-based studies. However, our intent was not to be comprehensive in this brief analysis of published articles but to give a broad overview of the terrain. We are confident that, despite the aforementioned possible inaccuracies, this does give us a rough picture of what the coaching and mentoring research terrain looks like, in terms of published academic research.

Considering Table 2.1, we observe the following:

- How research is classified, in methodological terms, differs according to different publishers and databases.
- Research approaches such as survey research and case study research appear to transcend neat categorizations into quantitative, qualitative or mixed methods studies.
- The general trend (excepting mentoring articles on survey research in Business

Source Premier) is that more than half of the articles, on both databases, have been published in the last 10 years.

- Although the caveat about classifying research approaches still stands, there do seems to be more articles that have qualitative research methods at their core (interviews, focus groups, case studies) than quantitative research methods (surveys, experiments, mixed methods).

Whilst the preceding analysis of coaching and mentoring research is somewhat useful in setting the scene for coaching and mentoring, it lacks depth. In order to better understand the different approaches taken, we need to engage with the concepts of gaze (where the researcher looks) and mindset (what they are likely to see when they look). This brings us into the realm of research philosophy to some extent. Whilst we are not writing a research methods text on coaching and mentoring, we do think that it is important to draw, selectively, on that literature to inform our understanding of coaching and mentoring research.

We explore this now, using the idea of truth theories within research philosophy. We will then apply these ideas to four different archetypes of coaching and mentoring research.

## WHAT IS TRUTH IN COACHING AND MENTORING?

In his article in 2010, Darwin examines the philosophies of Kuhn, Popper, Lakatos and Feyerabend to arrive at four theories of truth which he uses to make a contribution to the philosophy of management. It is our view that this can be usefully adapted and used as an analytical framework for looking at different philosophies and approaches to research within coaching and mentoring. Borrowing from Darwin's (2010) analysis, we therefore propose four ways of assessing the truth claims of a piece of coaching or mentoring research. These are summarized below:

### Correspondence theory of truth

Where data on coaching and mentoring is collected in order to prove or disprove a theory we already have about coaching and mentoring, we refer to this as trying to demonstrate a correspondence between our theory and the practice we observe in the world. Darwin (2010: 40) provides us with some useful questions to ask here which we have adapted:

- Does the theory provide validated explanations as to what is happening?
- Does it predict coaching/mentoring outcomes?
- Can we rule out alternative explanations of what might be happening?

A correspondence theory of truth often underpins positivistic research, i.e. research based on experimental protocols used in natural science disciplines. Hence, statistical techniques applied to larger sample sizes are often used to demonstrate a cause and effect relationship or correlation between two variables, e.g. coaching and improved leadership skills. This theory of truth is likely to underpin the truth claims made by the authors of the articles using an experimental design, referred to in Table 2.1. The case in this chapter, written by Dr Rebecca J. Jones, is also an example of this.

## The coherence theory of truth

A coherence theory of truth is where claims for the truthfulness of research rest on the ability of the researcher to generate a plausible and consistent narrative which provides a persuasive account of the phenomena being examined. We argue that, in some ways, this is the theory of truth that managers often employ although they 'dare not speak its name' in an organizational context. This is because it is radically different from the above correspondence theory as it draws not on the external validity principles of proof common in natural sciences. Rather it draws on the internal consistency of its theoretical frames and constructs. However, we argue this is more commonly used in organizations that it at first appears. For example, it is possible to see a good business case for a particular organizational strategy in these terms. We propose the view that most leaders/managers in organizations, when making decisions on a business case, will not interrogate them by requiring 'proof' of their validity using natural science protocols to either accept or reject a hypothesis. Instead, they are more likely to look for consistent themes in the case and compare them against their lived experience to see if they are plausible. We have adapted Darwin's (2010: 45) questions here to assess coaching and mentoring research truth claims from a coherence perspective :

- Is the coaching and mentoring theory proposed consistent?
- Does the theory relate coherently to other theories, values and assumptions about coaching and mentoring?
- How plausible is the proposed narrative in explaining the coaching and mentoring phenomena observed?

In our archetypes below, Andy Pendle's approach to narrative coaching research has coherence at its core as a claim for truth about coaching.

## Pragmatism as a theory of truth

A pragmatic truth test is fundamentally based on the concept of usefulness. Hence, an approach to research that has pragmatism as its claim for truth is principally interested as to whether the phenomena being examined – in our case, coaching and mentoring activity – are useful to the stakeholders engaging with them. In other words, pragmatism in coaching and mentoring research is about whether it 'works' or not for its participants. This is different from trying to understand how it works or to prove that it works, using natural science methodologies. Adapting Darwin's (2010: 45) questions once more, we ask here:

- Is the coaching or mentoring useful?
- Does it work?
- Does it provide useful ways of understanding the system within which it is located?

The clinical mentoring programme evaluation discussed below is an example of where a pragmatic theory of truth is adopted.

## A consensus theory of truth

A knowledge claim based on a consensus theory of truth focuses on where accounts of particular phenomena concur with each other. In other words, where the accounts of various stakeholders agree, we can trust in this as knowledge about it. Applying this to coaching and mentoring research, we can argue that, where participants in a coaching or mentoring scheme within an organization agree about outcomes and benefits, this is warranted knowledge about coaching and mentoring from a consensus theory of truth perspective. Adapting Darwin's (2010: 45–6) questions here again, we ask:

- Does the coaching and mentoring fit with the shared theories, values and assumptions of the community of practice?
- Is the language of coaching and mentoring shared and enriched as a result?
- Does it provide interpretations of coaching and mentoring practice that are accepted by those who participated in it?

The account below by Dr Duminda Rajasinghe (example 3) provides an example of research which adopts a consensus theory of truth.

## COACHING AND MENTORING RESEARCH ARCHETYPES

### The positivist archetype: A correspondence theory of truth

#### Dr Rebecca J. Jones

This example is based on the following study conducted for the article: Jones, R.J., Woods, S.A. and Zhou, Y. (2019) 'The effects of coachee personality and goal orientation on performance improvement following coaching: A controlled field experiment', *Applied Psychology: An International Review*. DOI: 1111/apps.12218.

In this study, we sought to address the question: What are the individual characteristics that influence whether coaching is beneficial for people's performance? The role of individual differences in learning and development at work has typically been examined around attribute-treatment interaction (ATI) theoretical mechanisms, which propose that the individual differences of learners will influence the outcomes from specific development interventions. We focused our attention on the Big Five personality traits, core self-evaluations, and goal orientation.

The type of question we posed in this research makes the underlying philosophical assumptions of the research clear. For example, the use of the word 'influence' in our research question highlights the belief that we are able to establish causal explanations (in this instance that differences in coachee characteristics can cause there to be a different effect of coaching on performance).

Implicit in this question is that it is possible to identify a universal law in relation to coachee characteristics and outcomes that can be applied across all coachees. Furthermore, the presentation of attribute-treatment interactions as an explanatory theoretical mechanism suggests that this study involved deductive theory testing. These underlying assumptions combined (establishing causal explanations, belief in universal laws and deductive theory testing) highlight the positivist assumption underlying this piece of research.

In the positivist orientation, the research methods adopted are characterized by the presence of controlled observation and measurement. Accordingly, in this study we conducted a field experiment with an experimental group who received coaching and a control group for comparison. Participants were randomly assigned to either the intervention group or a control group. Participants in the intervention group were all provided with four one-hour coaching sessions with sessions generally spread over a monthly period. Participants completed questionnaires one month after completing the final coaching session and again three months later. As each control cohort was matched to a coaching intervention group cohort, two questionnaires were emailed to control group cohorts when the final coaching session was completed for their matched coaching intervention group. There was no further contact between the participants in the control group and the research team. As an assumption of positivist research is the ability to measure and quantify constructs of interests, participants completed questionnaires related to their personality characteristics and their performance. In addition to collecting data from participants, supervisor ratings of performance were measured over the same three time points.

By examining the interaction of coaching with individual differences of coachees across multiple time points, and compared to a control group, we found that in respect of self-rated performance, coaching was most beneficial for people high in openness, low in CSEs, and high in avoidant orientation to goals, although we found no significant effects for supervisor ratings of performance. Especially positive among our findings was the prospect that coaching can be a potentially effective development technique for people who may respond less well to other forms of instructional learning (i.e. those low in CSEs, and high in avoidant orientation to goals); in short, people who appeared to benefit most from coaching were arguably those most in need of a form of development intervention to fit their characteristics and styles.

## Discussion

Jones et al.'s (2019) case above provides a good example of the positivistic strand within coaching and mentoring research. We note their strong emphasis on the rigour of their scientific method and the careful definition of terms, such as influence. The strength of this method is that it enables researchers to make specific claims about the impact of coaching on specific groups which are supported with evidence; furthermore, the clarity and specificity of their methods suggest that there is a strong chance that, were other researchers to try to replicate their experiment, they would get similar results. Hence, they are able to argue that their truth claim is generalizable beyond their specific sample and can be applied to other coachees who have similar personality traits and characteristics. What it remains silent about are the 'lifeworlds' of the coaches and coachees in terms of what they understood the coaching to be, the impact it had on them and how they understood the quality of the relationship between them. There is also relatively little examination or evaluation of the coaching process (the GROW model) itself and how it was enacted between the participants. To be fair, focusing on these things was not the intent of the authors – this point relates to the 'gaze' of the researchers that we raised at the beginning of this chapter. However, we highlight the 'blindspots' in this approach in order to support our view that any knowledge claim can be challenged from other perspectives and that no one perspective is likely to give the complete picture. We now move on to consider a radically different perspective on coaching research using a coherence theory of truth.

## NARRATIVE COACHING – A COHERENCE THEORY OF TRUTH – ANDY PENDLE

### The construction, composition and performance of coaching identities

I came to coaching a practising humanistic therapist and trainer. As such I am clear that many of the positive elements of encounters between coaches and coachees are derived from the individual personas of the participants meeting in a joint enterprise of enquiry (de Haan, 2008b). While coaching is clearly a different field to therapy, my sense is that much of the coaching research produced to date lacks a curiosity about the person of the coach. Many of the top-end coaches appear to be trading on a high degree of personal charisma while at the same time producing texts that to some degree erase the individual coach from the coaching equation by replacing them with formulaic frameworks for coaching (e.g. Downey, 2003; Whitmore, 2009). These narratives, whilst apparently promoting coaching, have the potential to diminish the significance of both the individual coach and the coachee. Therefore, a PhD research project that focuses on how coaches construct their sense of professional identity seemed both timely and purposeful.

In devising this project I concluded that rather than focusing on top-down competencies imposed by external organizations, it is more conducive in understanding coaches' professional identities to develop an inferential discourse that has as its foundation a bottom-up analysis of how successful coaches construct and perform their professional coaching identities. It was clear from the outset that a qualitative approach was appropriate for this project due to its inferential character. After considering various methodological approaches, a broadly narrative approach was settled on due to the assumptions that the identities we inhabit are contained within the narratives that we promote (Brockmeier and Carbaugh, 2001). Because identities are also embodied and performed, a narrative-performance methodology (Reissman, 2008) was chosen that could simultaneously focus on both the content of the interview and the performance-event of the interview itself.

The first task of the study was to establish a working conceptualization of identity as this is the cornerstone of the entire project. This involved moving between essentialist (e.g. Cardinal et al., 2011) and non-essentialist (e.g. Butler, 1990; Moran, 2014) perspectives until an original conceptual framework was formulated that was both credible and served this study. Following this I produced a meta-ethnographic literature review (Noblit and Hare, 1988) of the texts and publicity materials of three practising and published coaches. By doing this I was able to synthesize the artefacts these coaches had produced in pursuit of the construction of their professional identities and so note the emergent themes and patterns. This in turn produced a foundation that was able to facilitate my passageway into the fieldwork by informing the creation of interview schedules and broadening my awareness of the materials and strategies employed in coaches' identity construction. I then drafted a further literature review chapter that focused on the wider terrain of the coaching field in order to identify the various generic platforms available to coaches (e.g. Western, 2012) on which to construct their professional identities. For the fieldwork, 13 coaches who could credibly be regarded as successful and recognized within their fields were contacted and meetings requested. Nine interviews were conducted and data from eight of these are in the process of being analysed.

At the start of the process I had imagined that the construction of professional identities by coaches might be a generally superficial process largely concerned with marketing. However, in the event, I have encountered greater levels of authenticity and a sense of a wider purpose than I expected. Whilst data analysis is ongoing, results tentatively suggest that the achievement of a credible and highly functioning coaching identity is a more rigorous and testing process than might have been imagined. Elements of this often include significant encounters with mentor figures alongside a meaningful and challenging life journey.

## Discussion

Pendle's (as yet unpublished) research is a good example of a piece of research where the focus of the researcher's attention is to develop a strong and plausible narrative about the coaches he is looking at. We notice how he is framing himself and his engagement with the coaches in relational terms and places emphasis on the making of meaning. He describes his research process as an iterative one where he is developing a credible and coherent narrative about these coaches as he engages and re-engages with it. Whilst he is working with narrative techniques at a meta-level, he is also engaging with the process of how the 13 coaches go about constructing and enacting their identities. Ultimately, any judgement on his contribution to coaching theory and practice will rest on the extent to which his own account plausibly and coherently offers a framework for how these coaches operate in terms of their construction and maintenance of their coaching identities. It does not focus on testing a theory he already has about coaching but rather on engagement between theory and practice as he crafts the narrative. In some ways, Pendle's approach has similarities to Rajasinghe's (below) in that they are both focused on meaning making, although, as we will explore below, there are some differences in approach and philosophy.

## How do leaders interpret their dyadic executive coaching experience? An interpretative phenomenological analysis (IPA)

### Duminda Rajasinghe

This PhD study was carried out to understand how executive coaching helps leadership development from the perspective of both the coachee and the coach. I asked, 'how do leaders make sense of their dyadic executive coaching experience?' The literature review of both the academic and practitioner literature revealed that the question of 'how executive coaching works' is relatively under-researched. Therefore, my aim was to develop a deeper understanding of how executive coaching works by employing a case study within an organization.

This qualitative research was conducted using IPA, a health psychological research methodology which offers a cross-disciplinary application due to its inclusive nature (Wagstaff et al., 2014). It is informed by three philosophical underpinnings: phenomenology, hermeneutics and idiography (Smith et al., 2009). IPA helped me to place emphasis on the leaders' experience of executive coaching (phenomenology) and how they made sense or gave meaning to their experience (hermeneutics). IPA acknowledges that human beings are active interpreters of their lived world, which is informed by their experiences and predispositions (Brocki and Wearden, 2006). This complies with my position on coaching that it is a social activity informed by humanist philosophy (see Garvey, 2017). Therefore, IPA offers a relevant methodology for analysing how individuals experience coaching and the meanings that they attach to the experience. This is in line with the conversational engagement that coaching promotes to develop different understandings by challenging the predispositions of individuals (questioning hermeneutics) and engaging in conversations (interpretative engagements) to develop understanding (Rajasinghe, 2018).

I used purposive sampling to recruit a small (five participants) homogeneous sample and conduct two semi-structured interviews with each participant. The interviews are transcribed verbatim and subjected to line-by-line analysis. Respecting the ideographic commitments of IPA, first, I analyse the data from the three coachee participants and then the coach participants (see Rajasinghe, 2018). IPA's combination of both phenomenology and hermeneutics helped me to develop a deeper understanding of the phenomenon, because 'without phenomenology there would be nothing to interpret, without hermeneutics, the phenomenon would not be seen' (Smith et al., 2009: 37)

My findings comprised seven themes, namely that coaching:

- helps to create and develop new understanding
- creates and develops opportunity
- generates motivation
- encourages action
- supports the entire learning process
- ensures continuity
- helps tackle specific problems.

These themes appear as a narrative that demonstrates how executive coaching works. This narrative offers a unique contribution to the literature. This study also demonstrated that executive coaching can be used to tackle problems that leaders face. It reveals that an organizational agenda exists in executive coaching despite claims in the literature that the agenda is led by the coachee. I also found that coachees become coaches themselves due to their executive coaching engagement and that coaching resulted in contagious and continuous development within the case study organization. These appear as theoretical contributions in this study. Moreover, incorporating IPA into coaching research, together with the innovative research design, also stands as a contribution to research methodology. My findings may also serve as an evidence base to inform future coaching practice.

## Discussion

Rajasinghe's account above is an interesting example of Interpretative Phenomenolgical Analysis (IPA). As doctoral supervisors ourselves, we note the increasing use of IPA in coaching and mentoring theses as a useful way of making sense of qualitative data, particularly when the researcher is interested in how individuals make sense of things: in this case, executive coaching. However, as Rajasinghe himself says, he is construing coaching as a social activity and conducted his research within a case study organization which uses executive coaching. Hence, in inducting his seven themes from the data, he is arguably interested in how the executive coaching as experienced by the participants fits with the shared theories, values and assumptions of the community of practice, i.e. the case study organization. By focusing on the meaning making of the participants, his research has provided interpretations of executive coaching which are accepted by those who participated in it. Furthermore, he argues that the narrative presented is useful in enriching our understanding of how executive coaching works in this context. By drawing on where the different accounts of the executive coaching agree, he also makes claims regarding the organizational agenda (versus the individual coachee's agenda) in executive coaching, as well as suggesting commonalities in the way that coachees become coaches through their experience of being coached. Whilst his account is not typical of studies that claim consensus (in that it is a small, homogeneous sample), the truth claim is consistent with consensus as it is situated within a social context, inducts common themes from different participants, and makes claims about coaching on the basis of their accounts which have been recognized by those producing them.

## Evaluation of clinical mentoring in an NGO: Pragmatic theory of truth

One of us (Stokes) was commissioned to undertake an evaluation of a clinical mentoring programme for an NGO. The evaluation intervention was designed to assess the appropriateness and effectiveness of the defined mentoring framework as a learning and teaching process within this context. This included addressing three main objectives:

- to assess the extent to which the approach used had been sufficiently adapted to the local context
- to examine the extent to which the mentees' competences improved
- to explore how the mentoring component of the project is currently being implemented and to identify possible improvements/amendments.

The data collection was undertaken in two visits, the first in July/August 2019 and the second in February 2020. Both quantitative and qualitative data were collected from mentors, mentees, local officials, staff and patients. The methods used were interviews, focus groups, direct observation and analysis of objective assessments of mentees' knowledge, skills and attitudes. Purposive sampling was used to determine who would participate in the evaluation, and data was collected until saturation was reached. In summary, it was determined that the mentoring process was an effective learning and teaching strategy which has enabled new knowledge, skills and attitudes to be developed by the mentees.

The evaluation was considered at four levels – theoretical; how mentoring is conceptualized within the NGO; the design of mentoring within the local project; and the actual experience.

Focusing on the actual experience, the mentoring approach was found to be largely adapted to the context within which it is set. However, an analysis was conducted of what had worked and what had not which formed the basis for some practical recommendations for improving the implementation of the mentoring programme.

Some questions were asked as to whether the relationships constructed between the mentoring participants were truly adult to adult. Whilst there was evidence of some mentoring skills and processes being used within the programme, it was not accurate to describe the intervention as being a mentoring scheme/programme per se. This was because what was being taught and learnt was being defined by the relevant protocols and guidelines for medical practice rather than by the mentees' own learning agendas. Suggestions for improvement were offered, including having a consistent and collective approach to feedback and education of mentees, and using a wider range of teaching and learning strategies.

## Discussion

In some ways, this account has something in common with a consensus theory of truth in that insights and themes were generated from a range of stakeholders within a given context to engender some recommendations for practice. However, the primary agenda of those controlling and commissioning the research was whether the clinical mentoring process being evaluated was useful (or not) in improving the competences of the mentees. Hence, the commissioning group who ultimately decided what research questions were asked were less interested in why the mentoring worked and were more interested in establishing the extent to which it worked in that particular context, how sustainable the process was and whether it could be usefully adapted/ scaled up to be used in other contexts. Hence, the evaluator conducting the data collection and analysis was expected to generate a practical report which contained useful recommendations for those commissioning and supporting the mentoring work in the field, rather than making a theoretical contribution to clinical mentoring. Ultimately, the extent to which the knowledge generated in the report is trustworthy or not rests on how practically useful it appears to be to those assessing it.

## CONCLUSIONS

Based on our analysis so far, it seems reasonable to argue that, due to the development of coaching and mentoring discourses, it is harder to sustain the view that there are distinct research archetypes of the two terms. In previous editions of this text, we have characterized mentoring research as being more positivist in orientation, using protocols of natural science research to generate hypotheses about the impact of mentoring. We have characterized coaching research as being more qualitatively focused and based on insider accounts, often with an agenda of promoting coaching as a process. We argue that, due to the increased research activity, particularly in coaching, this distinction is no longer as clear-cut. As we have shown in this chapter, there are a range of perspectives in both discourses, which cut across all research philosophies and approaches. Of course, positivistic mentoring articles and insider coaching articles still exist and are still being published. However, the range and scope of research activity seems to have broadened across both discourses.

In this chapter we have proposed an alternative approach to understanding research activity, which draws on Darwin's (2010) typology of truth claims within research philosophy. We have offered some examples of how these truth claims are enacted within live research contexts and discussed the basis of the truth claims. We have done this against the backdrop of the 'terrain' of coaching and mentoring research, which we have categorized in terms of data collection methodologies used. In Figure 2.1, we offer a basic framework for thinking about the concepts of researcher gaze and mindset that we introduced at the beginning of the chapter.

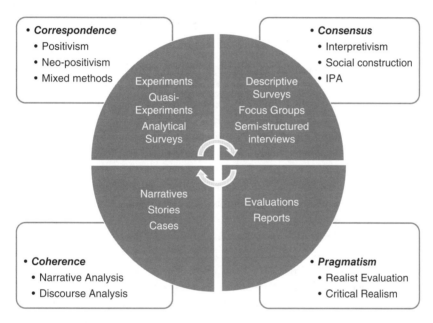

**Figure 2.1** A basic framework for thinking about the concepts of researcher gaze and mindset

Here, we have sought to make a connection between data collection methods, methodological approach and theories of truth. To explain the framework, it is our contention that coaching and mentoring researchers who adopt a positivist or neo-positivist position are likely to evidence their claim for truth by trying to demonstrate a correspondence between their theory and the practice they observe. Hence, they are most likely to adopt the protocols of natural science, using hypothesis testing and statistical analysis, and will collect data through conducting experiments or developing analytical surveys which seek to test relationships between coaching/mentoring and other variables, e.g. coachee personality. In our analysis of published research above, we found nearly 9,000 examples of survey or questionnaire research and over 4,000 examples of experimental work in coaching alone, on one database. Following Darwin (2010), it is also possible to argue that the use of mixed methods might constitute a correspondence approach, in that methodological triangulation might be seen as an attempt to demonstrate the strength of the findings as against natural science protocols. Nevertheless, we accept that it would be reasonable to argue that the intent of the researcher may be to establish consensus.

Moving on to consensus, we argue that those who adopt interpretivist, phenomenological or social constructionist perspectives, as coaching and mentoring researchers, are most likely to apply a consensus theory of truth to their claims about their research. As a result, they are most likely to use focus groups, descriptive surveys and series of semi structured interviews as data collection methodologies, in order to generate common themes around which there is participant consensus. In saying this, we do recognize that it is possible to use these data collection methodologies from other perspectives. Researcher mindset will tend to determine how these are conducted and analysed. It is our view that these methodologies are more often used by those adopting a consensus theory of truth due to a shared intent to induct common themes from the qualitative data collected.

We also argue that coaching and mentoring researchers who are interested in analysing coaching and mentoring discourses in terms of what is said and written about them are more likely to use coherence as a truth claim for their research. This is because they are more likely to be collecting data to inform and develop narratives on coaching and mentoring activities themselves. Hence, their data collection and analysis methods, like Pendle's in our above example, will focus on collecting stories and accounts that inform those meta-narratives. Again, we must acknowledge that data collection methods such as collecting life histories, discourse analysis and other ideographic techniques are not exclusively based on a coherence theory of truth, but we argue that coaching and mentoring researchers are more likely to base their truth claim on this perspective as opposed to others.

Finally, a pragmatic truth claim is more likely to be made by coaching and mentoring researchers who conduct evaluations of coaching and mentoring practice. This would apply to realist evaluations (see Pawson and Tilley, 1997) as well as critical realism approaches (Bhaskar, 1975) as they are both concerned with seeing research as an ongoing process through which researchers improve the concepts they use to understand the mechanisms that they study. The concept of generating theories about coaching and mentoring that are useful to practitioners is core to conducting evaluations and generating reports about them and their application. As we have continually stated, evaluations of practice are not exclusive to pragmatism, but this is the more likely truth claim to be made by coaching and mentoring researchers who engage in these sorts of data collection.

 ──── Future Direction ──────────────────────────

In this section, we offer our view on the routes forward that mentoring and coaching research might usefully take. There is a need for increased debate about the criteria by which claims for knowledge creation are made within coaching and mentoring. As we will argue in other chapters of this book, coaching and mentoring are currently still dominated by what Western (2012) calls the managerial discourse, which is based, in turn, on scientific rationality. We have asserted in this chapter that it is through adopting natural science protocols that a correspondence theory of truth is established. Our prediction, however, is that as the coaching and mentoring discourses continue to mature, significant challenges to the dominance of the managerial discourse will rise and this will give increased prominence to other forms of truth and their associated research approaches. However, we also predict that research approaches to coaching and mentoring will be increasingly sensitive to power relations between key stakeholders. This will present particular challenges for those using a consensus theory of truth position within research. In the current climate of COVID-19 and the Black Lives Matter movement within the UK, there are questions being asked of government in terms of how these tensions and challenges are being politicized and whether there is evidence of collusion on the part of powerful stakeholders in maintaining the status quo. Furthermore, the almost ubiquitous use of the term 'fake news' suggests that the foundation for knowledge claims about these issues, and others, is starting to be questioned. We will explore the issue of dominant discourse further in the chapter on power. However, our expectation is that we will see more accounts emerging from the pragmatist, consensus and coherence perspectives, as those research approaches gain more traction due to a desire to understand whether and how coaching and mentoring 'work'. We predict that 'plausibility' and 'sensemaking' will become more widespread criteria for judging knowledge claims about coaching and mentoring in the future.

---

 **Activity**

Choose a recent piece of research that you have read and analyse it against the frameworks provided in this chapter. What strengths do you see in the research in the light of this chapter? What weaknesses are highlighted? How does this leave the conclusions that you can draw from the research? As a scholar or scholar-practitioner, what could you do to improve the research? As a practitioner or scholar-practitioner, what could you apply with conviction having analysed the research?

---

 **Questions**

- How far do you agree that an individual's commitment to a particular research tradition leads them to ignore and downplay research in other traditions?
- How far does your research commitment leave room for you to embrace other approaches?
- How might you ensure that you follow best practice for research in your chosen tradition?

**Further Reading**

For a discussion on discourses in coaching and mentoring see Chapter 3, and for a critique of skills and competences see Chapter 4 of: Garvey, B. (2011) *A Very Short, Slightly Interesting and Reasonably Cheap Book on Coaching and Mentoring*. London: SAGE.

For a discussion of the evaluation of coaching and mentoring see Chapters 6 and 13, and for an exploration of research in coaching and mentoring see Chapter 13 of: Gray, D.E., Garvey, B. and Lane, D.A. (2016) *A Critical Introduction to Coaching and Mentoring*. London: SAGE.

# 3

# CREATING A COACHING AND MENTORING CULTURE

## CHAPTER OVERVIEW

In this chapter, we look at creating or developing coaching and mentoring cultures with organizations and offer both theoretical and practical insights into the development of environments supportive of coaching and mentoring. This chapter explores the literature on the subject of coaching and mentoring cultures. We present various models of mentoring and coaching culture while outlining strategies and practices for leaders, managers and specialist coaches and mentors to widen the impact of what they do. The chapter raises some challenging questions and issues for organizations wishing to develop coaching and mentoring.

## INTRODUCTION

One of the frontiers in the field of coaching and mentoring is how to harness organizational impact. We have seen the variations of meaning of coaching and mentoring in Chapter 1 and the approaches to gathering evidence to justify and understand coaching and mentoring in Chapter 2. Here, we continue with the same themes of variation and move away from the tired and well-worn track of 'one best way'. Coaching and mentoring are social phenomena and are therefore influenced by social processes. One size does not fit all. There are many choices that relate to specific contexts. However, in the business world dominated by the rational, pragmatic manager (Garvey and Williamson, 2002), coaching and mentoring advocate risk, losing much of their potential to influence how people manage and work in organizations unless the organizational implications of a coaching and mentoring way of working are considered and acted on.

Coaching and mentoring have traditionally been seen as one-to-one practices and so those studying, researching and working in the area have tended to ignore the wider social and organizational implications of their work. However, more recent research across the whole range of sectors including higher education (e.g. Hakro and Matthew, 2020), the electronics industry (e.g. Wong et al., 2017), the public sector (e.g. Ellul and Wond, 2020) and banking (e.g. Koshksaray et al., 2020) supports earlier work (McGovern et al., 2001; Garvey and Garrett-Harris, 2005) which suggests that the impact on the organization is considerable. This chapter seeks to address this issue.

## METHODOLOGY

We approach the concept of coaching and mentoring cultures in this chapter from both a theoretical and practical position by drawing on some of the literature on coaching, mentoring and culture as well as practical experience. Consistent with the themes already established in Chapters 1 and 2, we recognize that the form coaching and mentoring take is related to the social context and its perceived purpose. Consequently, we try to avoid prescription and, instead, raise what we see as important questions about the idea of developing a cultural environment that will support and sustain coaching and mentoring activity. We also raise some critical questions concerning the very concept of a coaching and mentoring culture. The implications of these insights will be discussed in the conclusion. We begin by examining the mentoring organization.

## THE MENTORING ORGANIZATION

Megginson et al. (2006) build on case study research in Clutterbuck and Megginson (2005b: 7) to identify the characteristics of a mentoring culture. Eight features of mentoring schemes that pay attention to the organizational dimension are:

1.  clear link to a business issue, with outcome measured
2.  part of a culture-change process
3.  senior management involvement as mentees and mentors
4.  established link to long-term talent management

5. mentees in the driving seat
6. light-touch development of individuals and scheme

7. clear framework, publicized, with stories
8. scheme designed to focus on business issues and change agenda.

Reading the case examples on which this list is based highlights the perspective noted elsewhere in this book (Chapter 12) that mentoring is often actuated by a social impulse to support those disadvantaged in employment and elsewhere (schools, for example) – women, ethnic minorities, people experiencing bullying, and so on. Nonetheless, in all the cases cited, there was also an emphasis on supporting the development of talent, on working with people at the top of the organization and on future potential leadership. Choi et al.'s (2019) commentary on introducing a culture of mentorship into academic medical centres is a good example of this sort of leadership development discourse.

Carden (1990: 276), when suggesting that mentoring works with the dominant culture of the organization, stated that mentoring could 'exclude(s) the socially different, clone managers and administrators, and maintain a status quo based on "accumulation of advantage" and replication of hierarchical systems'. And Garvey (1994a, 1995b) indicates that mentoring cannot be a 'cure-all' for organizational ills and is least effective when viewed as a 'new initiative' rather than a natural process and part of normal behaviour at work. Such findings would suggest that mentoring, on its own, is neutral with regard to fundamental organizational cultural change. However, the challenge of mentoring, as argued by, for example, Caruso (1996) and Turban and Dougherty (1994), is to recognize the need to synthesize individual and organizational aspirations as a central condition of organizational success. This coincides with Nonaka's (1996) recognition of the importance of personal commitment in a knowledge-creating organization.

Caruso (1996) also introduces the concept of power (see Chapter 7) in the organization when he says that often the mentee's agenda is replaced by the mentor's or the organization's objectives (see Chapter 11 for a full exploration of the problem of goals). Given the point made so far in this book that learning happens in a social context, an organization can make it more or less possible for people to learn by its values, processes, policies and actions. Caruso (1996) argues for a theory of mentoring in which the qualities of learning, as conceptualized, for instance, in the theory of situated learning (Lave and Wenger, 1991), and the potential benefits of mentoring move away from the traditional one-to-one mentoring relationship to characterize relational activities in the organization as a whole. In practice, this means that a mentor can be a 'variety of individuals and/or institutions who provide help to a protégé' (Caruso, 1996). It then becomes appropriate to talk about a 'mentoring organization'. We characterize this as:

- the compatibility of individual and organizational aspirations
- high employee commitment
- a focus on collaboration and team development

- a complex web of practices and relationships that are supportive and developmental of the individual and the organization.

Above all, people who have a developed an enthusiastic sense of themselves as learners inhabit a 'mentoring organization'. This concept resonates well with Higgins and Kram's (2001) notion of 'multiple mentoring relationships' (discussed in Chapter 8) where any one individual may have a range of developers, including coaches and mentors. Therefore, the links between mentoring, coaching and organizational development are strong, and this is perhaps why so many different types of organization engage with it. However, there are relatively few recent examples of where there is a stated organizational intention to develop a mentoring culture/organization. This is perhaps because, as we argue elsewhere in this text, the more dominant current focus is that of developing a coaching organization.

 **Reflective Questions**

- What does an effective mentoring network look like?
- How might the boundaries between what is and what is not mentoring be understood?

## THE COACHING ORGANIZATION

The literature on the coaching organization is more robust and fuller than that on the mentoring organization. This is often tied in with the notion of creating a coaching culture, explored later in this chapter. It is nonetheless very thin compared with the huge amount of writing (both academic and professional) on the one-to-one coaching relationship. We speculate that one reason for coaching organization literature being more developed than mentoring organization literature is that coaching has been more widely seen as a mainstream way of managing in the past (Zeus and Skiffington, 2000; Whitmore, 2002; McLeod, 2003; Pemberton, 2006). An early example of this strand in the literature is Megginson and Boydell (1979: 5), where they describe coaching as 'a process in which a manager, through direct discussion and guided activity, helps a colleague to learn to solve a problem, or to do a task, better than would otherwise have been the case'. This definition sees coaching as being the responsibility of the line manager, and sees it as being centrally 'concerned with improved task performance' (1979: 5). With this focus on performance, it is easier to justify coaching as being a fundamental way of managing work relationships rather than mentoring, which is seen as a special intervention to be called on for certain particular and unusual purposes (making major transitions, challenging inequalities, increasing opportunity, and so on). Wiginton and Cartwright's (2019) research into the impact of business coaching supports this view of coaching. In their survey of 87 companies, coaching was seen as being integral to supporting leadership effectiveness, strategic clarity, short-term decision making, customer satisfaction and employee engagement – in other words, fundamental leadership and management practices.

Clutterbuck and Megginson (2005b) have developed one framework, grounded in the practices of major organizations, for creating a coaching culture. This study produced a model of four levels of depth against six main areas that are divided into four sub-areas to produce a 4 × 24 matrix for assessing a coaching culture (2005b: 99–100). They describe the four levels as:

- nascent
- tactical
- strategic
- embedded.

This framework marks a multi-strand journey from:

- having the idea of making an organizational impact
- to doing disjointed things to bring it about
- to doing integrated things
- to establishing these things in the DNA of the organization.

The 24 areas identified from the case studies are listed below – the items in italics are those that were found in a high proportion of the cases studied (Clutterbuck and Megginson, 2005b: 28–9):

1. Coaching linked to business drivers:
   i. Integrate coaching into strategy, measures and processes
   ii. Integrate coaching and high performance
   iii. Coaching has a core business driver to justify it
   iv. Coaching becomes the way of doing business.

2. Being a coachee is encouraged and supported:
   i. Encourage and trigger being a coachee
   ii. You can challenge your boss to coach
   iii. Extensive training for both coach and coachee
   iv. External coaches used to give coaches experience of being coached.

3. Providing coach training:
   i. Integrate coach training for all
   ii. Coaches receive feedback on their use of coaching
   iii. After their training, coaches are followed up

   iv. *Coaches are accredited, certificated or licensed.*

4. Rewarding and recognizing coaching:
   i. People are rewarded for knowledge-sharing
   ii. *Coaching is promoted as an investment in excellence*
   iii. Top team are coaching role models (who seek and use feedback)
   iv. Dedicated coaching leader.

5. Systemic perspective:
   i. Assume people are competent
   ii. Organic, not process-driven
   iii. Initiatives decentralized
   iv. Constructive confrontation.

6. The move to coaching is managed:
   i. Senior group managers move to coaching
   ii. Line manager takes responsibility for coaching culture
   iii. *Integrate coaching and culture change*
   iv. Coaching supports delegation and empowerment.

This study clearly points out that developing culture change in an organization is not a quick-fix process and that there are many approaches and options.

Other authors who have written about coaching culture include Whitmore (2002), Caplan (2003), Hardingham et al. (2004), Pemberton (2006), Hunt and Weintraub (2007) and Hawkins (2012).

Hunt and Weintraub (2007) offer a US perspective on the topic. They adopt a similar case study methodology to Clutterbuck and Megginson (2005b), so comparison is possible. They focus on what they call 'developmental coaching', which they define as 'relationship-facilitated, on-the-job learning, with the most basic goal of promoting an individual's ability to do the work associated with that individual's current or future work roles' (2007: 27). Within this definition, however, they include 'whole life' issues such as 'career direction and work–life balance' (2007: 34).

Their approach focuses heavily on organization readiness. They also develop an assessment framework that helps individuals or organization representatives to assess readiness to create a coaching organization, and to identify areas for further work within the organization. As such, their list seeks to serve the same function as the one from Clutterbuck and Megginson (2005b) outlined above. However, Hunt and Weintraub (2007) focus more on the cultural context and social qualities; for example, they emphasize trust, employees and relationships as ends in themselves, valuing learning, truth-telling, diversity and continuous improvement, and they place a high bar on entry into the process of developing a coaching culture.

The Pemberton (2006) study is from the UK (rather than the USA) and examines how to spread coaching practice widely in an organization. Her book focuses on the manager as coach and she argues (2006: 3) that a tipping point (see Gladwell, 2002) has been reached with coaching so that it is now a pervasive phenomenon in the life of staff in organizations. Pemberton (2006) argues that staff members expect to be coached and the only people who can deliver this coaching in the amounts required are line managers. In summary, Pemberton (2006) suggests that all managers need to work in a coaching way because:

- there is now a growing expectation from the organization that managers should coach
- employees have experienced coaching outside work and expect it at work too
- it responds to what is sought by demanding and egocentric staff
- it delivers the 'deal' that employees expect
- it harnesses the motivation that employees have to contribute to the organization.

Some sources, particularly those that focus on externally provided, psychologically grounded coaching, seek to emphasize the weaknesses or dangers of coaching. Berglas's (2002) much-cited article is an example of this literature. Another is the chapter in de Haan and Burger entitled 'Limitations of Coaching with Colleagues' (2005: 151–9). At the centre of their concerns are the points that 'the internal coach is less free with respect to the coachee's organization' (2005: 153) and 'the internal coach has a less well-defined relationship to the coachee' (2005: 154). They make the challenging but reasonable point that coaching managers 'sometimes find it hard to put the coachee and his/her issues truly at the centre and to intervene in a way that respects the autonomy of the coachee' (2005: 155). This difficulty is related to points made in Chapters 6, 7 and 8 of this book about the power, control and obedience expectations of managers. It may also be another example of either 'mindset' or 'gaze' raised in Chapters 1 and 2. While these points have legitimacy, it is also important to remember that these authors have an agenda and a position to defend.

To extend this argument, we are grateful to Bruno Rihs, a Swiss colleague, for drawing to our attention Platt (2001), who highlights the weaknesses of a particular and specific approach to coaching:

I have generally found that people who practice NLP [neurolinguistic programming] are not receptive or even prepared to countenance critical reviews of this field of study. Indeed, I have come to recognize that 'Hell hath no fury like an NLP practitioner scorned' as a result of daring to question some of the practices framed by NLP … When I published the negative findings of a large number of clinical trials focusing on NLP techniques and also the research of Dr Heap, Principal Clinical Psychologist for Sheffield Health Authority … the response almost universally condemned the findings stating that they were 'unscientific' or that the particular aspects of NLP could not be clinically trialled, or that the areas studied were minor and insignificant when viewed against the entire gamut of the NLP approach. A mass of anecdotal evidence was also cited to challenge the clinical research findings.

In our view, there are two points here. Coaches adopting a strong frame for their interaction need to also have a robust approach to critiquing that frame if they are to avoid the defensive, cult-like reactions noted by Platt (2001). Additionally, we argue for a celebration of difference rather than viewing it as a problem or a challenge to one's very being. In a world of increasing polarization and extreme positioning, we suggest that an accepting and tolerant position is a more constructive way forward. Creating a coaching culture, even more than individual coaching, requires an ability to liaise and co-operate with others who have differing views of the organization and of the purposes of coaching – in other words, a diversity perspective, as discussed in Chapter 13.

A more recent book, *Creating a Coaching Culture* by Hawkins (2012), is also the one most clearly focused on the topic in the title. It has added to Clutterbuck and Megginson (2005b) by presenting a larger number of case studies (30 compared with 8 in the earlier book). Hawkins's book is actuated by the question, 'What can coaching uniquely do that the world of tomorrow needs?' (2012: 1). He sees coaching culture as being about informal, on-the-job learning (2012: 15) and sees it as having three pillars:

- coaching strategy
- coaching infrastructure. (2012: 24)
- alignment with organizational culture change

From this he develops a model which, in keeping with much of his earlier work, focuses on organizational learning as an outcome. This seven-step model is then spelt out in the second part of the book, picking up on many features of the Clutterbuck and Megginson (2005b) model outlined above. In the final part of the book, he surveys pitfalls on the journey to a coaching culture, examines the link to continuous professional development and to his work on supervision (Hawkins and Smith, 2006), and positions evaluation and return on investment in the journey. More recent contributions to the debate, for example Lawrence (2015), have tended to focus, like Hawkins (2012) and Clutterbuck and Megginson (2005b), on the pragmatic implementation of coaching cultures, but Lawrence (2015), in particular, has emphasized that simply introducing coaching into an organization is not sufficient. In order to move an organization towards embeddedness (in Clutterbuck and Megginson's (2005b) terms), additional mechanisms such as internal coaching skills training need to be introduced.

 **Reflective Questions**

- What is a good measure of whether coaching has become embedded in an organization?
- To what extent is it possible to specify appropriate timescales for movement towards an embedded coaching culture?
- Are such timescales useful or desirable?

## COACHING AND MENTORING CULTURE: THE NEW FRONTIER

The above literature review has helped to both define the field and identify the parameters to address in taking coaching and mentoring organization-wide.

What is needed next to develop this frontier is a series of organizational quasi-experiments, where scholars and practitioners can co-operate to build a long-term development alliance to make an impact on an organization. To start this process of developing a range of models for creating a coaching and mentoring culture fit for a variety of contexts, we believe it is necessary to examine a number of cultural features. This section introduces these features and offers a rationale for making choices about each. The features, similar to the dimensions framework presented in Chapter 1, are set as opposite points on a continuum as follows.

### Change or stability

This variable is key to the development of a mentoring or coaching culture. Megginson and Clutterbuck (1995) noticed that in some companies such as the Swedish part of Nestlé, Svenska Nestlé, retired executives were invited to mentor up-and-coming high-potential managers. This seems to be an example of a strong culture, confident in itself and wanting to perpetuate 'shared meaning, shared understanding, and shared sensemaking' (Morgan, 1986: 128). In another organization in Megginson and Clutterbuck (1995), each of the 20 members of the top team had an external coach because the chief executive was convinced that no one in the firm (with the possible exception of himself) had the characteristics necessary to drive the organization forward. In our view, this is a weak culture because there is little within the organization to sustain the desired culture. Balancing the amount of help offered to individuals in a culture change process therefore represents a major challenge and leads to the question, 'How can just enough help be provided from outside to develop coaching so as not to swamp internal efforts and thus to avoid the possibility of dependency being created?'

In one bank we studied some years ago, we found evidence of dependency being deliberately created by a coaching firm that was widely used throughout the bank, in order – it seemed to us – to maximize revenues for the coaching provider. However, strong cultures also present challenges. If people in an organization are good at replicating what they already do well, what happens when the environment changes and what is needed begins to change? Many strong cultures, for example in the UK retail sector (i.e. Marks and Spencer), suffer when market circumstances change. For some organizations, a pattern of using internal or quasi-internal coaches (such as ex-staff who have gone 'independent') needs to change to engaging genuinely external resources to prepare experienced staff to deal with the new situation in new ways. Clearly, this has never been as pertinent as in the current COVID-19 pandemic. As we will argue later in this text, cultural certainties about work and leadership development have been significantly challenged. Two obvious examples of sectors of where this has particularly impacted on ways of working are the hospitality sector and the travel industry. Staff in these industries have been required to think of radical ways of changing the nature of what they do in response to these organizational pressures. Hence, change is likely to be a strong factor in coaching or mentoring cultures.

Being clear whether the culture that is desired is a changed or a stable one is the first question to ask and will influence the form of the answer to many of the questions that follow (see Figure 3.1).

| | | |
|---|---|---|
| Change | or | Stability |
| Deficit | or | Appreciative inquiry |
| Problem | or | Solution |
| Internal | or | External coaches |
| All managers | or | Master-coaches/mentors |
| Performance | or | Whole life |
| Roll-out | or | Creep-in |

**Figure 3.1**   Dimensions of coaching and mentoring culture

## Deficit or appreciative inquiry

Implicit in much writing about coaching is a very traditional human resource development (HRD) model based on identifying needs, planning, implementing and evaluation. This sometimes glories in the name 'gap analysis', which implies that there is a gap between what the job requires and what the employee can provide (for a thorough-going critique of this position, see Roy Jacques's 1996 book *Manufacturing the Employee*).

Models of individual and organizational functioning based on standards and competencies (see Chapter 13 for a fuller account of this issue) are grounded in a similar understanding to the HRD gap analysis model.

Some psychologists also adopt a 'needs' model. This bases coaching on what the learner may need to develop into a fully functioning person. For example, Hardingham et al. (2004: 71–7) suggest that coaching must address such topics as belonging, control and closeness needs. A summary of these views is provided in Megginson (2012).

Standing in contrast to these deficit perspectives is positive psychology. This cluster of inter-related theories and practices suggests that creating a coaching culture will involve building on strengths. Strands of this movement are interested in 'flow' (Csikszentmihalyi, 2002), 'apprecia-tive inquiry' (Cooperrider, 1995) and, particularly in the world of coaching, the 'solutions focused approach' (Berg and Szabó, 2005). Auxier et al.'s (2020) study, using coaching to help long-term care facility staff work effectively with older adults on their management of pain, is an interesting example of this perspective.

Many HR systems in organizations are posited on the gap model, for example appraisal, perfor-mance management and, in many instances, coaching and mentoring. The psychological effect of such a perspective, where people get training, education, development, coaching or mentor-ing because there is something missing or wrong with them, is considerable. As Garvey and Williamson (2002) suggest, those entering a developmental session of any form may not engage in a positive state of mind if they think they have been sent to be mended. While honouring the benefits of positivity, it is well to be aware of two critiques of this orientation – Ehrenreich (2009), who emphasizes the coerciveness of the demand for positivity, and Burkeman (2012), who values in a coherent and elegant fashion the *via negativa*.

If one is to develop a coaching or mentoring culture based on strengths, a major piece of work will be to address the challenge that these embedded systems place in the way of a culture that celebrates, extends and develops strengths. In one such attempt we made some years ago in an insurance company, the biggest challenge the strength-oriented developers faced was the opposition from the HR department. The systems we were advocating would have required a rewriting of every HR policy. After working with HR, the challenges of engaging line management seemed relatively straightforward!

We leave this dimension with a question: do you think that you are better off going with the grain of existing policies or seeking to develop an alternative set of assumptions about how best to engage people in their own evolution?

## Problem or solution?

Related to the dimension about deficit or appreciation is this simple dichotomy in coaching and mentoring thinking. Many well-established models of coaching and mentoring suggest starting by identifying a problem that the client wants to work on. Flaherty (1999) and McLeod (2003) are examples of needs orientation. Flaherty, being a psychologist, emphasizes assessment as a process for determining needs; McLeod, with his performance coaching perspective, focuses on organizational issues such as communication, 'Who's the boss?', and interpersonal conflict.

Grant and Greene (2001), Jackson and McKergow (2002), Berg and Szabó (2005) and Pemberton (2006) offer an alternative perspective based on attention to solutions rather than problems. So, where do the efforts to create a coaching and mentoring culture need to focus? Should they focus on fitting in with the problem-focused orientation so prevalent in our wider culture, or on seeking to create a new orientation to building on strengths, which may set people against powerful organizational interests and societal taken-for-granted assumptions?

## Internal or external coaches/mentors?

This dimension relates to the change and stability dimension – in particular, to the question of whether the power-holders believe that there are managers in the organization who display the characteristics sought by change leaders. However, other considerations also shape where the emphasis is placed. One such factor is the extent of the proposed spread of coaching or mentoring. If it is for a relatively narrow group, top management or high-potential employees, for example, then the costs of using external, professional coaches may not be prohibitive. On the other hand, if the intent is to coach everyone in the organization, then clearly the costs of external help become too huge to bear. For some organizations, budgets for development are so modest that external coaching for anyone is out of the question.

Many authors (see Caplan, 2003; Hardingham et al., 2004; Clutterbuck and Megginson, 2005b) argue that there is a great advantage in engaging managers in the coaching enterprise. There is also considerable evidence that mentoring is beneficial to the organization, the mentor and the mentee (see Wilson and Elman, 1990; Garvey, 1995a; Devins and Gold, 2000). In fact, many authors on culture in relation to coaching and mentoring suggest that this is a crucial plank in its creation. So does necessity (or capacity) push the organization in the direction of using internal coaches? Do the benefits of engaging people widely in coaching others justify the expenditure of money and effort in enabling everyone to perform in this way?

## All managers or master-coaches/mentors?

Some companies seeking to create a coaching or mentoring culture have relied on a cadre of skilled leaders to develop high-level coaching and mentoring skills. In Clutterbuck and Megginson (2005b), a case study example of such a company would be Kellogg's. In the mentoring literature, Garvey and Galloway (2002), for example, illustrate the skills approach to developing a mentoring culture. A number of banks in the UK, prior to the banking crisis, for example HBOS, developed internal mentors while others, such as Lloyds TSB, created a job role of internal coaches, giving this aspect of the manager's role to specialists. Other cases from Clutterbuck and Megginson (2005b) focus on giving all managers the same training, for example in Vodafone.

An argument for specializing is that the master-coaches/mentors can then use their enhanced skills to coach/mentor other managers in coaching/mentoring skills. An argument for the 'train everybody' orientation is that it sends a signal that coaching/mentoring is a central part of the manager's job and not something that can be delegated to anyone else. Sometimes the choice is a function of the size of the business. Sometimes it is a cultural choice based on perceptions of power (see Chapter 7), democracy, individualism or collectivism within the organization, and sometimes it is a function of cost. So, which strategy should be emphasized – a specialist cadre or the widest possible engagement?

## Performance or whole life?

Some developers of a coaching and mentoring culture will want to narrow the coaching or mentoring manager's attention with laser focus onto performance. Authors who support this view include McLeod (2003). Paradoxically, Whitmore's book *Coaching for Performance* (2002) has a much wider remit than the title suggests. Other sources, such as Brockbank and McGill's 2006 book *Facilitating Reflective Learning through Mentoring and Coaching*, direct their attention more widely, while Alred and Garvey (2000) advocate a wider application of mentoring for a more holistic development of people. And the same can be said for the radically participative, content-free coaches as advocated by exponents such as Downey (2003). So, how focused on performance should coaching and mentoring be in any particular organization?

## Roll-out or creep-in?

The picture in the heads of the leading coalition about how to introduce change will dictate to which end of this spectrum organization leaders are drawn. The choice is between 'driving the change through the organization', which leads to a tendency to roll out training to all in a high-cost, high-profile campaign on the one hand, and on the other to a systemic perspective based on 'creep-in'.

The creep-in approach was characterized by the engineering company cited in Clutterbuck and Megginson (2005b: 68–9), which focused on key decision makers, took time to explore options, thought through the integration of coaching with other initiatives the company was exploring and did not go for extensive training of large numbers as a separate initiative. So, should an organization favour roll-out or creep-in? Is the greatest chance of success achieved by following the organization's norms or by trying something different?

## Summary

By examining these variables – change or stability; deficit or appreciative inquiry; problem or solution; internal or external coaches/mentors; all managers or master-coaches/mentors; performance or whole life; roll-out or creep in – it becomes possible to set out the broad direction and strategy for a favoured approach within a specific organization to creating a coaching/mentoring culture.

 **Reflective Questions**

- Are there other dimensions that should be included in any analysis of coaching culture?
- If so, what might they be and why are they important?

## SITUATIONS TO FOCUS ON TO CREATE A COACHING AND MENTORING CULTURE

We have found from working with organizations in recent years that the strategy of focusing on creating a culture can seem abstract to some decision makers. In such cases, an approach that can be followed is to attend to opportunities to build coaching and mentoring (C&M) into the fabric of the organization. Some impactful examples of these opportunities are:

- C&M as preparation for new roles
- C&M as delegation
- C&M as management style
- C&M as problem solving.

We discuss each of these below.

### Coaching and mentoring as preparation for new roles

Ever since Levinson et al. (1978) first suggested that mentoring was associated with transition, mentoring and, latterly, coaching have been linked to supporting people in new job roles.

The first 90 days in new roles is a period of intense learning (Porter et al., 2004; Neff and Citrin, 2005; Watkins, 2005). For example, Porter et al. (2004) say that a new CEO is faced with seven surprises:

- You can't run the company.
- Giving orders is very costly.
- It's hard to know what's really going on.
- You are always sending a message.

- You are not the boss.
- Pleasing shareholders is not the goal.
- You're still only human.

This represents a strong agenda for coaching and mentoring, and similar issues face new job-holders at every level in the organization.

Thinking about the strategic options addressed in the previous section, decisions will need to be made about the extent to which external and internal coaches or mentors will be used. If they are internal, will this be line managers or specially appointed and trained people?

## Coaching and mentoring as delegation

Building the expectation of delegation in encounters with managers is the fundamental basis for creating a developmentally aware culture. Companies starting from here do not even have to use the word 'coaching' or 'mentoring'. If it is known that asking a boss what to do will lead to the following sequence of questions, then a delegation culture and thus a coaching/mentoring culture will have been established:

- What are the options?
- Which of these would you prefer or recommend?

- Why don't you try that and let me know how it goes?

## Coaching and mentoring as management style

Building a coaching and mentoring approach into all leadership training is a starting point for this opportunity. There are implicit views about how to manage in all leadership training programmes. Advocates for a coaching and mentoring culture need to spend time exploring with development and training colleagues what these messages are and how they integrate with what is being done and said to propagate coaching and mentoring. They are not two processes, but one.

## Coaching and mentoring as problem solving

Coaching and mentoring are not soft forms of managing staff; in fact, they are not even a form of managing staff, hard or soft. They are a means of addressing issues and problems (or, as solution-focused coaches would say, achieving solutions) that can be used in a wide range of contexts. We have frequently remarked on the enthusiasm with which managers have grasped a coaching framework, like GROW, and found that they can use it in a team setting to deal with a big issue. Thus, an issue to be considered is how an organization's project management approach fits with its coaching and mentoring approach.

Perhaps the best way of making sense of this issue, in a pragmatic sense, is to use the example in Case Study 3.1.

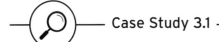 **Case Study 3.1**

### Towards a mentoring culture

One company we have worked with over a number of years is an international scientific consultancy firm. The company has grown substantially over the last 40 years to become a global leader in commercial intelligence for the energy, metals and mining industries. It has grown, in part at least, by the acquisition of smaller specialist businesses, and mentoring has been at the heart of this growth strategy. With the acquisition of new businesses come many social challenges and the need to help people integrate quickly into a new and sometimes alien culture. Mentoring has therefore been employed to support the psychosocial (Kram, 1983) development of people within the business as well as playing an important role in leadership and career development. Being international, the business extensively employs technology to support its business communications, and its HR and learning and development activities are no different.

The business first piloted mentoring in 2006. The plan was to:

- formalize the mentoring process
- build a cadre of senior and departmental business-wide mentors
- offer mentoring as a leadership development and induction support activity.

The company was also clear about what mentoring is not, in its own words:

- supervision
- checking up
- providing a hand up
- criticizing or hand holding.

Mentoring became part of the firm's learning and development (L&D) programmes, a handbook was created, an annual podcast produced to support the programme, case studies on mentoring relationships are regularly published and the names of all trained mentors are public information. The L&D manager manages with a 'light touch', offering support and guidance, and participants are invited to let the L&D coordinator know if the relationship comes to an end.

Potential mentors may volunteer or be nominated by their line managers following a developmental discussion. All potential mentors participate in a mentor skills workshop. Participants are invited to review their relationships regularly. The L&D function also offers mentors ongoing support in the form of refresher programmes, more advanced skills programmes, troubleshooting phone-ins and webinars. By 2015, over 120 mentors had participated in mentor skills training with over 90 current relationships.

The year 2016 marked a shift in the training programmes for mentors. Rather than face-to-face or through video conferencing, which had been the norm since 2008, the skills workshop was produced as a series of international webinars where many people from around the world could interact together for short but intensive periods of learning. This had the advantage of cost saving as well as providing an intensification of the training and an opportunity for participants to practise and try skills between sessions and then report back and raise issues and questions.

Coaching is also employed within the business, and although it has engaged external coaches from time to time, the main focus has been on coaching within the line management function. In the company's own words, 'coaching is typically provided to enhance capability and skills in a performance management context or in anticipation of a future role. A Line Manager is well placed to provide coaching.'

NB: Through all this, much credit must go to the dogged determination of a small number of committed managers to continually work with the process, adapt, adjust and change.

## DISCUSSION OF CASE STUDY 3.1

Looking at coaching and mentoring as practised in this organization, we can see that, in terms of our analysis above, the emphasis is on management style as the focus for the intervention. This is also done, principally, by a more traditional route of developing master mentors and coaches who are internal to the business via internal training and development. As the intention was to formalize the mentoring process with a scheme, the approach was more akin to roll-out rather than a creep-in approach. While the organization is very successful and did not face a 'burning platform', there was clearly a recognition that, given the organization's expansion plans, the mentoring process and, later, the coaching process were developed in response to an organizational problem of integration within the organization's culture. Therefore, while those sponsoring coaching and mentoring were clearly focused on performance, within a changing organizational context, the overall intent was towards stability and maintaining the success of the organization in the future. However, as we suggest above, there is a challenge for those organizations which principally seek to drive towards a coaching or mentoring culture by mainly or solely drawing on the mentoring that occurs in the organization. As Lawrence (2015) suggests, mentoring and coaching itself may be insufficient to embed the activity as part of the taken-for-granted assumption (Schein, 1985) within the organization. Hence, while the organization has, at the present, a core number of willing advocates of coaching and mentoring who seek to perpetuate it within the system, it is, perhaps, telling that there is an implicit need for them to keep this up within the organization, or else the organization may 'revert' to a more traditional, deficit model of performance which is typical of the dominant managerial discourse (Western, 2012) in many organizations. We are also assuming – as we have so far in this chapter – that it is appropriate to talk about one culture for the entire organization, although this can be questioned, given the organization's acquisition strategy. Given our experience of this organization, we recognize that it is possible to argue for the existence of sub-cultures within the organization, which tend to respond to coaching and mentoring in different ways, depending on the context in which they are introduced. This leads us on to some critical questions about the concept of a coaching or mentoring culture, which we consider below.

## WHAT DO WE MEAN BY A COACHING OR MENTORING CULTURE?

According to, for example, Drake and Pritchard (2016) and Hawkins (2012), developing a coaching culture is only possible under certain conditions; others, for example, McComb (2012) and Wilson (2011), assert that organizations are increasingly striving to achieve a coaching culture. However, a few authors (Nielsen and Nørreklit, 2009; Rajasinghe, 2018; Reissner and Du Toit, 2011; Western, 2012) argue that many emphasize the positive aspects of coaching and downplay the problems. In the majority of literature that we have cited in this chapter so far, the writers appear to make two key assumptions. The first is the uncritical assumption that an organization has one culture, a set of values, beliefs and expectations that are shared by and that influence people who work in that organization.

However, cultural researchers such as Debra Meyerson and Joanne Martin (Meyerson and Martin, 1987) have long since challenged what they refer to as an integrative perspective. To use a phrase from the popular Disney franchise *High School Musical*, the integrative perspective assumes that we are 'all in this together' and that conflict with dominant core values is an exception rather than the rule. This also suggests that any divergence between the individual and organizational voice is dysfunctional and undesirable. In this sense, it has much in common with Fox's (1974) unitary perspective on organizations. However, as Meyerson and Martin (1987) argue, there are two other perspectives on organization culture – differentiation (which recognizes the existence of sub-cultures within organizations) and fragmentation (which argues against hard and fast distinctions about values and recognizes the contingent and uncertain nature of organizational life). Why do these alternative perspectives go unrecognized in organizations? One reason may be that those who have written about creating a coaching culture, in particular, have tended to have a background in organizational consultancy and have tended to work at a senior level with senior management teams and boards, in whose interest it may be to portray a united front. Also, moving onto the second assumption that is made, there is a tendency for those who work within coaching and mentoring to engage in what we have already referred to here as 'misplaced concreteness'. In other words, it is easier to consider culture as something clear and unambiguous as it renders the behaviour of employees and other stakeholders as being knowable, reliable and predicable. This brings us into the realms of power within organizations, which we explore in much more detail in Chapter 7. Garvey (2019a) links the idea of 'misplaced concreteness' to the tendency of HRD professionals and managers to refer to coaching and mentoring as 'tools'. He argues that viewing them as 'tools' is directly associated with the managerialist discourse and contradicts the humanist values which underpin coaching and mentoring. However, suffice it to say that, at this point, organizational interventions which focus on the values, beliefs and expectations of organizational members are intimately bound up with power relations within organizations. Hence, related to the idea of concreteness, there is, in the literature we have examined thus far, a tendency to view organizational culture as something that can be used to control the behaviour of others by influencing 'hearts and minds'. This perspective requires culture to be seen as something almost physical but malleable that can be constructed within an organization. Indeed, we have a colleague with whom we have worked for many years who describes how they have 'put a mentoring culture' into their organization. This seems to afford a coaching or mentoring culture a real ontological status (existing independently of those who create it and work with it) as opposed to it being seen as a social construction (Burrell and Morgan, 1979). Case Study 3.1 does seem to indicate that the scheme is only really 'alive' while those key stakeholders seek to socially construct it. It raises the question of whether a coaching and mentoring culture is better seen as a useful metaphor for an organization (Morgan, 2006) as opposed to a real entity which has a separate ontological and organizational status. In this way, we wonder whether it makes more sense to see it as being similar in nature to the concept of a learning organization (Argyris and Schön, 1996), which arguably proves to be a useful concept that a range of stakeholders can recognize and buy into. Therefore, while we are for coaching and mentoring and their wider application, as we argue in Chapter 1, we remain somewhat sceptical as to the usefulness of universal prescriptions for creating coaching and mentoring cultures, although we recognize the useful contributions made to the area in terms of defining important dimensions and useful language.

Another important aspect of a coaching and mentoring culture to consider, which we have touched on throughout this chapter, is the set of relationships that exist between leaders and followers. Garvey (2019: 132) argues that: 'It is also clear that executive egos, particularly in relation to coaching and mentoring can be problematic.'

In terms of the creation of coaching and mentoring cultures, these relationships can be usefully examined using two well-known theories from psychoanalysis: transactional analysis (see Berne, 1968) and transference (see McAuley, 2003). Transactional Analysis (TA) is a useful way of conceptualizing human relationships in that it views interactions between people as transactions. These transactions can be analysed in terms of the roles and 'games' (Berne, 1968) that people play in these relationships. In TA terms, it is possible to draw parallels between leader-follower relations within organizations and parent-child relationships within families. It is relatively easy to imagine how a relationship between, say, an older, more experienced leader and a more junior, less experienced follower might resemble a relationship between a strict, critical parent and their submissive, obedient child! In cultural terms, the parent can be seen as setting the tone for the relationship in terms of what values, beliefs and behaviours are acceptable within the family culture. Furthermore, if the parent is strict, it is likely that there will be little tolerance of alternative perspectives on how the family should operate, in terms of deviating from what might be seen as appropriate behaviours for the child to engage in. Again, the parallel is fairly obvious if we move back into the organizational context of leaders and followers. If leaders adopt a unitary/integrative perspective on how they see organizational culture, they will see themselves (unconsciously) as the parent who sets the tone for how work is to be done in the organizations and will see their followers as adopting these behaviours. This goes for introducing a coaching or mentoring culture as for any other way of leading and managing. A more pluralist perspective on organizations may see the leader being more tolerant (we will explore this idea further in Chapter 13) of difference and expecting there to be more variation within the organization. This is perhaps more akin to an adult position in TA terms. This raises the interesting question as to whether a mixed message is created when people attempt to 'put' coaching and mentoring cultures into organizations. As we have argued in this text so far, coaching and mentoring discourses tend to have espoused theories of coachees and mentees as being adults who are capable of making their own decisions about what to do in their life and work. However, unconsciously adopting an integrative perspective in the implementation of such initiatives may encourage other stakeholders to notice a dissonance between the directive process used to implement a non-directive process!

Moving on to transference and countertransference, we will explore further when we examine 'Supervision in Coaching and Mentoring' (Chapter 12). However, in leadership and cultural terms, this also has a connection with TA. Arguably, followers and leaders can easily fall into relationships with each which mirror parent-child relationships. Followers may, unconsciously, expect their leaders to act like parents, giving them clear guidance about expectations of behaviour and norms to observe; in other words, they may be acting, in their employment relationship, as if it were a relationship with their own parents, or other parental figures from their past. Similar to TA, the leader may cement this unconscious transference by their own counter-transference (their response to the follower's feelings and expectations). Again, as we have argued in this chapter, coaching and mentoring culture discourses have embedded in them assumptions around appropriate behaviours of challenge, questioning and constructive feedback, which may be at odds with these transferred feelings. Hence, in Case Study 3.1, we could see take-up of the mentoring initiative as being evidence of follower compliance and obedience to the 'way we do things round here, now', as opposed to an affirmation of challenge questioning and constructive feedback.

Nizet and Fatien Diochon (2012) remind us that coaching is an ambiguous and complex practice, and therefore we argue that coaching has the potential to enable the desired managerial performance as well as contribute to change, or to become a mechanism for a new form of surveillance and control aimed at extracting compliance. In relation to mentoring, Carden (1990) pointed out over 30 years ago that mentoring works with the dominant culture of the organization but also has the potential to 'exclude the socially different, clone managers and administrators, and maintain a status quo based on "accumulation of advantage and replication of hierarchical systems"' (p. 276). She also maintains that it has the potential to facilitate a learning and development agenda. Garvey (2019a) argues that:

> Coaching and mentoring are complex social processes and as such are subject to the complexities and vagaries of our human existence. They can both help support people through these complexities or make them worse. They can be emancipatory and subtle forms of control. The extent to which they can contribute to culture change is in the hands of the people who want such change. With genuine humanistic values and genuine desires to make life better for people, coaching and mentoring can achieve great things for people. Without these values, they simply become tools with which to manipulate people and extract a bit more from them for the benefit of the business owners. (p. 133)

This raises some interesting questions about how such initiatives might be designed and evaluated, which we will explore in more detail in the next chapter. Our intent in this chapter has been to identify some perspectives and language through which the issue of the creation of such cultures might be usefully and critically considered.

## CONCLUSIONS

In this chapter, we have sought to introduce some dimensions of coaching and mentoring that are directed towards impacting the organization as a whole, rather than the usual focus on an individual or a tranche of individuals. We have explored what the literature says about the process and have outlined our sense of the strategic decisions that have to be made and the tactical opportunities that exist to progress this agenda. Finally, without seeking to diminish the contribution made by the literature, we have raised some critical questions about that literature and how it should be used.

In the next chapter, we focus on questions of the design and evaluation of coaching and mentoring schemes.

 **Future Direction**

We discern a widespread interest in creating coaching culture, less so in creating a mentoring culture. This seems appropriate in so far as mentoring is seen as an offline process and coaching as something that can be done by a line manager. However, much can be learned by those interested in developing a coaching culture from the mentoring literature. Here, it is clear that finding ways to minimize the power difference between mentor and mentee seems to have considerable benefit. Perhaps this learning could be applied within the coaching context.

An emphasis on paid external one-to-one coaching takes the eye of the coaching leaders in organizations off the question of creating a coaching culture – indeed it could be seen as threatening the market for external coaching. Similarly, external coaches can leave the topic alone because they are the ones who may feel supplanted. So, if coaching is viewed as 'a good thing', then perhaps the future is to find a balance between internal and external coaching work within organizations. A way forward would be to link the drive to the outcomes of coaching with the organizational purpose. This may be considered as a force in shaping the approaches to coaching and mentoring as organizational interventions.

 **Activity**

Identify an organization that you know well in terms of its key personnel and activities. Using the dimensions framework described in this chapter, seek to position it within this framework in terms of its progress (or lack of) towards a coaching/mentoring culture. What are the barriers to making more progress? What might need to change for this to happen?

 **Questions**

- How far do/does the organization(s) you work with want to push the development of a coaching/mentoring culture?
- What is the business case for developing this culture?
- To what extent is it useful to think of organizations as having only one distinct culture?
- To what extent should a coaching style be seen as the default style of leading and managing in the organization?

**Further Reading**

For a rigorous and thoughtful discussion on organizational culture, see the classic text by Joanne Martin: Martin, J. (2001) *Organization Culture: Mapping the Terrain*. London: Sage.

For a more practical 'how to' text, read Jones, G. and Gorrell, R. (2014) *How to Create a Coaching Culture*. London: Kogan Page.

For those interested in cross-cultural working, read Rosinski, P. (2003) *Coaching across Cultures*. London: Nicholas Brealey.

For a critical look at the notion of creating a coaching or mentoring culture, see Garvey, B. (2019b) 'How far is culture change through coaching and mentoring possible?', in: Hamlin, R., Ellinger, A., Jones, J. (eds) *Evidence Based Initiatives for Organizational Change and Development* (IGI Global Premier Reference Source Book). Hershey, PA: IGI Global.

# 4

# DESIGN AND EVALUATION

## CHAPTER OVERVIEW

This chapter mainly focuses on practice and practitioners. It places emphasis on the pragmatic issues of scheme design and evaluation that confront those who organize formal coaching and mentoring schemes in an organizational context. We start by exploring some approaches to evaluation and then consider some key issues in relation to scheme design. We also attempt to bridge theory and practice and argue that positivistic thinking tends to dominate organizational life, and this is a further example of 'misplaced concreteness', as discussed in Chapter 1. To address this, we suggest that an action-oriented approach offers a way forward.

## INTRODUCTION

In an organizational context, there are many competing demands on managers. Organizations, however conceived, are complex places and, with such complexity, there can be a tendency to simplify and reduce an organization to a set of principles or rules. When an organization is attempting to develop coaching and mentoring, there is no less a demand to simplify and attempt to position, control, ignore or smooth over social factors. The inherent risk of this approach is that those practising coaching or mentoring within a scheme may encounter difficulties. As we argued in Chapter 1, both coaching and mentoring are associated with a range of discourses, and it is these that are likely to shape the approach to practice. It is the same when it comes to scheme design and the evaluation of mentoring or coaching programmes. The assumptions that underpin any particular discourse, and the resultant choices made in relation to the dimensions framework presented in Chapter 1, will shape the choices made in the design of the scheme and the approach taken to evaluation.

## METHODOLOGY

Keeping in mind the points raised in Chapters 1, 2 and 3 about the perceived purpose of mentoring or coaching and the social context, we explore the challenges of scheme design and evaluation. Additionally, we, the authors, are practising coaches and mentors, consultants and academic researchers. As a result, we intend to put forward an approach to the scheme design and the evaluation of coaching and mentoring which draws on the strengths of these different approaches. In doing so, we acknowledge the possibility, as Gill et al. (2010) argue, that multi-methodological processes can be difficult and time-consuming. Nevertheless, our intent is to suggest a process that can encompass a range of approaches. In doing this, we draw on some selected literature and previously presented themes, and we celebrate, as a virtue, a blend of theory and practice on the basis that there is nothing as practical as a good theory!

## APPROACHES TO EVALUATION

Beginning a discussion on scheme design with a discussion on evaluation may seem strange. Evaluation is often an afterthought! This is because it seems to be axiomatic to argue that it is only possible to evaluate something once there is something to evaluate. Furthermore, it seems to make sense to think about how to evaluate something once it is known what there is to examine. For example, if a scheme coordinator has exceeded their recruitment targets for a mentoring programme and has a far greater number of participants than anticipated, it seems sensible to adjust the evaluation methodology accordingly. Additionally, and perhaps the most persuasive of all these arguments: it is only possible to evaluate something once the outcomes are known!

All too often schemes are evaluated later in their development, and the success factors are identified post hoc. According to Megginson et al. (2006: 9), it is important to be clear about the success criteria before the scheme starts. For us, this seems to depend on the answers to three key questions:

1. How will I know whether the scheme has been successful or not?
2. What criteria will I use to make these judgements?
3. What measures will I use to assess the scheme against these criteria?

## MODELS OF EVALUATION

### Kirkpatrick

Perhaps the best-known goal-based model of evaluating training interventions is Kirkpatrick's (1959) model. Kirkpatrick bases the model on four different levels:

1. Reaction – participants' responses and reactions to the training, whether they themselves found it useful.
2. Learning – whether participants have increased their capability or knowledge as a result of the training.
3. Behaviour – what impact the training has had on participants' behaviour.
4. Results – what impact the training has ultimately had on business results or the wider environment.

Although this model was developed to evaluate training, it is useful in the context of coaching and mentoring evaluation because it draws our attention to three main issues.

First, it recognizes that the success of a scheme is multi-layered and not just about whether participants thought it was useful or enjoyable. Often, training event evaluation is limited to the reaction level because this is easy and quick to measure. This has led to the handing out of evaluation forms at the end of training events being somewhat derisively known as 'happy sheets'. However, the Kirkpatrick model recognizes that this is only one measure.

Second, it also acknowledges that participants are not the only source of data for judging the success of a training intervention, even if the focus is on them and their capability. Ely et al. (2010: 596) explore this issue in their comprehensive review of evaluation models used in leadership coaching:

> Although 24% of studies in our review included multi-source data, the reliance of the majority of studies on client self-report data reflects a major limitation of the coaching evaluation literature. Leadership coaching is a very personal process – making the client a natural source of information. However past research suggests that individuals tend to inflate self-assessments of their performance. Additionally, meta analyses investigating the validity of self-assessments have shown self-assessments to be only moderately correlated with other measures of knowledge and performance. This suggests that assessments of leadership behaviour and performance should also be collected from relevant others in positions to evaluate the client's behaviour and performance (e.g. the client's subordinates).

The Kirkpatrick framework offers other stakeholders the opportunity to identify the positive impact of an intervention on an individual's learning or behaviour even when that individual's reaction to it is a negative one or vice versa. It also recognizes that, as in the case of formal mentoring and coaching schemes, the ultimate aim of a development intervention is to improve organizational results in some way, for example increased profits, improved performance, greater employee retention or reduced costs.

Finally, it also recognizes the importance of time as another key element in the process. The difficulty with this is that we are less likely, in studies that take a 'snapshot' approach, to be able to identify the distal outcomes. However, what the framework does not do is completely resolve the issue of different research paradigms that we explored in Chapter 2.

A positivist approach to evaluation is likely to seek to prove a causal link, for example between coaching and improved business performance, with the researcher attempting to discount alternative and competing explanations for such an improvement.

With a phenomenological approach, the researcher is attempting to evaluate the scheme in terms of the subjective understandings of the impact of the intervention. Further, it is not clear what happens if multiple levels of evaluation conclude that there are competing conclusions about the effectiveness of the intervention. Similarly, different stakeholders may have different reactions, learning, behavioural responses and impacts on business results, the net effect of which make outcomes difficult to measure.

Finally, perhaps the most important drawback with Kirkpatrick's model is that while allowing for the possibility of different stages of evaluation, it does not lend itself to ongoing evaluation and feedback, throughout the life of a coaching or mentoring scheme. As will be seen in Chapter 6, this form of evaluation has also led to the pre-specification of learning outcomes that are independent of and detached from the learner.

Another approach to evaluation is the Return on Investment (ROI) approach. This was a favoured approach in coaching from the early 2000s as executive coaching was burgeoning. This approach sits firmly within the managerialist discourse. Grant's (2012) analysis of ROI evaluation within coaching is critical for the following reasons:

1. Financial measures of ROI in coaching often use different approaches so make comparison across studies problematic, e.g. some build in a conservative estimate.
2. It is difficult to attribute a direct causal link between coaching and financial return.
3. It is even more difficult to attribute coaching to its impact on those that the coachee manages.
4. Even if these flaws can be controlled for, the ROI is problematic as, to compare rates with others, factors such as costs and opportunity to shape the outcomes must be similar.
5. The impact of using a financial ROI may be to stress the coachee to achieve the financial returns which may militate against the coaching itself.

Grant (2012) argues for the use of well-being and engagement measures as they may give a more holistic view of coaching impact, using well-validated instruments. However, Yates (2015a, 2015b) seems to call into question whether the above discourse has had much influence. In her survey of HR, OD and L&D managers in 69 large UK organizations, she found that:

- More than half (57.4%) do not know how many of their employees are currently working with an external coach.
- More than half (57.4%) do not know the status of each of their coaching relationships.
- 47.5% do not know the total annual spend on external coaches.

This relative lack of focus on the precise details of who is coaching who and what it costs seems to mitigate Grant's (2012) claim that too much emphasis on ROI stresses participants. Nevertheless, Yates's (2015b) response to this put forward a 12-step process for the effective evaluation of coaching programmes:

1. Identify the business case.
2. Check out cultural readiness.
3. Emphasize contracting and code of ethics.
4. Agree a robust and consistent process for coaching.
5. Determine ideal coach specification and build coach pool.
6. Involve the line manager throughout the coaching process.
7. Set the context for coaches.
8. Ensure management information (MI) reporting.
9. Link results to internal surveys and metrics.
10. Report on evaluation and organizational intelligence.
11. Work in continuous partnership.
12. Share success stories to increase buy-in.

This appears to be an attempt to respond to what is seen as a deficit in process on the part of the organizations involved. While having a clear evaluation structure and integration with organizational metrics can be helpful (see Chapter 3, 'Creating a Coaching and Mentoring Culture'), it is important that Yates's (2015a, 2015b) research was conducted with large organizations, and it must be understood in that context. Mentoring and coaching are social processes that depend on the active engagement and positive participation of individuals, and the social context is important. Consequently, the personal commitment and personal involvement inherent in a coaching or mentoring scheme mean that it is important to treat evaluation as an ongoing developmental process. The consequences of an evaluation that discovers a problem 12 months after it occurs could be serious for the future of coaching and mentoring in that organization. Hence, while there is a strong argument for thinking through the rationale for a coaching or mentoring scheme in organizations, and designing the evaluation with this in mind, there is a risk in overly linear-rational evaluation models. This is because they can, inadvertently, close off an iterative approach to evaluation, which allows for this active multi-stakeholder engagement.

Additionally, there are tensions in scheme design and evaluation. As we will discuss in Chapter 7, power and surveillance impact on coaching and mentoring schemes. For example, Ben-Hador's (2016) study examines the idea of coaching as a form of tacit performance evaluation. Her multiple case study research was conducted using text analysis between coachees, their managers and HR staff, across eight organizations in Israel. It revealed that the coaching process itself was being used to evaluate executive performance and, in some cases, was militating against the coaching process, which by implication undermines any evaluation of the coaching process within those organizations. Hence, this raises a tension between what evaluation is being espoused and what evaluation is occurring underneath. This fits with the more overt manifestation of power observed by Weer et al. (2016) in their longitudinal study in the USA – they refer to it as 'pressure-based coaching' – where coaching was used to magnify existing power mechanisms, with the intent of improving performance. Similarly, this pressure-based coaching, as in Ben-Hador's (2016) study, seemed to undermine, rather than enhance, performance, which, in turn, detracts from effective evaluation.

Another tension in scheme design and evaluation is acknowledging that not all possible outcomes will be or can be recognized, and therefore measured, before the coaching or mentoring intervention begins. Therefore, this lends weight to the argument that an ongoing, development-focused evaluation is the best strategy for capturing this learning throughout the life of a scheme. Case Study 4.1 is an example of such an evaluation. It employs a 'realist approach' (Pawson and Tilley, 1997).

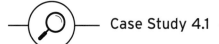 **Case Study 4.1**

### London Deanery Mentoring Service evaluation: A realist approach

Chadwick-Coule and Garvey (2009) report on their evaluation of the London Deanery Mentoring Service. The London Deanery embarked on a service to develop a network of trained mentors for London's medical and dental professionals in 2008. The Deanery co-ordinates, trains and quality assures the network of mentors and acts as a broker (and paying agent) between mentee and mentor for a diverse mentee client group.

The Deanery commissioned the Coaching and Mentoring Research Unit at Sheffield Business School to undertake a formative, developmental evaluation of the Mentoring Service's working practices and outcomes. The evaluation took place between January and July 2009.

The aim of this report was threefold:

- to enrich understanding of the effectiveness of current partnership mechanisms in the delivery of the Mentoring Service
- to identify potential benefits for the participants
- to understand the impact of mentoring and the Mentoring Service on participants.

The evaluation involved five key elements: scoping work with members of London Deanery to establish the evaluation framework and 'theory of change' underpinning the scheme; stakeholder interviews with London Deanery staff/external representatives involved in project governance through the Mentoring Advisory Group; a survey of London Deanery Mentoring Service mentors and mentees to assess the extent to which the Mentoring Service meets its purpose; client case studies with eight pairings (i.e. involving mentor and mentee) across different client groups and specialisms; and a review of project documentation relating to the governance and management structure processes and procedures of the Mentoring Service. The intent in conducting the evaluation in this way was not to provide a summative evaluation of whether the London Deanery Mentoring Service initiative had been successful or not, in hard and fast terms. It was recognized that the Mentoring Service was unlikely to develop in a neat, logical or predictable manner. Chadwick-Coule and Garvey (2009) instead chose to use a 'theory of change' approach to the evaluation. This approach involved trying to understand the intent of the various stakeholders and the change that they were trying to make and using this logic of change (see Figure 4.1) to inform the data-collection process. In this way, it was possible to design data collection and analysis that reflected different aspects of the approach and, as the service progressed and further evaluation took place, to refine the questions asked and the issues that were explored. It was also possible to reflect back to participants, and strategic stakeholders, the consequences of the approach they adopted, what it achieved and what problems were encountered.

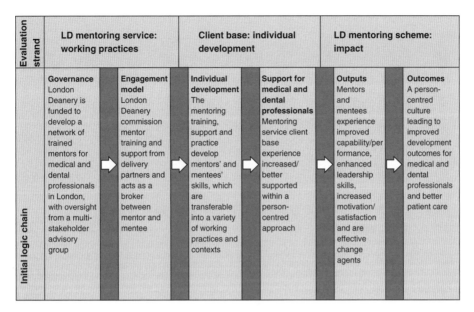

**Figure 4.1**   Theory of change evaluation framework

## DISCUSSION OF CASE STUDY

Chadwick-Coule and Garvey (2009) recognized that different stakeholders within this scheme are likely to hold different views on what it means to be a 'good mentor' or what constitutes 'good mentoring' or even being a 'good doctor'. Some, for example, may have defined a good mentor in terms of knowledge, others in terms of having qualities such as empathy, experience, etc. It was therefore important to surface such divergent and potentially conflicting philosophies (or theories) as they led to different images and socializations of programme participants. As we will discuss in Chapter 7, there are dangers in having a single dominant discourse because powerful stakeholders (e.g. funders, scheme sponsors) can dominate the evaluation.

Chadwick-Coule and Garvey's intent was to understand the complex web of arguments, orientations and actions which constituted the theory of change with regard to this intervention. This then enabled them to position the views and opinions of the various stakeholders in the study as representing the ongoing social factors which strengthen or weaken the theory of change, as articulated in Figure 4.1. In this sense, they were trying to develop a 'rich picture' of the intervention which encompassed working practices, individual development and impact on outcomes.

Overall, the evaluation revealed that the Mentoring Service was well received and all stakeholders reported positive responses that were in line with the theories of change. Nevertheless, this orientation towards evaluation also allowed them to identify some areas for future development and consideration – for example, challenges around administration, access to experienced mentors for novice mentors, training for mentees, impact of pressures on budgets and impact of changes in the Deanery. Most of all, however, the evaluation presents a sophisticated, rich picture of the various social and organizational dynamics involved in such an initiative, thus enabling key stakeholders to make more informed decisions about the future of the service and, indeed, of the Deanery itself, to some degree.

The benefit of looking at this evaluation process is that, due to the richness of the picture, it is possible to anticipate some of the challenges and issues that need to be resolved in terms of designing an effective coaching or mentoring scheme.

A PhD researcher, Sally Lawson, took the basis of the above evaluation much further. She argues that it is essential to understand the 'theory' of mentoring, and thus the theories of change associated with specific mentoring programmes to inform, evidence, evaluate and communicate what we do.

## WHO NEEDS A THEORY OF MENTORING? WE ALL DO, SAYS SALLY LAWSON

Mentoring is based on valuing and working with individual differences and is predicated on beliefs about individual and collective agency and the collaborative potential to effect meaningful change. Once established within mentoring, these are then externalized to influence ways of being and working in the real world. Yet despite a wealth of writing about how to do 'good mentoring', there has been limited progress on 'good theory', i.e. substantive causal explanations of how it works (Bozeman and Feeney, 2007).

Mentoring is more than a recipe, the sum of its artefacts. Change through mentoring comes from those involved and not the intervention per se, although the construct of mentoring creates an enabling social environment in which change occurs. It is transacted through personal and interpersonal engagement in developmental relationships and purposeful conversations. Outcomes are individually defined and meaningful. Each relationship is unique and yet contains elements and links that point to the way other mentoring relationships might also work, across levels and phases (Megginson et al., 2006). Acknowledging this complexity, new knowledge such as theory should be generated from a sympathetic, congruent methodology. The author's PhD (Lawson, 2017) established how mentoring worked as an intervention and an approach within a mentoring programme. This was offered to a group of specialist health and care practitioners as an opportunity to learn differently, work differently and make a difference. The evaluation used realist methodology (Pawson and Tilley, 1997). It was chosen for the way it reflected the philosophy and approach of the very thing it was evaluating and its potential to generate transferable theory of how mentoring worked from mentoring's extensive literature, expert opinion and the experiences of those involved. The ontological position in realist methodology is that the world is real, complex and organized in social systems within which and with which people interact, individually and together. In considering what can be known about this world, the realist approach seeks to understand how interventions work and, as a result, to improve knowledge about them.

In her research, bringing this causal perspective to mentoring enabled the researcher to accommodate its complexity in practice and, when generating theory, in terms of what worked for whom and how. Attention shifted from the presence or absence of particular mentoring artefacts to the individual and interpersonal responses to them, situated in and impacting on their real world as they better came to understand it. The evaluation process enabled the researcher to identify the parts played by the individual mentors and mentees as themselves, in their interactions with each other and the many resources mentoring afforded, influenced by the circumstances that informed what they thought, felt, decided and did. These ranged from the most personal and interpersonal, to those situated at organizational or even infrastructural levels. Together, these highlighted the way mentees and mentors moved to meaningful outcomes that encompassed learning, development and change. Appreciating the patterns in the way these linked elements played out, through the contexts, mechanisms and outcomes identified in the literature, and amplified by experts and personalized by what the mentors and mentees themselves identified as significant for them, was the basis for generating theory about mentoring. Such theory was necessarily dynamic and complex.

An experienced mentor recognizes the importance of enabling their mentee to explore and use these processes for themselves. This is part of their expertise. What is needed for the wider mentoring community is to uncover these processes and patterns at a collective level and express them as theory or theories that can then be scrutinized, validated, amended or refuted. Good theory can then support good mentoring.

The following sections of this chapter explore these challenges and issues in more depth.

## SCHEME DESIGN

### Purpose

First, as we have already argued in previous chapters, it is important to be as clear *as possible* about the intended purpose of a coaching or mentoring scheme. Different stakeholders within a scheme – senior managers, coaches, mentors, other managers, customers – may have different and competing views about the purpose of the scheme. Again, this can be linked back to our earlier discussion about different ways of dealing with evaluation research. A phenomenological approach to evaluation, as was taken with London Deanery, will tend to emphasize the exploration of different subjective views of the purpose within a scheme in a relative way. However, a positivistic approach will tend to emphasize the need for clarity around purpose. This is because the positivist research agenda is focused on 'testing' or 'proving' a causal relationship between coaching and/or mentoring and the dependent variable, for example organizational performance. In doing this, the evaluator must be able to isolate the effect of the coaching and mentoring on organizational performance. If organizational performance improves after coaching and/or mentoring has been used as an intervention, the evaluator must be able to discount other competing explanations for this variance in performance – for example, the arrival of a new managing director, a general economic upturn, other developmental interventions (see Gill et al., 2010, for a summary of other research design problems using this approach).

Our preferred plan is to adopt a phenomenological approach to understanding purpose. This approach does not downplay differences in understanding but acknowledges them as sources of further questions leading to deeper and fuller discussion. Inevitably, however, *initial* responses to the questions reproduced below tend to be decided on by the most powerful stakeholders, for example the senior managers or sponsors of the scheme. In Case Study 4.2 later in this chapter, the purpose of the scheme seemed to expand in an attempt to cover as many organizational ills as possible!

## Reflective Questions

- How will I know whether the scheme has been successful or not?
- What criteria will I use to make these judgements?
- What measures will I use to assess the scheme against these criteria?
- What is the theory behind coaching or mentoring in my organization?

In Colley's (2003) work, the 'agency' of the mentors and mentees within engagement mentoring schemes meant that the purpose of the mentoring, as defined by government and other powerful stakeholders, was fundamentally altered and undermined by these seemingly less powerful stakeholders. In a different way, in Beech and Brockbank's (1999) work, we can see how different understandings of what mentoring was about and what people's roles were in it led to 'psychosocial dysfunction' (1999: 24), as power dynamics (see Chapter 7) emerged in unexpected ways within the mentoring relationships and within the mentoring scheme.

## Recruitment and selection

Along with the question 'What is the scheme for?', a further question might be 'Who is the scheme for?' Often, this question stimulates a statement around purpose and an intended target for an intervention. However, as Case Study 4.2 shows, the answer to this question is not always obvious.

## Eligibility

Organizational schemes consume resources; therefore, scheme sponsors need to make decisions about who they will allow to be involved in the coaching/mentoring process. They need to be clear about the criteria for acceptance as either a coach or coachee. For example, a FTSE 100 company based in the north of England offered external one-to-one coaching for a range of aspiring senior managers as part of a 19-day development programme. They talked in terms of 'targeted' coaching, using a 'push' approach, rather than offering it to all and working via a demand-led system. Additionally, these managers had an internal mentor to support their application of the learning from the programme into the workplace.

In Case Study 4.2, the eligibility question seems clear, but was this the right choice given the outcome?

## Credibility

Coaching and mentoring work best when both parties are willingly involved and make active choices about who they want to work with. Therefore, each party must be credible to the other in terms of their willingness to invest the time in the process. This can lead to competition for key organizational members as coaches or mentors and does suggest that, inevitably, not everyone can have exactly who they want to work with. Some years ago, we were involved in creating a mentoring programme, putting together senior executives from experienced exporting organizations with those from less experienced exporting organizations, as part of a publicly funded project (see Megginson and Stokes, 2004). Mentees were often quite fastidious in terms of who they would work with (see the section on Matching below) and were often very clear at the outset about what their mentor should have achieved and what sort of business they would like them to be in. Conversely, the mentors were happy to work with anyone from any background. Garvey and Galloway (2002) also found examples of what they called 'mentee fastidiousness' and 'mentor indifference' in the mentoring scheme they developed. In practice, if mentees were matched with someone not meeting their specification, they found that the relationship could still be very useful to them. In this sense, the mentees were clear about what they wanted, but wrong about the importance of their pre-specification.

## Availability

Related to the above, the scheme organizer must consider the likely availability of both coaches/mentors and mentees/coachees and the impact of any imbalances on the success of the scheme in terms of its stated purpose. At the time of writing the first edition of this book, we were working with South Yorkshire Police and their Positive Action Mentoring Scheme (PAMS) (see Chapter 12). The intention of the scheme was to make progression and development within the organization accessible to under-represented groups within its hierarchy. One of the challenges facing newly trained mentors was that there were relatively few formal referrals via the scheme; because of the confidential nature of the scheme, mentees either made direct contact with the mentors or mentors made offers to prospective mentees. This also presented a challenge when it came to evaluating the scheme because of the lack of information about the outcomes of the scheme.

## Motivation

It is important to be aware of possible motivations for being involved in a scheme that both coaches/coachees and mentors/mentees might have. Our experience with a range of schemes (see Megginson et al., 2006) suggests that it is often more helpful if the coach or mentor has a clear idea about what they want to get out of the relationship, in addition to being helpful to the coachee/mentee. In contrast, a desire to 'give something back' and to 'offer people the benefit of my experience' can suggest that the coach/mentor has more of an interest in being admired and having a willing and receptive audience than actually focusing on what they might do to help their partner further their agenda. There is nothing wrong with altruism as a motive for becoming a coach or mentor, but we have found that if it is the only motive, then this is a contra-indicator. It is often better that mentors/coaches are also interested in learning for themselves. Asking a potential mentor or internal coach 'what do you hope to gain from mentoring or coaching?' could be a productive question in uncovering motivations.

## Coaching and mentoring education and development

Once the decision has been made about whom the coaching or mentoring is for, and methods of recruitment and selection have been established, it is important to consider the mode and methods of development. The one that we shall focus on here is our preferred approach to development, which is rooted as it is in adult development theory.

## A curriculum for mentoring and coaching education

The term 'curriculum' is important here. It is about thinking about learning and development over time, rather than as a one-off event, and it is about what a programme of learning should consist of. The curriculum specialist Basil Bernstein (1971) posed four key questions in relation to curriculum design and suggested that these need to be addressed in any curriculum design as follows:

What is:

- valid knowledge
- valid pedagogy

- valid evaluation
- valid realization?

In relation to mentor or coach development these questions are relevant. However, pedagogy is about teaching and Bernstein (1971) suggests that high teacher control in education can result in low autonomy for the learner. In the context of mentoring and coaching where a mentor or coach needs to 'consciously seek out their own way' (Megginson and Stokes, 2004: 94) an andragogic (Knowles, 1980) approach is more appropriate. Knowles (1980) outlined six elements of andragogy for adults:

1. need to know the reason for learning something
2. learn experientially
3. need to be responsible and involved in the planning and evaluation of their learning

4. are most interested in learning things relevant to themselves
5. need a problem-based approach for learning rather than a content-based approach
6. tend to be self-motivated rather than need external motivation.

The risk of a pedagogic training programme is that it has the potential to disengage the learner, and Broad and Newstrom (1992) have argued that this approach simply does not deliver. The andragogic approach resonates with the concept of 'the mentoring way' (Garvey and Alred, 2000) (perhaps more appropriate to think in terms of the 'coaching and mentoring way') and is therefore an important element of the curriculum design for coach or mentor education. This approach is more empowering for the adult learner, coach or mentor and provides an alternative model of learning. This may subsequently influence the coach's or mentor's approach to their practice, potentially reducing the tendency to instruct and advise and helping them to become more andragogic and non-directive in their practice.

Therefore, we propose the following content for a coach or mentor programme:

- establishing the purpose of the mentoring or coaching in the context in which it is employed
- mentoring/coaching philosophies
- exploring a range of possible definitions of mentoring/coaching and considering how these apply individually and in the context of the scheme
- some psychological education on transference and countertransference and parallel process
- power dynamics and how to work with them in a nondirective way
- considering at least two process models, comparing and contrasting them
- skills practice including listening, questioning, use of summary, challenge and support
- the importance of establishing ground rules and reviewing them
- working with expectations
- establishing a good relationship
- considering and discussing organizational issues which may impact on mentoring/coaching activity
- ways of ending the relationship.

Learning takes time, and whilst learning, ongoing support is necessary. This can take various forms, from one-to-one support to peer group support.

## Matching

Matching coaches and coachees, and mentors and mentees is often messy and difficult. Megginson et al. (2006) argue that it is important to take account of a number of factors when matching.

### The criteria for matching

These should follow from a clearer understanding of purpose and identification of who the coaching or mentoring is for. For example, in the export scheme referred to earlier (Megginson and Stokes, 2004), the focus of the matching was around putting people with experience of export together with those who had no such experience. As we later explore, this was not the only factor.

### Rapport

The quality of the relationship and chemistry is something that we have argued (Chapter 1) is particularly underplayed in the literature on coaching. In both the export scheme and the PAMS scheme mentioned earlier, the success of the intervention seems to crucially depend on the quality of the relationship.

## The balance between similarity and difference

In all coaching and mentoring, it is crucial to achieve a balance between there being sufficient difference, in order to add value, and sufficient similarity, in order to enable rapport. As mentioned above, the quality of the relationship and the strength of the rapport between the two individuals is referred to much more in the mentoring literature than in the coaching literature, although this trend is beginning to change (see Bluckert, 2005). Colley's (2003) work on engagement mentoring also reminds us that each individual will want different things from the relationship and that this may not always be consistent with the stated aims of the scheme.

## Marketing a scheme

Coaching and mentoring can sometimes be seen as 'nice to have' options within an organization. Our view is that, because coaching and mentoring is such an intrinsic and natural part of adult development (see Chapters 1 and 3), it should be recognized and embedded as a central and legitimate work activity. For those new to coaching and mentoring, it is important to give them an opportunity to find out about what is involved before committing to it. Consequently, marketing the scheme is important, but there are two key approaches that can be taken with marketing.

### Formal launch and new initiative approach

This is where the usual mechanisms for promoting any change are put in place in a formal and organized way, for example team briefings, formal papers, presentations. This has the advantage of legitimizing the activity, particularly if key players (see Chapter 8) are seen to be involved. This approach is supported by Clutterbuck et al.'s (2012: 15) analysis of successful diversity mentoring programmes, which concludes:

> In terms of management and leadership, one of the most important traits for most of these programs is that they needed someone to serve as the cheerleader/the torchbearer to motivate mentors and mentees and the organization and to keep things going.

Hence, the formality and structure help, according to their analysis. However, this formality also brings pressure to bear on people to be involved. This can militate against the spirit of voluntarism which underpins coaching and mentoring. Also, it can sometimes put too much pressure on the coaching and mentoring itself to solve a whole host of organizational issues and raise expectations too high (see Garvey's case study in Megginson et al., 2006: 124–33).

### The organic approach

This is where coaching and mentoring are promoted in a low-key way by using other, less formal channels of communication, for example newsletters, word of mouth, lunchtime get-togethers.

To draw on Gareth Morgan's (2006) work on metaphors, this approach tends to require scheme organizers to think of the scheme rather like an organism, as a living thing that needs to be nurtured and developed under the right environmental conditions. This has the advantage of relieving some of the pressure on a scheme that the formal launch approach brings, while still giving people access to the experience in a way that might pique their interest as opposed to pressurizing them to be involved. Case studies in Clutterbuck and Megginson (2005b: 137–45) of KPMG and the Scottish Executive illustrate this approach, where they conclude that it has the potential disadvantage of not seeming to have the full weight of the system behind it and, therefore, possibly fizzling out.

Cranwell-Ward et al.'s (2004: 68–9) book on mentoring provides a useful list of support tools which a scheme organizer may use to market their coaching or mentoring scheme. These include:

- booklets – giving details of objectives, benefits, roles and responsibilities of participants
- policy/process documents – giving details of eligibility, processes involved and possible content of meetings
- websites – giving details contained in the above two categories but also links to other resources, e.g. models, useful questions, FAQs

- use of champions – identifying people who have been coaches, coachees, mentors or mentees and who have benefited from the scheme
- information workshops – short lunchtime sessions to inform people about the scheme
- email and voicemail – two normal organizational communication mechanisms which might be used to promote the scheme.

In tackling this case study, consider the issues outlined above in your analysis. You may also employ some ideas from Chapter 3 to help.

 **Case Study 4.2**

### Background

Engineering Co. is a large, market-leading, multi-national engineering company. It is also constantly aware of the serious threat of competition. To tackle these threats, the business created a new corporate change strategy underpinned by a number of slogans:

- 'the battle for supremacy in the marketplace will be won on the factory floor'
- 'customer led'
- 'learning organization'
- 'continuous improvement'
- 'people are our most important asset'.

Senior management stated that change would only be achieved through the involvement and commitment of the whole workforce. The strategy was created by the senior team and 'cascaded' through the business.

*(Continued)*

Central to the change strategy was the notion of 'the common approach' for all people. This meant that the design, implementation and evaluation of all development programmes were carried out with constant reference to the worldwide company objectives. Through this approach of working to a common agenda, it was believed that all sections of the company would develop in the same direction and emerge with a shared philosophy.

At the heart of the Organizational Change and Development (OCD) programme was a mentoring scheme.

The Learning and Development Manager (LDM) employed Kram's (1985b) four stage process:

1. defining the scope of the project
2. diagnosis of the factors that will support and the factors that will hinder the scheme
3. the implementation plan
4. evaluation.

---

## The Case

### Scheme purpose

The overall purpose of the mentoring, as specified by the LDM, was to 'provide the yeast in the bread' for change. He saw mentoring as a key element in helping those on the OCD programme to apply their learning in the workplace. In the brief for mentors, he asked them to discuss career opportunities with their mentees as well as help resolve learning difficulties by creating a supportive environment. He was clear that mentors were not meant to control events but to act as 'independent counsellors and guides'.

He positioned the mentoring process as 'two-way'. In doing so, he hoped that the mentors would learn as well. Additionally, to the above purposes he added that mentoring was for new recruits and mentors needed to provide the opportunity for 'clients' to gain a better understanding of the internal and formal structures of the organization quickly. This was seen as particularly important for people new to the organization as valuable time was often lost in understanding these structures.

Further, the scheme was to address the following:

1. recent redundancies
2. the need for improved individual effectiveness
3. internal cultural change (from 'command and control' to a 'leadership culture').

The scope of the scheme was comprehensive.

### The issues

The LDM acknowledged that the business had no previous experience of mentoring and that some potential mentors had had no positive experience of mentoring in the past and some were opposed to the concept of the scheme.

The competitive nature of Engineering Co.'s business meant that the time scale for implementation of mentoring was short. However, Engineering Co. set about gaining information on the attitudes, skills and knowledge of the potential participants in the mentor scheme to help plan the approach to mentoring.

It was discovered that some potential mentors had a poor comprehension of how development impacts on the career progression and personal growth of people. This led to the view, held by some potential mentors, that people development was secondary and unimportant. Some potential mentors were experiencing blockages in their own career progression and therefore were not very keen to help others to progress.

Another issue identified was the overriding culture in the organization. It was felt that individuals might not consciously attempt to thwart the culture change but might be driven by a powerful subconscious force based on the notion of 'this is not the way I did it' and 'I did it the hard way and so should you'.

These attitudes were part of the deep internal politics of Engineering Co., and it was these that needed to change if the organization was to achieve the successful implementation of its new strategy.

## Implementation plan

The LDM developed criteria for the selection of mentors as follows:

- interest in being a mentor
- support for the change process
- position to influence
- ability to influence networks
- security in own position and sense of 'camaraderie'
- time to participate
- leadership – self-management abilities, ability to listen, interpret and comment, ability to manage time skills necessary to facilitate good interpersonal relationships.

This, the LDM believed, would mean that potential mentors would already be experienced by virtue of being 'senior' in the organization. But he wasn't specific about what being 'experienced' actually meant! The selected mentors received a half-day training programme that focused on developing counselling skills.

Following the training, the mentors were placed with mentees by the LDM, who claimed he 'knew everyone's needs'.

In some cases, the mentor was the mentee's line manager or the line manager of the mentee's manager. The mentoring pairs did not create any 'ground rules' of engagement and consequently there was no review process within the relationships.

## Evaluation

During the 14-month research period, the OCD programme had, according to the LDM, been running very well. However, the mentor scheme had many problems and went through a period of restructuring. As a result of this, it emerged that mentors needed further training and development, particularly in understanding the nature of adult learning and counselling skills.

*(Continued)*

There was also a need identified to consider the reward and recognition issues for people fulfilling the mentor role. Mentors said that they were too busy to give their time properly.

### Postscript

The official language of 'people are our most important asset' was promulgated. However, mentors and managers still spoke about the shop floor workers as 'animals who need their arse's reaming out'.

A comment from a shop floor worker seems relevant here, 'You can talk development all you like but if the product is not out of the door on a Friday night, you still get your backside kicked!'

### Discussion questions

Using Kram's framework for developing a mentoring scheme, discuss the case of Engineering Co. and consider:

- What did the LDM do well?
- What could the LDM have done better?

Using the criteria above and some ideas from Chapter 3, suggest some reasons for the scheme's failure. Suggest an alternative approach.
Consider the influence of culture on the mentors, the mentees and the scheme itself.
What role does 'power' play in this case and how is it manifest?
In an autocratic culture, what is likely to be the dominant management behaviour?

---

## CONCLUSIONS

In this chapter, we have chosen to focus the unit of analysis on the coaching and mentoring scheme itself. As mentoring and, in particular, coaching have become more popular and commonplace in organizations, it is noticeable that evaluation and return on investment have become more prominent as discussion topics, particularly within the practitioner-based literature. As we have suggested in this chapter and in Chapter 2, it is important to reflect on and be clear about the rationale for conducting such evaluations. Furthermore, the approach to evaluation that is employed has critical implications for scheme design and should be considered first of all.

Our own preferred position on evaluation is one that sees it as an ongoing and collaborative process; in research methodology terms, it is more akin to action research. Gill and Johnson (1997: 76) summarize this approach well:

Action research, then, is clearly an important approach to research in business and management, particularly given its declared aim of serving both the practical concerns of managers and simultaneously generalizing and adding to theory. Most researchers using this approach wish to do immediately useful work and at the same time to stand back from the specific so that their research may be more widely utilized.

It is unfortunate, in our view, that many publicly-funded coaching and mentoring evaluation projects seem to reject this approach in favour of a more positivistic evaluation strategy. This latter approach tends to emphasize distance between the evaluator and what is being evaluated, which, in our view, can militate against a deep understanding of what is happening within the complexities of a coaching and mentoring scheme. Crucially, evaluating any pilot coaching and mentoring scheme at the end of its life means that the scheme organizer, the participants and the organization as a whole do not benefit from the evaluation until the end, when, in fact, it might have been possible to improve the experience for all concerned had a more collaborative approach been used. As a result, this can have the effect of influencing the scheme organizer's behaviour so as to make sure they appear to 'hit their targets' at the expense of identifying useful learning that may come out of the scheme.

Furthermore, we have also argued, using Kirkpatrick's (1959) model of evaluation, that as well as adopting an ongoing approach to evaluation, there are some strong arguments in favour of extending the evaluation over a longer time period so as to capture the effects and implications for participant learning, behaviour and its impact on the organization's results.

Drawing on our experience of conducting evaluations, we have attempted, following the traditions of action research, to identify broader challenges in terms of scheme design that have come out of our work and that of others. We offer these to scheme organizers and practitioners, as well as other researchers, in the hope that they are useful in generating a deeper understanding of coaching and mentoring. We will continue to return to these issues and themes throughout the book.

 ## Future Direction

It is our contention that those who fund and commission research into coaching and mentoring need to recognize the situated, contextual nature of such activity. Our prediction is that, as the body of research in this area continues to grow, a more sophisticated and reflexive approach to scheme design and evaluation will emerge. Central to this approach will be some recognition of the impact of the evaluation process itself on the outcomes. We also predict that organizational coaching and mentoring schemes will become more and more aligned with and linked to existing development initiatives within the organization. This, in turn, will have implications for the way evaluation is understood, in terms of its scope and scale.

 ## Activity

Imagine this scenario: You have the chance to work as a coaching and mentoring consultant with a construction business. The business has grown significantly in the last five years and has plans to double its turnover in the next five years. This has partly been as a result of a successful acquisition strategy – the group is now made up of 15 separate smaller businesses, each with their own distinctive offers in different locales. The MD feels, however, that there

*(Continued)*

is a communication issue and cultural gap between those businesses and that, as a result, the group is not accruing all the advantages of working together as a larger group. In particular, he has identified that there are key pockets of knowledge and expertise within some of the businesses and that these need to be more widely shared. He sees mentoring as a way of achieving this. However, many of the businesses are characterized by him as having a 'macho' culture with little history of sharing and collaborating on such things and where asking for help is a sign of weakness. He is concerned that this will militate against a mentoring programme:

- As the consultant, what steps would you take, in terms of scheme design, to ensure that the scheme is successful?
- How would you evaluate how successful your intervention is?

---

 **Questions** ————————————————————

- How will you know whether your coaching/mentoring scheme has been successful or not?
- Who is the coaching/mentoring for?
- What criteria will you use to make these judgements?

---

 **Further Reading** ————————————————

For a strong analysis of qualitative research evaluation, look at: Creswell, J. (2012) *Qualitative Inquiry and Research Design: Choosing among Five Approaches*. Thousand Oaks, CA: SAGE.

For those particularly interested in action research as a mode of evaluation, look at: Ozanne, J.L. and Saatcioglu, B. (2008) 'Participatory action research', *Journal of Consumer Research*, 5: 423-39, for a strong example of how this might be planned and conducted.

In order to gain an overview of the key issues in mentoring scheme design, read Stokes and Merrick's 'Designing mentoring schemes for organizations' (Chapter 11) in J. Passmore, D.B. Peterson, and T. Freire (eds) (2013) *The Wiley-Blackwell Handbook of Psychology of Coaching and Mentoring*. Chichester: John Wiley, pp. 197-216.

For an in-depth look at mentor training see: Garvey, R. and Westlander, G. (2013) 'Training mentors: Behaviors which bring positive outcomes in mentoring', in J. Passmore, D.B. Peterson and T. Freire (eds), *The Wiley-Blackwell Handbook of the Psychology of Coaching and Mentoring*. Chichester: John Wiley, pp. 243-65.

# 5

# MODELS AND PERSPECTIVES ON COACHING AND MENTORING

## CHAPTER OVERVIEW

This chapter looks at the wide variety and range of models and perspectives in coaching and mentoring. We aim to reflect the breadth and depth of the field and to explore some of the assumptions that underpin the various approaches and models. This is not a detailed exploration of models and perspectives; rather, we attempt to capture the essence of each approach to raise more interesting research questions about mentoring and coaching as a domain of theory and practice. For a more detailed account of various models of coaching see Cox et al. (2014). In this fourth edition, we have included three updated case examples. One is an updated version of self-mentoring. The second reflects the increasing trend towards internal coaching schemes within organizations, and the third is an example of an inter-organizational model of coaching. Towards the end of the chapter we have included an updated discussion on the hybridization of coaching and mentoring referred to in Chapter 1.

## INTRODUCTION

Megginson and Clutterbuck (2005a) suggest that raising the issue of techniques in mentoring and coaching can be reductionist and lead to a formulaic approach to practice. They also suggest that, for some, having a model or framework to follow is contrary to the humanistic tradition that coaching and mentoring represents. This can inhibit empathy and a sense of giving oneself to another. However, they argue that, for others, having a conceptual framework that guides their practice is useful and does not necessarily inhibit an authentic and meaningful coaching and mentoring relationship. Additionally, Gray et al. (2016) argue that one of the tests for a profession to be called a profession is a set of common standards. With the exponential proliferation of coaching, specifically, many competence-based courses invite participants to create their own models of practice. Clearly this creates a problem for the professionalization agenda. Taking into account these different and equally legitimate positions and by linking to other chapters in this book, we debate these issues.

## METHODOLOGY

We developed this chapter using literature, general web searches and our own experience to uncover the wide variety and range of coaching and mentoring models. Given the content of this chapter, it is not possible to provide a case for every model presented; however, the four cases included in this fourth edition highlight a changing trend in mentoring and coaching and so deserve a proper amount of air time!

There are several distinct approaches to coaching which emerge within searches of both academic information databases and practitioner search engines. We briefly summarize some of the main or dominant perspectives and models below, starting with coaching models and then mentoring, and we examine some of these in more detail as the chapter develops. We suggest that coaching has become commodified into brands, and the form that mentoring takes is often related to its purpose and social context (see Chapter 1), which we refer to as 'modes'. Cox et al. (2014), in their handbook of coaching, refer to these modes as contexts, with our notion of brands being referred to as genres. However, their text seems to have a similar intent to this one, in terms of enabling the reader to compare and contrast different models and approaches. In a similar vein, Passmore et al. (2013: 6), in their edited text on the psychology of coaching and mentoring, examine theories and models and issues, with the aim of giving readers 'a full understanding of the depth and scope of the literature in their area of interest'.

## APPROACHES TO COACHING

### Main approaches

As we suggested would happen in the first edition of this book, there has been a significant growth in the number of brands of coaching. This is in part due to the proliferation of courses for coaches that include the development of one's own model and, perhaps, also related to the commercialization and commodification of coaching in particular, where creating a distinctive brand is a strong market motivation. In the first edition, we suggested that the approaches summarized below were those which seemed to have both a significant practitioner interest and application as well as having a research evidence base:

- Sports coaching – as we claim in Chapter 1 – constitutes one of the traditional roots of many of the other approaches to coaching.
- Life coaching – holistic approach to working with others. As raised in Chapter 1, we found a 19th-century reference to life coaching, but another root is in person-centred counselling.
- Executive coaching – while this is a market-driven approach, it is emerging as a distinct field with strong links to peer and sponsorship mentoring approaches.
- Team coaching – drawn from models of facilitation and action learning, this has become an increasingly popular field, which challenges the traditional dyadic approach to coaching.
- Brief coaching/solution-focused – this has its roots in therapeutic counselling and involves a goal-focused, time-limited intervention.

To these approaches we can add some additional brands which are now recognized as distinct approaches to coaching:

- Cognitive behavioural coaching – this approach has its roots in cognitive behavioural therapy and focuses on challenging negative automatic thoughts and thinking errors which inhibit effective personal performance.
- Gestalt coaching – drawn from gestalt therapy, this approach focuses on the exploration of the here and now, using heightened awareness of the client to promote growth and learning.
- Narrative coaching – focuses on the use of client stories and discourses to enable client development.
- Positive psychology coaching – seen as a departure from approaches rooted in traditional psychological and therapeutic models, this approach focuses on working with client strengths and what already works for them in promoting growth and learning.

It is interesting to note that of the nine approaches outlined here, six relate to the Psy Expert discourse outlined by Western (2012). This suggests, as we claim throughout this fourth edition, that the Psy Expert discourse is dominant in coaching.

## Other approaches to coaching

There are many other approaches found either through Google or in books written by practising coaches. These include: coactive coaching (Kimsey-House et al., 2011); ontological coaching (Sieler, 2003); person-centred coaching (Joseph, 2010; Gregory and Levy, 2013); existential coaching (Spinelli, 2010); transpersonal coaching (Brantley, 2010; Rowan, 2010); NLP coaching (Hayes, 2008); and, more recently, a hybrid between mentoring and coaching, as argued by Stelter (2019), or an 'integrated' model, as introduced by Stokes et al. (2020).

The majority of the above, and others not mentioned here, represent novel and distinctive approaches to coaching on the part of their creators, but they have not yet extended significantly beyond the originators to become distinctive bodies of practice about coaching. This is not to say that they will not do this in time. However, it is interesting to note that the proliferation of approaches to coaching reflects the commodification thesis that we referred to in Chapter 1.

For reasons of space, we now focus our attention on approaches that have expanded beyond one or two individuals and which have dominant theory and practical discourses.

## SPORTS COACHING

As argued earlier, sports coaching has perhaps the longest history as part of the modern discourse on coaching. The academic literature on sports coaching seems to fall into three main areas:

1. injury prevention/risk analysis (e.g. Blitvich et al., 2000)
2. biomechanical analysis of sporting techniques (e.g. Post, 2006)
3. the performance/development of sports coaches.

This latter category is of most interest to us in terms of developing an understanding of assumptions underpinning sports coaching, containing a body of research that is focused on coach and coachee commitment (e.g. Hollembeak and Amorose, 2005; Turner and Chelladurai, 2005). This could be characterized as the sports psychology approach to coaching. It is interesting to note that much of this research-based literature (rather like in other applications of psychology) employs statistical survey techniques, using large sample sizes. There are some studies that employ qualitative techniques. For example, Irwin et al.'s (2004) study looks at the origins of the coaching practice of elite UK gymnastics coaches. Interestingly, Irwin et al. (2004: 437) conclude that the 'most important resource identified by participants was mentor coaches'. This was the case for 91% of the coaches chosen in their study. While they do raise the issue of the ways in which coaches learn, they seem to stop short of critiquing sports coaching practice. However, writers such as Jones and Wallace (2005: 121) raise questions about the core assumptions of sports coaching: 'Despite its complex nature, associated literature has traditionally viewed coaching from a rationalistic perspective, a "knowable sequence" over which coaches are presumed to have command.' Jones and Wallace (2005: 121) challenge this assumption on the basis that this often equates to advice to coaches that is 'fine in theory' but that 'ignores the many tensions and social dilemmas which characterize their practice'. While they recognize that the importance of sequential practice and compliance (on the part of coachees) is important in sport, they also argue that an over-reliance on this approach ignores issues such as ambiguity, the importance of reflection in action, and the diversity of goals in sport. Instead, they propose adopting the metaphor of orchestration within sports coaching. This suggests that coaches 'are unlikely to have a free hand either in selecting coaching goals or in determining how goals are to be achieved with and through their charges'. Rather, their approach emphasizes 'challenging athletes' agency (autonomy or personal power) through encouragement and incentives' more often than 'delimiting their agency through sanctions' (Jones and Wallace, 2005: 129).

Potrac et al.'s (2002) study of a English soccer coach suggests that the rationalistic, instructional approach to sports coaching is rooted in the coach's desire to retain the respect of his coachees. From their case example, they suggest that the approach to coaching in this context is directive, with the coach imposing his view of how football should be played onto his players.

Those who have taken coaching concepts from sport and attempted to apply them in other contexts resist this controlling approach. For example, Downey's (2003) book draws heavily on Tim Gallwey's (1997b) concept of the inner game. Within this framework, the role of the coach is to help the player to overcome their fear and negativity. Following Gallwey, Downey (2003) calls this fear 'interference' and suggests that coaching ought to enable a focus on the performance of the task rather than a focus on a fear of failure. This approach entails focusing on 'self two', a version of oneself that is characterized by relaxed concentration, enjoyment and trust. While Downey (2003: 24) does not completely reject the notion of being directive, he argues that 'the magic inhabits the non-directive end of the spectrum'. Furthermore, Downey (2003: 57) also raises the issue of the coach's intent when asking questions or making interventions:

> In coaching [...] understanding one's own intent at any moment is a key component in becoming more effective. When I ask novice coaches the intent of a question, I get many kinds of answers. Mostly, they point to the coach's need to solve, to fix, to heal, to be right or to be in control.

We speculate that Downey's (2003: 57) view of the coach in Potrac et al.'s (2002) study might be that he is more about enhancing his own status rather than helping the coachee(s) 'become more aware or retain responsibility'.

 —— **Reflective Questions** ————————————————

- What is the appropriate balance between structured coaching activity and individual coachee agency?
- To what extent should the context of the coaching relationship influence the nature of the relationship between coach and coachee?

## LIFE COACHING

As Grant (2003: 253) argued, 'the general public has a thirst for techniques and processes that enhance life experience and facilitate personal development'. This has expressed itself in coaching, particularly through life coaching. A simple search on 'coaching' gives over 251 million hits; searching for 'life coaching' reveals over 74 million, suggesting that this is a growth area. In his article on work–life balance, McIntosh (2003) suggests that one of the drivers for life coaching is the relative imbalance that many people have in their work–life balance. He argues for life coaching as one way of redressing that balance.

However, in comparison, a search on the academic journal database Swetswise reveals only 136 different hits for 'life coaching' out of a possible 42 million journal articles. This suggests that despite the huge amount of popular interest in life coaching, there is still a relatively underdeveloped research base to support this interest.

There are exceptions to this. In response to the relative lack of research, Style and Boniwell (2010) conducted a study of a group coaching intervention in the UK. Working with a control and experimental groups (n = 40), they found that the group coaching intervention significantly increased participants' sense of well-being and happiness as measured against several well validated psychological tests. Also, Grant's (2003) earlier study concluded that there was 'preliminary empirical evidence that a life-coaching programme can facilitate goal improvement, improved mental health and enhanced quality of life'. However, he qualified the results by pointing out that these were self-reported successes by potentially already well-motivated goal-focused individuals, without the use of a control group. Nevertheless, it is still one of the few empirical studies of life coaching. It is worth noting at this point the content of Chapter 11, where we question the concepts of goal orientation.

Grant's study raises some useful distinctions between self-reflection and gaining insight. He views self-reflection as being about monitoring one's performance and understanding one's behaviour and motivations. However, gaining insight is 'a reflective process associated with goal attainment' (2003: 260). In an earlier study, Grant et al. (2002) found that when examining the impact of journal-keeping, individuals who kept journals have higher levels of self-knowledge but less movement towards goal attainment. In fact, Grant (2003: 256) suggests that the journal-keepers were 'stuck in a process of self-reflection' or, as we might call it, 'analysis paralysis', rather than gaining insight and making behavioural change to reach goals.

 **Reflective Questions**

- What processes best enable goal attainment?
- How far is goal attainment, as opposed to self-knowledge, the primary purpose of coaching and mentoring?

## EXECUTIVE COACHING

Executive coaching is perhaps the branch of coaching that has been most susceptible to the commodification of coaching services – this is particularly the case with larger organizations. Natale and Diamante (2005: 362) supported this in the US context: 'Leader organizations such as Alcoa, American Red Cross, AT&T, Ford, Northwestern Mutual Life, 3M and United Parcel Service offer executive coaching as part of their development and productivity programmes. Other organizations, such as Motorola and IBM, deploy executive coaching services regularly.'

Joo's (2005) survey of the literature on executive coaching is extremely useful in identifying some distinct patterns. This work involved an analysis of 78 articles on executive coaching and a classification of these studies. Joo (2005) argues that the literature based on the sample he looked at can be placed into three different categories:

1. definitions and designations of practice
2. description of specific executive coaching methodologies
3. case studies of executive coaching.

These categories certainly seem to resonate with what we have found in our survey of this literature.

Like ourselves, Joo concluded that relatively little research work (only 11 articles out of 78) underpins executive coaching, although 'there are a number of case studies portraying successful instances of executive coaching' (Joo, 2005: 465). Although there have been some significant reviews of the executive coaching field since Joo's work (e.g. Bono et al., 2009; Smith and Brummel, 2013), there still seems to be a relative lack of research on executive coaching. While Joo makes important contributions in several areas, for example definition, distinctions between approaches to counselling and coaching, perhaps one of the most useful conceptual distinctions he offers is the difference between proximal outcomes (behavioural change on the part of participants) and distal outcomes (the ultimate purpose of coaching). This framework, drawn from Wanberg et al.'s (2003) work in mentoring, leads us to ask the following questions about the contribution that executive coaching makes:

 **Reflective Questions** ─────────────────────

- What behavioural changes do we hope and expect to see in coachees and coaches?
- What are the ultimate individual or organization outcomes that we hope and expect to see as a result of executive coaching?
- What is the relationship between behavioural changes (proximal outcomes) and the ultimate outcomes of executive coaching (distal outcomes)?
- How might we understand and measure all of these things?
- What kind of measurement is appropriate?

## TEAM COACHING

A simple search on 'team coaching' reveals 470 million hits – a 33% increase on when we did the same search in the third edition. Many of these seem to be advertisements for independent coaches moving into this area of work. Educational and training providers are also increasingly offering new courses on team coaching. Practitioners appear to agree that team coaching is about developing a collective approach to goal setting and achievement. However, there are also disagreements about what team coaching is and how it is practised. Since the publication of our third edition there has also been an increase in practitioner books on the subject. Clutterbuck's (2007a) book on team coaching, for example, draws on Hackman and Wageman's (2005) work and tries to make clear distinctions between a team coach and facilitator; an individual coach and a team coach; a leader-manager and a leader-coach. His argument is that team coaches are more engaged with the team that they are working with and that the coaching role is more mutual (in terms of learning) and wider ranging than that of a facilitator. He suggests that leaders who operate as coaches to their teams are less output orientated and more process orientated than traditional team leaders. He views one-to-one coaching as similar to team coaching except that the team coach has more issues to consider. These would include, for example, group dynamics or leader credibility.

While these distinctions are helpful as a starting point, it is not immediately clear as to where the evidence for these distinctions comes from, and Clutterbuck (2007a) also points out that there is a major gap in the evidence supporting the claims for team coaching. The research base to support team coaching as a distinct form of coaching is extremely thin. However, one contribution is that of Hackman and Wageman (2005). In their conceptual article called 'A Theory of Team Coaching', they attempt to engage with the theory on group work, team dynamics, leadership and coaching to move towards a theory of team coaching. They base this on what they call four core conditions (2005: 283):

1. that key group performance processes (i.e. effort, strategy, knowledge, skill) are not too constrained by task and organization requirements
2. that the team is well-designed
3. that coaching behaviours focus on salient group performance, not on interpersonal relationships
4. that coaching interventions are timely, i.e. the group is ready for them.

As they themselves acknowledge, 'these conditions are not commonly found in traditionally designed and managed work organizations' (2005: 283).

Furthermore, they make very little reference to the existing coaching literature and much more to theories of group dynamics and team leadership. Therefore, it is by no means clear that the authors have succeeded in developing any form of team coaching theory that is distinct from other forms of group intervention or other forms of coaching. However, what does emerge very clearly is that there is strong support for a different approach to leading teams that moves away from traditional command and control models of management. Moreover, it is clear that leaders of teams, whether they are operational work teams or executive boards, need to pay more attention to group processes.

Mulec and Roth (2005) present one research-based study within two teams in AstraZeneca, the drug company. One of the coaches was external to the business and one of them was internal. They noted that 'in between team meetings, the coaches met with the project leaders of the respective teams in a follow-up and preparation meeting where the individual leader was coaching in her leadership role' (2005: 486). The results of the study seemed to be very positive, with respondents of the research pointing to better management of the agenda and greater participation in meetings on the part of team members. However, it is not clear from the study whether this was due to the direct interventions of the coaches in 'real time', as the authors put it, or whether this was as a result of the individual coaching, culminating in better leadership of the teams.

In 2017 Clutterbuck and Hodge conducted an online survey, 'Surveying Team Coaching Supervision'. The survey, with a response of just 55, indicated that there was a need for specialist supervision of team coaches because the role is complex and requires 'first rate coaching skills' as well as the abilities to facilitate a group, together with an understanding of complex organizational issues, systems and cultures. This raises four issues. First, for a survey, this is a very low response rate, and therefore it is difficult to place too much faith in the findings (see Chapter 2). Second, contrary to Clutterbuck's (2007a) argument that team coaching is not the same as facilitation, the discussion in this survey suggests that it is the same. Third, despite the poor response rate, there is an acknowledgment here that the team coach does need specialist contextual knowledge, perhaps in line with the hybrid version of mentoring and coaching we have raised in Chapter 1 and at the start of this chapter. Fourthly, we wonder how long it will be before there is a team coaching supervisor's qualification in the marketplace (see Chapter 7 on power)!

We are doubtful, as things currently stand, if there is any evidence that can be stretched to develop an independent theory of team coaching or even team coaching supervision. However, we do recognize that the concept of team coaching may have an appeal for organizations for two main reasons:

1. There could be a 'value for money' argument here. Individual coaching is expensive when it may be possible to coach a team for the same price and the coaching consultant is able to maintain their daily rate of pay.

2. For those subscribing to the managerialist discourse, the notion of team coaching is a return to the performance agenda and a move away from the person-centred humanist approach.

 **Reflective Questions**

- Is coaching primarily a one-to-one developmental dialogue or can coaching take place one-to-many?
- To what extent should coaching be based on direct observation of performance by the coach?
- How far is team coaching a rehash or rebranding of older ideas?
- How far are practitioners attempting to create another brand of coaching for commercial gain?

## BRIEF COACHING OR SOLUTIONS-FOCUSED COACHING

This model of coaching probably has the smallest current research base and output of the main approaches we have identified so far in this chapter. Nevertheless, it does seem to be a developing area.

Brief coaching and solutions-focused coaching are terms that are often interlinked but also referred to separately. They refer to essentially a very similar philosophy and process.

Brief coaching or solutions-focused coaching draws on solutions-focused brief therapy (Watts and Pietrzak, 2000; Berg and Szabó, 2005). The therapeutic approach moves away from a 'problem' orientation to a 'solution' orientation. Drawing on a range of therapeutic studies, Watts and Pietrzak (2000) argue that one of the key contributions that solutions-focused brief therapy (SFBT) makes is that it 'eschews the "medical model" perspective and takes a non-pathological approach' (Watts and Pietrzak, 2000). This also seems to apply to the coaching version of the approach. As Grant (2006b: 74) puts it, 'the idea is that the coach primarily facilitates the construction of solutions rather than trying to understand the aetiology of the problem'. The approach is rather like 'appreciative inquiry' (see Cooperrider, 1995) in that it focuses on what works by drawing on the resourcefulness of the client.

 **Reflective Questions**

- To what extent should coaching interventions be focused on understanding the roots of client problems?
- To what extent is it legitimate to focus on solutions as opposed to issues and problems?

## COGNITIVE BEHAVIOURAL COACHING

Cognitive behavioural coaching (CBC) is a brand of coaching that has become increasingly popular in the last five years or so. Palmer and Williams (2013) articulate the main tenets of this approach and trace the discourse of how cognitive behavioural theory approaches to therapy were adapted to be used in a coaching context. They emphasize the importance of facilitating the client's self-awareness, equipping them with thinking skills, building their internal resources, stability and self-acceptance, enhancing self-efficacy and enabling them to become their own coach (2013: 325).

Perhaps more than many other approaches to coaching, this brand is characterized by a number of process models – Palmer and Williams (2013) identify nine different models of CBC. Williams et al. (2010: 38) identify five main goals of using such a model to:

1. facilitate the client in achieving their realistic goals
2. facilitate self-awareness of underlying cognitive and emotional barriers to goal attainment
3. equip the individual with more effective thinking and behavioural skills
4. build internal resources, stability and self-acceptance in order to mobilize the individual to their choice of action
5. enable the client to become their own self-coach.

CBC, as an approach to coaching, seems to emphasize the importance of challenging negative or inappropriate patterns of thinking so as to enable clients to change their own behaviour. It is common within this approach to encourage clients to experiment with new ways of behaving and thinking (Williams et al., 2010: 41) by giving the client homework. At its heart, there is seemingly a faith in the rationality of the client being able to recognize and therefore overcome irrational thoughts and behaviour.

 **Reflective Questions**

- To what extent do coaches need to actively challenge the thinking and behaviour of their clients?
- How far can the application of self-awareness and rationality take clients in changing deep-seated habits and behaviours?

## GESTALT COACHING

Gestalt approaches to coaching, like CBC, have become increasingly popular in recent times. Bluckert (2010), when writing on gestalt coaching, articulates some of the main assumptions underpinning this approach, in particular, the emphasis that gestalt coaches place on working in the present moment, using what is 'in the room' to help the client grow and develop. Bluckert uses the arguments of Beisser (1970) to put forward a paradoxical theory of change, meaning that, for things to be different, we have to be fully in touch with the current situation before change can happen. Spoth et al. (2013: 392–3) argue that this is best achieved by 'co creating the relational field', where 'partnering with the person to co-create the relationship heightens the coach's impact'. As in the relational coaching work of de Haan (2008b), the relationship between coach and coachee is critical. However, a distinct offering that gestalt coaches make is the emphasis that they place on the use of self. Usually, this takes the form of noticing one's own experience of what is happening and using this in the service of the client. This approach contrasts quite sharply with CBC because it is context-specific, happens in the moment and is difficult to represent in the form of a model, acronym or key set of predetermined questions. Both Bluckert (2010: 80–94) and Spoth et al. (2013: 385–406) point to the paucity of research evidence within this field of coaching. Spoth et al. (2013: 402) are particularly vocal and direct on this:

> Gestalt coaching clients' experience and the concepts and methodology need further study and description in the literature. It is time for gestalt coaches to stop being the best kept secrets in the coaching world.

 **Reflective Questions**

- How appropriate is it for the coach to use their own feelings and perceptions in coaching?
- To what extent is it helpful to focus on the problematic feelings/issues of the coachee so that change (paradoxically) can take place?

## NARRATIVE-BASED COACHING

Based on theories regarding the social construction of reality (Berger and Luckmann, 1966), narrative approaches to coaching are based on the assumption that the coach can help the coachee reframe and retell the stories that they tell about themselves and about others. Following Stelter (2013), we can think of coaching as a process of sense-making, which takes place at two levels: the individual, making sense of their own experience, and the co-creation of meaning. Central to narrative-based coaching, therefore, is the use of stories. Stelter uses Jerome Bruner and his work in cognitive psychology to examine how the concept of coaching discourse can be used to understand how coaches can use narrative techniques. He uses three main concepts – agency (the ability to choose between alternatives); intentionality (the focus on meaningful behaviour); deconstruction (changing and rearranging stories) – to explain how this might be done. One technique that is often used, particularly in group-based approaches to narrative coaching, is referred to as outsider witnessing, where individuals or groups are asked to provide a subjective response to the story they hear (either their own or someone else's). This enables a uniquely reflexive approach to the experience where the coachee and coach, having co-created a story, can then ask themselves what the impact of that story is on them and their thinking and future behaviour. Drake (2010: 122) argues that narrative coaching has four main features:

1. Identity is situated – based on 'what is' in a particular situation or context.
2. Growth is liminal – coachees develop most significantly when their usual strategies of sense-making do not work and gaps in understanding appear when telling stories.
3. Discourse is powerful – telling stories enables coachees access to deeply held assumptions about their realities.
4. Re-storying is possible – changing stories coachees tell and using them differently is seen as possible, which requires them to loosen their 'narrative grip'.

A key feature of this approach, therefore, is that clients have access to their own stories and, crucially, those of others, including organizational discourse.

 **Reflective Questions**

- To what extent should coaches be helping coachees to access their own agency in terms of being able to re-tell/recreate their own/others' stories?
- How can clients influence the dominant discourses of their workplaces?

## POSITIVE PSYCHOLOGY COACHING

Interest in positive psychology approaches has exploded in the last five years. The popularity of the work of Martin Seligman (2008, 2011) on this approach has led to writers in coaching using this approach in their coaching work. For example, Biswas-Diener and Dean (2007) use the research base of writers like Seligman and others to support their claim that positive psychology represents a significant breakthrough in coaching research. Kauffman et al. (2010: 158) sum up this approach:

> Positive psychology coaching (PPC) is a scientifically rooted approach to helping clients increase well being, enhance and apply strengths, improve performance and achieve valued goals. The PPC orientation suggests that the coach view the client as 'whole' and that the coach focus on strengths, positive behaviours and purpose.

Freire (2013) provides a comprehensive review of the research and practice on positive psychology approaches to coaching. Within this she examines the various ways that the work on positive psychology has added to the field of coaching and mentoring, through various 'sub-brands' of positive psychology coaching: authentic happiness coaching; the flow-enhancing model; the co-active coaching model; positive organizational psychology. In particular, she highlights the trend of using psychological tools and instruments for assessing clients' strengths. This is also done in the work of Driver (2011) in his text on positive psychology coaching. PPC does have links with solution-focused approaches discussed above. For instance, Jackson and McKergow (2002: 3) emphasize the following aspects, amongst others, of this approach:

- What's wanted?
- What's working?
- Progress?

- Influence?
- Resources and strengths?

They contrast these aspects with problem focus, which they attribute to blame-giving, negativity and lack of progress.

 **Reflective Questions** ────────────────────────

- To what extent can a positive orientation reframe coaching?
- What place do/should psychological instruments/measures play in coaching approaches?

The above discussion has explored some of the main approaches to coaching found in today's marketplace. These approaches are largely ignoring the social context of coaching, but the next two examples represent a changing trend in coaching. Like team coaching, these two approaches recognize that there is something valuable in the coaching process but that it doesn't necessarily require trained experts, external to the organization, to deliver the coaching. Are we seeing a change in the marketplace? In this first example, Mark Robson, a former director of a large European manufacturing company in the UK, offers some critical insight into the challenges of internal coaching. The coaches in the scheme are from across Europe.

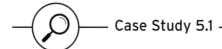 Case Study 5.1 ——————————————

Internal coaches emerged in the 1990s (Brock, 2011), and surveys consistently report that their use continues to expand. For example, the latest Ridler Report (2016) indicates that 70% of the companies surveyed used internal coaches, whilst a further 20% planned to in the future. Frisch (2001), one of the first to note the emergence of the internal coach, saw the benefits as being cost-saving, inside knowledge and broader availability, set against the issues of credibility, confidentiality and trust. Supporting this, Wasylyshyn (2003), in a survey on executives and internal coaches, saw knowledge of the company and its culture as the biggest positive, with the lack of objectivity and concern about confidentiality and trust as the key negatives. Today, the reasons stated (Ridler Report, 2016) for investing in internal coaches are development of a coaching culture, accessibility, and being able to offer coaching more widely for a given budget. The reasons for not using internal coaches are similarly unchanged, being trust, confidentiality and objectivity. However, for the coaching industry, internal coaches and internal coaching schemes have become a significant work stream: scheme design and implementation, coach training, accreditation and ongoing support, and of course coaching executives who are 'too senior' for internal coaches.

It is clear that internal coaching is now an important means of delivering coaching in organizations (Ridler Report, 2016), and yet it still attracts little research attention. The focus of the literature concerning internal coaching remains on setting up, managing and maintaining coaching schemes; a conversation between practitioners with something to sell and commissioners looking to buy. Whilst internal coaches are key to making coaching a success in an organization, there has been almost no attention paid to how internal coaches experience being a coach (Ebrahimi and Cameron, 2012; Mukherjee, 2012; Feehily, 2018) and what impact their experience of the coaching role has upon them. The impression given is that internal coaches are simply the tool or mechanism by which coaching is delivered but are otherwise passive. My PhD research set out to address this gap in our knowledge of how internal coaches experience the coach role.

The emphasis in the coaching literature, particularly around creating a coaching culture by embedding coaching in an organization, is on the need to create a supportive environment if coaching is to thrive (Clutterbuck and Megginson, 2005b; Hawkins, 2012; Clutterbuck et al., 2016). The responsibility for creating this environment is placed upon senior management, the delivery mechanism for a coaching scheme. However, some of the coaches I interviewed were not coaching in such an environment. They were coaching in the shadows of their organization, but they continued to coach. Key to understanding this was the realization that when it came to their coaching, the internal coaches I interviewed were not passive: for them, coaching was too important. That internal coaches actively managed their coaching role is illustrated by two findings from the research: access to support mechanisms and balancing the coaching role with other organizational responsibilities.

Whether coaching in a supportive environment or not, the internal coaches I interviewed took personal responsibility for accessing the support they needed to sustain their practice. When coaching in a supportive environment, what I called coaching under organizational floodlights, this meant making time to attend CPD events, supervision and meetings with peers. When coaching in the shadows it meant lobbying their organization to make available the support they needed or finding the support they needed through peer networks or by looking outside the organization. Surprisingly, and a watch-out for the coaching industry, seeking specific support – a CPD event of interest or supervision – was the only reason the majority of internal coaches I interviewed gave for engaging with the wider coaching industry.

A second way in which internal coaches actively managed their coaching role was to analyse the capacity they could commit to coaching and plan their formal coaching sessions around their other organizational responsibilities. In this way they protected their freedom to coach by ensuring that it did not visibly clash with their other roles. However, the coaches were clear their coaching was important: coaching commitments, once made, were defended and not cancelled if at all possible.

 ## Reflective Questions

- How far is the coaching literature dominated with 'good' stories?
- How far does the coaching literature treat internal coaching as simply an extension of external coaching?
- How far are the differences properly explored?
- How far is internal coaching a commercial threat to external coaching?

The second case example provides an interesting and innovative approach to internal coaching.

 ## Case Study 5.2

The Joseph Rowntree Foundation (JRF) is an independent organization working to inspire social change through research, policy and practice. The Joseph Rowntree Housing Trust (JRHT) is a registered housing association and care provider in Yorkshire and the North East. JRF and JRHT were established to search out the underlying causes of social 'evils', influence social advancement and demonstrate how that can be achieved.

JRF/JRHT has a progressive internal coach programme which was introduced in 2011 and is continually growing and developing. It started with eight staff coaches, all of whom worked in various roles within the organization and who coached on a voluntary basis. This has since developed into a team of 20 Institute of Leadership and Management (ILM) qualified coaches who have access to regular coach supervision and action learning set workshops and training, in support of their ongoing personal development (https://en.wikipedia.org/wiki/Institute_of_Leadership_and_Management).

Previously, coaches were appointed on a consultancy basis at significant cost and coaching was a little-known concept aimed only at senior staff. It was often used as part of management performance review, or even as an alternative to management, but with no overall clear

*(Continued)*

purpose. As such, coaching was an expensive, targeted and exclusive intervention which was outside the reach of most staff.

At the time, the organization was committed to transforming the organizational culture, to one in which staff were more engaged and empowered. The Chief Executive, Julia Unwin, had a long-term commitment to coaching and particularly a strong view that it could be beneficial to staff working at all levels. Together with colleagues, she discussed her views with York and Scarborough Hospital Trust, recognizing that in financially straitened times JRF could not afford to pay, but it could barter.

The hospital trust was an organization which shared many of JRF's values and ethics and already had an established and successful staff coaching model, so the development of a reciprocal arrangement presented an opportunity to provide a quality service, whilst still offering value for money.

A plan was subsequently devised by the Coach Leads of each organization, and this provided a framework for the implementation, development and delivery of internal coaching within JRF over a transitional three-year period. The hospital trust initially assumed the role of 'mentor/critical friend', but as internal expertise developed at JRF, this arrangement evolved into an equal partnership that now benefits both organizations through the provision of low-cost, quality coaching services shared between the two organizations.

There are a number of benefits to this approach. The shared coach resource, which includes some training and coach supervision, means that both organizations can be confident in the quality of coaching when promoting coaching to staff. It also means appropriate coaching is available for staff who might not feel comfortable having a coach who is perceived to be 'less senior' (an inevitable drawback of internal coaching programmes, regardless of the level of experience of the coach). As demand for coaching is unpredictable, this approach also solves the problem of overall availability as both organizations have access to a wider and more diverse pool of coaches.

This approach has enabled a quality and sustainable resource to develop which provides value for money, significant financial savings and numerous benefits to both organizations. At the time of writing, the Coach Leads are looking at extending this process to include the provision of mentoring and are looking at how they might build on the success of the reciprocal arrangement to include other local organizations.

Ros Jahnke (Head of Coaching, JRF/JRHT) has been Head of Coaching at JRF/JRHT since June 2015 but has managed and developed the programme since its early inception on a voluntary basis alongside a former substantive role.

 **Reflective Questions**

- How far in this example is coaching recognized as helpful to the organization and how far is it seen as a commodity?
- What are the implications for 'coaching as a profession' with examples such as this one?

# APPROACHES TO MENTORING

The applications of mentoring are extremely wide and range across all sectors. Megginson et al. (2006) provide an insight into the wide range of applications and features in 18 organizational case studies and 9 accounts of individual relationships. The applications in general include:

- mentoring young offenders and supporting victims of domestic abuse
- mentoring in schools
- mentoring in its various forms in the UK National Health Service
- teacher development and mentoring women into science, engineering and technology roles
- mentoring in higher education
- diversity mentoring at British Telecom and for the disadvantaged in the South African mining industry
- mentoring with engineering firms and e-mentoring for small businesses
- executive mentoring within the service sector and leadership mentoring in Denmark
- mentoring for manufacturing managers in Australia and within financial services in the UK and Switzerland.

Despite the variation of application, when compared to coaching, there are few distinct forms of mentoring. As suggested in Chapter 1, mentoring, perhaps due to its holistic, educational and voluntary roots, does not have the same propensity for commodification as does coaching. However, we do believe that publicly-funded mentoring, in particular, with its strong managerialist discourse, is moving towards commodification linked to a target and measurement agenda promoted by the UK and US governments. As a result, approaches to mentoring tend to be differentiated by mode and by the sector in which it is applied (sectoral application is explored more in Chapter 4). Like coaching, mentoring does seem to have some generic themes, albeit fewer. However, a new form of mentoring appears to be developing in the US in the form of 'self-mentoring' (Carr, 2012).

## Executive mentoring

Rather like executive coaching, this application of mentoring has its roots in traditional mentoring and is typically focused on developing so-called 'high-fliers'. However, rather than being exclusively goal-focused it enables the mentee (the executive) to identify the purpose and focus of the development. This type of mentoring is commonly linked to talent management programmes and leadership development.

## Diversity mentoring

Diversity mentoring (see Chapter 13) is a common application of mentoring, aimed not just at redressing perceived inequalities in the workplace but also at recognizing and valuing difference.

## Mentoring in education

Several foci exist here. One strand is about the educator's development. This commonly includes a more experienced teacher who mentors someone less experienced. Another strand is about developing mentoring skills in and between school/college/university learners. A further strand focuses on pastoral relationships between staff and learners and sometimes between peers in schools (see below). There is also a strand of professional mentors in secondary education called learning mentors. These people are employed in schools to work with children with special abilities or behavioural or learning problems. Managers from local businesses may also be part of a voluntary mentoring programme in schools.

## Voluntary sector mentoring

Sometimes known as befriending or buddying, this sort of mentoring is often undertaken to help vulnerable members of society, for example ex-offenders or young drug-takers.

We explore each of these further in subsequent chapters; however, it is important to examine the different modes which permeate the mentoring discourse as these have important implications for both mentoring and coaching.

# MODES OF MENTORING

## Traditional dyadic mentoring

As we have argued earlier (Chapter 1), the mentoring discourse can be traced back many hundreds of years. However, as Colley (2003: 32) argues, the work of Daniel Levinson and colleagues was one of the first to develop a 'classical model of mentoring'. Levinson et al.'s (1978) longitudinal study of 40 men as they develop through different stages of their life strongly influenced the traditional view of mentoring. The following passage from Levinson et al. (1978: 98–9) illustrates this:

> The true mentor, in the meaning intended here, serves as an analogue in adulthood of the 'good enough' parent for the child. He fosters the young adult's development by believing in him, sharing the youthful Dream and giving it his blessing, helping to define the newly emerging self in its newly discovered world, and creating a space in which the young man can work on a reasonably satisfactory life structure that contains the Dream.

While Levinson was at pains to point out that the mentoring relationship was not a parental one, it is nevertheless easy to see, based on this view, why the term protégé has been popular in the US mentoring literature (see Chapter 4). The mentoring relationship, in Levinson's view, is a close, sometimes stormy one which enables the 'protégé' to move more quickly through periods of personal transition. Sheehy's (1996) work resonates with this. Her original work, *Passages: Predictable Crises of Adult Life*, first published in 1974, covered female development in the same way as Levinson's work on men. She updated this work in 1996 in light of the changing social patterns of women's lives, and this work is now in its second edition (Sheehy, 2006). The 1996 edition, called *New Passages: Mapping Your Life across Time*, explored the development of both men and women. Like Levinson, Sheehy's research seems to indicate that the traditional notion of being mentored by someone more experienced or older is an important developmental factor for both parties. Bob Bookman, one of Sheehy's subjects, described as being 'comfortable in his own skin', drew his development from being mentored by a more successful agent in his industry and from mentoring younger people in his own organization (Sheehy, 1996: 86).

 **Reflective Questions**

- To what extent is mentoring needed in order to make effective life transitions?
- How important is age/experience asymmetry in mentoring?

## Peer mentoring

Clawson (1996: 11) makes a strong case for peer mentoring, as summarized in the following quote:

> In a context of rapid technological change and shifting organizational structures with confusing family and personal anchor points, there is no reason to assume that people of roughly the same age and experience could not engage in mentoring activities, especially if the natural competitiveness of the bureaucratic pyramid is replaced with an encouraging teamwork in the process oriented firm.

If we accept the rhetoric of rapid change (see Chapters 6 and 7), then peer mentoring is likely to become a more prevalent mode of learning. This echoes the earlier contributions of Kathy Kram (Kram, 1980; Kram and Isabella, 1985). In the later of the two, Kram and Isabella (1985: 118) argued that peer-mentoring relationships are distinct from traditional mentoring relationships in that they 'offer a degree of mutuality that enables both individuals to experience being the giver and receiver of these functions'. Hence peer mentoring, in their study, seems congruent with Clawson's (1996) view of teamwork. This 'mutuality' does imply some overlap with the term 'co-mentoring' (see below). Therefore, it is important to be clear about what this mutuality/reciprocity entails.

In Kram and Isabella's (1985) study, the boundaries between who is mentor and who is mentee do not seem to be strongly drawn. Indeed, their term 'special peer' is explicitly referred to as being the equivalent of a best friend, with wide personal and professional topics being 'on the table'. However, other studies seem to see peer mentoring as being less 'mutual'. For example, Fine and Pullins' (1998: 89) study of salespeople is very clear: 'Peer mentoring occurs when a more experienced salesperson (the mentor) takes responsibility for the development and guidance of a less experienced salesperson (the protégé).' While they do refer to mutual support, the discussion of results makes it clear that there is one 'giver' – the mentor – and one 'receiver' – the mentee.

Similarly, Fox and Stevenson's (2006) work in the UK higher education sector makes it clear that although the final-year students (the mentors) in the study did make gains in confidence, experience and awareness, the success of the scheme was still judged in terms of the academic performance of the first-year students (the mentees).

Peer mentoring is increasingly common in UK schools. Here, the form is often an older pupil mentoring a younger pupil, but Garvey and Langridge (2006: 46), in quoting users, offer a range of meanings:

> It helps young people understand the demands and expectations put on them when they start a new school, through to taking public examinations and everything in between. (Peer mentoring co-ordinator)

> It's about pupils supporting pupils. (Head teacher)

> Peer mentoring is when you work with someone in your own year group or below and build a relationship of trust and respect. (Year 10 mentor)

 **Reflective Questions**

- How important is it for successful mentoring that participants can relate to each other as peers?
- To what extent is mentoring a two-way process?

## Co-mentoring

Co-mentoring is a way of formalizing the mutuality within a mentoring relationship. It implies that both parties in the relationship are learning and that they are equal partners. However, as Kochan and Trimble's (2000) study of their own mentoring relationship highlights, there can be different understandings of how that mutuality presents itself. For example, the following passage from their account demonstrates this:

> Boundaries and roles began to shift. Our relationship transcended the hierarchical mentor/mentee roles and entered into a co-mentoring relationship. Fran began to view the relationship as one in which she was also learning. Often she would ask Susan for her perceptions as a teacher and use their sessions together to talk about issues important to her and her school. (2000: 24)

What is not completely clear from their study is how often and how much Fran (initially the mentor) was helped by Susan. As suggested above, peer mentoring and co-mentoring can often become blurred as both people in the relationship become more comfortable with disclosure. Sometimes, as with Kochan and Trimble (2000: 24), the relationship can move to one that has friendship as an important part. Indeed they talk of 'acting like friends, sharing personal hopes and frustrations, and talking about family issues'. This also appears to be similar with a case from Megginson et al. (2006: 190–5) featuring the long-term relationship – over 20 years – between two senior public-sector managers. As with Kochan and Trimble (2000), the two managers – Allen and Hinchliffe – acknowledge the mutuality of their relationship as well as the importance of friendship within it. However, what is still not completely clear (perhaps because it is not formalized and structured) is how that manifests itself within mentoring conversations.

In some examples, the arrangements may be more structured. For example, each person may take it in turns to be mentored by the other. The advantage of this more bounded use of co-mentoring means that time is divided equally between the two parties to ensure parity of benefit. On the other hand, the more fluid version of co-mentoring allows mutual exploration of interesting issues in which both parties are helped at the same time.

 **Reflective Questions**

- To what extent should mentoring be mutually beneficial to both mentor and mentee?
- What role does friendship play in mentoring?

## E-mentoring

Using information technology and other media for mentoring conversations has become increasingly popular (see Chapter 10 for further comment on e-development). Megginson et al. (2006: 64–7) feature three research-based case studies of e-mentoring. In his account of the east of England e-mentoring pilot, Hawkins (2006: 67) identifies several benefits of e-mentoring as a mode of mentoring:

- It is less time-consuming in terms of time off work and travel for mentors.
- It is easily accessible via the internet.
- It can help to equalize the power difference between mentor and mentee.
- It removes first-impression prejudice.
- It gives more time for reflection and learning.

The findings from an evaluation study of e-mentoring in Megginson et al. (2006: 134–41) support some of these findings. However, also in Megginson et al. (2006: 216–19), e-mentoring does have its challenges in terms of its richness, which is well summarized in the following extract:

> Virtual mentoring inevitably does not offer the wide range of communication and information that is available in face-to-face mentoring, depending as it does pretty much solely on the written word. I think this lack of opportunity to observe the mentor in action, 'read' his non-verbal messages (and he mine) and sense and hear complex intonation in the communication has affected the potential richness of the mentoring relationship. (2006: 218)

Furthermore, studies on e-mentoring such as that of O'Neill and Harris (2004) have raised some questions about the development of mentoring skills on the part of both mentors and mentees in an e-mentoring relationship. They strongly suggest that participants need time to grow into these new conventions in order to ensure their effectiveness.

In current times with the global lockdown due to the COVID-19 virus, e-mentoring has become the norm, as has e-coaching (see Chapter 10 for more on e-development).

 **Reflective Questions**

- What are the advantages and disadvantages of face-to-face mentoring?
- What are the key factors which influence the effectiveness and strength of a mentoring relationship?

## Reverse mentoring

Reverse mentoring is a relatively recent development. It takes place when the mentor is younger or more junior than the mentee. It focuses on the differences of experience, understanding and attitudes as mentor and mentee learn about each other's worlds. In Time Warner in the US, younger, technically-expert people mentor senior executives. In the UK Health Sector, patients mentor health care professionals.

## Self-mentoring

Self-mentoring offers a new development in mentoring modes. The following case study provides insights into this development.

 **Case Study 5.3**

Self-mentoring is for a learner of any age, profession, gender, race, or ability who is willing to initiate and accept responsibility for self-development by devoting time to navigate within the culture of the environment in order to make the most of opportunities to strengthen competencies needed to enhance their leadership skills (Carr, 2011, 2012, 2014; Beckford, 2013; Bond and Hargreaves, 2014; Carr et al., 2015).

The term 'self' as in self-mentoring implies individual effort and solitude. However, self-mentors do not work in isolation but are encouraged to invite a legion of colleagues at any time, when needed, to be involved in the learner's efforts to meet individual expectations. Such was the case for the former superintendent who, upon matching her skills with the organization's needs, built a legion of colleagues which she referred to as a community of leaders for conversation, reflection, insight, and feedback for support in areas where she lacked proficiency (Petty et al., 2016). Central to self-mentoring is the idea of self-reflection (Huang and Lynch, 1995), as it equips the learner with insight necessary to navigate through any environment or overcome a hurdle that blocks their success. For the former super-intendent, it addressed the shortfalls initially identified through peer engagement and reflection.

Self-mentoring is grounded in self-leadership theory (Carr et al., 2015; Petty et al., 2016), which further explains the process. As a normative theory, self-leadership is a theoretical con-struct focused on the internal mechanisms individuals use to intentionally focus their attention and efforts to lead and guide themselves in aspects of both self-direction and self-motivation in three key strategic areas: personal behaviours, natural rewards, and constructive thought patterns (Manz and Neck, 2004; Neck and Houghton, 2006). In terms of natural rewards, effective self-leadership practices emphasize the creation of positive elements or items within tasks and/or the redesigning of tasks, reducing the number of negative forces within the task and thereby increasing both the natural intrinsic motivational qualities of the task and the energy-producing qualities of the task (Houghton and Neck, 2002).

From the superintendent's experiences and studies that follow, four tiered levels in self-mentoring emerged. They are:

- self-awareness
- self-development
- self-reflection
- self-monitoring

The levels are sequential, self-paced and individualized. Each level builds on the skill devel-opment from the previous level. The first level, self-awareness, identifies leadership skills needed by the organization and often shrouded from the leader due to lack of use. Through the next two levels, self-development and self-reflection, the learner identifies expectations and masters strategy development and implementation for the self-monitoring level (Bond and Hargreaves, 2014).

Both quantitative and qualitative field studies in self-mentoring yielded analogous results. In each of the studies, participants experienced a heightened degree of perceived self-efficacy and confidence. Not only did they report more confidence in their ability to perform in a role or position in which they served, but they experienced a greater sense of self-efficacy (Bond and Hargreaves, 2014; Carr et al., 2015; Petty et al., 2016). Bandura (1997) defines self-efficacy as the perceived ability to perform or complete a task (Bandura and Locke, 2003).

Self-mentoring, as the studies suggest, can be applied in any situation or given environ-ment. While initial studies were in multiple public school districts, university faculty from two different universities have also been studied as well as high school students. It becomes increasingly apparent that self-mentoring can be applied to most professions or careers. It can be used in isolation or combined with mentoring or coaching to support individuals with the desire to achieve and increase performance. Self-mentoring is not limited to education, but business and industry can equally benefit.

*Dr Marsha L. Carr, University of North Carolina at Wilmington, USA*

—— **Reflective Questions** ————————————————

- How far might self-mentoring be Grant's (2003: 256) notion of 'stuck in a process of self-reflection'?
- How far might self-mentoring be associated with the aims of cognitive behaviour coaching as outlined by Palmer and Williams (2013: 325), roughly quoted here as: creating an environment for self-awareness, equipping an individual with thinking skills, building internal resources, stability and self-acceptance, enhancing self-efficacy and enabling an individual to become their own coach/mentor?
- What might be the implications for mentors and coaches if this mode is adopted?
- How far can this mode of mentoring be associated with the idea of developmental networks or a community of discovery? (see Chapter 9)

## HYBRIDIZATION

In the third edition, we raised the prospect of the hybridization of coaching and mentoring. In Chapter 1 of this edition, we raised the issue again, but this time we are beginning to see glimpses of this change in various places over the last few years. We first noticed changes through the findings in the Ridler Reports of 2011, 2013 and 2016. More recently, Stelter (2019: 11) suggests:

> I am often asked whether it might not be time to jettison the coaching concept. I agree that the concept is somewhat tired, and that it has become burdened with associations that I would want to distance myself from. In many regards, *mentoring* in its current meaning is a fairly apt term for the dialogue form I strive for.

Stelter (2019) appears to be striving for something other than what he calls first- and second-generation coaching, where in the former, goals and performance are the agenda, and in the latter, the system in which the coachee sits is important. His third generation is about facilitating a mutually beneficial dialogue. His is a call to a return to the humanist roots (see Chapter 1; Gray et al., 2006; Garvey, 2016) of coaching and mentoring.

Stokes et al. (2020: 10) argue that coaching and mentoring share the same skills and processes and that it is the agentic nature of the context in which coaching and mentoring happen that influences the variety of forms that they may take. This kaleidoscope results from the fact that context is multifaceted, heterogeneous and liveable. That is why we suggest that seeking to neatly separate coaching from mentoring in practice is ultimately futile as practitioners will inevitably borrow from both discourses when identifying practical behaviours that work best for them. (Stokes et al., 2020: 10).

Nadeem and Garvey (2020) call for a coachee-centred approach where a 'repertoire' of skills is necessary to adequately help the learner. This is clearly a move towards integration of mentoring and coaching concepts.

## CONCLUSIONS

The primary purpose of this chapter was to recognize and acknowledge the variety of approaches to mentoring and coaching. In particular, the intention was to use selected literature as a way of representing approaches to coaching and mentoring, rather than exploring the structures of specific models or processes like the GROW model (Downey, 2003) or the three-stage process (Alred and Garvey, 2019). This generates a number of questions that inform our exploration of coaching and mentoring in theory and practice (see below), and they have been refined to reflect the fact that each domain examined has something to contribute to this exploration. The questions are also phrased to recognize that it is important to ask them, whether the label we are using is coaching or mentoring. In this sense, they may be seen as research questions that drive exploration.

 **Future Direction**

Looking at the range of coaching and mentoring models is likely to raise more questions than it answers due to the breadth and diversity of applications. However, our experience of working with and analysing these models is that each new perspective adds a different angle to a body of discourse which has more linkages and commonalties than differences. Our prediction is that there will initially be more models and perspectives to swell the existing ranks, but that researchers will increasingly look for ways to integrate and build on the work of others. This is already happening with an increasing blurring between coaching and mentoring, but we predict that, particularly within coaching, the multitude of approaches is likely to coalesce into a smaller number of broad approaches which will better represent the choices of approach that the coach/mentor has, including the possibility of an eclectic mix of models and perspectives.

 **Activity 1 (coaching)**

Consider this:

Looking to enhance the effectiveness of coaching in your workplace? Read on to discover the growing popularity of solutions-focused coaching and OSKAR. [....] So, where are we to look for new developments in coaching? The Solutions Focus (SF) approach to coaching has been gaining in popularity over the past five years. Developed from the brilliantly simple 'brief therapy' work of Steve de Shazer and Insoo Kim Berg, SF offers a new level of effectiveness to the coaching conversation. Rather than identifying what's wrong or looking for barriers to progress, the focus is simply on finding what works. [...] OSKAR stands for:

*(Continued)*

Outcome

Scale

Know-how

Affirm & Action

Review

(McKergow and Clarke, undated. Available at: http://sfwork.com/pdf/Coaching%20 with%20OSKAR.pdf, accessed 14 September 2016).

Using Western's (2012) discourses, analyse the above and consider which discourse the extract resembles the most. What might the implications of the discourse be and who is it aimed at?

---

 **Activity 2 (mentoring)**

Consider this:

> Traditionally, mentoring is the long term passing on of support, guidance and advice. In the workplace it has tended to describe a relationship in which a more experienced colleague uses their greater knowledge and understanding of the work or workplace to support the development of a more junior or inexperienced member of staff. This comes from the Greek myth where Odysseus entrusts the education of his son to his friend Mentor. It's also a form of apprenticeship, whereby an inexperienced learner learns the 'tricks of the trade' from an experienced colleague, backed-up as in modern apprenticeship by offsite training. (CIPD factsheet, 2012c, https://www.shef.ac.uk/polopoly_fs/1.110468!/file/cipd_mentoring_factsheet.pdf (accessed 14 September 2016))

Examine the language used in this extract. What view of mentoring is being presented here and who is its target audience?

---

 **Questions**

- What is the appropriate balance between structured mentoring/coaching activity and individual coachee agency?
- To what extent should the context of the mentoring/coaching relationship influence the nature of the relationship between coach and coachee?
- To what extent is coaching and mentoring a two-way process? To what extent should coaching/mentoring be mutually beneficial to both mentor/coach and mentee/coachee?

---

**Further Reading**

For a comprehensive discussion on many models of coaching with one chapter on mentoring see: Cox, E., Bachkirova, T. and Clutterbuck, D. (eds) (2014) *The Complete Handbook of Coaching*, 2nd Edition. London: SAGE.

For insights into many different forms of mentoring see: Allen, T.D. and Eby, L.T. (2007) (eds) *Blackwell Handbook of Mentoring: A Multiple Perspectives Approach*. Oxford: Blackwell.

# 6

# CONVERSATIONAL LEARNING

## CHAPTER OVERVIEW

This chapter is about the power of one-to-one developmental dialogue. It explores the influence of the social contexts in which learning takes place and discusses, as well as compares, the 'linear' view of learning with the 'non-linear' view. We look at the non-linear nature of coaching and mentoring conversations and present and analyse a transcript of a live learning conversation. There are links in this chapter to Chapters 1, 2 and 4 where we discuss various positions on research philosophy, mindset and gaze.

# INTRODUCTION

Within the wide business community, there has been a dominant rhetoric that change is the only constant in the 21st-century developed world (Garvey and Williamson, 2002). This rhetoric has extended in recent times to suggest that the pace of change in organizational life, which is influenced by technological innovation, competitive pressures and political initiatives, has accelerated. As we will argue in Chapter 10, the COVID-19 pandemic has added weight to that discourse via technological innovation, through the need to communicate and work online. Such is the dominance of this discourse that the implications of this fast-changing and competitive climate for people in organizations of all types and in all sectors are believed to be considerable. These implications have migrated into organizational policies for recruitment and selection, learning and development and health and safety. They manifest in learning and development and recruitment policies written with the assumption that the organization needs people who are able to:

- adapt to change rapidly
- be innovative and creative
- be flexible
- learn quickly and apply their knowledge to a range of situations
- maintain good mental and physical health
- work collaboratively.

These characteristics are acutely relevant in higher education, due to the requirements to teach in a 'blended' way (simultaneous face-to-face and online teaching). In this current COVID climate, where the pressure to perform is increased, it is also crucial for employees to have 'strong and stable personalities' (Kessels, 1995) and to be able to 'tolerate complexity' (Garvey and Alred, 2001).

Furthermore, the pandemic has also seen the rise of another tacit competence – the ability to cope with unexpected bereavement. In their article on bereavement due to COVID-19, Carr, Boerner and Moorman (2020) point out that so-called 'bad deaths' (where death is perceived as being unjust, untimely and unexpected) place a huge burden on us, psychologically and physically.

Yet, there seems to be a tacit expectation that we should be able to deal with these bereavements 'competently' in the same way that we are expected to deal with other expected bereavements. In sum, this is a very challenging list, which contains elements not often found in the competency frameworks so commonly promulgated by organizations! We speculate that this is because competency frameworks are products of the Psy Expert and Managerial discourses (Western, 2012) and are therefore essentially reductionist in nature. For this reason, they cannot account for the subtleties and complexities of human behaviour that the above list implies (see Hemmestad et al., 2010, on the complexities of sports coaching, for example). Kessels (1995) argued that reductionist approaches to learning are becoming increasingly redundant, and many managers observe that this type of development simply does not deliver (see Broad and Newstrom, 1992; Groot, 1993; Garvey, 2012). As presented in Chapter 1, at the heart of both coaching and mentoring is support for individuals to learn in context things of relevance to themselves by drawing on their own resourcefulness in times of crisis, transition and change. This is not the stuff of competency frameworks, and it is therefore strange that the mentoring and coaching professionalizing associations strongly promote training for coaches and mentors through competency frameworks.

The notion of meaningful learning conversations holds a response to this fast-changing climate and enables people to understand and appreciate the meaning of change for themselves and, as Garvey (2012) and Nadeem et al. (2021) have shown, without reference to the blunt instrument of a competency framework.

## METHODOLOGY

Overall, this chapter is adapted and extended from the publication which first appeared as Alred et al.'s (1998) 'Pas de deux: Learning in Conversations'. Here, we extend this article by drawing on some selected literature on learning and development philosophies, the importance of narratives and discourses within the context of human development. We then present a transcript of a live learning conversation and analyse it using Megginson and Clutterbuck's (2005a: 32–6) concept of 'the layers of dialogue'. We argue that the core elements of conversational learning presented here are still as relevant to the current context as they were before, if not more so.

## RATIONALITY AND LEARNING

In association with the rhetoric of change, there has been a growing tendency in both the public and private sectors towards 'objectivity' in all work activities. In Western's terms, the Psy Expert and the Managerial discourses in action within organization have become a dominant preoccupation of managers (see Chapters 2 and 4).

As with the strong move towards an assumed accurate, rational measurement of the performance of individuals and organizations, there is also a change in our understanding of the nature of rationality itself. Barnett (1994: 37) argues that the kinds of thinking available to people is changing: 'Society is more rational, but it is a rationality of a limited kind.' As far back as 1974, Habermas argued that the most employed and widespread models of learning presuppose the impersonal, 'technical' mode of rationality. According to O'Brien (2020: 1), this limited mode of rationality still exists and has been compounded by the technological advances in social media which have led to the rise in 'fake news' that we are witnessing today:

> The very concept of objective truth is under siege from forces that, in purely technological terms, didn't exist 20 years ago. Worse, it is a world in which empathy, perhaps second only to evidence as a catalyst for changing our minds about the most important issues, is increasingly denigrated and devalued.

This presents significant challenges to our notions of what learning and knowledge acquisition are. The current mode of thinking aims to establish systematic bodies of generalized knowledge or explicit rules and procedures, i.e. competency frameworks. It sets out to specify objectives and learning outcomes which make it easier to judge success in teaching and learning if these outcomes or objectives are met. This mode lies behind current competence-based learning, which dominates the learning and development agenda in many organizations.

This technical mindset towards learning is often accompanied by the strong inclination to think of learning as a linear activity (Bernstein, 1971; Habermas, 1974; Barnett, 1994). We have become so used to this that we no longer notice it, nor how it is only one, and perhaps not a very good, way of talking and thinking about learning. This view implies that, as we learn, we move along a straight line, or that the learner moves up a kind of road or staircase. The discourse of 'talent management' and 'fast-tracking' suggests that we may even be able to hurry people along this road or up the staircase (see Self, Gordon and Jolly's (2019) study of talent management in the hospitality sector as an example of this).

Clearly, the logic of this mode is particularly attractive and beguiling, for if we know the precise route that people take then (we might imagine) the most helpful thing we can do is to accelerate their journey and get them to their destination as quickly as possible.

Of course, we often do make progress in this way, such as passing a driving test, learning a new language or successfully filling a new role, but 'moving forward' is only part of the story, and the merits of this approach include the enhanced possibilities of accountability, quality control and the belief that we are accelerating the learning process. Despite the criticism (Jessup, 1991) that concentration on outcomes is unduly technicist in approach, this emphasis does not preclude attention to process and relational aspects of learning. However, the 'hegemony of technique' (Habermas, 1974) can only engineer what has been pre-specified (Bernstein, 1971). In other words, it gets us to where we want to go by the straightest and most direct route. However, this cannot develop our awareness of the different kinds of destination available (see Chapter 11 for a discussion of this in relation to goals within coaching and mentoring), the speed of travel or the choice of route, nor does it hold out any promise that we will be enriched simply by the travelling. (Enrichment in this sense is equivalent to the notion of 'holistic learning' discussed in Chapter 1 and is much more akin to the Soul Guide (Western, 2012) origins of mentoring and coaching.) Consequently, this technical mode of rationality cannot be adequate to develop the learner in the fast-changing environment where they need to be pre-eminently capable of collaborative working, flexibility, innovation, creativity and improvisation. It may actually be counter-productive because it has been argued that 'genuinely interactive and collaborative forms of reasoning' (Barnett, 1994: 37) or social learning are in danger of being driven out by technical or 'strategic' reasoning and individualism. This is one aspect of the way interpersonal relationships may weaken during times of rapid social change (Toffler, 1970; Bauman, 1989; Sennett, 1998; Arnaud, 2003, O'Brien, 2020).

There may be clues that this dominating technical mindset may be changing and lessening in its impact. Garvey (1994a) noted that despite the pressure for improved performance, linear and controlled learning, there is also a strong desire for people in the workplace to reach out for the more human aspects of life. Bachkirova (2011) argues that 80% of the world's population is interested in the spiritual aspects of life, and Western (2017) argues that the Soul Guide discourse is 'familiar to most coaches'. People seem to want to develop stronger and more supportive relationships at work (Bear, 2018) to enable them to learn from and with one another to develop their knowledge and skills, to enhance their performance and to assist them to progress in their chosen careers. As raised in Chapter 10, this is also a mental health issue, particularly in this COVID era, where people gain support from the people they work with as well as from others. Clearly, mentoring and coaching can be associated with this dynamic and are another way of interacting and learning. It is no surprise that coaching and mentoring activity is growing right across all sectors of society. This desire for support and for improved human relationships among people at work fits well with Erikson's (1995) concept of 'generativity'. According to Erikson, if we are not 'generative' we can stagnate, but by engaging with others in social interaction and dialogue and by developing others as well as being learners ourselves we may satisfy the generative motive and avoid stagnation.

## THE POWER OF STORIES

Another way of developing collaborative learning is through engaging in stories. The relationship between 'story' and learning is well established (Geertz, 1974; Daloz, 1986; Bruner, 1990). The main vehicle for story is metaphor, and it is through understanding the myths and symbolic representation of realities in a metaphor that a person may extract meaning (Morgan, 1986). While this can provide a positive vehicle for learning, it may also be at the heart of conflicts between people. The differences between the protagonists may not be in their knowledge but in their understanding of the 'meaning' of the story, its language, metaphors and symbols. As raised in Chapter 1, Bruner (1990: 32) explores the importance of meaning and suggests that this is important to the practice of human psychology: 'Psychology … deals only in objective truths and eschews cultural criticism. But even scientific psychology will fare better when it recognizes that its truths about the human condition are relative to the point of view that it takes toward that condition.'

Bruner's (1990: 33) view is based on two points. First, it is important to understand how the individual's experiences and actions are shaped by their 'intentional states'. Second, the form that these 'intentional states' take is realized through the 'participation in the symbolic systems of the culture'. It is Bruner's belief that interaction with the patterns inherent in the culture's 'language and discourse modes, the forms of logical and narrative explication, and the patterns of mutually dependent communal life' shapes behaviour and attitudes. Consequently, we are not isolated individuals, nor are we rootless in response only to the present. On the contrary, we take meaning from our historical pasts which gave shape to our culture, and we distribute this meaning through dialogue. It is Bruner's belief that 'meaning' is both individually and culturally constructed. So 'meanings' will inevitably vary and may be interpreted in the context of both the individual's 'intentional state' and the cultural frameworks from which they draw.

Coaching and mentoring conversations are one vehicle for such 'meaningful' dialogue and here, in our view, is the potential power of learning conversations to lead, shape and build changing attitudes, behaviours and performance in the workplace (see Koukpaki and Adams (2020) for a recent research example). We enact work through the story, and an organization is only as good as its narrative allows it to be. This implies that there may be 'good' stories which help to shape a 'good' view of an organization, but also 'bad' stories can equally become embedded as cultural norms. Bruner (1990: 97) suggests that a culture may be in conflict with itself and 'our sense of the normative is nourished in narrative, but so is our sense of breach and exception. Stories make reality a mitigated reality.' According to Bruner (1990: 97), conflict then is a product of:

- deep disagreement about what is ordinary and normal
- an overspecialized narrative – here stories become ideological or self-serving; this can create mistrust about the interpretation, and 'what happened' is discounted as fabrication or is rewritten
- limited, controlled, suppressed or restricted narratives, i.e. extremist groups, dictatorships and propaganda.

The value of exploring story through conversation is in addressing these issues and in the ability of conversationalists to develop new and alternative meanings so that a fuller picture is developed, thus giving more choice of action. A conversation with a mentee or coachee may reveal that they 'know this story already'. They are not encountering anything new but may be helped to revisit and find new insights, understandings and meanings in old truths, such as the importance of team-building or of maintaining distance from and perspective on work. With these topics, we seem to be dealing with basic and apparently simple ideas, but in reality they are so complex, so deceptive in their simplicity, yet so important, that they have to be approached again and again from different angles. Here, a 'technicist' approach to learning is simply inappropriate because conversational learning does not seek right answers but rather possibilities and options.

Conversation plays a major part in learning for, as Bruner (1985: 23) says, 'language is a way of sorting out one's thoughts about things'. Discussion can help the learner to re-frame an idea, think new thoughts or build from old ones (Garvey and Williamson, 2002). Vygotsky (1978) would agree: he viewed dialogic learning as a 'higher mental function'. This is because the engagement in ideas through dialogue externalizes the idea in a social context and enables new perspectives to emerge. These perspectives are then internalized and integrated into the individual's mental frameworks and functions. Conversational learning develops wisdom and practical judgement – the products of holistic critical learning. These are the real alternatives to competency-based learning and are of far more use to both business and wider society in developing the list of attributes outlined in the introduction of this chapter.

## THE SOCIAL CONTEXT

It is clear then that learning is also contextual and that the organizational context can influence the ability of those working within it to function (see Chapter 8). The notion of 'environments' put forward by Vygotsky (1978: 86) as the 'zone of proximal development' plays an important role in the learning process. He described this as 'the distance between the actual development level as determined by independent problem solving and the level of potential development as determined through problem solving ... in collaboration with more capable peers'. The implication here is that a greater potential for enhanced understanding and learning is unlocked if there is guidance or collaboration through dialogue.

These notions have major implications for coaching and mentoring conversations and for how we organize for learning in the workplace. The influence and power of the social context in the learning process is not in doubt. As Bruner, writing on Vygotsky, states, 'passing on knowledge is like passing on language – his [Vygotsky's] basic belief that social transaction is the fundamental vehicle of education and not, so to speak, solo performance' (1985: 25).

Lave and Wenger (1991) developed the idea of learning as a social activity within a social context in their notions of 'communities of practice' and 'legitimate peripheral participation'. Vygotsky saw learning as a holistic, continuous process which should be pursued until the issues are resolved or, in Kolb's (1984) or Jarvis's (1992) terms, with full consideration of the models of experiential learning. In Vygotskian terms, this means a 'unity of perception, speech and action, which ultimately produces internalization' (Vygotsky, 1978: 26). So, mentoring and coaching conversations have the potential to develop great insight, new thoughts and enhanced meaning within the social context of the discussing pair and, at the same time, the social context of the organization.

## NON-LINEAR CONVERSATION

Non-linear learning and meaningful conversation are natural bedfellows. However, conversations take place in any number of situations, and while all share a common factor of involving at least two people talking, they may in fact serve a variety of purposes, of which non-linear learning is only one. For example, many of us have fallen into conversation with a stranger when travelling, both parties being in transit. This can be an occasion for more expansive talk, or less inhibited talk, than when in a familiar context. Unexpected things can emerge: we can be surprised at what we are ready to share with a stranger, and such 'brief encounters' are sometimes remembered with fondness and appreciation (Simmel, 1950). The contrasting situation of talk over a meal among intimates in a domestic setting can be similarly valuable as a space to explore, to touch on matters that really matter, to connect the mundane with the fundamental – in short, to learn in a non-linear way. Any one conversation may serve a number of purposes.

Mentoring and coaching conversations are associated with the development of both the affective and the rational (see Chapter 1). These conversations assist in the development of human qualities such as trust, openness, honesty and integrity, as well as supporting those notions crucial to workplace learning such as the enhancement of skills, applications from training, understanding and sense-making through experiential learning (Daloz, 1986). Coaching and mentoring can bring together those who view learning as a means to an end, such as improved effectiveness and efficiency, and those who emphasize the wider psychosocial (Kram, 1983) contexts in which people are regarded as 'ends in themselves'.

In their book *Techniques for Coaching and Mentoring*, Megginson and Clutterbuck (2005a) provided a helpful typology for coaching and mentoring conversations. While they refer to this as the 'seven layers of dialogue', which in itself may imply a linear conversation (it is presented as a progressive and hierarchical framework), if conceived as a series of equal status elements in which all may play a part (see Figure 6.1), it offers a way of analysing and understanding the non-linear movements that may be made within a conversation. We have found this to be most helpful in educational programmes for coaches and mentors.

Social dialogue is aimed at establishing a social connection in a friendly manner, a central feature of both mentoring and coaching (Chapter 1). Social dialogue helps to develop mutual understanding, empathy and trust. It is therefore an important element and not to be underestimated as a contributor in establishing a learningful relationship. Social dialogue is a constant

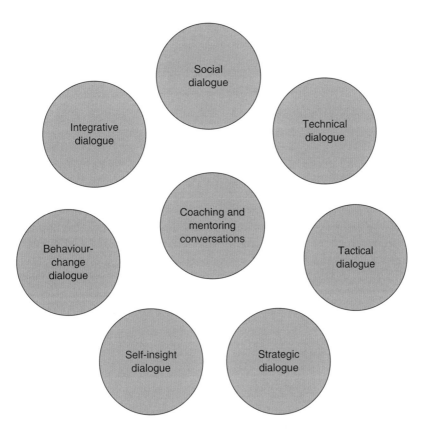

**Figure 6.1** Coaching and mentoring conversation typology (adapted from Megginson and Clutterbuck, 2005a)

element of coaching and mentoring in that it needs to be present on most occasions, particularly at the start and the end of a conversation.

'Technical dialogue' is another element of a coaching or mentoring conversation identified by Megginson and Clutterbuck (2005a). Here the focus is on clarifying existing knowledge about work policies, procedures and systems. It tends towards the short term.

'Tactical dialogue' is also short term, where the conversation is aimed at discovering practical ways to deal with the issue in hand.

'Strategic dialogue' has the purpose of taking a wider perspective and of putting the immediate challenges into a broader context. This is often a discussion about the longer term and develops a sense of direction and scale. Strategic dialogue assists with decision making over time.

'Self-insight dialogue' is where the learner gains an awareness of their hopes, fears, thinking patterns or emotions. This may occur over time or it may be a 'eureka moment'. Self-insight is one of the core purposes of coaching and mentoring and therefore a key element in the coaching or mentoring conversation.

'Behavioural dialogue' is often a product of self-insight dialogue. It is aimed at bringing together understanding from the other layers to effect change. Like self-insight dialogue, behavioural change is a core purpose of coaching and mentoring activity and therefore is also a key element. In relation to time, this can also be short, medium or long term.

'Integrative dialogue' moves through the different elements, not in a linear fashion but more like a dance where both partners take the lead in turns, making use of the different elements in order to learn and progress.

Any one element of this conversational typology can be helpful and develop ways forward for the coachee or mentee. However, from our experience, some coaches or mentors have a 'comfort zone' for conversation. In business settings, for example, social, technical, tactical and strategic conversations are more the norm. This is often despite the coach or mentor being aware that a 'self-insight', a 'behavioural change' or an 'integrative' conversation may be what is needed. We have also learned that the nature of the conversation may be controlled by the coachee or mentee as they attempt to stay in their comfort zones. In either case, much of this is influenced by the dominant discourse of the social context. For example, in a small business setting, it is not surprising that technical, tactical or strategic conversations are the norm, and while this undoubtedly offers potential for change and growth, they may not offer the depth or breadth of transformation that may be necessary in an individual case.

## CONVERSATION AS DANCE

As we have established, in a mentoring or coaching conversation, the learning is often non-linear as the two conversationalists explore and probe ideas and come to conclusions or new viewpoints.

As an illustrative example, here is a transcript from an integrative mentoring conversation. This is put forward to highlight not so much the content of the conversation but more the process of mentor and mentee talking together and what the mentee learns from it.

The mentee has recently been promoted within his organization. He talks about the nature of the new job, the changing relationship with his line manager and an aspect of his personality. The conversationalists know each other well and they have talked before. Their relationship and shared understanding enable the conversation to be respectful and purposeful. Knowledge is assumed and hence, to an observer, may appear understated, but both parties recognize its significance as the conversation proceeds. They explore the themes of the conversation, getting closer to new learning, refining understanding and meaning as they go. There are repetitions, restatements of themes and variations in pace and the balance of support and challenge. The conversation has two distinct sections and hints at a third. The first is an exploration led by the mentor, the second is a refocusing based on a different understanding of the mentee's situation and the third is movement towards action (Alred et al., 2006).

At the outset, the mentor mentions that he has observed a slight change of behaviour in the mentee. Normally, the mentee is very open about all aspects of his life. In taking on this new role, it seems to the mentor that he has been uncharacteristically reticent.

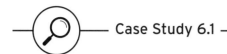

## Case Study 6.1

### A live mentoring conversation

**Mentor:** Can I take you back to this week, and the start of your new job? Usually, I know what's happening in your working life, and I usually know what's happening in your personal life, because you're very chatty – you share a lot. But this week, it's a big new beginning and you've said how you would have liked your boss to show some interest. I wonder if you could say a bit more about that. It seems like a quiet start…

**Mentee:** Yes, a quiet start … um … previously, he's been very supportive, but this week he's been very busy with other things, with another colleague actually. He says you have to manage him [laughter]. When I was in charge of the last area, he would leave me to get on with it and I would feed him information from time to time. But this new job is different.

The mentor intuitively senses that there is an issue to be explored. He leads gently.

**Mentor:** It sounds like there is something you want from him?

The mentee is challenged to move in this direction and brings the conversation round to a well-trodden issue.

**Mentee:** Er … I think I would like more information … I think there's this other issue which comes up … that he suffers from 'last minuteism', in time management, and you know what I'm like with time management. You know, if it's not in the diary three months ahead, I find difficulty with it really. For example, there is a very important meeting today that I was just told about on Wednesday. Well, I'm sorry, there's no way I can go to it … [laughter] … so there's that issue.

The mentor follows by opening up the issue.

**Mentor:** That's his style …
**Mentee:** Yes, yes … worries me a touch …
**Mentor:** Really? He is somebody you are having to work to … yes … and that's a problem for you …?

**Mentee:** Yes, generally he's very good, the 'last minuteism', it gets a bit close for comfort, and personally I find that very difficult. I like a more planned future.

The mentor maintains momentum by offering a suggestion.

**Mentor:** You're usually very upfront with people. Have you thought about going to see him to discuss it?

After some hesitation, the mentee stays in step.

*(Continued)*

Mentee: I think I should, although ... I've not really thought about it ... [pause] ... I think ... [pause] ... yes, I do need to go and see him and say, 'That meeting was important and you knew it was coming up, would it have been possible to have let me know more in advance?' With a lot of things, the administrator has put in place some of these dates and we now have them. And I think he needs to learn some of that ...

The mentor now moves the focus from the manager to the mentee/manager relationship.

Mentor: This issue has come more to the fore this year with the shift to your new role as director. It's something to do with the last job being less important than the new one and here you are with a high profile. And it means you've got a different sort of relationship with him.

Mentee: Well, it's bigger business, it's worth a lot of money, in the picture of things, the last job is worth peanuts really, actually, in financial terms, whereas this one is worth a lot of money to the organization.

Mentor: So the stakes are higher?

Mentee: Absolutely.

The mentor holds the line.

Mentor: This relationship with your boss is perhaps more important than it's been before ... is it?

The mentee begins to look at things differently.

Mentee: I think it is. [Pause] I just wonder, just sometimes, I wonder whether it's me that's got the problem with this time management business ... um...

Mentor: It's bit of a running joke, isn't it ...?

Mentee: It is really. [Laughter]

The mentor stays with the theme, leading the conversation and challenging.

Mentor: I have a simple man's diary ... [laughter] ... you ... have a different sort of diary ...

Mentee: Absolutely ... absolutely, [laughter] ... and you seem to survive all right [laughter] ... um ...

Mentor: So is that another issue ...?

The conversation takes a significant turn.

Mentee: I don't know ... but I wonder if, personally, it's a bit of an obsession. I think the busier you are the more you need to be organized. My view of time is ... [pause] fundamentally ... Well ... it's a negotiable thing and something around which you have choice ... but I don't think everyone sees it like that [laughter] ...

Mentor: Well ...?

Mentee: I don't think he sees it like that. I think he feels he has a right to my time on request.

The mentor seems to feel that this is a significant moment so, rather than probe further, he feels it is time for some consolidation through summary.

Mentor: Interesting, I'm conscious that we've been talking for some time … I wonder if it would be useful for you to summarize …

The mentee, to his surprise, is given responsibility to lead.

Mentee: You want me to do that?

Mentor: You start and I'll chip in …

Mentee: All right … well, I suppose the first thing is the issue of the past, what went on then, but I don't … that's gone now, that was tense but I got out of that responsibility … so in a sense that was quite satisfying. But it wasn't like frying pan to fire, it's a new thing opening up. What I have now in terms of budget well that's a bit nerve racking. And then there's … [pause] … then there's the time management issue … um … which is … I'm not sure whether it's my problem or his. Either way, we've got to sort it out. And I think that's probably the key issue. When people are busy you've got to sort out some sort of organization around that.

The mentor takes back the lead and the conversation moves toward action.

Mentor: So when we take this further, we'll pick up these issues. You're in the early, very early stages, the first days of the new responsibility …

Mentee: Yes.

Mentor: And working on the relationship with your line manager is a priority …

Mentee: Yes, I think it is, I think you're right, and I think I shall tackle that … although, I've always got on well with him …

Mentor: Yes.

Mentee: I don't have a problem with that. Because the stakes are a bit higher, the relationship is likely to be a bit closer.

The mentor reflects back the mentee's words.

Mentor: On the other side there's what you've described as being obsessive about time management. Perhaps it will be helpful to explore that more, so that you can get clearer about it, and that may help you with your manager.

Mentee: Yes, because it does create tensions. Last-minute things create tensions for me, because my sense of responsibility says I should be doing that, and my sense of time management … which is 'my time and we negotiate' – thinks – I'm not going to be there because I've already made previous arrangements. So that's complicated. Feelings of guilt, I suppose [laughter] are around.

The conversation is coming to an end. The mentor ensures they end as a pair, looking ahead to the next conversation.

*(Continued)*

Mentor: So we've explored what the new responsibility is like and two issues, one to do with your line manager and one more personal. I wonder if that is a suitable place to stop.

Mentee: I think it is. I mean, what it's done for me is draw out this time management issue which ... [pause] ... I think it does have the potential to be significant and it does have to be resolved. Before we started this, I didn't really know where we were going to go. There was a concern there and I think I've clarified what that concern is.

Mentor: Can we agree to pick that up next time?

Mentee: Yes, that will be useful.

 **Reflective Questions**

- What do you notice about this conversation?
- In Western's (2012) terms, what kind of discourse(s) do you find here?

## DISCUSSION AND CONCLUSIONS

There are at least two stories inherent in this conversation. One story is the mentee's story that planning and organization are important. There is also a fairly sophisticated story about autonomy and independence versus compliance and interdependence between the mentee's manager and the mentee. Both these stories present potential problems for the mentee, the manager and the organization, particularly because the financial stakes are quite high and the mentor is working hard to achieve 'self-insight' and 'behavioural change' in the mentee.

This example also serves to illustrate non-linear learning and the conditions that promote it. The conversation starts in a 'social' way and moves through 'tactical', 'technical' and 'strategic' quite quickly. Prompted by his new role, the mentee revisits issues he has addressed before. Time management is a perennial issue, and here the idea that it is an 'obsession' is new and this is conversation leading towards 'self-insight'. He states explicitly that he didn't know at the outset where the conversation would go but it has been productive, leading to insight, clarification and a commitment to action. Following a linear model, the mentor could have proffered these outcomes himself by giving advice and thus holding the conversation in tactical or technical. However, with a complex subject like time management, advice would be inappropriate at this stage. The mentor could have moved the conversation into strategic but, instead, he initiated a non-linear conversation. The mentee provided the content and the mentor facilitated a process of crisscrossing the issues, looking at them from different angles, gently prompting the mentee to take risks, such as voicing a criticism of his line manager and admitting to an 'obsession'. In this way, self-insight develops. This conversation is also about the culture of the organization. The topic of time management is often influenced by the behaviour and values of those who lead. So, 'last minuteism' is the way the manager behaves, and this is at odds with the mentee's behaviour. The self-insight here presents the mentee with choices so that the next level of conversation at future meetings may be within 'behavioural change', but this may take some time to action and establish.

When the mentor asks the mentee to summarize, it is a further challenge to the mentee to lead the process, as well as explore the content. This pushes the conversation to 'integrative'. The mentee is learning about specific issues and about the non-linear conversation. He is learning to learn, and what he has learned is of considerable value both to himself in developing Vygotsky's (1978) 'higher mental functions' and to his organization in terms of collaborative working and adjustments in behaviour towards others. The conversation is also helping to maintain stable mental health by examining the meaning the mentee attributes to his behaviour and the behaviour of others. The mentee could quite easily become stressed if he fails to understand his manager's behaviour and fails to consider adjustments in his own. There is also potential for misunderstanding in this example, leading to potential conflicts because the manager's and the mentee's meanings about time are differently constructed.

 ## Future Direction

As we move to a future where learning conversations may become common in everyday life and work, there is a challenge to engage not only in learning conversations that work, but in learning conversations at work. A further challenge is to those who wish to 'manage' others in a changing dynamic in the workplace. The old methods of purposeful planning, systematic arrangement, command and control, status and hierarchy may now no longer be the best approach when learning, knowledge exchange and development are the key business drivers. These values may need to give way to greater autonomy, experimentation, exploration and the genuine facilitation of learning as a process that adds value. This requires space and time for different kinds of conversation and new conditions to enable people to perform at their best. The greater the desire to strictly control the conversation, the less it produces true creativity, freedom of movement and expression – valued attributes in the new business model of the 21st century. These are found in organizations that encourage learning through conversation.

As we have argued elsewhere in this edition, the boundaries of what we mean by being and learning at work have now been challenged due to the current context of COVID-19. For us, it has raised the possibility of how legitimate peripheral participation (Lave and Wenger, 1991) might be conceptualized in one of three 'lifeworlds' that we as individuals can be said to inhabit. The first world – the most familiar to us – is one where we physically travel to our workplaces and engage in conversational learning as part of formal development activities, e.g. training courses and, of course, formal coaching and mentoring relationships on a face-to-face basis. We might call this the Outer World. The second lifeworld is what we might call the Inner World and has some connection with Gallwey's (1997b) concept of the Inner Game of Work, where learning and reflexivity are focused inwards and where we work on ourselves using our own internal resources. This has long since been considered the domain of coaching and mentoring practice but, following Alain de Botton's (de Botton, 2006) notion of the architecture of happiness, we predict that there will be further work on how we reflexively engage

*(Continued)*

with conversational learning with our inner selves. Finally, and most pertinently to the current context, there is the Virtual World. Clearly, this world has existed for some time for all of us in terms of our emerging online identities through platforms such as LinkedIn, Facebook, etc. However, the current context has meant that, for many of us engaged in coaching and mentoring work (see Chapter 10 for a further discussion of e-development and home working), we have been required to further develop and attend to our online identities and further reflect on how effective conversational learning can be enacted on platforms such as Zoom, Microsoft Teams and other domains. It is our view that this experience will have a profound, long-term effect on how learning conversations are conducted, that will transcend a technical process for hosting such conversations. As with our inner and outer architecture, we predict that much more emphasis and energy will be focused on the design stage of our virtual worlds where we consider how we integrate the three worlds together so as to maximize individual, group and organizational development, and the 'limits of competence' will start to become exposed.

---

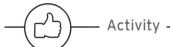 **Activity** ———————————————

Consider this extract from the start of a coaching conversation:

> I feel kind of, well, errm that my cultural orientation is strained in this new job. I mean the way people talk to each other is different, their politics are different, there are different skill requirements on me. Things have really changed and I feel bad and think I may have made the wrong choice. There was a time when I just wrote my report as an expert and gave the Board the information they needed to make a decision but now they expect me to make the decision myself and then for me to persuade or influence them to make the decision I recommend! It's mad. They get paid to make decisions and I don't. I mean, I'm not a salesman, I'm an industry expert – that's very different.

If you were coaching Fred, what would you ask him next? Using Figure 6.1, analyse your question and consider what kind of conversation you would have with Fred following this opening paragraph. What sort of conversation do you think Fred wants or, indeed, needs?

---

 **Questions** ———————————————

- Are we too shy, inexperienced, constrained, discouraged or lacking in opportunity to have more non-linear conversations in the workplace than we may currently do?
- If a manager is a coach for their team, where does 'power' sit, who holds the agenda and what form might the conversation take?
- How might an underpinning discourse shape the culture and impact on business performance?

---

**Further Reading**

For an exploration of learning and development through reflective practice: Koukpaki, A.S.F. and Adams, K. (2020) 'Enhancing professional growth and the learning and development function through reflective practices: An autoethnographic narrative approach', *European Journal of Training & Development*, 44(8/9): 805-827.

For a critique of competence-based learning, you might find the following book interesting: Barnett, R. (1994) *The Limits of Competence*. Milton Keynes: Open University Press and SRHE.

For an interesting account of various learning theories, try Chapter 3 in Daloz, L.A. (1999) *Mentor: Guiding the Journey of Adult Learners*, 2nd edition. San Francisco, CA: Jossey-Bass.

# PART 2

## INFLUENCES ON COACHING AND MENTORING

# 7

# POWER IN COACHING AND MENTORING

## CHAPTER OVERVIEW

In this chapter, we discuss power in coaching and mentoring. We believe that power is a key concept that permeates through all units of analysis in coaching and mentoring. First, we introduce an established typology of power and then present and critically discuss three established examples where power influences coaching and mentoring. Whilst these cases may have been written some time ago, we believe that they still serve the purpose of our arguments and therefore they remain. We then draw the themes together and raise some key questions about power in coaching and mentoring.

## INTRODUCTION

Throughout the book so far, we have argued that it is important to move beyond a technical-rational approach to coaching and mentoring. We have emphasized the importance of seeing coaching and mentoring schemes as human systems, often operating within larger human systems, i.e. organizations and societies. A key concept that permeates through all units of analysis in coaching and mentoring – the conversation, the relationship, the management triad (i.e. coach, coachee, manager), the organization, and so on – is that of power. This is for two main reasons.

First, power is a central concept in organizations, and therefore in organizational theory. Power is used to explain relationships between people within organizations and organizational structures; it is also used more widely to explain relationships between organizations, societies, countries and regions. Coaching and mentoring relationships are inevitably located within a given context – for example, organizational schemes, mentoring engagement schemes – and therefore power has relevance.

Second, it is often said that 'knowledge is power' (we explore this notion later); coaching and mentoring, whatever their nature, are often intended to enable some sort of exchange of knowledge, wisdom and understanding between their participants, so inevitably power will be involved. Further, coaching and mentoring are often associated with transition, development and growth. Therefore, it is inevitable that, as people grow and develop (often at different rates and times), this will alter the power dynamics between them. It is therefore important to try to understand power and the extent of its impact.

## METHODOLOGY

Our approach in this chapter is to use an established typology of power, present some interesting and contrasting case examples and critically discuss these by employing three models that relate to power found in other literature on the topic. In particular, we employ McAuley's (2003) model of transference to help understand some power dynamics within some specific relationships, power in discourse and the concept of power bases. Our overall purpose is to raise key questions.

## WHAT IS POWER?

Jackson and Carter (2000: 76), in their textbook on organizational behaviour, define power as 'the ability to get someone to do something that they do not particularly want to do'. This ability to influence behaviour seems to be a key part of most descriptions of power as a concept (see Clegg and Haugaard, 2012, for a more detailed discussion of the various theories of power in organizational theory).

In our view, coaching and mentoring are essentially voluntary in nature, and this value position is rarely explored. Power is often explained by referring to sources or bases of power, and one of the best known of these frameworks is French and Raven (1962), who argued that power can be understood as being one of five sorts:

- reward power – the ability to provide rewards such as promotions, pay rises or developmental projects
- coercive power – the ability to withdraw or withhold the rewards mentioned above or to make life difficult or unpleasant for those who do not comply
- legitimate power – derived from someone's formal authority or position within an organizational hierarchy
- expert power – derived from being perceived to hold knowledge, experience or judgement that others value but do not yet have
- referent power – based on personal qualities, i.e. likeability, being respected, charisma.

Clearly, this raises some interesting initial questions. If we take the first two categories of reward power and coercive power:

1.  What implications does this have for a manager who is trying to coach someone whom they also line manage?

2.  How honest and open can the subordinate be in a relationship when they know, or perceive, that their coach has the power to influence their career?

Turning to the impact of legitimate power on the matching process:

3.  Does this mean that all coachees and mentees vie for the most senior person within the scheme because they represent the best chance for career progression?

Moving on to the expert power category:

4.  What implications does this have for empowering the coachee to aspire to acquire this expertise?

5.  Do individual coachees' perceptions of the value of their coach change as they begin to acquire more knowledge and expertise?

Referent power is also a key issue and relates to issues of dependency:

6.  How likely are you to end coaching and mentoring when the powerful person you are working with makes you dependent on them?

 — **Case Study 7.1** —

### Beech and Brockbank (1999) on power/knowledge and mentoring

Perhaps the best way of exploring some of these issues is via a case study. Beech and Brockbank's (1999) article provides an excellent account of how power, knowledge and different understandings of mentoring play out within a mentoring scheme in the British National Health Service (NHS). From a study of 35 mentoring pairs, they identified four pairs to focus

*(Continued)*

on in their journal article. From these eight open-ended interviews, the researchers identified four main categories of data:

- the relationship and psychosocial functions
- management style
- power/knowledge
- career functions.

With the first pair, they examine a relationship between a line manager and their subordinate. In terms of the power and knowledge issue, we note that the mentor (referred to as Judith) paid relatively little attention to the knowledge transfer aspect of their relationship, preferring to focus on the psychosocial (Kram, 1983) aspect of it. The mentee (known as Hannah), however, placed much more emphasis on knowledge transfer as being an important part of mentoring. Consequently, as the relationship progressed, Hannah's perception of Judith's 'expert power' decreased, as Hannah's own knowledge base grew. Beech and Brockbank (1999) also use transactional analysis (Berne, 1964) to explain Judith's strong need to fulfil a nurturing parent role with Hannah. This contrasts with Hannah's account of the relationship. Hannah rejects the closeness of the relationship. Beech and Brockbank describe this as 'the typical embarrassment of a child who is over-nurtured by an over-involved parent' (1999: 13).

In French and Raven's (1962) terms, power does seem to be an issue in this relationship. The power seems to revolve around different understandings of what the mentee wanted and was getting from the relationship in terms of expert power.

Judith's account suggests that she was trying to minimize the effect of her legitimate power within the organization and, indeed, reward power and coercive power do not seem to be a feature of this online mentoring relationship. However, this contrasts sharply with the relationship between Juliet and Harry.

In this relationship, Juliet is Harry's line manager, but reward power and coercive power are very noticeable in Juliet's account of the relationship. She refers several times to her power to influence Harry's career adversely. Beech and Brockbank (1999: 19) confirm that this is also Harry's perception. Although Harry is conscious of the reward and coercive power displayed by Juliet, he, like Hannah in the previous pair, questions the expert power of his mentor.

Jane and Hazel's relationship (the third pair) seemed to operate from an adult–adult position in Berne's (1964) terms and seemed not to suffer from some of the problems of the other relationships referred to in the study. This may have been because Hazel was not being line managed by Jane at the time when the mentoring study took place, though she had been, prior to that. We note that although Jane (the mentor) sought to play down her knowledge, that knowledge was nevertheless important to Hazel; again, the 'expert power' seems pertinent here.

In Jackie and Hillary's case (pair four), Jackie had used her legitimate power to promote Hillary within the organization and, in her view, had invested in him. Despite achieving promotion, Hillary did not acknowledge Jackie's contribution to his development. Instead, Hillary started to question Jackie's knowledge and ask if it was of use to him anymore.

## DISCUSSION

Clearly, there are a number of patterns in this case study. First, the power dynamics are particularly significant when the mentor has some direct control over the mentee's future in terms of rewards and punishment, i.e. reward and coercive power. Second, power and perceived knowledge do seem to play an important part in determining how 'powerful' a mentee perceives their mentor to be. Of course, it is important to recognize that this may well be a function of the particular study and the individuals involved. However, the findings do seem to resonate with the power model found in McAuley (2003).

McAuley's model (see Figure 7.1) looks at the role of transference and countertransference in mentoring. Transference is a form of projection or enactment of previous relationships. De Vries and Miller (1984: 8) argue that transference happens within a relationship when an individual, often unconsciously, treats that relationship as though it were an important one from the past. Phillips (1995: 2) states that transference is the 'unwitting recreation and repetition of earlier family relationships'.

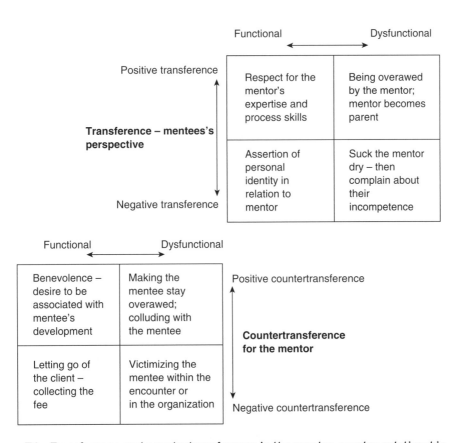

**Figure 7.1** Transference and countertransference in the mentor–mentee relationship

*Source:* McAuley (2003: 14). Reprinted by permission of the publisher (Taylor & Francis Ltd, http://www.tandfonline.com).

Within mentoring and coaching relationships, there is the possibility that the mentee or coachee may project or enact a significant previous relationship with their mentor or coach. Countertransference occurs if the mentor or coach responds to the projection. This could be either positively and supportively or negatively. Either response has the possibility of creating either positive or negative inappropriate behaviour within the mentor.

McAuley (2003: 21) argues that 'the ambivalence in mentoring – the manner in which it is poised between more humane organizational practice but also supports the notion of management – creates a number of tensions'. He goes on to argue that an understanding of transference would help in understanding and perhaps dealing with some of these power tensions.

Figure 7.1 shows ways in which transference issues can have an impact on a mentoring relationship. At the start of the four mentoring relationships in Beech and Brockbank (1999), there is clear evidence that there was positive functional transference on the part of all mentees towards their mentors. They appeared to have respect for their mentor's expertise and process skills. Similarly, there is some evidence (with the probable exception of Juliet) that mentors were exhibiting positive functional transference towards the mentees, in that they were happy to be associated with their development. However, as the relationships deteriorate, we can see evidence of the mentees 'sucking the mentor dry and then complaining about their incompetence' (McAuley, 2003: 14) or dysfunctional negative transference. Furthermore, in Juliet and Harry's relationship, we can see evidence of negative dysfunctional countertransference on the part of Juliet. She seems to demonstrate a destructive tendency towards Harry, the mentee.

What appears to have happened, following Beech and Brockbank's (1999) analysis, is that mentees developed in their understanding and expertise while they were working with their mentors. As a result, all mentees reported a perceived reduction in the disparity of knowledge, expertise and understanding between them and their mentor. Their response to this perception was to begin to withdraw from the mentoring relationship and to question the quality of their mentor; in other words, the expert power that had attracted them to the mentor in the first place had, in their eyes, begun to diminish. This deliberate withdrawal served to protect them from any psychological damage as the mentoring relationship deteriorated. Unfortunately, this was not the case for the mentors, who were left confused and with a sense of unfinished business, for the most part, despite their apparent powerful positions due to their legitimate hierarchical power as well as the reward and coercive power that many of them could have used towards their mentees.

An understanding of the mentoring process itself seems to have been missing among the participants. In particular, there appears to be little awareness of Levinson et al.'s (1978) work on adult development. This work highlights age-related transition stages in human development. Levinson, probably the first writer in modern times to acknowledge and highlight the contribution of mentoring to adult development, was interested in the question, 'What happens psychologically as we grow older?' He noted that adult development is made up of a series of transitions where our thinking patterns and value systems change (also noted by Jung, 1958; Erikson, 1950, 1995; and Sheehy, 1996) as we grow older and a mentor can assist with these transitions. Had participants been aware of this, it might have prompted them to see their mentoring partner in a different light. For example, mentors might have recognized that it is normal for mentees to want to separate from their mentors at certain stages in their development and that this is a helpful thing for them to do. They could have taken steps to: (a) work with the mentee's negative functional transference to encourage the mentee to establish their own expert power in relation to that of the mentor; or (b) worked with their own negative functional countertransference so as to enable them to let go of their mentee in more deliberate fashion to minimize the damage to themselves as mentors.

Unfortunately, the lack of this understanding and the power dynamics implicit in hierarchical managerial relationships within organizations, coupled with the power dynamics within mentoring conversations, led to an unsatisfactory outcome for most of those involved in the programme.

 **Reflective Questions**

- What might be useful about understanding the power dynamics within a particular coaching/ mentoring context?
- What alternative actions might such an understanding throw up for the participants/ scheme designers?

 **Case Study 7.2**

### Mentoring in the Big Six accounting firms

Dirsmith et al.'s (1997) account of mentoring within the so-called Big Six accounting firms (pre-Enron) also provides some insights into how power manifests itself in mentoring. In this study, the researchers undertook 180 interviews in two phases. They found two key mechanisms present in these organizations: management by objectives (MBO) and mentoring.

Mentoring in this context was focused around career progression as opposed to psychosocial support (Kram, 1983). Dirsmith et al. (1997) argue that mentoring was broadly informal and imply that, at least partly, mentoring became important in these organizations because 'MBO was found to be ostensibly mute on organizational politics' (1997: 13). Also, MBO was mainly organizationally driven in its focus and did not really address itself to individual firm members. MBO was, therefore, perceived as technical and being about 'looking after the numbers'. Mentoring, by contrast, was predominantly a political discourse, aimed at individual firm members. Dirsmith et al. (1997: 15) summarize it as follows:

> Largely off the record and enunciated among trusted people, the mentoring guidance and advice could be highly specific and 'gritty', covering the protégé's relations with clients and key partners, the business aspects of the firm, the protégé's appearance and behaviour and the politics of practice.

However, despite this apparent disparity between MBO and mentoring, Dirsmith et al. (1997) point out that the two discourses were connected. This was because many of those within the firms understood the role of 'a good mentor' to be one of 'looking after the numbers' of their mentee; in other words, defending and interpreting their performance against classic MBO

*(Continued)*

targets: realization rates, client billings, time budget averages, revenue and profit per partner. Those who had mentors that would perform these roles for them were known as being 'on the bus' towards partnership or greater power. A fascinating feature in this study is that mentoring in this context benefits the mentor by enhancing their power base. Again, Dirsmith et al. (1997: 18) summarize this as follows:

> Mentors [who] successfully sponsored protégés through the promotion process found themselves better connected with the new cadre of partners than non-mentors, which stabilized their own social network. Furthermore, practice office managing partners who had served as mentors often proved disproportionately effective in gaining promotions for their office's managers, so much so that they 'exported' many new practice partners to other offices and thus extended and further stabilized their own social networks.

In other words, mentors and their protégés both have a great deal invested in the mentoring relationship.

## DISCUSSION OF CASE

This account, similar to the previous case study, draws our attention to a number of issues that relate to power in coaching and mentoring.

First, it is essential to recognize the importance of language. For example, in Dirsmith et al.'s (1997) account, the person being helped to find promotion in the mentoring dyad is referred to as 'the protégé'. If, following the lead of Foucault (1979), we explore the genealogy of that term, the word protégé comes from the French verb protégér, which means 'to protect'. In the *Oxford Reference Online* (2006c), protégé is defined as being 'a person under the protection, patronage, tutelage of another'. This definition of the term very much describes the mentoring process within Dirsmith et al.'s study. However, the terms 'mentee' or 'mentoree' do not necessarily carry those associations, and these terms are much more common in European writing than in the USA (for an in-depth discussion of mentoring and coaching in the USA, see Chapter 14 by Dawn Chandler in Dirsmith et al., 1997).

In our view, the terms protégé and mentee, as well as the term 'coachee', imply passivity. They suggest that the person referred to is a passive recipient of the help, whereas much of the modern literature emphasizes the importance of dialogue and of two-way learning. Downey (2003) tackles this issue by preferring the term 'player'. This is perhaps a link to the sporting roots of coaching.

Megginson et al. (2006: 131) (also now presented in a rewritten form in this fourth edition in Chapter 5) discuss the use of the term 'client' to describe the learner or mentee in a mentoring scheme in Engineering Co. and state:

> This has confused and misleading meanings. This term implies a customer–provider relationship and seems to be born out of the 'customer-led' concept [in Engineering Co.]. However, whilst the term itself may have been an attempt to alter the existing relationships within Engineering Co., mentoring is not a customer–supplier relationship.

The word 'client' has become common in the literature on coaching. This positively acknowledges the interaction as being a business one where 'the client' is someone who pays for a service. However, in coaching, this 'business' relationship is not always clear and provides an opportunity for some confusion and misunderstanding about where power sits. For example, the 'client' in a business context may not be the person who pays. Payment may come, for example, from the Learning and Development budget or from the 'client's' manager's budget. This has the potential to create conflict as to whose agenda is being serviced here. Case Study 5.1 hints at this challenge in relation to internal coaching. The mentoring arrangement described above was voluntary and internal to the organization, and the use of the term client does seem to equate coaching and mentoring with other professional services such as law, psychotherapy and accountancy, for example. However, as Hawkins and Smith (2006) point out, there are a number of different ways of seeing clients. They talk about there being three clients:

- the person in the room
- the organization or network of which they are a part
- the purpose of their joint endeavour (serving customers and other stakeholders).

Again, this notion of multiple clients is seen in Dirsmith et al.'s (1997) account, with individual mentoring firm members engaging with three clients:

- their mentees and their development issues
- the firm, as represented by the MBO discourse
- other stakeholders, i.e. senior partners, customers.

All of these different clients have an impact on the power dynamics both within the organization and within the mentoring dyad itself. This is also present in the following coaching intervention.

 **Reflective Questions** ─────────────

- To what extent is it helpful to recognize that multiple stakeholders are 'in the room', in coaching and mentoring conversations?
- Is it useful to separate out the coaching client from the organizational client?

 **Case Study 7.3** ─────────────────

**The successful adventure of a downwardly mobile executive (Blattner, 2005)**

In this case study, Blattner (2005) presents an account of his own executive coaching work with his client, Terry. Terry is presented as a fairly senior executive who is experiencing some problems with a 'lack of professional fulfilment'. In power terms, it is interesting to note the issues Blattner chooses to focus on and those he chooses to play down or leave out.

*(Continued)*

Blattner says very little about himself and why Terry might have chosen to come to him. In fact, all he says is that 'a colleague referred him' (2005: 3). At this stage, Blattner gives no indication of who the colleague is or what being 'referred' means. However, in his author's description, Blattner refers to himself as 'a psychologist-consultant-coach with PAS International Ltd'. Upon searching for Blattner on Google, we found that he is listed as an Illinois-based psychologist (www.psychologyinfo.com/directory/IL/illinois-directory_15.html). This may or may not indicate a referral from a psychologist – Blattner does not tell us.

His biography is phrased in such a way that is intended to emphasize Blattner's expert power as a consultant, describing him as having '25 years experience as an organizational consultant and executive coach' and being 'highly versed' in doing this sort of work. Organizational consultancy and executive coaching would appear, rather like in Dirsmith et al.'s (1997) study, to involve two different units of analysis – the organization and the executive respectively. However, Blattner does not engage in any attempt to differentiate the two areas of work; indeed, he seems to deliberately conflate them. For example, he says that 'as consultants, we still do not know how the process of coaching actually works' (2005: 3), but he does raise the question as to why organizational consultants should engage in executive coaching.

The use of language in this article is interesting, particularly when it comes to his description of his own interventions. These are often framed as 'suggestions' from the coach. For example, Blattner (2005) 'suggests' that he and Terry agree to a three-month coaching contract with a view to reviewing it after that. In the second session, he suggests that Terry complete a questionnaire. This appears to be a psychological instrument for assessing Terry against four measures: dominance, influencing, steadiness and compliance. It is only after this is completed that Blattner asks Terry to identify goals for the next three, six and twelve months.

As to the issues not discussed in this article: first, it is not clear why Blattner asks Terry to sign up for three months. Why not two weeks, four sessions or ten sessions? Second, it is not clear why Blattner has chosen to use a self-reporting psychological instrument to evaluate Terry. Why this one and not another one? Why use one at all? Third, the scores that emerge from the instrument are taken, uncritically, as being representative of Terry's actual behaviour, as is illustrated in this example:

> Also, the scores provided some feedback regarding Terry's behavioural style. Some of the positive findings indicated that Terry was people orientated – building confidence in others; he was service orientated – a dependable team player, and he was cordial and helpful when dealing with new clients or customers. (2005: 4)

The discussion in the article omits any evidence from anyone, other than Terry, that this is how others perceive him. Nevertheless, Blattner and Terry then use the data to agree on Terry's goals. The chronology of this process is interesting. Terry agrees to paid coaching for three months, then completes a self-assessment and then agrees the goals. Notwithstanding our questioning of the ubiquity of goals in coaching (see Chapter 10), it is not clear as to the basis on which Terry agrees to pay Blattner for three months. On what basis is Terry making that decision, when, as implied by Blattner, Terry is not clear about what he wants out of the coaching until session three? Furthermore, although Terry is presented as someone with significant legitimate power, he also seems very amenable to Blattner's 'suggestions', as compared with our mentees in the mentoring case studies examined.

As the coaching progresses, we hear about Terry's ups and downs and his frustrations with his new boss and his anxieties about his position. Notice, however, that despite the fact that Blattner is a self-styled eminent psychologist, there is no examination of transference and countertransference in Blattner's account of the relationship, even when it seems to be particularly merited. For example, on page 10, Blattner recounts how he felt that Terry 'had just wanted me to roll out a formula, give him the answers and that would be that'.

However, Blattner recounts how he 'resisted that approach and responded by repeatedly reframing his questions and asking thoughtful and clarifying questions in return'. It seems reasonable to assume that Blattner was working with Terry's transference, in putting him in the role of expert, which had started to move towards being positively dysfunctional in nature (see Figure 7.1). By being aware of his own potential positive dysfunctional countertransference in wanting to remain being seen as the expert, Blattner appears to have avoided this danger in the service of the client. However, despite Blattner's use of Daniel Goleman's work on emotional intelligence and a demonstrable awareness of important phases in managing the relationship – for example, on page 12 he talks about arriving 'at a place to start working on closure for our coaching session' – the account is noticeably bereft of any emotional challenges within the coaching relationship.

## DISCUSSION OF CASE

Blattner's account of this coaching relationship and our previous discussion of language draw our attention to an important aspect of power in coaching and mentoring that we have used several times already, that of 'discourse'. McAuley et al. describe discourses in the following way:

> Discourses are sets of ideas and practices that condition our ways of relating to and acting upon particular phenomena; a discourse is expressed in all that can be thought, written or said about a particular topic, which by constituting the phenomena in a particular way, influences behaviour. (2007: 265)

If we apply this understanding to writings on coaching and mentoring, we could argue that the 'gaze' or mindset of the writer influences how people coach and mentor. In particular, following Jackson and Carter (2000: 66), a dominant or powerful, legitimated discourse determines 'who can say what, where – and why'.

The arguments made, particularly by postmodernist writers, for example Gutting's (2005) overview of Michel Foucault's work, is that writing about something is inevitably a powerful activity – as the Prophet Mohammad said, 'The ink of the scholar is more powerful than the blood of the martyr.' Referring back to Blattner (2005), we can see how he uses his power as the author of the text to convey certain impressions about coaching. Blattner decides that, despite his training as a psychologist, he has chosen not to use psychological constructs in order to talk about his relationship with Terry. Blattner's position on his own article is that it 'offer[s] some insights into one process and to create or stimulate ideas for the professional currently engaged in such activity' (2005: 3).

However, an alternative reading of this text is to see it as a sales document. Blattner is presenting himself as writing for 'the professional' and hence associating himself with that professional discourse. Furthermore, he chooses to represent himself as a process expert making suggestions, but nevertheless hinting that he has an overall plan for Terry – using the term 'phases' presents these developments as milestones along a journey that he has travelled many times before. Consequently, we believe that Blattner wishes to play up Terry's seniority and his desire for development and stretch but seeks to minimize or play down the view that Terry is in an emotional crisis and, in particular, that this is not played out within the relationship with Blattner. Instead, Blattner is using his power as the author of the text to present himself as a senior expert who works with other senior people in an organized way and who has good personal outcomes in both personal and professional domains. He seems to distance himself and his work from being therapeutic and moves towards developmental language. And, like all good sales testimonials, he even has the client's – Terry's – endorsement at the end! However, the discourses that remain silent or subdued are those of Terry's wife, his boss and his work colleagues – we only ever hear from Blattner or an edited version of Terry's 'voice'.

## COACHING, MENTORING AND LEADERSHIP

If we look at all three cases examined in this chapter, a common theme that runs through each of them is that of leadership. As we have seen, how leadership is understood within organizations is fundamentally intertwined with power and with the concepts of coaching and mentoring. Indeed, many of the schemes we discuss in this book are in some ways leadership development initiatives. Therefore, it makes sense to pay some attention to the concept of leadership in a discussion about power in coaching and mentoring. Grint (2010: 4) offers a useful typology of leadership, which he presents as four questions:

- Leadership as position: is it where leaders operate that makes them leaders?
- Leadership as person: is it who leaders are that makes them leaders?
- Leadership as result: is it what leaders achieve that makes them leaders?
- Leadership as process: is it how leaders get things done that makes them leaders?

Grint offers these as 'ideal types' which are unlikely to exist in exclusion to each other, rather suggesting that we need to decide between these perspectives as definitions of leadership. Similarly, Jackson and Parry (2018) pose three questions that most often come up when people examine leadership as a concept:

- Are leaders born or made?
- What makes an effective leader?
- What is the difference between leadership and management?

Clearly, all seven of these questions raise interesting and vital issues about what constitutes leadership and to refer to Chapter 3, where we introduce Porter et al.'s (2004) seven surprises for a new CEO:

- You can't run the company.
- Giving orders is very costly.
- It's hard to know what's really going on.
- You are always sending a message.

- You are not the boss.
- Pleasing shareholders is not the goal.
- You're still only human.

We begin to see layers of complexity building up for the concept of leadership. Adding to this, the current situation in the world with COVID-19 has highlighted many different approaches to leadership. Some, particularly women leaders, have handled the pandemic differently and the outcomes appear to be different. Western (2020) argues that:

> Covid-19 evolved within a network consisting of animals and humans, viruses and marketplaces, urban density and social etiquettes, political actions and decisions, economic practices, globalised trade, mass travel and digital information networks. ... A stable network formed allowing the new virus to become a pandemic.

He goes on to say that complex issues, such as the pandemic, cannot be worked through with 20th-century linear thinking – the thinking we raise throughout this book of simple cause and effect reductionist managerialism. Rather, it requires eco-leadership where the leader puts themselves on the line, acknowledges that they don't know, and works beyond the established norms in an ethical way for the good of society. Those who have done this appear to be making progress; those that haven't have fuelled the crisis.

Whilst our book is on coaching and mentoring, and not leadership, we need not be overly concerned with debating leadership. This would be a nigh-on-impossible task anyway; we recently did an Amazon UK website search (May 2020) and found over 70,000 books on leadership listed. Reviewing just this material would keep us busy for quite some time! However, as Northouse (2019: 12) acknowledges, 'Leaders have an ethical responsibility to attend to the needs and concerns of followers [...] Leaders are not above or better than followers. Leaders and followers must be understood in relation to each other.' (See Chapter 3 on TA and transference in leadership).

This recognition that leaders and followers co-construct their relationship can also be applied to coaches and mentors in their relationships with coachees and mentees and, indeed, the potential for both coaching and mentoring to assist leaders to 'tolerate complexity' (Garvey and Alred, 2001) is ever present.

In Chapter 6, we examine the utility of stories in coaching and mentoring conversations. It seems to us that the way that leadership is understood within organizations contributes significantly to many coaching and mentoring conversations. For example, in the Blattner study above, we have already commented on the way that Terry's seniority and achievements are played up by the author. Blattner is perhaps seeking to link his analysis to broader societal discourses about what makes an effective leader. In Grint's (2010) terms, this may refer to Terry as a leader in terms of his position within the organizations he has worked in, or to the business results attributed to him, to his somewhat 'bullish' style or to his personality as a 'natural' leader. Similarly, in the other two cases above, we can analyse the participants in both schemes as being influenced by the social constructs of what is understood by being an effective leader within their respective organizations. In the Dirsmith et al. (1997) case, this includes 'looking after the numbers', whereas in Beech and Brockbank's (1999) case, being an effective leader seems more tied up with specific competencies and knowledge. The fact that many coaching and mentoring interventions tend to focus on developing leaders suggests that the sponsors of such schemes have the often implicit view, following Jackson and Parry's (2018) questions, that leaders can be 'made' or developed. Based on our experience of working with organizational scheme development (see Chapter 4 for a more detailed analysis of coaching and mentoring scheme design), we also argue that many schemes seem to focus on developing leaders as opposed to developing managers. This might suggest that despite the fact that many people in the organizations we work with have the job title of manager, some are seen as leaders and some are not. Indeed, we could also argue that there is an implicit hierarchy as well as a clear distinction here between leadership and management. Again, this discourse that seems to distinguish between leadership and management appears to parallel the distinction between coaching and mentoring. This raises the question of how useful distinguishing between leadership and management, for the purposes of coaching and mentoring scheme design, really is. Gosling and Mintzberg (2003: 54–5) address this point specifically:

> Most of us have become so enamoured of 'leadership' that 'management' has been pushed into the background. Nobody aspires to be a good manager anymore; everybody wants to be a great leader. But the separation of management from leadership is dangerous. Just as management without leadership encourages an uninspired style, which deadens activities, leadership without management encourages a disconnected style, which promotes hubris. And we all know the destructive power of hubris in organizations.

They suggest that it is probably unhelpful to artificially separate management out from leadership in terms of professional practice because most managers engage in aspects of management and leadership. In doing so, and encouraging a focus on leadership at the expense of management, this may serve to weaken the 'leader' and make them susceptible to their own ego. This alternative discourse supports earlier work by Collins (2001) examining the importance of humility and professionalism in what his research identified as level 5 leaders. In this research, the most effective (level 5) leaders were seen as people who had the drive, vision and competencies to make sure things got done, coupled with personal humility in terms of their own ego and reluctance to claim sole credit for the results of their organizations. As we have argued thus far in this book, much of the coach's and mentor's work is about helping coachees and mentees work on their own self-awareness in terms of what it is possible for them to achieve. The danger is that the coachee's or mentee's agenda may be informed by dominant discourses about 'strong leadership' or 'good management' from the organization they work in, from leadership development programmes or even popular media that may work against the interests of the organization.

For example, at the time of writing, there seems to be a plethora of reality television shows on UK television channels, some of which deal with leadership, coaching and mentoring together. In one particular programme, *The Apprentice*, Lord Alan Sugar, a prominent UK industrialist, seeks to employ one of a number of aspiring leaders as his 'apprentice' in a competitive reality game show, where the winner gets a real job in Sugar's company. In this show, potential recruits are 'mentored' by Sugar and colleagues on various tasks but, at the end of each episode, one of them is removed from the competition using Sugar's catchphrase – 'you're fired!' The recruits have to persuade Sugar that they are worth keeping in the show. While this could be construed as merely a game show, it is nevertheless watched by millions of people in the UK who are presented with a successful industrialist seemingly operating in a very directive, forceful no-nonsense style with followers desperate to please a dominant authority figure. Inevitably, we are invited to link together Sugar's success with this style. It seems inconceivable, given its popularity, that this discourse of leadership and followership has no influence on the audience in terms of their practice within their respective organizations, however much it is presented as 'entertainment'. In terms of coaching and mentoring, this might influence us, for example, to be more amenable to a sponsorship model (Clutterbuck, 2007b) of coaching and mentoring, where coachees and mentees are seen as protégés of powerful figures within organizations, and the agenda for the coachees/mentees is to identify the person who is most able to influence their career progression through their personal sponsorship. It is therefore important for those of us involved in coaching and mentoring work within organizations to recognize the power of the discourses around leadership and followership and what these mean for our clients and other stakeholders. We explore the impact of this organizational discourse in the next section by contrasting this with the individual agency of the coachee/mentee.

 **Reflective Questions**

- What impact do popular culture TV shows have on coaching and mentoring initiatives in organizations?
- To what extent, if any, do the producers of TV programmes contribute to the discourse of coaching and mentoring?

## ORGANIZATIONAL DISCOURSE AND INDIVIDUAL AGENCY

Inden (1990: 23) defines human agency as:

> the realised capacity of people to act upon their world and not only know about or give personal or intersubjective significance to it. That capacity is the power of people to act purposively and, reflectively, in more or less complex interrelationships with one another, to reiterate and remake the world in which they live, in circumstances where they may consider different courses of action possible and desirable, though not necessarily from the same point of view.

This ability to act purposefully and to proactively create one's own world is explored in the work of Bachkirova (2011). In her text on developmental coaching, Bachkirova (2011) examines the role of the 'self' using literature from neuroscience, psychology and sociology. She examines three versions of the self. The first metaphor that she uses is that of the self as 'operator', which is a part of human beings that receives experiences and data and then decides what to do with them in terms of action. In coaching terms, this affords the coachee and the coach a considerable amount of agency with regard to their actions. However, the second metaphor that she offers gives the opposite view. This second 'story' is that there is no self:

> To summarise, the second story treats conscious will as an illusion. Our actions spring out of innumerable combinations of forces and connections in our brain/mind/organism constantly interacting with environment. More often than not all of these are made not by a conscious rational agent, but by underlying process. The rational self only notices the decisions being made and thinks that it is the author of these decisions. (Bachkirova, 2011: 41)

She settles on the third notion of the self as evolving and developing, which, therefore, draws heavily on adult development and developmental psychology research. She refers to the work of Kegan and Lahey (2009) within which they develop a typology of adult development, which has three broad stages of cognitive complexity:

1. The socialized mind – a sense of self shaped by expectations and perceptions of other people.
2. The self-authoring mind – people use their own criteria, judgements and values to drive things forward.
3. The self-transforming mind – people can stand back from their own ideology and point of view and recognize the value of multiple perspectives.

Self-transformation, in this story, is seen to be of a higher order for both coachees and coaches. In this sense, their work has some connections with Knowles et al. (1998: 64), who provide a useful set of alternative definitions of what it means to be an adult, which are paraphrased below:

- Biological adulthood – we become adults at the age we can reproduce, typically in early adolescence.
- Legal adulthood – we become adults when the law says we can vote, marry without consent, etc.
- Social adulthood – we become adults when we start performing adult roles like buying a house, being a parent, working full time, etc.
- Psychological adulthood – we become adults when we arrive at an understanding of being responsible for our own lives and being self-directed.

Knowles et al. (1998) argue, in a similar vein to Kegan and Lahey (2009), that the psychological domain is a critical one in terms of being self-directed. This has some commonality with Bruner's (1979, 1990) notion of intentional states. Summing up the implications of her own analysis, Bachkirova (2011: 54) argues that 'one of the important implications of the third story of self is the actual fact of the possibility of change in the self'.

Using the notion of the emerging and developing self and applying this to the coaching process, it is possible to conceive of a coachee who, with a self-transforming mind, may be able to exercise individual agency. In their research study into executive coaching, Louis and Fatien Diochon (2014) do raise this as a possibility. Their research agenda was focused specifically on the coach and their awareness of power dynamics in the coaching relationship within an organizational executive coaching context. Using critical incident theory, they interviewed 20 coaches about their organizational coaching experiences. As a result, they identified a typology of agendas that impact on executive coaching relationships. Of the 13 agendas they identify as being played out in coaching relations, the three principle agendas that were coachee driven were:

1.  The Organization Excluded – the coachee wants to work with the coach on their exit strategy and future career without telling anyone in the organization that they intend to leave.
2.  The Apparent Compliance – the coachee agrees to be coached but then withdraws psychologically from the relationship, agreeing behaviour changes with no intention of following through.
3.  The Imaginary Hidden Agenda – the coachee suspects a hidden organizational agenda for the coaching and therefore does not develop a trusting relationship with the coach.

In each of these cases, the coachee demonstrates their ability to influence the coaching process and agenda. In the first example, the coachee uses their agency in terms of the organizationally sponsored coaching process to divert the attention of the coach away from the organizationally approved agenda to the personal agenda of the coachee. In the second example, the coachee demonstrates skilful behaviour in seeming to acquiesce to the coaching process but, in reality, not engaging with any behavioural change, while in the final example, the coachee protects themselves from disclosing personal feelings or information to avoid this being exploited. Similarly, Welman and Bachkirova (2010: 148) also suggest that the coachee may lead the coach 'into territory that is not of their choosing and resist attempts to move in the direction that is'.

In her analysis of coaching conversations in Germany, Rettinger's (2011) research supports the view that individual agency can be exercised by all parties in the coaching relationship. This study is principally conducted through a discourse analysis of coaching conversations drawing on the concept of discourse identities (Zimmerman, 1998). In this account, she suggests that the principal roles of coach and coachee can be broken down into what she calls activity identities – smaller roles that each party plays within the main role of coach and coachee. In terms of coachee agency, what is interesting about her findings is that these roles are signifiers for the competence and identity of both parties, not just for the coach. One of the activity identities that the coachee is deemed to perform within this is that of expert in their own life, which reverses the usual role that the coach plays in terms of process expert. Hence, the client/coachee assumes the role of evaluator, problem teller and expert at certain stages in the conversation, which challenges the usual power dynamic of the coach being the person that drives the process.

In contrast to this notion of individual agency, the rise in organizational interest in coaching described by many commentators (e.g. Passmore et al., 2013; Cox et al., 2014; Garvey et al., 2014) could be reframed as a mechanism for the control of employees on the part of powerful stakeholders within organizations. Nielsen and Norreklit (2009) examine this phenomenon in their research. They conduct a critical discourse analysis of two well-known coaching texts: Hunt and Weintraub (2002) and Anderson and Anderson (2005). They argue, from a critical theory perspective, that the ways in which coaching is written about in these texts have a particular manner of construing the coachee and the coach, within which managerial control and discipline are retained on the part of the organization:

> Executive coaching signals that the coach has an authentic interest in helping the manager and promises the development of his potentialities. However, whatever room there is, it is not a free room for self-realisation; it is a room controlled by the organization. Consequently, while management coaching as represented in employee coaching may result in the disciplining of the body,

i.e. action, management coaching as represented in executive coaching may result in the disciplining of the spirit, i.e. values. (Nielsen and Norreklit, 2009: 212)

These ideas resonate with the works of Townley (1994, 2008), where she uses a Foucauldian analysis of power to examine the role that organizations play in controlling and influencing the individual. In her text on HRM practices (Townley, 1994: 124–5), she likens mentoring to the religious confession, which encourages 'the renunciation of one's own self and will'. Like Nielsen and Norreklit (2009), she is arguing that coaching and mentoring have the potential to allow the agency of the individual coachee to be subordinated to that of the organizational agenda, as represented by the coachee's line manager. Reissner and Du Toit (2011), on the other hand, argue that all three types of stakeholder in an organizational coaching programme – the organization, the coach and the coachee – have the opportunity to influence the discourse in different ways. In their conceptual paper, they put forward the idea of 'storyselling' in coaching as opposed to storytelling. In this framework, the coachee involves themselves in selling a version of their personal story, first to the coach based on the view of themselves that they want the coach to see, and then to the organization of the change in them and their behaviour. These discourses may compete with those put forward by other stakeholders, and, as Reissner and Du Toit (2011) point out, the way may be open for manipulation and abuse of these stories as a result. This idea of competing discourses and manipulation of agendas features in the work of Colley (2003) on mentoring. Examining social inclusion mentoring schemes, Colley points out, using a number of case studies, that mentees in the study were adept at influencing the process and content of the mentoring conversations to fit their own needs, even though there were strong alternative discourses coming from other stakeholders, such as government agencies and mentors. Colley (2003: 100) is careful not to overstate this mentee agency, given the strength of other discourses, but, nevertheless, argues that 'young people can exercise power rather than being passive recipients of mentoring'. This editing and selling of stories is evident in several, more recent, research projects such as the work of Schwabenland (2015) in her work on voluntary agencies in war zones, so that outcomes might be more palatable to funding stakeholders, or Kwon et al.'s (2014) study on discursive strategies that senior stakeholders use in team meetings to achieve sub-group agendas. However, this only deals with a deliberate and conscious use of power by individuals or groups. Lukes (2005) makes the point that power can be exercised through inaction or a lack of awareness of consequences, which can prevent conflicts or challenges from ever being consciously raised in the first place. Applying this to the purchase of coaching services, it could be argued that, by undervaluing coachee skills and qualities, for example (see Chapter 8), powerful stakeholders are limiting the efficacy of these interventions. However, these stakeholders may believe that their actions are in the best interests of the coachees or may simply not be aware of any negative consequences. In his text on organizational theory, Morgan (2006: 323) acknowledges that, often, perceived manipulation/exploitation can be systemic, accidental and/or reversible. Nevertheless, the individuals' autonomy and agency are being curtailed, even if this is not deliberate. This is certainly reflected in Colley's (2003) account of engagement mentoring programmes, where mentors' and mentees' behaviour is constrained and regulated by systemic forces rather than by a single person or a group of powerful individuals. Individual mentors are, argues Colley, as much constrained by the system as the mentees are. However, it is nevertheless noticeable, from

Colley's (2003) account, that mentees, to some extent, do manage to evade these pressures of employability and exercise their own agency in relation to the help that they receive. This individual resistance can also be seen in Dey and Steyaert's (2014) research into social entrepreneurship and ethics, where, by problematizing tensions between managerialism and service delivery, the individual entrepreneur retains their sense of self and successfully avoids their activities being prescribed by other agencies. In summary, we can say that there are competing discourses about coaching in organizations, some of which emphasize the dominance of the organizational voice, whilst others emphasize the ability of individual agents to subvert that dominant discourse.

 **Reflective Questions** ─────────────────

- To what extent are participants in coaching and mentoring programmes able to change/influence programme outcomes/objectives such that they are different from the stated aims of the programme?
- Is it always possible to identify power dynamics at play within coaching and mentoring initiatives?

## CONCLUSIONS

In this chapter, we have used four main frameworks: bases of power, transference, discourse analysis and agency to look at the issue of power within coaching and mentoring. We have raised some important issues about coaching and mentoring when seen through the lens of power. To summarize, the power relations between coaches/mentors and their coachees/mentees are influenced by at least five different factors.

First and most obviously, there is the impact of line-management power relations on coaching and mentoring. As shown by our case studies, this can serve to influence mentee/coachee engagement with the process by either establishing collusion (see Dirsmith et al., 1997) with the manager in terms of the use of legitimate power to enhance the career progression of the mentee/coachee, or causing withdrawal from the process. Our discussions in Chapters 1, 3, 5 and 6 suggest that trust is a key component of the coaching and mentoring process. Adding the notion of power to the trust condition means that if coachees and mentees feel restricted in their openness with their coaches or mentors, due to managerial or hierarchical relationships, then the process is likely to be limited in the extent to which it can be successful. Furthermore, both parties can use their individual agency to influence the process so as to limit their perceived vulnerability.

Second, and related to the first point, it appears that the line-management relationship can often crowd out the psychosocial aspect of mentoring (Kram, 1983) in particular, but can still be helpful for both parties in terms of career progression. However, this appears to be dependent on both parties in the dyad understanding the purpose of the process and their role within it. This was not the case within the NHS case study (Beech and Brockbank, 1999), where a limited understanding of the mentoring process appears to have contributed to psychological damage for the mentors and withdrawal and lack of satisfaction for the mentees.

Third, the statement that 'knowledge is power' appears to hold some water in terms of the evidence considered here. In each of the case studies, the coach's or mentor's expert power was a critical feature of the process. Correspondingly, as the asymmetry in terms of knowledge and expertise between, in particular, mentor and mentee begins to reduce, the mentee's perception of the expert power of the mentor begins to diminish. However, how this is handled in the mentoring and coaching dyad is critical to the outcomes.

McAuley's (2003) analysis of transference and countertransference is useful in that it offers us a conceptual framework for understanding and anticipating the various traps and challenges facing us in coaching and mentoring relationships. Indeed, although Blattner (2005) does not use the terms (for reasons we will explore below), there is evidence that he did use these ideas within his coaching intervention with Terry, which seems to have helped Terry develop.

A further and related point is that the dominant discourse in much of the literature on coaching in particular, and mentoring to some extent, focuses on the position of the coach and the skills and competencies he or she either needs to acquire or has in place. In popular texts such Whitmore's (2009) practitioner book *Coaching for Performance*, we hear that the coach's role is one of facilitation: 'Coaching is unlocking people's potential to maximise their own performance' (Whitmore, 2009: 10). Others, for example, Downey (2014), Rogers (2012) and Starr (2008), place emphasis on the coach's skills and process whilst also asserting that the coachee is central to that process: 'The task of the coach is to use advanced skills of listening, questioning and reflection to create highly effective conversations and experiences for the individual' (Starr, 2008: 20). In Chapter 8, we seek to address this imbalance by exploring the concept of 'the skilled coachee'.

Fourth, all of the analysis above leads us to recognize that, although thinking about individuals having or possessing power may be a useful analogy, to some extent, power is relational. The work of Foucault (1979) and others (see Gutting, 2005, and McAuley et al., 2007) helps us to recognize that power resides not in individuals but is co-created in the relationships between people. Key components of that co-creation are the various discourses that are created around coaching and mentoring, particularly those around leadership and management, as related concepts. Following Jackson and Carter (2000), it is important to recognize that the dominant discourses that emerge are inevitably power-laden and are concerned with who is able to say what to whom, when and why. In these different case studies, it is easy to see how the writer has certain purposes and agendas, be they academic, financial or a combination of these. One of the advantages of deconstructing discourses and developing a genealogy (as we do in Chapters 1 and 2) of coaching and mentoring is to recognize that it is possible to draw very different and often contradictory conclusions from a piece of writing, and much depends on the lens used to view it. For example, in our sceptical critique of team coaching in Chapter 5 it may be that the authors of the survey are attempting to influence and shift the marketplace in their favour.

Finally, to be fair, we should also recognize that we ourselves, as writers of this text, are choosing to privilege certain discourses above others in this book. Because of our mutual background, areas of interest and power interests in aspects of coaching and mentoring, we cannot hope to escape from the same challenges and criticisms that we have posed to others in this chapter and throughout the entire book. Clearly, we are seeking to influence the dominant discourse of coaching and mentoring and our own status within it as a result of writing this book, but hopefully in a way that helps others become aware of those challenges and choices as a result.

 **Future Direction** ————————————————

We should recognize that as coaching becomes a more commonplace activity, issues of power, voice and discourse will become more important. Coaching and mentoring can seem attractive because there is the possibility of emancipation from dominant forms of control and oppressive power relationships. However, this does not mean that coaching and mentoring are immune from such power issues – far from it.

International professional bodies, like the European Mentoring and Coaching Council (EMCC) or the International Coach Federation (ICF), and national bodies, like the Mentoring and Befriending Foundation (UK), will increasingly need to work with the power dynamics. For example, at the 2020 EMCC conference, out of 40 sessions, 16 used the word 'coaching' in the title and both pre-conference sessions were on coaching topics and 3 used the word 'mentoring'. We conclude from this observation that the current popularity of the term 'coaching' may be crowding out the positive contribution of the mentoring discourse. The impact of this is not yet clear but will increasingly become an issue over time.

 **Activity** ————————————————

Consider the following brief case study scenario. The organization in question is a medium-sized private sector manufacturing business with units in various countries around eastern and southern Europe, but its head office is located in the north of England. The organization culture might be characterized as a 'work hard–play hard' culture – fast-paced, energetic and 'macho' in nature. The organization makes products in the UK that supply some of the large supermarket chains in the UK but, as a supplier that is relatively small in relation to those organizations, it is vulnerable to share price fluctuations and pressure exerted from these customers. Coaching and mentoring are seen as critical by the HR manager as a way of achieving the organization's goals, and he has been instrumental in driving through C&M initiatives throughout the business. However, the resourcing for delivering on these initiatives is continually questioned by the chief executive and other senior managers. This has meant that the HR manager has had to advocate for the programmes on numerous occasions. This has, to some extent, been politically risky as it has involved challenging senior managers about their support and behaviour; however, he has tended to prevail in terms of getting some qualified support for C&M, even when the environment is tough, financially. Nevertheless, due to strong financial pressure, the existing CEO is forced to resign and a new CEO is recruited. As before, the HR manager advocates, strongly and passionately, for the C&M initiatives. However, on this occasion, the political damage is considerable and the HR manager is forced to exit the organization.

*(Continued)*

- How might this scenario be understood, in terms of the power discussion in this chapter?
- What alternative political strategies might the HR manager have adopted?

---

 **Questions** ———————————————————

- Who or what is driving the content of the discussion in the coaching/mentoring relationship?
- What might be being denied or avoided in your coaching or mentoring scheme?
- Who is being empowered or disempowered in your coaching and mentoring work?

---

 **Further Reading** ———————————————————

Perhaps the best theoretical account of power in organizations is Stephen Lukes's classic text: Lukes, S. (2005) *Power: A Radical View*, 2nd edition. Basingstoke: Palgrave Macmillan.

Stewart Clegg's text on frameworks of power provides a strong overview of a range of key theoretical perspectives on power: Clegg, S. (1989) *Frameworks of Power*. London: SAGE.

For a strongly critical, research-based perspective on the triangular relation in coaching with regard to power, read: Louis, D. and Fatien Diochon, P. (2014) 'Educating coaches to power dynamics: Managing multiple agendas within the triangular relationship', *Journal of Psychological Issues in Organisational Culture*, 5(2): 31–47.

---

# 8

# THE SKILLED COACHEE

## CHAPTER OVERVIEW

As has been raised in previous chapters, there seems to be a shift in thinking about the nature of coaching and mentoring. One of those shifts has been in how coaching and mentoring appear to be merging into a hybrid and differentiation between them is becoming less clear (see Chapter 1). Another shift we are detecting is in the emerging interest in the helped as opposed to the helper. So far in this edition, we have focused on the role that the helper - the mentor or coach - plays in coaching and mentoring. In this chapter, we wish to examine coaching and mentoring from the helpee's point of view. For the purposes of readability, we shall refer to coaching and the coachee, but we maintain that the ideas discussed here are equally applicable to the label of mentoring as they are to coaching. The analysis and fieldwork are based on the PhD work of one of us (Stokes). We will examine the role of coachee, as described in the coaching literature, and then use the fieldwork to develop a new understanding of the coachee and the skills.

## INTRODUCTION

Over the last 15 years, attempts to professionalize coaching have increased significantly in the UK. As well as the EMCC, there has been a rise in the number of professional body organizations within the UK: the International Coach Federation (ICF), the Association for Coaching (AC) and the Association for Professional Executive Coaching and Supervision (APECS) are the three other main bodies in the UK. In addition, there are other professional organizations with an interest in coaching, such as the Chartered Institute of Personnel and Development (CIPD) and the British Psychological Society (BPS). What is noticeable about this rise in the professionalization agenda and popularity of coaching is that it has occurred not only in business coaching but also in life coaching. Steve Peters, author of *The Chimp Paradox* (Peters, 2012), is one prominent example of a celebrity coach, working with prominent British sports stars such as the snooker player Ronnie O'Sullivan and cyclists Chris Hoy and Victoria Pendleton. This idea of celebrity coaches and mentors has extended into British reality television shows such as *The Apprentice*, *The X Factor* and *The Voice*. Furthermore, a number of lifestyle 'gurus' such as Paul McKenna, Scott Alexander and, in the USA, Tony Robbins, have developed a range of books, events, mobile phone applications and YouTube messages, and their websites boast of celebrity endorsements. What each of these examples may show is that there is a cultural predisposition to the idea of the coach or mentor being a key player in individual success – some human need for gurus. Further than that, however, we argue that these celebrity coaches are claiming some of the success for themselves, as if they are the ones who are, in some sense, responsible for inventing that person and their success. Aspects of this can also be seen in professional sports managers, particularly in men's professional football, where managers appear to be personally associated with the success of their playing staff and much of the football club's on-field success is attributed to the coach.

The reason for discussing these celebrity coaches and managers is that we believe that they are heavily influential in terms of the discourse that exists regarding coaching.

Hatch and Cunliffe (2013: 43) argue that power 'is exercised through practices that arise in discourse to regulate what will be perceived as normal'. Therefore, a prevailing discourse refers to a way of thinking, writing and acting in relation to something that sets the boundaries of what are considered to be normal for that phenomenon, in a way that crowds out or dominates other possible ways of seeing it. Hence, it is likely that popular television programmes such as *Dragon's Den* and *The Apprentice* contribute to the discourse about coaching as they offer those who view these programmes a version of 'normal' business behaviour where strong, direct challenge and criticism are portrayed as developmental and necessary. The dominance of these perspectives is in danger, we believe, of crowding out different and alternative views of leadership and, particularly, coaching. Given, as we have argued above, that discourse has a direct influence on future behaviour, we are therefore concerned about the popular image of life coaches, in particular, and its impact on coaching theory and practice. We will examine these issues as described below and seek to redress the balance in a small way by taking a coachee-centred view of coaching.

## METHODOLOGY

In this chapter, we will examine the concept of a skilled coachee by first critically examining the coaching and mentoring literature and then seeking to reframe some of the coaching skills discussed through the lens of the skilled coachee concept. Following that, we will introduce some fieldwork conducted by Stokes in order to develop a framework for thinking about coachee skills. The implications for a range of stakeholders will then be examined.

## COACHING LITERATURE

In his practitioner book, *Effective Modern Coaching*, Downey (2014) introduces the reader to the notion of coaching and chooses to avoid the usual term of 'coachee'. Rather, he prefers the term 'player' because, as he argues, coachee 'has the suffix –"ee" at the end, which denotes someone who has something done unto them – think divorcee' (Downey, 2014: 24). Based on the work of Tim Gallwey, author of texts such as *The Inner Game of Tennis* (1997a [1974]) and *The Inner Game of Work* (1997b), Downey argues for a model of coaching which puts the 'player' at the centre of the coaching and emphasizes the importance of 'following interest' in the service of the player. He resists labelling this approach as non-directive, as he does in his previous books (Downey, 1999, 2003), but, in keeping with Gallwey's (1997a [1974]) approach, argues against a more directive approach to coaching – where the coach tells or advises the coachee/player – as reducing 'the opportunity for the player to think or be creative, limits the possibility of their taking responsibility and takes any satisfaction or joy out of what limited achievements there might be' (Downey, 2014: 44). Downey is clear, throughout his books, that the coachee's agenda should be at the centre of what the coaching is about. What is noticeable about his approach is that he places almost exclusive emphasis on the skills of the coach in achieving a successful coaching intervention. Although he includes, in his 2014 text, a chapter on the genius of the player, this does not extend to his being explicit about their skills in coaching and being coached. Instead, he again focuses on the coach's skills: 'A huge part of enabling genius is coaching, and the effective coaching model embraces many approaches, from following interest to teaching, that give the skilled coach a lot to play with' (2014: 218).

However, an analysis of some of his coaching examples seems to belie this impression. For instance, Downey (2014: 101) gives an example of part of a coaching conversation where the coach is talking to the player about what direction to follow in the coaching conversation:

Player: I am really concerned about the new strategy Bob presented yesterday.
Coach: How concerned, on a scale of one to ten?
Player: That's a really good question. Actually, only about three or four.
Coach: So do we need to discuss it now?
Player: No, it's more important that we talk through the conference next week.

Downey puts forward this account as evidence of skilled questioning in coaching in terms of the coach helping the coachee decide where to focus their attention. While there is clear use of scaling techniques and some challenge in this small excerpt, the player also seems to be displaying some skills here in terms of deciding how best to use the coaching time and prioritizing what is most important. Similarly, the following excerpt is from a coaching session where the focus is on the coachee's management of time:

| Coach: | So what is your longer term goal for your time management? | hours a week, processing less paper and getting the weekly reports out on time, that would be just great. (Downey, 2014: 185) |
| Player: | If I could get to a position within the next month, where I am saving three | |

Once again, in his analysis, Downey focuses on the coaching skills and initiative demonstrated by the coach in focusing the player on his long-term goals. However, he pays little attention to the skills required from the coachee in terms of their ability to reflect on their own practice, to decide relevant and appropriate goals and to articulate them to the coach.

Whitmore's (2009) practitioner book *Coaching for Performance*, like Downey's, draws on the work of Gallwey (1997a [1974], 1997b) in terms of emphasizing the coach's role as one of facilitation: 'Coaching is unlocking people's potential to maximise their own performance' (Whitmore, 2009: 10).

Whitmore also, in common with Downey, seems to caution against an approach which tells the coachee – or performer, as Whitmore sometimes refers to them – what to do. As a strong advocate of goal-focused coaching, using the GROW model of coaching, he emphasizes the importance of the coachee having ownership of a coaching session in terms of its outcome: 'If the coachee has sought a session, clearly it is he (or she) who needs to define what he wants to get out of it' (Whitmore, 2009: 58).

However, this ability to clearly state goal outcomes seems to be treated as unproblematic and not identified as a skill on the part of the coachee. Like Downey, Whitmore offers sample quotes from coaching conversations to illustrate his argument. In an excerpt from one of these conversations, shown below, Whitmore (2009: 65) shows how a coach is helping a coachee to commit to a physical fitness programme – Mike is the coach and Joe is the coachee:

| Mike: | Let's look long term for a moment. What is the purpose of getting fitter for you? | Mike: | Fine. How fit would you like to be by when? |
| Joe: | I'm just feeling lousy about myself and my work is suffering. I want to feel good again. | Joe: | I would like to lose 15 pounds or so, and within a few months be able to not only run upstairs and for the train without getting out of breath but to actually enjoy running. |

Whitmore (2009) offers this example as part of an illustration of the goal-setting aspect of the GROW model. While it does illustrate this, it also seems to show Joe's ability in being able to articulate exactly what he wants in a way that Mike can then work with. However, it is noticeable that, like Downey, Whitmore pays much more attention to what the coach does in the conversation in terms of process than that of the coachee. This is ironic given that both are emphasizing the importance of the coachee in the relationship and the process, and both are critical of an instructor-led model of learning.

In her book *Coaching Skills*, Rogers (2012) articulates similar values to those of Downey (2014) and Whitmore (2009) in that she emphasizes equality, self-awareness and focusing on the coachee's agenda:

Coaching is a partnership of equals whose aim is to achieve speedy, increased and sustainable effectiveness through focused learning in every aspect of the client's life. Coaching raises self-awareness and identifies choices. Working to the client's agenda, the coach and client have the sole aim of closing the gaps between potential and performance. (Rogers, 2012: 7)

Rogers goes on to articulate six key principles of coaching, the first of which emphasizes the client's resourcefulness in being able to solve their problems. However, this resourcefulness is attributed to those personal characteristics that the client can use (e.g. self-reliance, self-worth) in their lives, to resolve challenges and issues, rather than to any skilled behaviour as a coachee. She seems to be seeing the resourcefulness of the coachee as a content issue for the coachee to work on, rather than as a coachee process skill.

Julie Starr in her book explores coaching from the point of view of the basic skills and processes needed to start coaching other people. Like Downey (2014), Whitmore (2009) and Rogers (2012), Starr (2008) focuses on helping coaches to develop the skills she feels they need to operate successfully as a coach. In a similar vein to the authors already mentioned above, she places emphasis on what the coach does but also asserts that the coachee is central to that process:

> The coach believes in the ability of the individual to create insights and ideas needed to move their situation forward. The task of the coach is to use advanced skills of listening, questioning and reflection to create highly effective conversations and experiences for the individual. (Starr, 2008: 20)

While Starr clearly acknowledges some ability in the coachee, she does not focus on this in her text, for the most part. In her Chapter 8 (Starr, 2008), she comes closest to this when discussing the concept of emotional maturity. As with the rest of the text, the focus of her attention in this chapter is on using emotional competences from the work of writers such as Goleman (1996, 1998) to inform the practice of the coach. She does, with each emotional competence, make a link to the coachee, but this is principally in terms of seeing these competences as outputs for the coachee from the coaching process, as opposed to acknowledging the process input that the coachee makes to the coaching process. For example, when discussing self-awareness, Starr (2008: 281) describes the coachee's development in terms of being more aware of their own talents:

> As you work with a coachee over several sessions, their overall self-awareness tends to improve. For example, they might shift from feelings that they have few development needs to realising that there's quite a lot they can get better at. Alternatively, they may begin to appreciate some of the finer qualities and talents that they have.

While she does focus on coachee skills here, they are skills that are seen as an output to the coaching interventions made by the coach and are more about the content issues within the coaching than how the coaching is conducted.

In his text on Neuro Linguistic Programming (NLP) in coaching, Phil Hayes (2008) explores coaching 'with an NLP accent' as he puts it (Hayes, 2008: 2). As with Downey (2014), Whitmore (2009) and Starr (2008), Hayes's emphasis in his work is on the coachee being the focus. His definition, like that of Jenny Rogers, suggests a coachee-centric focus: 'The coach helps the client increase their effectiveness in areas of life and work chosen by themselves, to goals and standards defined by them' (Hayes, 2008: 6).

However, despite this rhetoric, the text mainly focuses on the skills of the coach in helping the coachee progress and there is little space afforded to any process skills on the part of the coachee. Again, looking at examples of coaching conversations offered in the text, there does seem to be an acknowledgement that coachees need to offer metaphors and other linguistic patterns for the coach to be able to engage with. In the example below, the coach works with the client's metaphor for conceptualizing his decision making at work:

Client:   When I think about all the decisions I've got to make, it makes me feel as if I am coming up to a huge crossroads – more like Spaghetti Junction in fact.

Coach:   And what does Spaghetti Junction feel like to you right now?

Client:   Well it's really big and busy and confusing, and the traffic is coming up to it really fast – it feels like it's going to be difficult to slow down enough to judge which way I should go! I feel like I'm going into it out of control.

Coach:   OK, so how about we slow down now and think about it? We could even sit in the lay-by for a while so you can make a few calm decisions well before you get there! (Hayes, 2008: 44-5)

As with other examples quoted above, the author uses this snippet to emphasize the skill of the coach in matching and engaging with the metaphor offered by the client – in this case, getting them to manipulate the metaphor of Spaghetti Junction so that they are able to change their behaviour. While this is the case, it is also noticeable that Hayes does not focus on the skill of the coachee (client) in generating the metaphor and articulating it to the coach in this way. The client in this example has made the connection with an image and a sense of panic and is able to communicate this in a way that the coach can ask questions about. This is not, however, labelled as skilled behaviour in the same way that the coach's behaviour is. As with the other authors discussed so far, there is a clear assumption that the coach drives the process and the coachee/client responds to these promptings in relation to their life or career, without allowing for the possibility that coachee skills are involved in these interactions.

Megginson and Clutterbuck's (2005a, 2009) books focus on the skilled behaviour/techniques that coaches and mentors can use in their conversational work. In both texts, the authors are careful to offer some critique for the use of the techniques they examine in the books. The techniques are drawn from a range of approaches to coaching – for instance, narrative coaching, cognitive behavioural coaching and gestalt, with all emphasizing a sensitivity to the clients' agendas. Indeed, in the conclusions to their second text (2009), the authors argue strongly for a movement away from a coach-centric agenda, asking the following critical question: 'Given that the value of coaching and mentoring often lies in enabling the client to view their issues from other perspectives, is it ethical and appropriate for the coach or mentor to limit those alternative perspectives to those which fit the coach's or mentor's own philosophical approach?' (Megginson and Clutterbuck, 2009: 238).

Nevertheless, there is, similarly, no voice in the account for coachee skills or agency in terms of the coaching process. Clients/coachees are principally construed, by all contributors to the texts, as being the recipients of processes offered by the coaches, with the resource, in terms of intervention or technique, coming from the coach.

In their book *Brief Coaching*, Berg and Szabó (2005: 1) argue that the process that they outline 'utilizes what clients bring to the coaching relationship and conversation; that is, they already have skills, views and many other tools'. This is essentially a solution-focused approach to coaching. In the text (p. 40), they include a section which is entitled 'Using Client Skills'. However, it becomes clear that Berg and Szabó are referring to clients' experience and resources from other situations that they can use to bring to the coaching session, as opposed to utilizing any process skills within the coaching session. The emphasis, as with all of the approaches discussed so far, is on the coach directing the client to focus on a particular area, with the client essentially providing the content for the coach to work with:

> We hope we have shown you that being effective and efficient can work side by side with a respectful approach to utilizing the abilities and competencies that clients bring with them to the coaching process. It is often the case that many clients have been so pre-occupied with their problems that they need a slight nudge from the coach to look in the right direction. (Berg and Szabó, 2005: 43)

Again, while placing the client (coachee) at the centre of the intervention, the coach, nevertheless, is the focus for the text, with the client's contribution principally being one of bringing the issue and the content so as to enable the coach to have something to work with. Similarly, in *Co-Active Coaching* (Kimsey-House et al., 2011), while a great deal of emphasis is placed on the coachee as the focus for the coaching, there is still a sense – despite the emphasis on co-action – that the coach is the primary decision maker in terms of process and that it is their skills and abilities that need to be focused on:

> Coaches play a key role by holding a vision of what is possible and through their commitment to transformative experience. Coachees still choose the topic, the action and the results they want. But by taking a stand for the greatest possible impact from even the smallest action, coaches encourage and ultimately evoke transformation. (Kimsey-House et al., 2011: 9)

Kimsey-House et al. (2011) emphasize the resourcefulness of the client in terms of generating solutions, but in examining what they call the five contexts of coaching – listening, intuition, curiosity, forward and deepen, self-management – all efforts are directed towards the skills of the coach. In the sample dialogues included in the text, the majority seem to emphasize the clear-sightedness of the coach and their ability to see things that the coachee does not recognize. In the example below, the coach is said to be demonstrating the skill of articulation, within the context of listening:

Coachee: ... so that's why I came up with this alternative plan. I think it's a reasonable alternative. I think I can make the deadlines they've set.

COACH: Can I tell you what it sounds like over on this side of the line?

Coachee: Sure. You see a hole in there somewhere?

COACH: Actually, no. I'm sure the plan is sound. What I see, though, is an old pattern of accommodating other people's demands, almost no matter how unreasonable, at personal cost to you. It's one of the things you said you wanted to change. This looks like backpedalling. (Kimsey-House et al., 2011: 41, capitalization in original source)

While there appears to be evidence (albeit self-reported) within the examples that the coachees find the interventions helpful, the composite picture, developed in the text, of a typical coachee is one of a confused, stuck individual who seems to lack confidence and insight. The coach, in contrast, is portrayed here as an individual who is resourceful, has insight and is prepared to hold the coachee to account in terms of focus and in facing what is 'really' going on for the coachee. In summary, this analysis of these texts reveals a strong emphasis on the coach as process expert and, for the most part, the coachee is positioned as a recipient of that process, rather than being seen as having a process role to play in the conversation and in the relationship.

As we have raised in Chapters 1, 4, 5 and 7, we believe that there is a change beginning to develop – for example, Stelter (2019), in repositioning coaching as more akin to mentoring and referring to a coach as a facilitator of dialogue. We also see in Stokes et al. (2020) a new set of dimensions of coaching and mentoring which emphasize context, time and purpose, and in Nadeem and Garvey (2020) we see the learning experiences of the coachee coming to the fore as a way of assisting the coach to adapt and develop a repertoire of skills and processes to facilitate the coachee. Additionally, Rajasinghe's (2018) unpublished PhD focuses on how executives experience executive coaching – another piece of work that is exploring coaching from the coachee's perspective.

Despite these signs of change, for us, however, the coach centric discourse remains central to the coaching profession. In the next section, we will examine the fieldwork conducted by Stokes in relation to the concept of a skilled coachee.

 **Reflective Questions** _____

- To what extent does the coaching literature capture how you are when you are coached by someone else?
- Does the map describe the territory for you?
- What changes have you become aware of in recent times?

## FIELDWORK

The focus of the fieldwork was to answer the following questions about coachees and their skills within coaching conversations:

- How do they use conversational devices and strategies?
- What impact do these have on the coaching process?
- What skills do they demonstrate in using these conversational devices and strategies?

To examine these questions, the research methodology adopted was neither purely grounded theory nor action research but one which has aspects of both within it and one which has at its centre a commitment to address issues regarding power and agency within coaching relationships. Without wishing to engage in a protracted academic discussion about research methods, we think it would be helpful to briefly outline what these terms mean. A grounded theory approach to research (see Fendt and Sachs, 2008, for a rigorous discussion of the approach) means that, rather than seeking to start with academic theory, the researcher starts by grounding themselves in the phenomena under investigation and seeks to build understanding from that social world first. As we have argued above, the coaching literature is relatively muted on coachee skills and hence this meant that looking at coachee skills directly in order to theorize what might be going on in coaching conversations made good sense. Action research is based on the idea that something can be understood by making an active intervention/change and then seeking to capture and understand what happens as a result.

Gray (2009: 313) argues that, despite the many different modes of action research, all such approaches have three things in common:

1. Research subjects are seen as researchers or involved in a democratic partnership with the researcher.

2. Research is seen as an agent of change.
3. Data are generated from the direct experiences of research participants.

To offer an alternative perspective on coaching that includes coachee skills, it was important to recognize that any attempt to understand what these skills are, by directly observing coaching in action, would constitute an intervention. The intervention would have an impact on the relationship and future conversations, in some ways similar to that of coaching supervision (see Chapter 12 for a discussion of supervision), in that it would encourage participants to reflect on the skills and processes of both participants. This would, in all likelihood, change future conversations and the relationship. Hence, it was important to recognize this change effect and to acknowledge the importance of the participants being co-enquirers into the coaching process.

The fieldwork that was done can be summarized as follows:

1. Observe a coaching session (approx. 1 hour in duration) and video it.
2. Directly after the session, interview the coaching pair as a pair, inviting them to reflect on the conversation they have just had.

3. Review the interview notes and video.
4. Interview coach and coachee separately at a later date (several weeks after), using the provisional observations from stages 1-3 to inform the questions and prompts.

This was a small-scale, qualitative study involving seven coaching pairs with the agenda of making a contribution to understanding what skills coachees may have in coaching conversations.

## COACHEE SKILLS

By analysing the data that came out of this fieldwork, it was possible to generate a heuristic which illustrates a number of domains of skilled activity on the part of the coachee that are similar to those for the coach as articulated by, for example, Downey (2014), Starr (2008) and Whitmore (2009). We summarize these below:

*Framing the Conversation* – being able to set the path and scope of a coaching conversation and to iteratively develop where the conversation is going as it progresses. Framing the conversation refers to the conversational skills that the coachee employs to move the coaching conversation to the areas that they would like to focus on. All of the coachees in the study seemed able to articulate the outcomes they wanted from the coaching but in different ways. For some, this was done by clearly spelling out what outcomes they wanted, while for others it was about presenting the coach with a summary of an issue(s) or problem that they wanted to work on. This helped the coaching process by giving the coach some scope and context via which they could make interventions by asking questions and probing what these outcomes might look like. By stating clearly what they did/did not want in their coaching conversations, this then sets the conversation on a particular path. Hence, the coachee frames the conversation for the coach so that the coach can intervene. An example of this is shown in Case Study 8.1.

 **Case Study 8.1**

In this case example, the session had just begun and the coach had asked an open question about what the coachee wanted from the session. The coachee responds:

Coach:    So what would be a good outcome from this conversation?

Coachee:  I think a **good outcome for me** would be to just explore I suppose the thoughts I have about why I'm maybe not taking, I'm going to say the words 'a tougher line' but I don't even think it is about a tougher line. It's just **about me being more clear** about what I need from this person and then going away, **being able to have another discussion** with her.

It is noticeable that the coachee, by offering the phrase 'tougher line' and then giving further information about a good outcome, is helping the coach to know where to focus her questions and interventions and what her desired outcomes will be, in relation to the coachee's challenges in terms of her management role at work.

*Understanding Coaching Processes* – being able to be open to and engage with different coaching techniques and processes and having awareness and understanding of key personal development terms and their implications. In all of the coachees in the study, each had some familiarity with developmental work, hence developmental language; in most cases, the coachees were actually coaches in training themselves. As a result, this enabled the coachees to articulate their challenges and issues in ways that their coaches could recognize and engage with. This manifested itself in two main ways – being open to different processes and techniques within coaching, and being able to engage with developmental language.

## Case Study 8.2

In this case example, the pair were discussing the coachee's empathy with someone they line manage in terms of how difficult a time they had had in the coachee's organization during the previous year:

Coach:  Because of the work that we've done together in the last year, I know you've had a tough year and I'm wondering if you're **discounting** how tough this year has been for you and actually what the empathy or support that you want to give her is what's been missing for you and I'm wondering how that lies for you, 'cause it's my hunch and not yours.

Coachee 1:  Well certainly, you know, the review process was really tough and I think there wasn't a lot of support given. We were cast out to get on with it and if it all went pear-shaped then I think my head would have been on the block, so yeah, I do relate to that. I do relate to that. And I think that is right. I feel there's a **parallel thing** going on.

It is noticeable here that the coachee labels her own behaviour by using a term from Transactional Analysis (and Freudian psychology) – that of a parallel process. The coach is clearly aware that the coachee has an understanding and awareness of coaching, due to their mature and longstanding relationship. Therefore, she is able to offer this challenge to the coachee's behaviour, safe in the knowledge that the coachee has the skills and knowledge to understand and interpret this.

*Reframing Thinking* – the ability to change the way an issue or challenge is conceptualized using experimentation and practising different conversations, engaging with different metaphors and being aware of and engaged with one's own values and emotions. In the study, coachees were able to reflect on and challenge their own dominant ways of thinking. Most often, this was done by engaging with and using metaphors. While using metaphors is not necessarily particular to coaching, coachees in the study were comfortable with engaging with their own metaphors and those of others, in the service of developing their own thinking and self-awareness. Hence, they were adept at bringing metaphors to the session that the coaches were then able to work and help them re-engage with. This had the impact of enabling the coach to challenge dominant ways of thinking and to use the metaphor to help the coachee to bring new insight to their experiences.

## Case Study 8.3

In the extract below, the coachee has been asked a question about what progress she has been making in her life and work:

*(Continued)*

Coachee: I think I've gone from still having lots of business ideas and lots of ideas with career and stuff in that area. I've cleaned my house from top ... not cleaned, like done stuff, like totally emptied it, which has felt really good. And not just a room, like literally the whole house. I've pulled up carpets and painted floors and done ... And I was thinking about that in terms of like **my body as well, thinking how the top is my head and the cellar being my heart**. Don't know why the cellar's my heart. It probably should be my feet or something. So that's kind of happened. I've been seeing a chiropractor for my back.

Here, the coachee demonstrates skill in being able to move between the figurative and the literal, which then allows the coach to probe about why she has attributed her heart to the cellar and what that means.

*Deflection* – the ability to distance oneself from difficult topics, feelings or emotions by use of language outside the self or engaging with concepts in an intellectualized, abstract way. Deflection skills are used by coachees, often unconsciously, to move the relationship and conversation away from areas that are too challenging or risky for them. This can be enacted in a number of ways, as the following examples illustrate. One way coachees seemed to do this was by using conversational strategies that distanced them from the topic under discussion. One practical manifestation of this was when coachees used 'you' instead of 'I', in response to a challenge or question from their coach.

 Case Study 8.4

In the example below, the coaching pair is talking about the coachee's challenging relationship with a member of her management team.

Coach: Okay. So how easy do you find it to be vulnerable with her or let her in?

Coachee: I mean **she'd** be party to, you know, on Monday **we** have an executive management team for a couple of hours and that is informal and ... It's **an interesting question** because she was the ... I've totally blocked off on Thursday for the funeral of my niece and so I'm going to take Friday off because my son's back from Kuwait to go to the funeral. She was the last person I told in the executive team that I wouldn't be in. So maybe there is something in that.

Whilst the coachee, at first glance, appears to be answering the question in an open way, when re-examining it, it is clear that the coachee successfully manages to avoid discussing how easy she finds it to be vulnerable. This is shown by the way her language shifts towards the third person and moves away from feelings to logistics.

*Diversion* - the ability to use humour and self-deprecation to shut down or change conversational routes that involve consideration of difficult behavioural change. Here, as with deflection, the coachee uses conversational devices to close down areas of conversation that are challenging by diverting the coach away from those areas. One such mechanism is that of the coachee being openly critical of their own behaviour. This can come across to the coach as being honest and open and as evidence of the coachee facing up to their challenges and shortcomings. However, it can also have the impact of holding the conversation and relationship in its current state and restricting options for moving forwards.

This is done in a number of ways but often seems to have the benefit of protecting the coachee from having to take a risk, do something different or move into a conversational area that they are not comfortable with. This is often done at a deeply unconscious level.

 ## Case Study 8.5

Coach: Yeah. Would you be able to envisage different social work environments where you would be able to talk about yourself in that way?

Coachee: Yeah, I think so. Not work. You know, I've been with this organization so long I know a lot of people, I don't think that that would be too stretching 'cause you already either know people well or carry an assumption about them and it wouldn't be a test. But I think socially, yeah. I was just thinking there, I was talking about the split with my wife, if I ever want to go back on the dating game and find somebody else to share my life with, that is absolutely going to be a crucial test of that. Get on dating sites and go on dates. Thanks! [laughs]

Coach: Can I make a suggestion at this point? Maybe you could go on one of those dating programmes on TV. I'm sure they're really good. [laughs]

While it was clear that there was warmth and humour in the conversation, it is also clear from the ensuing conversation that the coachee has successfully diverted the coach away from a sensitive personal area, in this interaction.

 ## Reflective Questions

- As a coach or a mentor, how do you tend to respond if someone introduces humour or seems to resist going to a difficult place? Do you always notice?
- What impact does your response have on the relationship, going forward?

In summary, we argue that this framework extends the current notion of coachee skills beyond that of coachability (Bluckert, 2006) and recognizes that coachees both help and hinder the progress of the coaching relationship, rather than simply the more general technical skills involved in being a good learner (Carroll and Gilbert, 2008). However, as we have argued in relation to coach skills, an over-emphasis on coachee skills is susceptible to the same critique of only representing one side of the coaching relationship. Hence, it is important to understand how the skills of the coachee might complement those of the coach. We discuss this below, using the above coachee skill domains as the starting place for this.

## DISCUSSION

Coaching relationships, like any other personal relationship, develop within a social context. As we have argued in Chapters 1 and 7, the context for coaching is significantly influenced by the power and social relations within which it is located. Key stakeholders – coaches, managers, government officials, professional body representatives – have tended to dominate what is said and done in coaching. This has led to a version of the self as client, helpee, coachee and member of society portrayed as enterprising and discerning in terms of making purchase decisions about professional help (Rose, 1999). In keeping with Western's (2012) notion of the celebrated self and du Gay's (1996) view of the entrepreneurial self within the workplace, getting support is portrayed as a positive step in terms of taking control of one's life and career. However, this proactivity does not extend to these customers having agency in terms of how they engage with these helpers. In this sense, the discourse contains within it a mixed message/contradiction. On the one hand, clients of helping professionals, coaching in particular, are portrayed as discerning autonomous agents who seek to make an informed purchase of process expertise from a service provider. However, once within the process, an examination of what is written and said about coaching tends to reduce their role in this process to one of recipient of the helper's process. This, as we have argued, can be attributed to those powerful stakeholders, referred to above, having a vested interest in privileging their process expertise above the lived experience expertise of those being helped (Rettinger, 2011). However, despite this, as with Colley's (2003) study of mentees' engagement (or lack of it) in mentoring schemes, this study suggests that coachees can and do influence the process of coaching, despite the dominant rhetoric regarding the coaches. Her work also suggests that the mentors themselves were as constrained as the mentees in terms of what they could and could not do within the confines of the mentoring relationship. It is also worth noting Carr's work presented in this book in Chapter 5 on self-mentoring. Here the mentee is in control of the feedback process from others in order to learn and develop. Additionally, the concept of 'self-coaching' is beginning to emerge. This is often positioned within the arena of mindfulness and is based on the 'know yourself' philosophy. In both these examples, the role coach or the mentor is removed from the discussion.

Taking all this into account, it is important to recognize that our intention is not to replace a coach-dominant rhetoric with that of a coachee-dominated one. Rather, it is to argue for a reframing of our understanding as to how and why coaching or mentoring are effective and why they might not be.

By examining these connections, it is possible to draw some conclusions that underpin the alternative discourse of coachee skills:

1. **Coaching is a skilled collaborative partnership** where coach and coachee skills are integrated to form a conversation and a relationship. Power in the relationship is relational and created between the participants, rather than being principally held by one participant. Following Lukes (2005), it could be argued that coaching represents a context-bound, rather than context-transcending, relationship; in other words, I, as a participant in a coaching relationship, will only be able to exercise power over the other party within the context and conditions stipulated as part of the contract between both parties – outside of those, my influence is limited. Furthermore, it is important to recognize that inaction – a failure to make an intervention when it is possible to do so – can also be seen as powerful. Lukes (2005) refers to this as inactive power. Hence, by withdrawing literally or psychologically from the relationship or the coaching conversation, the coachee has the power to equalize that of the coach. By the same token, if the coachee willingly engages and actively commits to the coaching, and uses their skills to further the progress of the relationship, the coaches in this study suggest that the coaching is likely to progress more quickly and effectively than with others who do not have this commitment and engagement. This view of the coaching relationship strongly challenges the image of the skilled helper working with a fundamentally unskilled helpee (Egan, 2014).

2. **Defensiveness does not mean dysfunctionality** – we argue that all behaviours that the coachee exhibits in the coaching relationship have a function. Defensive behaviours on the part of the coachee serve to protect the coachee from too much embarrassment or threat in the coaching relationship and conversations. They are,

following Argyris and Schön's (1996) notion of defensive routines, fundamentally about preserving the status quo in the conversation and the relationship. Cavanagh et al. (2011: 1) argue that the primary purpose of coaching is 'to enhance well being, improve performance and facilitate individual and organisational change', which has, at its essence, an assumption that coaching is fundamentally about change, not staying the same. However, the data analysis reveals that a more sophisticated understanding of defensive behaviour is required which moves away from Bluckert's (2006) notion of 'coachability' – the idea that an individual is somehow a better coachee than another – to one where the coachee is acting skilfully so as to protect themselves and their autonomous self from perceived threat. It is more useful to recognize that, at a given moment in time, a coachee may be more or less skilled in both enabling and defensive behaviours and that both are necessary for an effective working alliance between coach and coachee. Furthermore, personal change as a process can be seen more as a transition that is gradual (Bridges, 2003), rather than an abrupt, discrete shift within which there may be a number of false starts and regression (Daloz, 1999).

3. **Responsibility comes with perceived process expertise** – as a number of the coaches in the study experienced, it is worth recognizing that a process where the expert is expected to dominate and dictate the methodology places significant pressure on the expert. In coaching discourse, the coach is seen as the skilled actor who is responsible for the design and implementation of the coaching methodology. With the rise of professional bodies, with their code of ethics, as argued in the literature review, there is increased pressure

on the coach to be responsible, ethical and professional. Professional bodies like the European Mentoring and Coaching Council (EMCC), the International Coach Federation (ICF) and the Association for Professional Executive Coaching and Supervision (APECS) each have codes of conduct, requirements for continuing professional development and supervision (Bachkirova et al., 2011). This professionalization of coaching has led to more focus from buyers of coaching in terms of the return on their investment. As Nielsen and Norreklit (2009) have argued, this has brought the voice of the organization into the coaching room as well as the two participants in the conversation.

Drawing on these three basic propositions, we are therefore proposing a view of coaching where there is equality between coach and coachee in terms of the process and skills involved. While the coachee may struggle to achieve their purposes and goals without the skills of the coach, the coach will also struggle to operate effectively as a coach without engaging with and acknowledging the skills of the coachee. We argue therefore that coaching development within coaching schemes, leadership programmes as well as educational programmes, should be extended to recognize and work with this largely unrecognized and untapped resource base. Ultimately, we agree with de Haan (2008b) that the key ingredient to coaching processes is the strength of the relationship, but we assert that the coachee needs to be recognized as a joint partner in this collaborative endeavour.

 ——— Future Direction ————————————————————

### Coaches

The theoretical implication of these findings for coaches is that they should be properly considered as comprising one half of the coaching relationship in terms of the process skills required to make the conversation and the relationship work. Recognizing the process skills implications for coachees means that coaches need to become more aware of these skills – both enabling and defensive – and adapt the application of their own skills to fit those of their coachees, as described above. For example, coaches may need to reflect on how persistent they are when challenging their clients. As a result, coaches could question themselves as to whether they always follow through on this challenge and ensure that the coachee is addressing the issues that they need to be addressing. This could involve developing new elements to their contracting processes and recognizing the importance of striking a balance between appropriate levels of challenge and acknowledging the functional (for the coachee) aspects of defensive behaviours (diversion and deflection). These defensive behaviours, as has been argued above, enable the coachee to persist with the conversation and the relationship.

This also means that coaches can rely more on their coachees in terms of their responsibility for making the conversation and the relationship work. The study suggests that coachees often have a good understanding of the coaching process and the tools, techniques and language that go with it. Hence, coaches can be more confident of challenging their coachees to work with coaching approaches/theories explicitly within the coaching conversations and be willing to use creative methods with their coachees, in the service of helping them achieve their goals and desired outcomes.

## Coachees

Coachees, as suggested by this research, can, alternatively, be thought of as skilled coaching practitioners who are not merely passive recipients of the expert coach's process but who make skilled and significant contributions to the coaching conversation and relationship. However, the converse applies to coachees – coachees have, therefore, a responsibility to use these skills and to recognize when they enable and when they limit progress within the coaching relationship. The implications of this responsibility may mean that coachees might need to invest more time and energy in the coaching process, particularly in terms of their abilities to frame the coaching session and, indeed, to reframe their thinking. In addition, the research suggests that, contrary to the prevailing discourse in coaching, coachees have significant agency within the coaching conversation. Therefore, this raises the possibility of coachees seeking/needing development in how to ensure that their coaching relationships are effective by utilizing their own process skills. Furthermore, there is the possibility that coachee supervision might be an effective way of understanding (a) how to enable effective coaching conversations and (b) how defensive coachee skills might undermine coaching conversation depth and how these protective behaviours might be used in a more self-aware fashion. In a wider sense, this research also draws attention to the way in which coaching discourse can serve to disempower the coachee and render them more dependent on the perceived process expertise of the coach. By re-casting the coaching relationship in a more collaborative light in terms of process skills, coachees may feel more able to take some control and ownership of their personal development processes.

## Scheme designers

In practical terms, these findings suggest that, for internal coaching programmes, more emphasis should be placed on developing coachees to become more aware of the skills that they have in relation to coaching. In particular, these conclusions we have drawn from this research suggest that coachee development should be focused on the coachee's responsibilities in working in collaboration with their coach in order to maximize the chances of the conversations being useful to the coachee. However, the heuristic offered above also suggests that it would be important to work with both coaches and coachees on coaching schemes (rather than just coaches) to help each party (a) to understand and develop their own process skills but also (b) to recognize how and in what ways these skills might be employed to complement those of their dyadic partner. Hence, we are suggesting that there is a place within coaching scheme development to argue that, alongside conventional coach-related skills, such as active listening, paraphrasing, summarizing and skilful questioning, we also include coachee skills such as framing, reframing and understanding the coaching process. This would require a significant re-examination of where organizational sponsors of coaching schemes might invest their resources, rather than continuing with the current position of focusing, principally, on coach development.

*(Continued)*

## Academics

Academics working in coaching, like ourselves, have three roles to play. One is by contributing to the literature on coaching, through their writing on coaching models and theories. This research suggests that there is some merit in revisiting such models and theories to incorporate coachee skills. However, as we have argued, this should not be in the form of a coachee-centric, as opposed to coach-centric, model. Rather, there seems to be sufficient merit in the research to suggest this development.

Second, they have a role to play in training and developing coaches and supervisors as part of courses and programmes that they design and teach on. The research suggests that more emphasis should be placed on helping prospective coaches work more effectively with skilled coachees, and that the prevailing discourse which places them in the expert role and, by the same token, the coachee in a passive recipient role, should be challenged. Furthermore, following Bachkirova (2011), coaches need to reflect on the coachee position themselves in terms of working with themselves and their personal reflexivity. Finally, academics have a role to play in investigating coachee skills further.

## Professional bodies

As we have argued elsewhere in this book, professional bodies have a great deal invested in preserving the status quo within coaching, as with professionalization comes notions of expertise and specialism (Rose, 1999), which allow claims for greater fees and social status to be justified. Making claims for coachee process skills and an equalization of the relationship between coaches and coachees might in this sense challenge this position. It is noticeable that, although all of the professional bodies mentioned have a code of ethics and guidelines for practice, these typically do not extend to govern the conduct of coachees. This indicates where the professional bodies sit in terms of who is deemed to be responsible for the conduct and outcome of coaching processes. The research suggests that this position needs to be revisited, with a recognition that, as with coaches, coachee empowerment confers great responsibility as well as great process influence. Furthermore, as we have suggested above, a recognition of coachee skills – both enabling and defensive – also implies that coaches may need to refine and develop new skills that work in complement to those coachee skills. Thus, professional bodies – particularly those who accredit/audit training providers – may need to consider how greater coachee agency and skill should be incorporated into professional coaching standards for coaching education. Further, professional bodies need to consider if their over-reliance on competence frameworks for coach education remains appropriate, not only in the light of this study but also in relation to the changing views on what coaching and mentoring actually are (see Chapter 1).

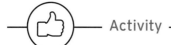 Activity

Reflect on when you have been coached, mentored or supervised yourself and bring to mind a session/moment where you felt particularly challenged or uncomfortable. Try to recall some of the things you said or did in that session:

- What do you notice about your own behaviour?
- To what extent do you recognize aspects of the behaviours described above in your own approach as a coachee/mentee/supervisee?

---

 ## Questions

- What constitutes skilled behaviour in your coachees/mentees?
- What are the implications of such skilled behaviour for the coaching/mentoring relationship?
- How would you describe the balance of responsibility – between coaches/mentors and coachees/mentees – for a successful outcome?

---

 ## Further Reading

For an interesting piece of research on coachee characteristics, look at Bozer, G., Sarros, J.C. and Santora, J.C. (2013) 'The role of coachee characteristics in executive coaching for effective sustainability', *Journal of Management Development*, 32(3): 277–94.

For an excellent discussion of power dynamics and coachee agency, examine Louis, D. and Fatien Diochon, P. (2014) 'Educating coaches to power dynamics: Managing multiple agendas within the triangular relationship', *Journal of Psychological Issues in Organisational Culture*, 5(2): 31-47.

See also for research on a learning informed process for coaching Nadeem, I., and Garvey, B. (2020) 'Learning experiences for academic deans: Implications for leadership coaching', *International Journal of Evidence Based Coaching and Mentoring*, 18(2): 133–151.

# 9

# MULTIPLE LEARNING RELATIONSHIPS

## CHAPTER OVERVIEW

Coaching and mentoring conversations are social interactions facilitated in specific contexts for a variety of purposes. This chapter explores the idea of multiple coaching and mentoring relationships and considers this in the context of the knowledge economy and the consequential implications for organizational structures and practices.

# INTRODUCTION

It would be difficult to conceive of any economy which was not driven by know-how. According to Garvey and Williamson (2002), all economies are knowledge economies and they always have been. Clearly, many different factors fuel economic progress but it is the development of ideas that enables progress – for example, in agriculture, the seed drill and the tractor, crop rotation methods and contour ploughing; in manufacturing and transport, the steam engine and the internal combustion engine; and in electronics, the valve, the transistor and the microchip. These advances are the products of learning processes facilitated in environments suitable for learning. This argument is supported by recent research by Mazhar and Rehman (2020: 796) who state: 'One undisputed determinant of the long term income growth of a country is the level of knowledge and technical knowhow of its workers.'

As discussed in Chapter 6 and as many other writers have suggested (see Rogers, 1969; Habermas, 1974; Vygotsky, 1978; Bruner, 1990; Lave and Wenger, 1991), learning is a social activity and people learn through and with others. Therefore, organizational structures and practices play an important role in creating and developing such environments. With this in mind, Western's (2012) network discourse is particularly appropriate. The idea, arguable at least, relates to a reconceptualization of business and the organizations which support it. The development of new technologies (see Chapter 10) has created new and emerging ways of working as well as new business forms designed to develop and apply knowledge, to innovate.

Kessels (2002) argues that a knowledge-productive environment is an essential requirement for a work-based organization to be able to operate in a knowledge economy. Neilson and Eisenbach (2003) support this view, referring to both Drucker (1993) and Pfeffer (1995); they suggest that 'knowledge is the only meaningful resource in today's economy ... people within which that knowledge resides become the primary sources of competitive advantage'.

Clutterbuck (1998) describes a range of one-to-one dialogic partnerships that could contribute to knowledge work. Garvey and Alred (2000) suggest that mentoring activity in the workplace offers the potential to develop a knowledge-productive environment. Hamburg (2013: 219) argues that 'mentoring is a human resources development process supporting learning and knowledge transfer'; Rosinski (2003: 245) suggests that a coach is a 'knowledge transferer'; Bowerman and Collins (1999) are clear that coaching is a vehicle for knowledge transfer; and Grant and Hartley (2013) argue that coaching helps to complete the learning transfer from workshops and seminars. These views suggest that developing people through coaching and mentoring to support and facilitate others becomes an important consideration for active participation in the knowledge economy. Furthermore, Whittington's (2020) work on systemic coaching constellations has examined the impact that coaching can have across individuals, groups, organizations and wider systems.

# METHODOLOGY

In this chapter, we critically discuss some literature related to the concept of the knowledge economy, developmental and social networks. The chapter starts with a discussion of changing employment trends over the last 15 or so years and the implications of these changing trends for organizations. We then go on to look at the notion of multiple coaching and mentoring relationships and consider how these might relate to Western's (2012) notion of the social network discourse. Following this, we apply the concepts of complexity and social network theory to the discussion. Finally, we examine a new notion of social organization for learning put forward by Williamson, drawn from his unpublished notes on communities of discovery. This chapter raises some key challenges for coaching and mentoring as well as organizational design.

## CHANGING EMPLOYMENT TRENDS

More than 20 years ago, Higgins and Kram (2001) noted four important trends in employment in the USA:

- changing contractual arrangements
- technological change
- changing organizational structures
- increasing diversity.

They argued that these trends were influenced by increasing competitiveness, a strong trend towards outsourcing, increased organizational restructuring and globalization. The changes in technological applications, products and services were leading to the developing notion of 'knowledge workers' and to consequent changes in the requirements of workplace skills. This was leading to the development of more 'expert' environments at work. Along with these issues, employers were attempting to change their structures to facilitate faster action, flexible working and flatter hierarchies. The pressure for employees to perform was increasing and a more personalized approach to learning and development, as new networks and relationships opened up in the new environment, was manifesting in the increase in coaching and mentoring activity.

With these issues they noted, by citing Thomas and Gabarro's (1999) work on black and white managers, that diversity among the workforce was a reality. Thomas and Gabarro (1999) showed that successful black executives develop strong developmental relationships drawn from multiple sources both inside and outside the workplace in preference to a single mentor. Krackhardt (1992) argued that strong links to others in a network are important for building trust and are shown to be particularly helpful in uncertain and insecure times (Krackhardt and Stern, 1988). Mentoring activity was becoming part of the diversity agenda.

These trends, outlined above, were also observed later in the UK and supported in the CIPD's paper *Managing Change: The Role of the Psychological Contract* (2007a), and, more recently, in the Confederation of British Industry's (CBI) employment trends survey 2015, *The Path Ahead*.

Over a decade ago, the 2008 global financial crisis clearly had an impact on both private and public sector business worldwide. However, more recently, there have been signs that a recovery was becoming established and one of the consequences had been a change in employment trends and business forms.

According to Hatfield (2015), self-employment was rising. She reported that since 2010 there has been a 40% rise in self-employment across Europe. It was also interesting to note that self-employment is a more common option for older males and that the female self-employment rate was also rising. This gives credence to the idea that disadvantaged groups, including women, are more likely to be self-employed because the general job market is difficult to break into (Hatfield, 2015). This suggests that diversity is still an issue 20 years on from Higgins and Kram's (2001) work reported at the start of this section. However, it is important to recognize that much of this recovery has been undermined by the COVID-19 pandemic.

At the time of writing, the immediate economic outlook for the UK is grim with multiple job losses being reported across a range of sectors but most notably in hospitality and cultural sectors. The UK government has extended the furlough scheme to protect jobs and income and the climate looks intimidating for those considering moving into self-employment.

For some, the pandemic has also produced new ways to work and to find new markets and opportunities. For example, a young entrepreneur known to one of the authors ran, up until COVID, a £1 million, high-end catering business. He catered for events, weddings and various tourist outlets around the UK. All that stopped with COVID. His mentor helped him to think differently about what he did and how he did it. As a result, his business started producing meals for hospitals and for community groups. Although his profit margins were hit, he managed to keep his 12 chefs employed. Recently he started doing 'pop-up' take-away restaurants as well as developing the idea of providing restaurant quality food delivered to the home for the customer to heat up and eat.

In the USA, recent investment research conducted by Heo, Grable and Rabanni (2020) points to a drop in tolerance of financial risk – including personal investment – particularly in relation to the COVID-19 pandemic. Whilst this research is specifically about investor confidence, it also signals a drop in business confidence more generally in the USA. In the UK, the CIPD report *Resourcing and Talent Planning* (2015b) suggested that UK employers were facing eight key issues:

- resourcing and talent planning
- recruitment difficulties
- employer brand
- diversity

- age diversity
- attracting candidates
- selecting candidates
- talent management.

The biggest issue for employers in resourcing at that time was similar to the USA: a lack of appropriate skills, particularly technological ones. However, organizations were recruiting more young people, particularly graduates, and were looking to develop this pool for the future. This survey also indicated that employers were looking to recruit more employees aged 50 plus with a view to encouraging more knowledge transfer between the generations – a possible role for mentoring? These trends are recognized by Lyons and Bandura's (2020) study of skills trends. In this article, they argue for learning approaches which, in particular, enable 'the development of high-level problem-solving, making use of individual and group assignments to encourage the merging of conceptual and practical knowledge via collaboration, reflection, information sharing and informal leadership' (Lyons and Bandura, 2020: 487). Organizations were reporting the use of diversity practices, with the public sector being the most proactive in this regard, although Ely and Thomas's (2020) recent work on diversity in the US context sounds a cautionary note on how effective this is (see Chapter 13).

While all the issues raised above may be of interest to the coaching and mentoring worlds, the issues of resourcing and talent, learning and development, employee attitudes and youth unemployment are probably the most important.

One organization, Youth Business International (YBI), had made huge strides in helping young people start and grow businesses. During 2015, for example, YBI supported 19,463 entrepreneurs with 11,213 active volunteer mentors in 42 countries. All mentors are trained and supported during their time with the young entrepreneur. During COVID, YBI launched its 'SOS Mentoring Programme' to support mentors in supporting their entrepreneurs (see Chapter 10)

As stated in Chapter 6, particularly in this economic climate, where knowledge and expertise are at a premium, the pressure to perform increases and it becomes crucial for employees to have 'strong and stable personalities' (Kessels, 1995) and to be able to 'tolerate complexity' (Garvey and Alred, 2001). As acknowledged throughout this text, these attributes are particularly challenging to realize in the current COVID-19 context. However, the opportunities offered may be for a new, personalized approach to learning and development as new networks and relationships open up in the new environment. While the pandemic has had an impact on all types of organization, coaching and mentoring activities still seem to offer a positive contribution in the circumstances outlined above; however, organizations are attempting to be more innovative in the ways in which coaching and mentoring are employed and adapted to meet the changing needs of organizations (see Chapter 5). The next section offers ways in which new forms of coaching and mentoring, based on their core values, are starting to develop.

## MULTIPLE DEVELOPMENTAL RELATIONSHIPS IN COACHING

In preparing this chapter, it became clear that the material available on multiple relationships in the area of coaching and mentoring is limited. Some of the developmental network and social network writers link their ideas to mentoring – for example, Collins (1994); Higgins (2000); Higgins and Kram (2001); de Janasz et al. (2003); Chandler and Kram (2005); Dobrow and Higgins (2005); Molloy (2005) – but there are very few links to coaching, although there are signs that this is changing.

We suggest that there are three main reasons for the lack of attention, until now at least, to developmental networks in coaching.

First, although we argue (see Chapter 2) that the discourse of coaching is changing, there is still a dominant thread of this coaching literature that is practitioner dominated, with a particular focus on improving coaching practice and impact. The practitioners are mostly independent coaches who work externally and therefore there is little impetus for them to consider this development in thinking.

Second, the rise in interest in coaching (in the UK at least) is mainly linked to external coaches. The CIPD learning and development survey (2015a) indicated that 65% of all responding organizations were now employing internal coaching as a preferred approach to learning and development. In the 2020 CIPD Learning and Skills at Work: Mind the gap survey, it is interesting to note that, despite a more gloomy picture in terms of organizational investment in learning and development, 45% of those who used coaching as a developmental tool reported that their use of it was increasing, with only 8% reporting a decrease in its use. In the second edition of this text, we reported that internal coaching was most often associated with performance improvement (CIPD, 2007b) rather than specific learning and development. This trend has also changed, according to the CIPD (2015a, 2020) surveys. Within the context of the knowledge economy, abilities such as 'time management, relationships, communication skills and sharing what you know, problem solving, creativity, emotions, metacognitive skills and a capacity to reflect upon behaviour and experience' (Alred and Garvey, 2000: 262), as well as 'flexibility, adaptability, creativity and innovative thinking' (Garvey and Alred, 2001: 526), are generally agreed as the desirable attributes of knowledge or 'expert' workers. We welcome this shifting trend, particularly if it marks a movement away from a compliance mindset and towards acknowledging the behaviours and attitudes needed in a knowledge worker. The CIPD 2020 survey in particular focused on the impact of COVID-19 and the rise in the use of mobile technology so as to enable learning (see Chapter 10 for a more in-depth focus on e-development). As established in Chapter 3, enabling robust and critical thinking is essential if a true learning environment is to become established. Most coaching literature holds the view that the coachee's agenda is paramount or crucial – this is also the case even in some specifically performance-related coaching writing. In Chapter 8, we consider the implications of this assumption, and in Chapter 5 the case example of internal coaching asks how far this is actually the case. There is clearly a tension here and McLeod, for example, states, 'I may have to set the scene in the corporate context ... Only then will we go to the issue that they have brought to the session' (2003: 166).

An early publication which acknowledges a coaching network is the paper by Bowerman and Collins (1999), where the main purpose of the coaching network was to develop a knowledge-development and sharing environment. In developing this coaching network within Canadian businesses, they note some interesting features:

- an emphasis on cross-functional relationships
- individuals to work together on the basis of learning needs
- mutuality
- skills development for both coaches and performers
- linking individual and organizational outcomes
- seeking continuous development through opportunities to apply the newly acquired skills.

The programme was established with an underpinning humanitarian and liberal philosophy which employed Lievegoed's (1993) humanitarian perspective on development, Flores's (1999) interpretations of language work, Argyris's (1977, 1986) concept of 'undiscussables' and 'skilled incompetences' and Revans's (1983) views on action learning. Within the coaching network, there were multiple definitions of coaching which tended to relate to the learning requirement of both parties. This we view as normal. All too often, organizations are tempted by the lure of simplification and misunderstand something as complex as coaching and fail to realize its full potential by trying to reduce it to something simple, or insist on a 'one size fits all' approach. In our view, this position, based on the Managerial discourse (Western, 2012), is unhelpful.

In this scheme, seniority was put to one side and relationships could be constituted with the senior person being in the 'performer' role. This status inversion is very difficult to achieve and requires a visionary leadership and a quality of humility on the part of business leaders. A number of controls were put into the process. These included a time boundary of 20 weeks, formalized reflection sessions and just-in-time skills workshops as appropriate and according to need.

Limited evaluation data exist to date and there is no longitudinal aspect to this paper. However, the authors believe in the potential of coaching networks.

## MULTIPLE RELATIONSHIPS IN MENTORING

Many conceptualizations of mentoring have positioned it as an exclusively one-to-one relationship with those in learning alliances (Levinson et al., 1978; Clutterbuck, 1992) engaging in the practice of having a single or perhaps a primary mentor. However, Garvey and Alred (2001), Higgins and Kram (2001) and Burke et al. (1995) suggest that many people, particularly in their workplaces, are in fact part of a 'learning network', with mentoring and coaching being among many other developmental roles. Higgins and Kram suggest that, in the past, we have simply been 'studying different types of mentoring' (2001: 266). This work has been built upon by Chanland and Murphy (2018) and Chang, Baek and Kim (2020), which will be discussed below.

However, Higgins and Kram's (2001) original observation is illuminating, particularly for the points made in other chapters in this book about the similarities and differences found in coaching and mentoring. Higgins and Kram (2001) classified these different types of mentoring as roles performed by the mentor and offer the following typology:

- *entrepreneurial* – those relationships with high developmental network diversity and high developmental relationship strength
- *opportunistic* – those relationships with high developmental network diversity and low developmental relationship strength
- *traditional* – those relationships with low developmental network diversity and high developmental relationship strength
- *receptive* – those relationships with low developmental network diversity and low developmental relationship strength.

The authors suggested that these various roles provide 'an important new lens through which to view mentoring at work' (Higgins and Kram, 2001: 264).

Clutterbuck and Megginson (1995: 237) present a model with the learner at the centre, emphasizing that the mentor is one of many who can make developmental alliances. The crucial point in both these ideas is for the learner to manage this network.

Burke et al. (1995) throw some light on the importance and impact of interpersonal networks in the workplace. They build on Kram's (1985a) idea of 'relationship constellations' in mentoring and look at a range of 'supportive' relationships for both men and women inside and outside of the organization. Burke et al. (1995) note that the participants (in the main in middle to senior management positions) in their study found a range of career support both inside and outside the work environment. Those who described their work environments in positive terms indicated:

- greater career and job satisfaction
- better organizational integration
- reduced intentions to leave.

Interestingly, the authors noted that men and women who reported a greater percentage of males in their outside networks also reported greater satisfaction in their career progress. They also noted that those participants with more family dependants reported greater organizational commitment.

However, they were unable to find any linkage between the structural nature of their participants' interpersonal networks and a wide variety of work or career outcomes. Their explanations for this finding are as follows:

1. It is unlikely that interpersonal networks affect work and career outcomes.
2. Interpersonal networks may be more significant at earlier stages of a career than later.
3. The effects of interpersonal networks, although present, are modest but may be dependent on other work setting characteristics.

It is our view that point 1 is contrary to other social network research findings (see, for example, Cross and Parker, 2004). Additionally, the participants in the sample were all in early or mid-career and therefore this may explain point 2. However, point 3 relates well to Garvey and Alred's (2001) assertion that the form mentoring takes within an organization may indeed be dependent on the cultural characteristics within that organization.

While offering a helpful perspective, Higgins and Kram's (2001) and Burke et al.'s (1995) work does not illustrate the complexity of either the subject under investigation or the changing dynamic of organizational life, as articulated at the start of this chapter. While the Higgins and Kram's (2001) typology of networked mentoring relationships helps provide a framework for discussion, it only provides a limited snapshot in time. Clearly, interpersonal relationships both inside and outside of the workplace are many and varied. Therefore, attempting to isolate variables and consequently draw cause and effect conclusions as well as a precise definition can be challenging (see Chapter 1). Chang, Baek and Kim's (2020) study, however, tries to do this and, in doing so, builds on Higgins and Kram's work and takes it in some interesting directions in terms of developmental networks in particular. Their study examined the developmental networks of 427 female workers in Korea using a quantitative methods approach. Essentially, they concluded from this data that the level of intimacy attained between people in the developmental network as well as the size of the women's networks had a positive impact on career satisfaction whereas contact frequency and range had the opposite effects. In other words, the amount and quality of support mattered but too much contact from too wide a range of 'developers' militated against positive perceptions of career satisfaction. Interestingly, the impact of role modelling – a key aspect of mentoring – was seen as a significant mediating factor in the study. In contrast to Burke et al.'s (1995) study, the gender of the higher status developers was not significant – the women reported higher satisfaction from their mentoring experiences through both men and women.

## A COMPLEXITY-INFORMED PERSPECTIVE

As raised earlier in this chapter, simplification in management has its appeal but social processes like coaching and mentoring are inherently complex. Clifford Geertz (1974) offers us an alternative perspective on social systems by suggesting that they are better understood in terms of a 'thick description'. Geertz explains that a rich description is a term for the systematic exploration *of*, an interpretation *of* and the search for meaning *in* social action. Consequently, other insights may be gained from a complexity-informed perspective.

We make a distinction between 'complicated' and 'complex'. If we give a kitten a ball of wool to play with, it will make a complicated mess with it! However, it would be possible, given enough time, to unravel the mess. With complexity, on the other hand, it is not possible to unravel the mess. All we can do is attempt to understand small, localized parts and keep exploring to understand how the localized parts interact with other parts. At the same time, as our understanding grows, further complexities appear. Complexity is ongoing and continuous. There is no solution, only temporary 'holding positions'.

Garvey and Alred (2001) argue that mentoring activity is complex and the organization in which it is operating is also complex, or, as Stacey (1995) suggests, in a 'bounded state of instability'. Here they suggest that mentoring is analogous to Boolean algebra, which is often modelled using a series of networked, interconnected light bulbs. As the different switches are flicked, the bulbs illuminate in different and unpredictable patterns, some bright and some dull: 'A light bulb in a Boolean array makes a difference because it is part of an open system, it is well connected, responds unambiguously to other light bulbs and sends clear messages' (Garvey and Alred, 2001: 524).

In a human developmental network, the system rests on similar qualities in that a good learner is well connected with an array of strong and weak connections with each participant offering different perspectives, insights, skills and knowledge. The learner draws on this network to further their learning but, in turn, they may help other members of their network to develop and change. There is a natural symbiosis here, rather like the bee visiting flowers and gathering pollen for its own survival while fertilizing the plant for its continued life.

This is similar to the perspective on mentoring first described in Homer's epic poem *The Odyssey* (see Chapter 1). Despite the challenge to the legitimacy of the Homeric poem as the root of mentoring (see Chapter 1), Telemachus, perhaps the first mentee, had several 'mentors' in his network. Some of the relationships in his network were long-term and strong partnerships, while others were shorter-term and weaker. Some were opportunistic while others were more formalized, almost appointed. Each, however, provided something different and unique to aid his development.

Mullen (2007: 129) noted in relation to student mentoring that members of a developmental network often have multiple and interchangeable roles. She suggested that those who are developmentally aware actively seek to support others as well as seek support for themselves. Another set of layers may be found in Garvey and Alred (2001) where they suggest that factors such as power structures (see Chapter 7), organizational culture, management style and the 'dominant logic' of an organization affect the nature and form of mentoring. This may also be the case in the influence of social networks on career progress.

## SOCIAL NETWORKS

Cross and Parker (2004), in their work on social networks, conclude that 'well-managed network connectivity is critical to performance, learning and innovation' (2004: 10). Their findings suggest that when activities and decisions are focused primarily on the boss, or if a team is poorly networked, performance is significantly reduced compared with well-networked and more loosely controlled groups. They also note that neither the use of technology nor significant individual expertise alone created high performance. Rather, high performers in the petrochemical, pharmaceutical, electronics and consulting industries were consistently part of larger and more diverse personal networks. More importantly, in the context of learning, their research demonstrates that 'whom you know has a significant impact on what you come to know, because relationships are critical for obtaining information, solving problems, and learning how to do your work' (2004: 11). Furthermore, in no cases explored in their research did they find that the use of technology or a knowledge management system outweighed the significance people placed on their personal network for learning.

Cross and Parker (2004: 5) illustrate a social network by comparing it with an organizational structure chart as shown in Figure 9.1. Using social network analysis, this translates as shown in Figure 9.2, where Cole is clearly the centre of the network and it is likely that most of the information flows through him. If Cole were to leave the organization, a knowledge gap would appear. It is particularly interesting that Jones, the boss, is not networked very well, although he is networked with Cole and therefore has access to the key player and his networks. There is a lesson here, in that organizational hierarchies do not necessarily present the sources of 'social power' within an organization. Additionally, if this business wanted to bring about change, the key player to work with is Cole. If Cole agrees and accepts the change, then others will as well. This is relevant if, say, a developmental network approach was to be developed in this business.

To illustrate, in a recent discussion with an organization wishing to develop coaching, it became clear that there was a fear of uncertainty and difference. The organization in question is large, growing, multinational and complex. The issues raised by coaching in one country are not the same in another. Management attitudes to coaching are also different in different countries (see Chapter 16 for an in-depth analysis of these different perspectives). Therefore, to try and impose

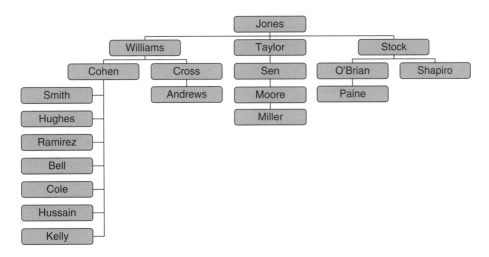

**Figure 9.1** Formal structures

*Source:* Adapted from Cross and Parker (2004: 5). Reproduced by permission of Harvard Business Publishing.

a coaching model (with the assumption of one best way) is asking for problems. The organization here anticipated issues of definition, skills, culture, meaning and acceptance. In their uncertainty, the HR managers in this group were seeking simplicity and practical steps – an understandable but not a sensible position. Eventually, they agreed to a unifying definition but accepted localized variation in implementation. The definition was not about such platitudes as 'we are all singing from the same hymn sheet', but rather about diversity and complexity being natural and normal in human systems. Perhaps this statement challenges managers to develop a new level of sophistication in thinking about organizations, particularly in a knowledge economy.

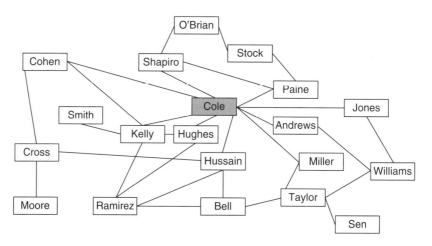

**Figure 9.2**   Informal networks

*Source:* Adapted from Cross and Parker (2004: 5)

Bringing all the above ideas together, in the context of a coaching and mentoring developmental network, the layers of complexity may be found in, for example:

- the numbers of people involved
- the network's scope and purpose
- the roles adopted within a developmental network
- the nature of the organization's business
- cultural considerations including attitudes and values
- the views taken on the purpose of mentoring and coaching
- the ownership of the developmental agenda
- the skills and processes employed.

In practical terms, living with or tolerating complexity is important to organizational progress. The natural desire to control and simplify needs to be moderated in order to allow for difference, disagreement, challenge and openness. Taken together, it seems that extensive social and developmental networks are important to human development and progress, particularly in the context of a knowledge economy. If this is the case, then there are clear challenges for organizational structures and management practices, and in the organization of coaching and mentoring.

The concepts of e-coaching and mentoring cultures (critically examined in Chapter 3) provide some insight into how to achieve this. Additional help may be found in Lave and Wenger's (1991) 'situated learning' and 'communities of practice'. They refer to learning as a social activity being a form of 'participation'. The consequences of situated learning manifest in relationships with other members of the organization, for example through engagement in the organization's social practices, by contributing to the achievement of the goals and aspirations of the organization, and in the ways in which people relate to their concept of *self* within a social context. The notion of Lave and Wenger's 'community of practice' relates well to the idea of developmental networks where the 'person' of the learner is emphasized. This is similar to the value placed on the learner in mentoring and coaching relationships. A prerequisite of this kind of learning environment is that 'Learners are engaged both in the contexts of their learning and in the broader social world within which these contexts are produced. Without this engagement there is no learning, but where the proper, wholesome and full engagement is sustained, learning will occur' (Alred and Garvey, 2000: 266).

Culture, mindset and practices are therefore very important simply because an organization can make it more or less possible by its actions that learning can occur. Traditional hierarchies, simplification of complexity and a 'tell' approach to learning do not lend themselves to a developmental network culture.

 Future Direction ───────────────────────────

The concept of 'communities of practice' is not without its problems. As first raised in Chapter 3, the tendency for 'defensive and cult-like reactions' in groups is great. Groups often create a power base of those who are 'in' with a desire to keep those who are not 'in' out! Cultures enable this to happen through cultural rituals, language, assumptions, symbolic displays and narratives. A community of practice may have similar tendencies and thus openness to new ideas and creative innovation may become reduced. An alternative concept is a 'community of discovery'.

### Community of Discovery

To be creative, innovative and able to change requires new thinking, the discovery of new ideas and new ways of working. The challenge, therefore, is to find ways forward for people to discover these. Clearly, we cannot learn about things that have not yet been discovered but we can learn about how to make discoveries and encourage learners, enquirers and innovators to experience their learning as discovery. A community of discovery is a philosophical position with practical implications.

### The Known World

We thank Bill Williamson and Stuart Martin for introducing us to the concept of communities of discovery. We draw from Bill Williamson's unpublished notes for some of this section.

*(Continued)*

In a meaningless world, human beings have a strong desire to attribute meaning. Human attempts to do this may help to explain the tendencies to reductionism and simplification, as discussed earlier. Religion, culture, science and the arts also provide a means for people to create meaning.

No one human has the knowledge to understand all there is to know about creation, evolution and the structure of both the material and social worlds. Consequently, human discoveries have been collective, social achievements. As has been attributed to Sir Isaac Newton as a classic truism, 'I have seen further because I stood on the shoulders of giants.' However, we contend that what there is to know or what is potentially knowable is not there already waiting to be discovered. It is through a sense of discovery that we will create and transform everything we currently claim to understand. The known world is not something that is just given; it is a world constantly being discovered.

What it means in practice differs from one person to another and these differences amplify across cultures and through different periods of history. Such differences are the subject of comparative history, anthropology and cultural studies. To understand the many ways people have constructed their worlds, we need to discover how to map out the different *ways of knowing* (see Peat, 1995; Pickstone, 2000) from different cultures and societies. We also need to explore those differences to reveal the subtlety and complexity of the interaction between experience and worldviews, social position and ways of knowing, circumstances and beliefs. This task requires us to understand these interactions at different levels:

- whole culture level
- organizations and other groupings within their level
- individual level.

Additionally, we need to understand how we come to know how to think within the frameworks of different cultures, social settings and the complexities of work. This involves at least two key questions: How do people learn the fundamental categories of thought that bring coherence to the worldview of their society? How are people able to use these categories as a *grammar of understanding* and interpretation that enables them to live in and adapt to their world in ways that allow them to bring order and coherence to change and uncertainty? As we have seen, in relation to the US 2020 election aftermath, developing such a grammar of understanding has never been more important.

These issues are central to that domain of inquiry known as the sociology of knowledge where, unfortunately, there has been both a concentration on political and ideological beliefs and a failure to consider how human beings actually assemble meaning in their lives through learning.

Finally, we need to inquire about:

- where new ideas come from
- how people come to change their thinking
- how, through that, their worlds change.

These really would be discoveries!

## The Applications of the Concept of Communities of Discovery

These points may seem at first very abstract, but they are, in fact, very practical. If we seek to understand the learning and development needs of a group of people in any organization, we have to find credible answers to the kinds of questions raised above. For example, suppose a company, like the one discussed earlier in this chapter, wanted to develop multi-developmental networks. Using the themes cited above, we can ask the following questions:

- How do people in an organization perceive and understand coaching and mentoring?
- How does coaching and mentoring fit into their way of knowing about the world?
- What explains the differences in knowledge of coaching and mentoring competency among them?
- How far are such differences a product of their previous experience of coaching and mentoring?
- How does the prevailing work culture shape attitudes to coaching and mentoring?
- How can members of the organization best be helped to think about engaging in coaching and mentoring in their organization?

None of these questions has answers found in a file or provided by a consultant. The answer to each would have to be discovered through analysis, reflection, dialogue and experimentation, so that members of the organization can share their views, learn from one another and continue to discover new ways of engaging in coaching and mentoring conversations. Either organizations can be managed in ways that nurture discovery or they can be left just to get on with their work. The difference between the two explains why some companies, projects, institutions and organizations are innovative and successful and why others are not.

Given the competitive pressures of change in the global economy, these are not matters that can be left to chance. The *necessary* conditions of successful innovation include:

- investment
- expertise
- leadership and management
- diversity of knowledge and experience, culture and background.

These break down into many more discrete qualities and actions, including:

- extensive social and developmental networking
- the development of appropriate reward systems
- product and service development
- marketing
- benchmarking.

The *sufficient* conditions for success include subtle factors such as:

- a commitment to learn on the part of members of a group
- extensive communication and dialogue
- a diverse culture of excitement about change and ideas.

*(Continued)*

Above all, there has to be:

- curiosity and a commitment to and delight in discovery
- determination to live in the world of ideas
- toleration of complexity, a celebration of success
- recognition that not all is controllable
- a sense of mutuality in the learning process.

When there is a prevailing sense among members in a group of belonging to a community where new ideas are valued and acknowledged, these conditions will be met. We describe such communities as *communities of discovery*.

---

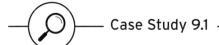 **Case Study 9.1**

### A community of discovery in action

Engineering Company was established in the 1940s and specialized in making pressed metal ladies' powder compacts. In the 1950s, it built the body shells of washing machines and other white goods. In the 1960s, it developed techniques to press automotive sub-frames from heavy steel as a market niche. In the 1980s and 1990s, it continued with its niche approach to engineering and service contracts for Boeing and the aerospace industry followed. Engineering Company is now a global multinational player supplying specialist parts to the big names in the automotive industry. Now operating in 22 different countries, its original site in the north-east of the UK now employs 1,400 people and turns over £160m per year – and it is still growing.

Much of this innovation and development have come from a relatively stable staff team. The company gives priority to interdisciplinary working, problem solving and in-house train-ing, skill development and total quality management. It offers its own apprenticeship scheme and funds its employees to study for university degree courses. The company is very proud of its investment in training and education and is willing to support employees who wish to take up further studies. Development is supported through mentoring activity and coaching is employed as an approach to problem solving. The leadership of the business is facilitative, committed to innovation, development and change. It is very supportive of its staff, who are highly skilled. The leadership keeps a close eye on the market and anticipates and responds to trends quickly. The staff believe that it is a good company to work for and that their futures are secured through good leadership, high-quality products and innovation. The career of its managing director is part of the 'folk wisdom' of Engineering Company. He rose from appren-tice to MD and firmly believes that this is a career pattern in principle open to all. True or not, he is widely admired for his achievement and is someone who takes an active part in the local economy and in the regional economy through business networks and government policy initiatives.

**Reflective Questions** ———————————————

- What are the cultural issues you notice here?
- What is the nature of leadership in this business?
- What hallmarks of a 'community of discovery' can you identify?

 **Activity** ——————————————————

Within a large, UK-based retailer employing some 180,000 people, the opportunities for developing learning networks are considerable. Like all organizations, this retailer needs a career development programme to produce a succession network of motivated, upward-moving employees. Those not identified as having potential or not desiring career progression also require development to help them adapt to changing job roles or requirements. It is recognized that one way to assist this is through coaching and mentoring activity. Most mentoring relationships are internal, and colleagues can access the company intranet where the names of colleagues who have volunteered, been trained and have mentoring experience are published. Most coaching relationships, on the other hand, are external. However, an interesting hybrid of expectations for an external coach is now emerging. Coaches are expected to have appropriate knowledge and relevant experience. For the future, this retailer is considering developing the idea of learning networks. This, it is believed, will help coachees and future leaders to think beyond the confines of the dominant management discourse of efficiencies, output and goals to develop their capacity to think strategically. However, the business may struggle to create such networked thinking because the managerialism discourse is so strong.

- How do you account for the apparent paradox within this business between the managerialism discourse and the network discourse?
- Given that, while substantial, this business is under strong competitive pressure from the 'discounters' and is losing market share, how might it tackle the paradox between what it thinks is necessary and the dominating managerialist discourse?

 **Questions** —————————————————

- How would an organization go about establishing a community of discovery approach to learning and development?
- How do coaching and mentoring fit into the idea of a community of discovery?
- How can members of the organization best be helped to think about engaging in a community of discovery in their organization?

**Further Reading**

For an interesting read on an approach to organizational change and development without the standard prescriptive models, and for an account of 'living' with complexity and acting with intent into the unknown, try: Shaw, P. (2002) *Changing Conversations in Organizations: A Complexity Approach to Change*. London: Routledge.

For a 'thought' paper which considers the role of mentoring within complex work-based situations, have a look at: Garvey, B. and Alred, G. (2001) 'Mentoring and the tolerance of complexity', *Futures*, 33(6): 519–30.

In relation to developing a grammar of understanding, look at: Kavannah, J. and Rich, M. (2018) *Truth Decay: An Initial Exploration of the Diminishing Role of Facts and Analysis in American Public Life*. Santa Monica, CA: RAND Corporation.

# 10

# E-DEVELOPMENT

## CHAPTER OVERVIEW

In the previous editions of this book we wrote, almost prophetically:

> E-development is the most future-orientated of all the chapters in this book. This is because currently there is insufficient research or experience of how to use the 'newest' of new technology within coaching and mentoring. However, there are already signs of where this might go.

Whilst it is true that there is little research as yet, COVID-19 has meant that the majority of people around the world now have substantial experience of working online in many different ways. In 2019, one of the authors was invited to offer a coaching programme in the Middle East. The original contract was for four face-to-face sessions with four online interactions in between. The face-to-face sessions were successful but the majority of the participants were reluctant to engage in the online part of the programme, stating that they prefer face-to-face. The evaluation suggested that this was for a number of reasons, for example:

concerns about confidentiality
feelings that it is 'impersonal'
technophobia
can't gauge the non-verbal cues.

Now, we believe this would not be the case. COVID-19 brought no choice if people wanted to communicate with each other. It brought new ways of working on a grand scale.

In the years running up to 2020, at various CPD events for coaches and mentors, the debate was about the challenges and problems with online working and working with people in remote areas. There were some who would simply not do it, often for the reasons cited above. Not anymore!

Electronic media is now the vehicle to make social connections between people. Together with the more established conventions of the telephone and electronic mail, additional modes of communication have appeared and are in daily use around the world as the way to continue working and communicating with colleagues and friends. Applications such as Skype, WhatsApp, Messenger, Zoom, Webex and Teams, to name but a few, have become central to social, educational and economic activity. Added to these, there are now programmes available that provide artificial intelligence based (AI) coaching and virtual reality-based coaching (VR).

Whilst COVID brought new opportunities, it also highlighted ethical and economic issues because technological hardware and internet services are not available to all. COVID has also raised questions about the gross inequalities across many different societies around the world, including in developed and sophisticated economies. Additionally, COVID lockdown has also raised mental health issues concerned with people only able to communicate for business and social reasons online.

In this chapter, we investigate the sudden and exponential grow in the use of electronic media in all aspects of human interaction but in particular its impact on coaching and mentoring. We take a critical look at this development and consider the future impact on coaching and mentoring.

## INTRODUCTION

In the third edition of this book, we started the introduction to this chapter by referencing Headlam-Wells et al. (2006: 273), which stated that e-mentoring is 'a relatively new and under-researched field, particularly from a European perspective'. In the period running up to 2020, many descriptions of e-coaching and e-mentoring were confined to talking about the use of email in an asynchronous manner to fulfil many of the functions of coaching and mentoring described thus far in this book. Our own research in this area (Megginson et al., 2003a, 2003b) was focused on schemes that use email as the predominant mechanism for the delivery of mentoring. Clearly, this has changed with COVID-19.

Our starting point is still with the concept of e-development but, like others, our experience of this is now substantial. Initially, we will use the term e-development to refer to any coaching or mentoring process where the main mode of coaching and mentoring uses electronic means to connect people. This includes telementoring, video conferencing, Zoom, Webex, Teams, Skype, text, email, various apps and other mechanisms that use the internet.

As is the case with many areas in mentoring and coaching, there is much more published research material that has come from the mentoring literature than the coaching literature and, although this is now changing, it is still reasonable to argue that many of the advantages and disadvantages of e-development apply equally to coaching initiatives as mentoring ones. This is particularly because much of the discussion and comparison of such processes are between face-to-face interventions (common to both coaching and mentoring) and electronic ones. An additional term in common use is 'virtual coaching' or 'virtual mentoring' (Geissler et al., 2014; Murphy, 2011) and, more recently, 'digital coaching' (Kanatouri, 2020), to which a similar argument applies.

## METHODOLOGY

There is little research yet on the COVID effect, so in this chapter we draw on a combination of selected pre-COVID research and the now burgeoning practitioner comments on working online in order to explore how the issues and problems raised prior to COVID have changed.

We revisit our original table on the advantages and disadvantages of e-development and revisit our taxonomy of e-development to compare and contrast pre-COVID thinking to post-COVID thinking. We present three new, post-COVID case studies and discuss how attitudes and behaviours have changed. We consider the ethical and mental health issues that COVID has thrown up in relation to technology and we also look ahead and raise some further challenging questions about the future of technology-based coaching and mentoring.

## EXPLORING THE ADVANTAGES AND DISADVANTAGES OF E-DEVELOPMENT

Ensher et al. (2003) identified three broad archetypes of e-development within coaching and mentoring:

1. Pure e-development – this is where all aspects of the coaching/mentoring are done using electronic means, including recruitment, selection, development, matching, conversation, support and evaluation.
2. Primary e-development – this is where the majority of the coaching and mentoring activity is done using electronic media but interspersed with some face-to-face meetings.
3. Supplementary e-development – this is where employing electronic media for coaching and mentoring activity is seen as a useful add-on or additional aspect of the process but is not central to the scheme or process.

During the international COVID lockdowns, pure e-development has come to the fore.

In the third edition, Table 10.1 summarized the main advantages and disadvantages of e-development based on our own research and other selected studies (see Hamilton and Scandura, 2003; Megginson et al., 2003a, 2003b; O'Neill and Harris, 2004; Headlam-Wells et al., 2006; Kennett, 2006a; Murphy, 2011).

**Table 10.1**  E-development – advantages and disadvantages

| Advantages | Disadvantages |
| --- | --- |
| Often diminishes visual status cues – for example, ethnicity, gender, age | Diminishes opportunity to pick up on one or more sources of information, such as body language, tone of voice, facial expression |
| Can break down geographical barriers to coaching and mentoring | Being easy to make, e-development relationships can also be easy to break |
| Can increase pool of available coaches and mentors | Removal of context for the coach/mentor can make it more difficult to pick up on what is not being said/shared |
| Can break down time pressures on participants – convenient, easy to access in short, more sessions | If contracting is not carefully managed, it is easier to develop unrealistic expectations about the regular relationship |
| What is said is captured, recorded and can be referred back to | If the process is predominantly electronic, experiential learning can be more difficult, which may militate against learning |

If we examine the three cases below against this table, we see a different picture emerging.

 Case Study 10.1

### SOS Mentoring: Youth Business International (YBI)

When COVID-19 hit Europe and the first countries went into lockdown, we received feedback from mentoring programme managers that mentors felt overwhelmed and unprepared to support their mentees. In response, we set up a small working group to support mentors globally and developed a webinar series to enable them to deal with the crisis and their emotional responses to it better.

At YBI we believe in face-to-face mentoring. However, that became impossible due to the meeting and travel restrictions. Remote mentoring was the only way forward. During one of our webinars a young entrepreneur from Trinidad shared her challenges and asked for one thing: 'Don't give up on us.'

Remote training and mentoring is different from face-to-face and it offered an opportunity to do something new and different. Making use of 'the mentoring way' for the training sessions for mentors, we invited young entrepreneurs to the sessions and the mentors worked on their challenges using breakout sessions and feedback. It was good to see that mentors really benefited from sharing ideas and solutions, developing a better understanding based on their own experience, making use of traditional mentoring processes remotely by using online collaboration tools, i.e. shared Google docs, Mural, Miro, Mentimeter. This allowed the mentors to tap into resources, explore online tools to work creatively with their mentees and make use of their mentoring skills that they are familiar with in a digital environment.

Making the most out of available online tools for collaboration in a mentoring context requires a significant time investment from the mentor. Delivering training sessions online for mentors and mentees asks for careful planning of the sessions by creating time and space to work jointly on a challenge and practise the key skills of mentoring.

As a rule of thumb, we divided the sessions so that there was 15 minutes of input, 30 minutes of exercise and practice and 15 minutes of feedback and Q&A. This seemed to work quite well. We also allowed additional time to check-in before the session and some time at the end of the session to debrief and reduce the feeling of being driven by technology.

Over the six sessions mentors became more confident and improved their remote mentoring skills. They enjoyed working in smaller groups on real-life challenges presented by our young entrepreneur mentees. Getting the entrepreneur in the room made the webinars real.

Remote mentoring works but it is still a challenge. Working with underserved young entrepreneurs means that access to reliable and fast internet is a challenge. In many countries data volume is still expensive and internet connection not reliable. While many online collaboration tools are available and video calls are easy to set up, we have to think about those who cannot access such tools or do not have the physical space to have an undisturbed, meaningful conversation. Making use of collaboration tools has the potential to encourage the mentor to drive the relationship and the topics to discuss. We were careful not to let this happen. Building trust and rapport is more challenging online but it is the basis of a good mentoring relationship. The intensity (depth) of a remote mentoring session can be lower and mentor and mentees may feel more dissociated. Overall, the feedback was good and the participants found the webinars helpful. Making remote mentoring work needs dedicated preparation and commitment from mentors, mentees and mentoring programme coordinators.

Joerg Schoolmann, Head of Mentoring at YBI

 Case Study 10.2

**Coaching in COVID – Being 'forced online': Is it really that different?**

How times change. My formative coaching experience was all done over the phone a decade ago – I only ever met my coach a couple of times in person at group gatherings. As a result, being coached remotely was all I really knew, so it quickly came to feel entirely normal.

*(Continued)*

Since becoming a novice coach myself, I have had sessions face-to-face in an office setting, others in coffee shops or parks, and virtually over long distances and time zones using modern technology. But the coaching medium was always a matter of choice, selecting the mutually preferred option to fit practicalities. It was not a forced arrangement. Since the advent of the coronavirus pandemic many optional choices have been removed and we have all been 'forced' online. Now we spend our working days in homebound isolation staring endlessly at computer screens and, for us older ones at least, fretting about the 're-wiring' in our minds as we experience the daily sensation of fizzing neurons. We've even acquired a new name for the fatiguing phenomenon: 'screen frazzle'. Many of my coachees are of a younger, 'tech native' generation, seemingly better accustomed to such a digital endurance trial, but they feel the effects of enforced isolation and the suddenness of their new 'VUCA' reality every bit as keenly, perhaps even more so. The oft-used terms 'resilience' and 'adaptation' have never been more apt, nor the notions of self-compassion and empathy more universally relevant. To understand more, I asked Jen, a work colleague and my newest coachee, for her thoughts about adapting to forced online coaching.

> I think it definitely helped with the coaching that I knew you before, I don't think I would have felt as comfortable otherwise online. It has made a difference through a screen but I think it's because I'm more at ease with human contact. Through a screen always feels a bit more formal. You get so much from being in the office and the spontaneous conversations you have with your immediate team. Working from home online you miss the informal chats. The sense of community you get from the office helps to give you a sense of belonging and belief in the organization. We can still get a lot of the nonverbal aspect using a video technique so I don't feel the coaching diminished, but we're not in an environment where we can spontaneously share. Sometimes that's a very helpful part of the coaching conversation. Online is more a moment in time. It's like clunk, you're on the call, you do your thing. That said, I think we're all making huge steps to make it work by ourselves and we're figuring out what does work and what doesn't work and meeting people halfway. It's a big adjustment, but we just have to make it work. Having an independent outlet to share your feelings, be challenged by questions and find constructive ways to reframe how you're feeling is an asset in these times for anyone.
>
> Gareth Owen – Director of Humanitarian Services, Save The Children

 Case Study 10.3

### Rapid Response Coaching – Rapid response coaching during the COVID-19 pandemic

At the outset of the COVID-19 pandemic in Spring 2020, a large national third sector organization approaches an organizational coach that they have been working with for some three or four years to support their senior field staff as the pandemic hits. The organization has just become one of the government's strategic partners in responding to the emerging crisis and regional managers are starting to feel the impact of increasing pressure and pace.

In conversation with the organization's deputy chief executive, an enthusiastic advocate of coaching, a 'rapid response' coaching offer was developed almost overnight in which the coach offered online coaching sessions daily for those who wanted confidential space to offload and process their thoughts. The organization was already using an online platform to great effect and it was agreed that the coaching would take place using this same platform.

The programme was slow to get started with only those managers who had already worked with the coach accessing sessions. As word spread, however, and with continued encouragement from the deputy chief executive, an increasing number of managers started to access coaching. They reported that it was extremely helpful in supporting them as they navigated the complex issues presented by the pandemic.

Once the initial emergency started to ease, a number of the managers sought repeat sessions with the coach as they valued the coaching space for their own professional and personal development. The 'rapid response' contract was re-negotiated and replaced by a more bounded programme of team and strategic development intended to build on learning from experiences during the crisis phase of the pandemic, using a group coaching approach. This new work brought together managers working all over the UK and was all provided online using the same platform as before.

Offering coaching via an online platform enables the organizational coach to offer great flexibility and geographical reach. Depending on the availability of the coach, online coaching can be scheduled to meet the needs of the client and allows coachees from all over the UK to be coached at their convenience and, in some cases, almost immediately. As the organization is already well used to working remotely, coachees are familiar with the idea of meeting online and didn't see it as a second-rate alternative to face-to-face. Many of the coachees are warehouse-based and online coaching allowed them to make contact from the field on their mobile devices, thus adding to the immediacy. Providing coaching in this 'real-time' and technologically adapted way positions it as relevant and practical for a group of managers who were new to coaching and might otherwise have been reluctant to access it. It does, however, also call for the coach to be extremely thoughtful about their professional boundaries. 'Rapid-response' flexibility does not mean unbounded access, and there is always the need to contract carefully both with the organizational client and with individual coachees to clarify the scope of the work.

Auriel Majumdar, Creative Business Coach, Supervisor and Consultant

## THOUGHTS ON CASE STUDIES 10.1–10.3

It is apparent from these three cases that going online was, in some ways at least, an emergency and rapid response. It is also clear that the participants may have engaged with some reluctance at the start. All three cases report that this was a successful initiative. If we examine these cases against Table 10.1, it would seem that human creativity and ingenuity have overcome most of the disadvantages, even in the case of experiential learning. It also appears that the advantages, as listed in Table 10.1, come through rather strongly and, although there may be those who still have concerns about online working, overall, this relatively low-tech (in the sense that the platforms are easily accessible) approach worked for the participants. It could be argued that the disadvantages were proffered pre-COVID and could be seen as a natural scepticism or versions of technophobia. Interestingly, however, and contrary to the popular belief that technophobia is age-related, in Crabbe's (2018: 27) PhD study, she cites 11 pieces of research that all state that age is not a factor in technology anxiety. She found in her research that 25% of first year business students suffered from technology anxiety. This is as much as any other age group (see Chapter 13 for more discussion on this).

However, Case study 10.1 makes an important point about accessibility and cost. In our world of inequality, it is again the underserved who may miss out due to cost, despite many of these platforms being nominally 'free', or due to their geographical location. As high-speed fibre optic is installed around the UK, there will be places that are excluded for economic or geographical reasons. There are signs that new technologies are becoming available to overcome the geography problems, but whilst this technology is in the hands of the private sector, standard economic practices will ensue, and those that can afford it will get it while those who can't won't!

This is an infrastructure, a social and economic issue and therefore it becomes a challenge for governments to grapple with as internet access has now become as important as roads, airports, ports and railways.

 **Reflective Questions**

- What do you notice in the three cases above?
- What are your conclusions on the advantages and disadvantages of working with coaching and mentoring online?
- How far did the participants in these cases develop trust with the online arrangements?

## PRACTICAL ISSUES WITH E-DEVELOPMENT

Much of our practical understanding about what works in terms of e-development and coaching and mentoring comes from research conducted at a time when coaching and mentoring were much more geared towards the pure face-to-face end of our continuum (Figure 10.1). This view is supported by Ghods and Boyce's (2013) comprehensive review of the academic and practitioner-based literature in this area. Like us, they found little evidence of e-coaching in terms of published empirical studies and relatively little on pure e-development-based initiatives. In their review of the area, they offer some suggestions to practitioners interested in using this approach in their coaching and mentoring, and these are paraphrased here. They suggest that it is important to:

1. Be aware of and clear about the context and purpose of the coaching or mentoring intervention.

2. Find ways of assessing the participants' degree of comfort with using the relevant technology that will be deployed in the scheme.

3. Have a robust pre-assessment of the availability, functionality and feasibility of the technology being used.
4. Seek to manage expectations around desired behaviours during coaching or mentoring, such as avoiding doing other tasks at the same time as being coached remotely. (Ghods and Boyce, 2013: 518-19)

These suggestions raise some important questions which will be debated in the conclusions section below and raised in the questions at the end of the chapter.

## REVISITING THE CONTINUUM FROM THE THIRD EDITION

In the third edition we wrote:

> In our view, there are relatively few pure e-development relationships but it is important to point out that it is more helpful to conceive of e-development as a continuum (see Figure 10.1). This illustrates that, while the majority of coaching and mentoring relationships fall into the supplemental category, this is a broad category. Following the logic we have put forward, nearly all coaching and mentoring relationships will fall into this category (Garvey et al., 2018).

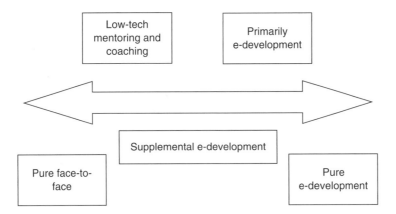

**Figure 10.1** A conceptual map of the e-development continuum

We don't believe that now this is the case. The genie is out of the bottle and with the continued presence of COVID around the world, it is likely that if people want and need coaching and mentoring support, it will come primarily through an e-development route. It is also clear that, potentially at least, many people find the new working arrangements satisfactory. For example, while Ellen (2020a) concedes that this is not the case for all, she writes: 'For many, WFH constituted a major lifestyle change, even a revelation. Sending work emails from sofas. Dumping "real" clothes for comfort. Ditching commutes. People aren't feeling any urge to return to help "Pret A Manger", or other high street businesses' (Ellen, 2020a).

However, potential mental health issues may remain in relation to e-development and interacting only online.

## MENTAL HEALTH

Some facts about mental health are quite stark. For example:

- 1 in 4 people experience mental health issues each year in the UK.
- 792 million people are affected by mental health issues worldwide.
- At any given time, 1 in 6 working-age adults have symptoms associated with mental ill health in the UK.
- Mental illness is the second-largest source of burden of disease in England.

Mental illnesses are more common, long-lasting and impactful than other health conditions.

- Mental ill health is responsible for 72 million working days lost and costs £34.9 billion each year.
- 75% of mental illness (excluding dementia) starts before age 18.

(Source: https://mhfaengland.org/mhfa-centre/research-and-evaluation/mental-health-statistics/ (accessed 5 October 2020)

Back in 1988, Zuboff argued that electronic media had the potential to isolate people from each other by replacing face-to-face contact with machines. Organizational behaviour, as a field of research, has a long history of studying these phenomena, and writers comment on how technology can lead us to become alienated from ourselves and our work (see Hislop, 2005). Additionally, as part of the narratives that surround technology, there have also been many references to the dangers of information technology as a replacement for human interaction within films and literature, from the dystopian vision of George Orwell's novel, *1984*, through to the Matrix trilogy of films. In each of these fictional and often cautionary works, the electronic machine or system represent something that militates against humanity.

As more people are working from home, the potential for alienation or a sense of isolation and the consequent mental health issues associated with disconnectedness have the potential to increase. Additional issues that have emerged in a COVID world where people are newly 'home workers' are that not everyone can cope with the challenges of home working (Ellen, 2020b). This may include prolonged periods of time sitting and looking at a screen and the lack of any suitable space in which to work uninterrupted at home.

Further, according to the Deloitte Survey (2020) (Working during Lockdown), 55% of those surveyed believe that they are more productive working from home. There are two potential sides to this coin. On one hand, working from home could, for some, lead to greater productivity, which may be a good thing. However, it could also mean that people are working longer hours at home and may also be working at different hours of the day (or night in some cases) than what they may normally work. Taken all together, there is the potential at least for these issues to impact on mental health. Individual resilience can come from 'self-esteem, self-efficiency, subjective well-being, self-determination, locus of control and support systems' (Bimrose and Hearne, 2012: 339). However, as Li et al. (2020) note, resilience may also be influenced by our institutional and occupational settings. It is here that both coaching and mentoring could play a role.

Various approaches to coaching have been shown to be helpful in supporting people with mental health issues. For example, narrative approaches have been shown to be helpful in enabling coachees to explore the narratives that influence their lives and, at times, rethinking these. Mentoring has also played its part in helping people with mental health issues as well as their carers by helping them to develop coping strategies. These services are now online and, whilst working online may be a trigger for mental health problems, it can also provide the vehicle to help people to recover. Applications like BetterPoints (Case 10.4) can also help with wellbeing issues.

We will now examine this relatively recent development in e-development.

## E-developments – High Tech

 **Case Study 10.4**

### BetterPoints by Sara Sanderson

BetterPoints™ is an incentives-led, evidence-based behaviour change platform. Users track certain activities – such as walking or eschewing their car for the bus – and accrue points that they redeem against rewards. Their tracking data are used to help local authorities and businesses improve their behaviour change interventions. The system is designed to motivate individuals to engage with the programme on offer to them, no matter what that is; it is unique in its flexibility and the range of activities that can be rewarded.

BetterPoints can be used as a standalone app or incorporated into a wider programme of behaviour change. The core elements of behaviour change models – moving from incentives to emotional engagement and personal involvement – are what BetterPoints programmes are built on. The app is a way to connect, not just to earn and track rewards, but to communicate, support and learn. The app is part of a broader behaviour change system that allows rapid customization, massive reward flexibility and sophisticated reporting. This includes a localized website, content management system, digital dashboard and API (application programming interface):

- BetterPoints is the digital currency that flows through our system. BetterPoints can be exchanged for high street rewards or donated to charity.
- The website offers many rewards and donation choices. It also provides an opportunity to earn greater rewards for increased engagement and data sharing.
- The content management system allows content customization, local, partner and event reward setting.
- The dashboard generates anonymizable reports and heat maps to understand and measure behaviour change trends.
- The API allows developers to rapidly integrate BetterPoints into other systems that want to add rewards to their programme.

A BetterPoints programme has the ability to engage participants in a particular activity or activities, which have the potential to change behaviour to support them as individuals and

*(Continued)*

also the wider community. Examples include health programmes such as weight loss, using local parks and walking; sustainable travel activities such as cycling, using public transport and car sharing, and community activities such as volunteering. BetterPoints have found the benefits of use are numerous and often surprising to the end user:

> Marie Claire, from Sheffield, told us how walking improved her mental health as well as her physical health. She set herself points goals each month to motivate her to get off the bus before her stop and earn points for walking. Marie Claire told us how she had suffered from depression during and after pregnancy and found that walking has enabled her to think differently and improved the symptoms of depression. (www.betterpoints.uk/page/work-with-us)

## DISCUSSION OF CASE

The above example is a commercial product to enable easier access to coaching principles. BetterPoints is not explicitly marketed as a coaching app but as a change programme. However, it is clear that the app has its roots in behavioural coaching models (see Chapter 5 for our discussion of such models) and is goal focused in nature. Following Ghods and Boyce (2013), the approach seems to recognize the importance of availability, functionality and feasibility of the technology in terms of its approach. Also, in Western's (2012) terms, it seems to be tapping into the concept of the 'celebrated self' in that individuals have the right to self-actualize (Maslow, 1943) and tailor their own development using filters and choices that are available when using an online system. Furthermore, the system has a built-in potential to amend and expand in terms of the domains within which it can be applied. This ability to tailor and individuate learning experiences is becoming more important. In our capacity as higher education lecturers, we have noticed a tendency for our undergraduate full-time students to expect to be treated more as individuals, even on large undergraduate business studies programmes, and to be able to sculpt their own learning experience. Perhaps this is, in part, due to their familiarity with social media, and with online on demand, streaming and content platforms (i.e. YouTube), where it is possible to construct one's own personal play/viewing list. With Higher Education becoming a more online process this is set to increase, and development systems such as BetterPoints seem to offer a way of embedding coaching principles which speak to this growing constituency of consumers of coaching.

## VIRTUAL REALITY BASED COACHING

A relatively new development in coaching has come in the form of virtual environments. Applications such as 'Second Life' and 'ProReal' are examples of desktop virtual reality (VR) applications. These allow coachees to not only express their issues but also to explore various solutions in a virtual environment. These systems often employ customizable avatars. A further development of this technology is known as 'Immersive Virtual Reality' (IVR). With the headset and hand controllers, it becomes possible to enter a virtual environment and physically interact with it in safety. Whilst there is still much to understand and explore here, it is possible that this development may suit certain types of learning situations better than others – for example, where something is physically inaccessible or there is a need to learn a practical skill. According to Kanatouri (2020), there have been a few studies and comparisons made between desktop virtual reality and Immersion. None of these have been associated with coaching or mentoring and were instead linked with educational settings in medical (Ekstrand et al., 2018), surgical (Pulijala et al., 2018), military (Stevens and Kincaid, 2015) and fire-fighting (Zhang et al., 2017). Whilst these pieces of research are not about coaching or mentoring, it is interesting to note that the results were mixed but both approaches were showing positive results, with the IVR slightly better than the VR results. There may be some future lessons for specific types of coaching and mentoring that may lend themselves to more technical solutions, for example, those that are:

- skills-based
- performance-oriented
- technically-oriented.

All of these may play a part in the coach or mentor's work.

Another variant of the VR and IVR is their ability to assist coachees through the creation of simulations. Here various common coaching issues maybe enacted and the coachee is able to play out various scenarios.

No doubt such applications will continue to be developed. However, some questions remain.

 **Reflective Questions**

- Can these forms of virtual reality replace online or face-to-face relationships?
- What might be gained and lost if they do?
- With reference to the 'theories of truth' outlined in Chapter 2, which version of truth are these developments coming from and what are the implications for human subjectivity and emotiveness?

## CONCLUSIONS

Overall, e-development remains an under-researched activity; however, we believe that this will change as the impacts of COVID are investigated and studied. The research that is published tends to be about e-mentoring schemes, and there are few published accounts of e-coaching. In a COVID world this is likely to change. The impact of e-development is now major and, in some cases, the only way of working that has yet to be fully understood in social, psychological and economic terms. Additionally, we speculate that the strong drive towards competency assessment for coaches in particular and mentors to some degree will lead to a reductionist view of the skills and abilities of the coach or mentor. This, we believe, could lead to high-tech computing with virtual reality, intelligent systems and robotic coaching and mentoring because these competency frameworks can easily translate into codable programmes (see Chapter 15).

In this chapter we have examined some of the issues and challenges around e-development pre- and post-COVID. The comparisons are stark! We can assert that e-development is here to stay and the detractors' voices have inevitably diminished. Our hope is that human creativity and ingenuity will find ways to enhance and expand our e-development opportunities.

 **Future Direction** _____

E-development is the most future-orientated of all the chapters in this book but, due to COVID, the future is now unfolding in front of us. In 2013, Ghods and Boyce reported that a research project was started in the USA to review the impact of Second Life on leadership development. In the third edition, we finished with their identified research agendas as follows:

1. There needs to be more research on what an optimal level of e-development might look like in coaching and mentoring programmes.
2. There has been relatively little work done on the impact of individual personality and working style differences and how these might impact on virtual coaching and mentoring.
3. Common coaching and mentoring strategies, particularly challenging, probing and supporting, may play out differently using e-development tools.

We could now add:

4. Research is needed on the impact on physical and mental health of homeworking and the role that coaching and mentoring could play in supporting people.
5. More research is need into more creative ways of making use of e-development.
6. Research is needed in relation to coaching and mentoring and VR and IVR.

Our predictions from the third edition have come upon us rapidly and e-development is now a central feature of organizational and individual development. It may be some time before coaching and mentoring can return to the predominantly proximal and social process we raised in the third edition. Undoubtably, innovations in software can bring some of that proximity into remote relationships, and now we believe this is set to develop further with the use of VR and IVR as well as platforms like 'Teams', 'Zoom' and 'Skype'. These technologies are now our main way of interacting and their potentials are still being explored. The human creative spirit, we believe, will find new ways to develop these to support and enhance the coaching and mentoring experience. For example, the ability to capture conversations electronically may mean that each session could have a more lasting impact because it could be returned to repeatedly. A recorded session could enable coachees and mentees to notice more nuances and patterns, and to become more self-aware more quickly.

E-development has extended into training, development and the supervision of coaches and mentors. As experienced developers of coaches and mentors, we have noticed the importance and impact of being able to see what 'it looks like'. The use of portfolios and videos in training programmes is already widespread. Through educational platforms such as Blackboard

Collaborate, it is possible to conduct coaching and mentoring supervisions on a broad scale, through the capacity of such technologies to develop protocols for linking large groups of people together across international boundaries and reduce the need for international travel – a benefit to the environment. One emerging example worthy of mention is the development of e-portfolios such as Mahara. In the UK, the Higher Education Academy is offering membership to academic colleagues through a dialogic assessment route. Here, the candidate produces evidence to meet certain criteria of their teaching experience using the Mahara e-portfolio. This is developed in conjunction with an appointed mentor who meets to facilitate the development of this e-portfolio. The portfolio is then made available to the assessor who questions the candidate on the evidence.

Therefore, not only will e-development influence the content of these helping interventions, but it will also affect the mode of delivery. The new post-COVID future will present challenges and difficulties for coaches and mentors but it will also open up another realm of possibilities for the field.

---

 ## Activity

Consider your own coaching and mentoring practice. How do you maximize interaction online? What, if any, ground rules do you create when working online? Are these any different from the ground rules in face-to-face work? How do you 'notice' the non-verbal signals your clients show you? In face-to-face coaching and mentoring, you may be able to employ various creative techniques to assist your clients. How may you do this exclusively online?

---

 ## Questions

- What is your response to the ethical issues thrown up by COVID?
- How far are recordings of sessions appropriate for your work? What are the ethical considerations here?
- What are implications of online working for organizational evaluation of the efficacy of such schemes?

---

 ## Further Reading

To consider learning and development issues related to COVID see: Li, J., Ghosh, R., Nachmias, S. (2020) 'In a time of COVID-19 pandemic, stay healthy, connected, productive, and learning: Words from the editorial team of HRDI', *Human Resource Development International*, 2(3): 199-207.

*(Continued)*

To consider innovative responses to COVID see: Bacq, S., Geoghegan, W., Josefy, M., Stevenson, R. and Williams, T.A. (2020) 'The COVID-19 Virtual Idea Blitz: Marshaling social entrepreneurship to rapidly respond to urgent grand challenges', *Business Horizons*, 63: 705–23.

To consider coaching during COVID see: Williams, H. and Palmer, S. (2020) 'Coaching during the COVID-19 pandemic: Application of the CLARITY solution-focused cognitive behavioral model', *International Journal of Coaching Psychology*, 1(2): 1–11.

# 11

# THE GOAL ASSUMPTION: A MINDSET ISSUE IN ORGANIZATIONS?

## CHAPTER OVERVIEW

This chapter examines some of the issues raised when introducing coaching or mentoring into organizations. It builds on the pragmatic discussions in Chapter 3 on creating a coaching culture and on the theoretical considerations on power in organizations in Chapter 7 and resonates with the issue of 'objectivity' in learning raised in Chapter 6. We focus on and debate the concept of 'goals' within coaching and mentoring, raising six key questions as a basis for our discussion. We discuss the belief that setting goals seems to be a taken-for-granted assumption about good practice, particularly in coaching but also in mentoring. In this chapter, we look at alternative possibilities to goals and ground these in our own research as well as other perspectives that relate to our findings. Finally, we turn to the organizational implications of these issues and show how these implications illuminate a number of key organizational practices in the use of coaching and mentoring.

## INTRODUCTION

The discourse on goals has practical implications for how individual coaching and mentoring relationships are conducted, and it also serves as a window opening a view onto many of the questions we seek to ask about organizational issues that surround the practice of coaching and mentoring.

Traditionally, there is a strongly established norm that working with goals is at the core of effective coaching. Indeed, it is embedded in the coaching process model GROW – Goals, Reality, Options, Will. The GROW model is perhaps the most widely known process model in coaching. It offers a structure to the coaching session based on establishing a goal. It is often the first process model that is taught to our students on the various coaching and mentoring programmes that we have been involved in. This practice is less firmly established in the literature of mentoring, but nonetheless it is discernible. Our research suggests that goals are not necessarily everyone's preoccupation and those that do not subscribe to the dominant discourse of goals still have a sense of direction and intent in their work and lives. For example, as raised in Chapter 15, we discuss the concept of 'purposive drift' (Oliver, 2006) or the old English word, to coddiwomple, which means to purposely go to a non-specific destination. That said, writers such as Grant (2020) in Passmore and Tee (2020) have defended goal setting in coaching conversations. We will explore these debates below.

In Chapter 7, we discuss the issue of power and in this chapter we argue that the discourse of goals is a power issue that raises some important questions about the way in which people interact and communicate within organizations.

Garvey and Alred (2001: 523) state:

> Mentoring is an activity that addresses a combination of short, medium and long term goals, and concerns primarily 'ends' as well as 'means'. Hence, mentoring is severely challenged in an unstable environment. It may become focused exclusively on short term goals, disappear or be displaced by friendships between people sharing a common difficult fate (Rigsby et al., 1998). Mentoring may slip into the 'shadow-side' (Egan, 1993) where it has the potential to be both destructive or add value.

Drawing on Kantian philosophy, in which treating people as a means to an end is morally wrong, whereas treating people as ends in themselves is morally appropriate, the above quotation stresses the social context as an influence on mentoring forms and highlights a problem associated with short-term goals – 'shadow-side' (Egan, 1993) behaviour. According to Egan, shadow-side is what happens unofficially in an organization. It is about conversations and actions behind the scenes and away from the overtly managed. We have mentioned the dominant discourse of compliance and obedience in organizations in Chapters 6, 7 and 8, and one consequence of this is shadow-side, which has the potential to influence coaching and mentoring agendas, collusion, spontaneity and authenticity in organizational life. Looking at the shadow-side in a broader societal context is also relevant. In the current COVID-19 pandemic, there have been concerns raised, in the UK, about the efficacy of subsequent lockdowns in curbing the spread of the infection, partly due to lack of compliance to isolation guidelines issued by the UK government. Here we can also see a fixation with various goals, e.g. reducing the R rate of the virus to below one, reducing infection rates per 100,000 people and, of course, daily infection and death rates. Putting aside political commentary for a moment, there is clearly a performative element to the discourse on the virus that is being developed by government and public health officials, which has been exacerbated by recent reports of vaccines for the virus. Deputy Chief Medical Officer Jonathan Van-Tam recently used the metaphor of being 'on the glide path' to resolving the challenges raised by the virus, hence playing to a destination-based discourse that seems to permeate through the government's briefings. Whilst it is beyond the scope of this chapter to comment on all goal-based discourse across society, we are simply making the point that these issues related to control and performance are not limited to organizational life. However, the organizational impact of this discourse for coaching and mentoring and goals is what we will examine in this chapter.

## METHODOLOGY

The above discussions generate for us the following organizational questions around the use of goals:

- Who dictates the agenda?
- Whose interests do the goals serve?
- Whose model of reality is privileged?
- How can the impact be measured?
- How can the usefulness of coaching and mentoring be focused?
- How can collusion be controlled?

We address these questions through the lens of goals and begin with a consideration of the place of goals in coaching and mentoring by drawing on our field data collected via a survey and four focus group discussions with over 50 coaches and mentors. We then examine the implications of this perspective for the questions listed above.

## GOALS

Most training and education bodies involved in coach or mentor development have encouraged their students to help coachees to set goals (Megginson and Clutterbuck, 2005a: Ch. 2), and we have, in the past, emphasized the importance of coaching schemes having an organizational goal (Clutterbuck and Megginson, 2005b: Ch. 4). In this, we have followed thought-leaders such as Downey (1999), Whitmore (2002), Berg and Szabó (2005) and Grant (2006a). Both Grant and Whitmore have been specific, and the others have at least implied that goal-setting is the very essence of coaching. It is probable that this view of development came from the ideology of management by objectives (MBO), advocated by Drucker (1955) in the USA and by Humble (1971) in the UK. Some consider the goal view as a dismal, reductionist, mechanical perspective that potentially corrupts behaviour, for example see Caulkin (2006) and Francis (2013). In Chapter 6, in the context of learning, we position the goal argument as an objectivity-driven perspective and offer the alternative view found in the notion of non-linear conversation.

Reflecting on our own practice as coaches and mentors, and on research into planned and emergent learning (Megginson, 1994, 1996), we wonder if the goal-setting ideology reflects lived practice and presents the whole story of conversational learning. The litera-ture on quality management is interesting on this point. Johnson and Bröms (2000), for example, confirm our concerns about targets at the organizational level. They argue that goal-free improvement led to Toyota's 20-year steady growth of profit and volumes, and that focused financial targets led the big three US auto manufacturers into constantly recurring trouble.

Another interesting perspective comes from studying mountain climbing and applying the les-sons from there to management. *Destructive Goal Pursuit: The Mount Everest Disaster* (Kayes, 2006) is an account from a business researcher of how the high-altitude expedition business can be a metaphor for the practices of some business executives in generating dependency and justifying the present suffering by fanatical devotion to a future desired state. And, of course, in the popular media on every side, there are articles about the UK government's obsession with goal-setting and targets, with warnings about how destructive and distorting of behaviour this is (for example, Caulkin, 2006; Francis, 2013).

A closer examination of academic and business journals in coaching and mentoring reveals a mixed picture. Megginson and Clutterbuck (2005b: 1), for example, state that, 'effectiveness depends on coach and learner having a common understanding of success'. Much coaching research (e.g. Parker-Wilkins, 2006) takes goals for granted and describes their achievement using measures of return on investment. Others use goals to measure skill development. An example of skill development as a measure is a study by Smither et al. (2003). This work is also interesting in that it introduces another theme, which was also found in our survey, namely that coaching gets people into the habit of setting goals. The authors found that those who were coached were more likely to set goals and that this led to improvements in their 360-degree feedback rating. Evers et al. (2006) also showed that goal-setting behaviour is an *outcome* of coaching. So, these sources indicate that coaching itself socializes coachees into the received wisdom of goal-setting. Graßmann, Schölmerich and Schermuly's (2020) meta-study examin-ing the relationship between working alliance and client outcomes across 23 coaching studies seems to lend weight to this interpretation.

There are, however, earlier sources (e.g. Ibarra and Lineback, 2005) who argue that goals are not central to transformation, but that a strong focus on an issue is what makes the differ-ence. Taking the argument a step further, Hardingham (2005: 54) says: 'The coachee may have achieved all the goals set out at the start of the relationship, but ... how can we be sure that in the long term those goals turn out to have been the right ones?'

Spreier et al. (2006) make a full-frontal attack on goal-setting. They highlight the destruc-tive potential of overachievers in a way that is reminiscent of Kayes (2006), referred to earlier. However, they see coaching as an *alternative to* goal-setting, in a way that contrasts with the lit-erature advocating goals.

One of the major critiques of goals in coaching comes from Ordóñez et al. (2009), who offer 10 questions to assess the place of goals in coaching practice:

1. Are the goals too specific?
2. Are the goals too challenging? (Especially, are the penalties for failure high?)
3. Who sets the goals? (How engaged is the goal holder? Who owns them?)
4. Is the time horizon appropriate?

5. How might goals influence risk-taking? (What does an acceptable level of risk look like?)
6. How might goals motivate unethical behaviour?
7. Can goals be idiosyncratically tailored to individual abilities and circumstances while preserving fairness?
8. How will goals influence organizational culture? (Would team goals be more effective than individual goals?)
9. Does the goal tap into intrinsic motivation?
10. What type of goal (performance or learning) is most appropriate in this context?

Western (2012: 186) challenges the goal perspective from his examination of what he calls the Managerial coaching discourse: 'Goals and targets are the "shock troops" of the Managerial Discourse in coaching – they break challenges into sizeable chunks taking a modernist managerial approach, whilst suggesting progress through a linear mindset.'

Western (2012) argues that this is a dominant discourse that positions managers and coaches as morally neutral in relation to the goals that are set (see Chapter 14 for a critical discussion on ethics in coaching and mentoring) and views the goals themselves as simply the most efficient means of achieving ends. Hence, Ordóñez et al.'s (2009) questions challenge these assumptions of moral neutrality and rationality.

David et al. (2016) have assembled a range of critical perspectives on simplistic SMART goal-setting; cumulatively these do not seek to demolish the practice of goal-setting but rather to finesse the practice to mitigate the dark side of goals while still maintaining the direction and purpose that goals can provide. This sentiment is also present in Hui, Sue-Chan and Wood's (2013) study of coaching style where they acknowledge the place that directive coaching has in relation to the achievement of direction and purpose, although they are relatively uncritical as to the place of goals in coaching. This also connects with Bozer et al.'s (2013) research into coachee characteristics for the effective sustainability of coaching. The study was conducted in Israel using an experimental research design, involving 72 coaches and 68 coachees – 29 peers and 28 supervisors were also involved in the study to ratify behavioural change in the coachees. The experimental group received coaching while the control group did not. All participants were given before and after surveys. In contrast to some of the research discussed above, the findings suggested that coachees who had a learning goal orientation and who were receptive to feedback (as evaluated by surveys) reported higher job performance as a result of coaching.

So, the jury is still out in the literature on coaching about the plusses and minuses of goals. The advocacy of goals is stronger in the books on coaching than it is in equivalent mentoring books, where there is an emphasis on the mentee's dream (Caruso, 1996). We now turn to what we discovered in our survey of coaches' and mentors' views about goal-setting.

 **Reflective Questions**

- What role do goals play in your own coaching and mentoring practice?
- To what extent do you find them useful?

# THE DARK SIDE OF GOALS - DATA

Overall, the literature still seems ambivalent on goals. As part of the previous edition of this text, we examined data from a sample of over 50 experienced coaches and mentors about their use of goals. Initially, we used a semi-structured questionnaire and then ran four focus groups to examine the data's meaning. Here, we re-examine the main themes and examples of verbatim quotes from respondents (italicized) below, in light of the current context of goals in coaching and mentoring. We focus on the respondents' reservations in an attempt to redress the widespread assumption that goals are an unequivocal good.

## Themes

### Organization issues

#### Seeking to serve organization goals at the expense of client goals

> *Goals are determined by the most powerful stakeholders, i.e. the coachee/manager/leader. They don't necessarily reflect the interests of people in the wider system (e.g. front-line workers) affected by the coachee's decisions.*

This quote is illustrative of a broader suspicion that is present within both coaching discourse (e.g. Nielsen and Norreklit, 2009) and organizational theory (see Morgan's (2006) discussion of organizations as instruments of domination).

> *Personal goals – the emergent can turn out almost unintentionally to fit with the organization.*

> *Goal-setting can be profoundly destructive of the coaching process ... but companies do need to have objectives for their investment in coaching. This is an ambiguity coaches have to manage in the contracting process.*

These two quotes illustrate the dilemmas that coaches have in terms of coaching and mentoring within an organizational context. Goal setting, as we argued earlier, can be aligned to managerialist discourse (Western, 2012). This can create dissonance for coaches, drawn to coaching and mentoring due to their humanistic roots (Rogers, 1961; Bluckert, 2006). Nevertheless, as our earlier primary data collection illustrated, coaches do recognize that for those sponsoring coaching, it is important that they are able to justify investment decisions (see Chapter 4 for a more in-depth discussion of evaluation). Hence, gaining organizational commitment often requires goals to 'appeal' to the positivist decision makers. We believe that conflict in goals between sponsor, coach and client diffuses motivation and creates confusion.

#### Setting goals as an unconsidered routine

> *Doesn't correspond with my [coaching] training but does with my non-directive/Rogerian training – and that makes a lot of sense to me.*

Again, similar to the above, coaches who experience dissonance find ways of resolving and overcoming these dilemmas. Related to this, some of our coaches pointed to the problem with goals in the sense that they are sometimes inappropriate in relation to clients' needs:

> *Goals spur for action. There are situations where 'relax', 'just be' or 'let go' are important. Not to make goals/ actions the key issue requires extra attention.*

The above quote, whilst seemingly critical of goals, also seems to echo David et al.'s (2016) call for nuanced goals. This nuance is echoed by Grant (in Passmore and Tee, 2020), who argued that goals are not monolithic entities but can be sub-divided into different types: distal and proximal goals, approach and avoidance goals, performance and learning goals, as well as higher and lower order goals. The quote below illustrates a coach's response to this recognition, in terms of nuancing the goal:

> *In this situation I frame the goal in a way that is more acceptable to them, giving them freedom to take action or not. My experience is that they outperform the 'goals'.*

This coach is pointing to the agency that they feel it is important to give to the coachee within the relationship (see Chapter 8 for a discussion of coachee agency in terms of coaching process). Below are a series of quotes which advocate for beginning the helping relationship from a position of curious 'not knowing', which they contrast with the certainty provided by a fixed, rigid goal.

> *I think that my belief that it can be very useful to start from a place of confusion, for which the only goal might be to find clarity about what the named goals might be, leads me to be confident that there is no need to have a precise goal to start off with.*
>
> *It's an unknowable world.*
>
> *Goals may distance us from connection with action/desire/focus, etc.*
>
> *Goals focus on what is perceived to be important at the expense of what is interesting.*

However, these positions might equally be challenged by arguing, as does Grant (in Passmore and Tee, 2020), that the different framing of goals in coaching might actually enable the focus on what is interesting, meaningful and emergent as opposed to the use of a precise, fixed performance goal. In this sense, we argue that, sometimes, coaches are setting up a 'straw man' when they criticize the use of goals in coaching.

Similarly, coaches can sometimes turn the critique in on themselves, as illustrated by the quote below:

> *I think goals are an aspect of my personal preferences for clarity and control. There are other ways which I fear I have not explored.*
>
> *Am I a goal junkie?*

In our work as educators in coaching and mentoring, we see this happening quite a bit as course participants develop their confidence and begin to recognize that an *exclusive* focus on 'looking for the goal' is unhelpful. It is often the case that coaches and mentors in training can become quite self-critical, following observed practice sessions, if they felt that they were unable to 'get their client' to an outcome by the end of the session. Conversely, they can feel, perhaps unduly, overly satisfied and confident in their abilities if they do. Furthermore, as they develop, we often see a pattern of more experienced coaches jettisoning what they see as rigid, goal-directed approaches in favour of more loosely coupled approaches, which have less overt structure, e.g. gestalt or Existential Coaching approaches (see Chapter 5 for a more in-depth analysis of these approaches). We argue that none of these binary positions are particularly helpful. Whilst it is probably healthy to recognize when our personal predilections for adding value dominate our helping, such an approach, when carried to its extreme, can mean that anything that is goal-related is rejected, even when it may well be what the client most needs at that time. Ironically, this can serve to push the coach to be more reductionist in their approach, even when the intent is to be the opposite!

## Client issues

As argued above, an overt use of the language of goals may well not work with some clients. The quotes below from our coaches illustrate some of the reasons why:

> Coachee may not be ready for goal-setting – resistance might slow the process down – need preparedness, maturity, confidence to set goals.

> If I am in transition, I can't commit.

> Goals don't work with people who are not in a positive place. They reinforce discomfort.

> Whenever I press someone about their goals for coaching, I find that they'll give me something because they feel obliged to meet my expectations that they should have a goal. Whatever they say at this point is almost never what they really want to work on.

It is also possible to find clients who have moved beyond goal-setting (Megginson, 1994). Nevertheless, these, again, all seem to be reasons why a careful, nuanced approach to goals is important, rather than suggesting an abandonment of them altogether. The quotes below from some of our coaches suggest a recognition of this perspective:

> Do goals act as a crutch/excuse to avoid what would be painfully beneficial?

> Perhaps the only goal is to do what is best for the client at the time. That may or may not include setting goals.

In summary, an over-application of goals and goal setting within coaching and mentoring can limit what is covered, prevent broad development of the person and prevent getting into deep and difficult issues that require a nuanced entry following lengthy dialogue. On the other hand, appropriately used and nuanced goals can provide a sense of purpose and momentum to a relationship and conversations and provide useful touchstones for review in terms of whether the coaching or mentoring is being useful to the client in terms of their development.

# ORGANIZATIONAL IMPLICATIONS OF LITERATURE AND OUR RESEARCH FINDINGS ON GOALS

As we said earlier in this chapter, the use of goals within coaching and mentoring raises broader questions about organizational life, particularly in relation to power, control and culture. The organizational issues that we address include:

- Who dictates the agenda?
- Whose interests do the goals serve?
- Whose model of reality is privileged?
- How can the impact be measured?

- How can the usefulness of coaching and mentoring be focused?
- How can collusion be controlled?

As well as providing the agenda for the ensuing discussion here, we also see these questions as useful Reflective Questions for readers to consider for themselves.

## Who dictates the agenda?

In most assignments involving an external mentor or coach, there is an organization stakeholder: the scheme organizer, a HR development executive, a member of senior management, who has a more or less clear perspective on what the coaching or mentoring is for. They may say that it is for driving change through the organization, to unleash performance, or to engender creativity in the achievement of organizational objectives. However this perspective is expressed, it can represent a significant constraint on the autonomy of helper and helped. The coaching or mentoring pair may get round this constraint, but, in that very act, they are giving attention to the issues that the promoter is interested in (see our discussion of Dirsmith et al., 1997, in Chapter 7). The ownership of the agenda is not a simple issue. Clearly, many have claims: perhaps the way forward is to raise and discuss these multiple perspectives with a view to arriving at a deeper understanding, the creation of more options for action and more rounded decision making. Fatien Diochon, Otter, Stokes and Van Hove (2019) suggest a methodology for examining this within a coaching context in order to understand the influence of these different stakeholders as well as the context within which the coaching takes place.

## Whose interests do the goals serve?

It was noticeable in our own research how often thoughtful coaches acknowledged that goals helped them to manage the ambiguity of helping. They did not necessarily see the goals as helping the client, but rather they gave the coach an opportunity to limit the discussion both to topics acceptable to power-holders and to the kind of issues which the coach felt they were resourceful in addressing. This returns us to the question of agenda and raises a challenge to the dominant discourse found in coaching and mentoring that the learner's agenda is paramount. Merrick and Stokes (2011) examined this in relation to the coach's ego. They found that, whilst espousing that the coachee's agenda was paramount and seemingly playing down their own contribution and influence, coaches were sometimes guilty of channeling the voice of the organization within the relationship and enabling it to dominate. Perhaps goals actually serve the coach's perception of their own performance? Coultas and Salas's (2015) research examined how coaches and coachees construct their identities, using information-processing theories. One of the key findings of their study was that, where coaches were seen to be more directive in terms of the goals that were set, there was seemingly less engagement with the coaching process by the coachee and less commitment to the goals set. Hence, while coaches might see goal-setting as a way of controlling the agenda, this study suggests that if, in the process of seeking to limit the coaching agenda, coaches restrict the engagement of their coachees, this tends to militate against their impact on the coachee's goal attainment in any event.

## Whose model of reality is privileged?

The practice of goal-setting can be located within a discourse of atomism (for further discussion of this process, see Chapter 13 on standards and competencies). By this we mean that goals help to divide up the world into manageable chunks. Our experience is that many clients address complex situations as a whole rather than looking through the optic of this skill or that competency. They can be socialized into changing their view to focus on competencies but only at the cost of deadening their perception of the issues and of marginalizing the relevance of the coaching or mentoring to their core concerns.

HR functions have advocated the use of competency models because they provide them with a common language for managing HR processes, from recruitment and selection through appraisal and performance management to discipline and redundancy. Another model of reality is the one embodied in SMART goal-setting, which suggests that if people have an unambiguous target then they will unquestioningly work towards it (see Grant in Passmore and Tee, 2020, for a critique of SMART goals). At a deeper level lies an almost entirely unchallenged assumption that growth is a good thing (especially economic growth), that the current situation is unacceptable and must be improved. In climate terms, this assumption has been heavily challenged, not least by Sir David Attenborough in his 2020 BBC documentary 'Extinction', where he points to the non-sustainability of the growth agenda. However, the modernist project of improvement through growth seems to be relatively unchallenged within the organizational and political spheres. Philosopher Alain de Botton (2014) argues that this is partly due to the narrow framing of what constitutes economic progress and debate via news agencies and outlets, which crowds out debates about what the aspired state is and whether it is a worthy aim to pursue.

In terms of popular culture, TV schedules are full of 'reality' programmes where goal-setting is an often explicit, essential part of the process. UK TV programmes such as *Grand Designs* and *Property Ladder* combine property development with self-development. There is much talk of bringing one's dream to life, creating an ideal home. The underlying assumption is that there is a desired or ideal state and that this can be arrived at via careful project planning and hard work.

So, the atomistic skills of competency models, the specification and compliance implied in SMART goal-setting, the growth orientation of political and economic rhetoric and the dream fulfilment of property TV programmes are all partial models of a taken-for-granted reality. In coaching and mentoring conversations, all such assumptions can usefully be deliberated on, so both parties can make conscious choices about what they want to achieve or be.

## How can impact be measured?

As we discussed in Chapter 4, evaluation tends to focus on return on investment or, failing that, on the development of specified and standardized competencies. Both these measures can be described as nomothetic rather than ideographic. By this, we mean that they are set along the same lines for everyone, rather than being crafted for and by each individual in the context of their own understanding of their unique situation. As a one-to-one relationship, coaching and mentoring seem ideally suited to ideographic measures, but they are often subordinated to a nomothetic measuring stick by other parties wishing to control what may legitimately be discussed in the privacy of the development dyad. The concept of non-linear conversations, discussed in Chapter 6, is relevant here. By hurrying, often in a straight line, towards a goal, we may miss the richness of the learning that comes from the journey itself.

## How can the usefulness of coaching and mentoring be focused?

Goals dominate the UK public sector and translate into an obsession with targets, action plans and the paraphernalia of performance management or measurement (e.g. Caulkin, 2006). They promote action which appears productive but often fails to achieve a meaningful outcome. They can be an outward form, often substituted for the thing that they are meant to be part of (for example, a well-thought-through purpose to which one is committed). Other cases of this are organizational policies or position statements (on the environment, diversity, etc.), the production of which becomes an end in itself and a substitute for having embedded a commitment to sustainability or equality in the organization. The concept of the rational and pragmatic manager raised in Chapter 3, which dominates modern business life, seems at odds with the professed qualities and behaviours outlined in Chapters 3, 6 and 8 that seem necessary for high performance in a knowledge economy:

- Adapt to change rapidly.
- Be innovative and creative.
- Be flexible.
- Learn quickly and apply your knowledge to a range of situations.
- Maintain good mental and physical health.
- Work collaboratively.
- Have 'strong and stable personalities' (Kessels, 1995).
- Be able to 'tolerate complexity' (Garvey and Alred, 2001).

Coaching and mentoring activity do seem to have the capability to make a useful contribution to these abilities, but this would require a shift from the rational pragmatic towards a more holistic and complexity-informed perspective on the workplace.

## How can collusion be controlled?

Can goals be used to sublimate, or repress, uncomfortable unconscious impulses? An example is the dean in William Golding's (1964) *The Spire*, who drives forward the construction of a cathedral with a huge spire, even though the foundations are not secure. It becomes clear in the novel that the spire is a symbol of his unadmitted lust for the builder's daughter. In terms of goals, it represents the use of outward busyness as a distraction from difficult unconscious material. Both coaches and mentors and their clients can engage in the busyness of goal-setting at the expense of digging a bit deeper into difficult issues. This tendency is reinforced by the organizational context that legitimizes goal achievement as the prevailing modus operandi. Additionally, while a goal may promote activity, it may, like the dean, distort behaviour. If a police officer has a goal for the number of arrests per month, there is more than one way to achieve it! In the recent case of George Floyd and the ensuing Black Lives Matter movement, we have seen where this sort of incentivized behaviour can lead if left unchecked and unreflected upon.

We suggest that it is not a case of being for or against goals but, rather, that goals need to be assessed honestly and with full knowledge of their complexities. A focus on goals only, without consideration of the attitudes and behaviours required to achieve them, simply invites negative collusion and distortion. Coaching and mentoring offer real and tangible opportunities for deep understanding of attitudes and behaviour, which in turn offers the prospect of:

- improved ethical decisions
- changing attitudes and behaviours
- transformational learning and development
- enhanced and informed strategic choice
- improved relationships and less conflict.

## CONCLUSIONS

The above research evidence and the literature suggest that goals are indeed an organizational mindset issue. Coaching and mentoring are pervasive phenomena in contemporary organizations. They can serve the goals of surveillance (see Chapter 7) and soft HR control (Legge, 1995; Jacques, 1996) or they have the potential to emancipate. Jacques (1996) warns against suggesting, rather simplistically, that a one-to-one relationship can free an individual from the thrall of organization and societal control; however, he does hold out the possibility of 'articulating different possibilities and implications that exist *within* these relationships' (1996: xviii). How it is played out in any particular context will depend, in part, on how the participants in coaching and mentoring activity engage with goals, purposes and issues of agency and ethics.

 ──── Future Direction ──────────────────────────

It seems to us that major organizations are still going through a phase of having the centre of the organization (often represented by the HR function) take control of the agenda for coaching. This is increasingly being done by careful, centralized selection of a pool of executive coaches, who will honour the company agenda and help clients to work towards it. Similarly, organizations are increasingly appointing more internal coaches, who are even more directly controlled in the service of the corporate agenda. It is hard to predict how long this trend will continue. It is clearly influenced by the immediate context of the pandemic but more fundamentally by the more enduring privileging of powerful stakeholders in organizations who wish to accrue the productivity and retention gains attributed to coaching and mentoring activities. We see a tension between, on the one hand, the focusing benefits of control and, on the other hand, the energizing advantages of liberation and personal responsibility.

 **Activity**

Before reading this case, put yourself in the role of an external coaching advisor. You will need to make the case to the Coaching Project board about how goals should be addressed in coaching in the organization.

In one organization we studied, there was no consensus on the place of goals. The parties involved held the following views:

The chief executive was an avid supporter of coaching and mentoring, and held a strong performance focus. For him, it was important to set goals, because otherwise there would be no way of measuring the impact of coaching and mentoring.

The Learning and Development head who was the principal designer of the scheme thought that goals should be set between the internal coach, the coachee and the coachee's line manager. She considered that goals would change during each coaching assignment and that outcomes could be explored to evaluate the scheme, but that they may not be about the same issues as the goals set in the initial tripartite discussions.

The internal coaches held mixed views. Some of them favoured setting goals at the beginning and working on them till they were achieved or abandoned. Others wanted more flexibility, but were conscious of the agenda of the coachees' line managers. Most wanted the goals to be learningful and developmental.

Line managers tended to have a view that coaching could address poor performance and wanted to set goals for their coachee.

Coachees mostly wanted their goals to be private and not to be owned (or even known) by their line manager.

The other party involved is an external advisor who is seeking to bring their own experience and wisdom to bear on the situation but also wants to use the insights from reading this chapter to weave a route through the complexities of the situation.

- What is your position on goal-setting in this context?

 **Questions**

- How would you progress this if you were in the position of an external coaching adviser?
- What is the place of goals in coaching and in mentoring and whose interests do they serve?
- What are the underlying assumptions embedded in coaching that influence the model of reality that is privileged?
- How can collusion in coaching be recognized and addressed?

 **Further Reading**

For the most comprehensive review of the issues covered in this chapter, read David, S., Clutterbuck, D. and Megginson, D. (2016) *Beyond Goals: Effective Strategies for Coaching and Mentoring*. London: *Routledge*.

On formal mentoring programmes and the importance of goal-setting within them, the following article provides an interesting empirical study on these issues: Matarazzo, K.L. and Finkelstein, L.M. (2015) 'Formal mentorships: Examining objective-setting, event participation and experience', *Journal of Managerial Psychology*, 30(6): 675–91.

# PART 3

## CONTEMPORARY ISSUES IN COACHING AND MENTORING

# 12

# SUPERVISION

## CHAPTER OVERVIEW

In this chapter, we discuss the complex issue of 'supervision' in coaching and mentoring. Although this is a relatively new term in coaching and mentoring, it has now become an established part of coaching and mentoring professional practice. We explore the reasons for the explosion of interest in supervision, particularly in the last 10 years, as well as examining the different approaches, functions and roles that supervision can play. Some argue that the demand to professionalize coaching and mentoring has created the need for supervision, and some also argue that supervision is a way of experienced coaches enhancing their income and extending their business to become the new breed of 'super coaches'. A further argument is that professional associations are using the issue of supervision to position themselves and control their members – supervision is about power. Additionally, it could be argued that supervision is a creation of therapeutic psychology and therefore it becomes an extension of the Psy Expert (Western, 2012) discourse. Others, for example paying clients, consider issues of quality control and competence. A further driver for supervision is the training or development of coaches and mentors. A central issue here is, as Gibb and Hill (2006) ask, what is the subject discipline we draw on to inform the education of coaches and mentors? They suggest:

> Understanding the nature of knowledge construction can help move us beyond a contest among favoured prescriptive models to situating theory and action in an integrative and inclusive framework for reflective practice. And it may also help guide both teachers and learners, writers and commentators, away from the traps of exchanging or mistakenly criticising unexamined preferences, and into debates where issues and matters, both critical and empirical, can be engaged with to the benefit of a broad and growing community. (2006: 74)

This chapter takes a critical look at some of these arguments.

## INTRODUCTION

Following on from our discussions on power found in Chapter 7, we can identify a dominant discourse that has emerged about coaching and mentoring supervision. One of the drivers for supervision has been the general professionalization of the industry (see Chapter 15 for a review of this). Organizations such as the European Mentoring and Coaching Council (EMCC) and the International Coach Federation (ICF) now expect their members to engage in supervision.

Related to this first point, there is a discourse, often coming from the membership of the professional bodies, about greater pressure coming from individual and corporate paying clients for coaches and mentors to be quality assured. Supervision does have the potential to offer a way in which clients can be more confident that they are dealing with a competent professional and perhaps be reassured that another professional is monitoring their work.

## METHODOLOGY

First, we discuss Berglas and Bluckert's earlier works with the question: Should a coach or mentor be 'psychologically minded' or 'psychologically trained'? We then examine two models of supervision, one drawn from the coaching literature and the other from the mentoring literature, and critically consider their application in practice. We conclude by presenting our own position on supervision and our argument for an ongoing developmental model.

## DEVELOPING COACHES AND MENTORS - KEY ISSUES

The literature on coaching specifically raises the importance of what Lee (2003) refers to as 'psychological mindedness'. Bluckert (2006: 87) describes this as 'people's capacity to reflect on themselves, others, and the relationship in between', and he suggests using an understanding and awareness of psychological processes to do this. Lying behind this point is a debate that continues within the coaching and mentoring field – do you have to be a trained psychologist, counsellor or psychotherapist to be effective and safe as a coach or mentor? This debate seems critical to the whole area because it determines the approach to and content of coaches' and mentors' education. An interesting take on the other side of this issue is Filipczak (1998: 34), who believes that psychological training for coaches is '*potentially harmful*'. He argues that this is because a psychologist may not have any understanding of the business environment and they may have a tendency to see a business '*as another dysfunctional family that needs to be fixed*' (Filipczak, 1998: 34). This reminds us that the context of the coaching or mentoring plays an agentic role (Stokes et al., 2020)

Berglas (2002) advocates that coaching, in particular, is something that should only be done by trained therapists. However, his position does not seem so clear-cut, as the quotation below illustrates:

My misgivings about executive coaching are not a clarion call for psychotherapy and psychoanalysis. Psychoanalysis, in particular, does not – and will never – suit everybody. Nor is it up to corporate leaders to ensure that all employees deal with their personal demons. My goal, as somebody with a doctorate in psychology as well as serving as an executive coach, is to heighten awareness of the difference between a problem executive, who can be trained to function effectively, and an executive with a problem who can best be helped by psychotherapy. (2002: 89)

Although Berglas is a coach himself, he is nevertheless deeply suspicious of those who coach without an understanding of psychological issues. In particular, he argues that such coaches, without an understanding of psychology, have a narrow focus on behavioural issues and find difficulty in recognizing the value of other perspectives. While Bluckert's (2006: 92) tone is more measured, he too is a strong advocate of the psychologically minded trained coach, as the following quotation suggests:

In the near future I believe we will see greater attention to the psychological development of the coach as a response to the growing awareness and acceptance in the field that psychological mindedness is one of the key higher-level proficiencies of executive coaching.

In fact, it is difficult to find anyone in the literature who will overtly demur from the view that it is helpful and probably essential that coaches and mentors have some awareness of psychological processes. Thus Western's (2012) Psy Expert discourse has become a dominant one and Ridler (2016) found that 64% of those surveyed believe that 'coaching supervisors should possess a high level of psychological training and development' (p. 50). Hence, the onus is shifting onto supervisors and not coaches, which is perhaps evidence of the development of the 'super coach'. However, the key questions appear to be: how much is enough and who should decide?

Bluckert's (2006) approach to being psychologically minded as part of coaching is to recognize that a key part of this is being aware of oneself and one's emotions so that they might be employed to help stimulate greater awareness in the client. Interestingly, this ties in with Grant's (2007) research into the link between emotional intelligence and coaching skills training. In this study, Grant (2007: 258) claims that coaching skills 'are inextricably related to emotional intelligence', as 'to move through the goal-focussed coaching cycle, individuals have to be able to regulate their thoughts, feelings and behaviours so that they can best achieve their goals'. Grant's (2007) study was also interesting because it shed some light on coach training. He compared the outcomes of two modes of coaching training: one over 13 weeks and the other over two days with a three-week break in the middle. He summarizes his conclusions below:

The main implications of these findings are that, whilst short, intensive programmes may improve participants' goal focused coaching skills, organizations seeking to deepen the impact of 'Manager as Coach' training programmes and improve the underlying emotional intelligence of participants, should use a spaced learning approach over a number of weeks. (2007: 257)

It would seem that a more extended learning experience helps coaches make the necessary connections with their own thoughts, feelings and behaviours, but also that this is possible to achieve by following a 'rigorous process of reflection, questioning and mutual support within an adult learning context' (Grant, 2007: 257).

This seems to fit with Bluckert's (2006) conclusions drawn from his own practice. He makes an important distinction between psychological training and psychological mindedness: 'Psychological training in an academic sense does not necessarily generate psychological mindedness as it may hardly touch on the awareness development of the student' (2006: 92).

While it is difficult to argue against the view that an awareness of psychological processes and one's own responses are important, psychological training – even that which is psychologically minded in nature – need not be the only route to self-awareness. As raised in Chapter 1, self-awareness, according to Caraccioli (1760), is achieved through a process of:

- Observation, leading to ...
- Toleration, leading to ...
- Reprimands, leading to ...
- Correction, leading to ...
- Friendship, leading to ...
- Awareness.

Returning to current times, Du Toit (2006: 53) suggests, 'In order to develop self-awareness the individual must have access to honest feedback.' And Garvey (2006) suggests that self-awareness is developed through a thorough exploration of an individual's story.

Our own approach to mentor and coach development has several strong connections with Bluckert (2006) and Grant (2006a), but perhaps has the strongest connection with Hawkins and Smith's (2006: 92) approach.

As coaches and mentors ourselves, as well as experienced higher-education lecturers, our philosophy is summarized using a slightly adapted, condensed form of Hawkins and Smith's (2006) core principles as follows:

1. Focus on self-awareness using experiential learning processes.
2. Teach theory only when experiential learning has started.
3. Learn iteratively by raising learner awareness of development need and quickly have an opportunity to put it into practice.
4. Use intensive feedback in small groups where learners work with each other as peers.
5. Teach basic skills in a way that brings them to life – demonstrations, illustrative stories, engagement and learners reflecting on their own lived experience.
6. Do real play – using real unsolved issues for learners – not role-play, which uses scenarios of case study issues from the past.
7. Have long periods of practice (which are supervised) that follow on from initial training in which learners establish their own connections between self-awareness, skills, theory and their experience of practice.
8. Challenge existing patterns of behaviour that may be unhelpful when coaching and mentoring.
9. Have a genuine belief in the learner's potential and ability to learn, and recognize that the learner's ability may exceed that of the teacher.

Like Hawkins and Smith (2006), our view of adult development recognizes that following a predominantly didactic model of teaching runs the risk of alienating experienced people who feel that their experience is denied. In addition, our view is that this approach is compatible with

Bluckert's (2006) perspective on psychological mindedness. We do not believe that this approach is exclusive to those with a psychology, therapy or psychotherapy background. In addition, we also argue, in line with Filipczak's (1998) argument, that it is important to be 'organizationally minded'. By that, we mean that it is important to recognize the contribution that base disciplines like philosophy and, in particular, sociology, play in coaching and mentoring. As much (though not all) of the coaching and mentoring work we do is located within an organizational context, having an understanding of sociological concepts that underpin organizations, groups and teams, e.g. power, culture, social structure, systems, seems critical to us.

Now that we have established some core principles and ideas around development, we move on to the issue of supervision.

## WHAT IS SUPERVISION?

As we observe in Chapter 1, Caraccioli (1760) believed that a mentor needs to 'form the heart at the same time that they enrich the mind' (1760: vii), suggesting an understanding of emotional intelligence; he also associated mentoring with a form of therapy long before such ideas were in the public domain when he stated: 'Melancholy, so common a complaint with the most voluptuous has no effect on the man who possesses reflection' (vs 35, 88). In a direct early reference to supervision in mentoring, Caraccioli (1760) believed that a mentor needs a more experienced mentor to work with. However, as Bluckert (2006) points out, although supervision has a strong tradition within the helping professions (see Hawkins and Shohet, 2006, for a review of this literature), it does not really feature in the coaching and mentoring literature until after the year 2000.

Hawkins and Smith's (2006: 147) definition of supervision is:

> the process by which a coach/mentor/consultant with the help of a supervisor, who is not working directly with the client, can attend to understanding better both the client system and themselves as part of the client-coach/mentor system, and transform their work.

From his mentoring research angle, Barrett (2002: 279) considers supervision as being based 'on the processes that occur between mentor and mentee during an interaction'. Bluckert (2006: 109), on the other hand, considers coaching supervision as being a 'time and place to reflect on one's work either with a senior colleague, in a led group, or with a number of peers', with the purpose of helping 'to make greater sense of difficult and complex work assignments and to gain more clarity going forward'.

While there are differences in terms of emphasis and focus between these two positions, there does seem to be a consensus that coaching and mentoring supervision is a process that has its primary focus on the supervisee's practice as a coach or mentor.

Bachkirova, Jackson, Hennig and Moral (2020) conduct a very useful systematic literature review of supervision in coaching. They distil a large number of sources down to 68 sources which meet their selection criteria for analysis. In this review, they induct four main themes out of this synthesis, that are present in this body of literature:

1. Clarifying the concept of coaching supervision – the studies examine definitions and functions of supervision (we will explore this further in this chapter).
2. The state of theoretical development demonstrated in the literature – they characterize the level and quality of theoretical underpinnings in the studies, exploring issues such as differing perspectives from other disciplines, relational dynamics particular to coaching supervision, mode of supervision as well as meta-models and frameworks.
3. The value attributed to supervision – they explore the benefits of supervision and the research methodologies used to examine those benefits.
4. The nature of the current use of supervision in the field – the challenges and applications of coaching supervision are examined.

From each of these themes, they generate a series of research questions/studies that they argue should be explored as well as offering some suggested methodologies that might be used to explore them. In essence, though, they argue for more research into coaching supervision so as to overcome criticisms of the current state of coaching supervision writings, which include that lack of empirical studies itself but also argue that the body of work is unevenly distributed across contexts and not sufficiently well integrated.

Back in 2011, Gray and Jackson (2011: 19–20) first attempted to deal with the integration issue by developing what they referred to as a meta-model of supervision, which brings these different strands together (although Bachkirova et al. (2020) may argue this is more characteristic of theme 1 above). They suggest that supervision has the following features:

1. It 'involves facilitating the development of the supervisee in terms of confidence, motivation and knowledge'.
2. It is 'complex and includes paying attention to what is happening both between the supervisor and the supervisee and the supervisee's relationship with the client'.
3. That 'the supervisee's development is not necessarily linear and can involve progressing at different speeds for different processes and functions' and that it can involve regression.
4. Teaching 'is at the heart of the relationship for both supervisor and supervisee'.
5. It is 'influenced by social and organizational contexts within which it occurs'.

As we explore the two models and the case study, we will see these features recurring throughout.

For our part, we define supervision as a process whereby the supervisee (who is a practising coach or mentor) is helped to make greater sense of their coaching and mentoring practice, with the goal of improving their practice as a result. However, we also acknowledge the intuitive appeal of de Haan's (2012) metaphor of supervision as being about two rather frightened people in a room who have no idea what is going to happen next!

 **Reflective Questions** ────────────────

- What role does supervision play in your personal practice?
- How much does the context of the coaching/mentoring practice matter for you, in supervision?

# HAWKINS AND SHOHET'S (2006) MODEL OF SUPERVISION

Perhaps Hawkins and Shohet (2006, 2011) offer the most useful and most widely known model of supervision. This is also examined in Hawkins and Smith (2006) (see Figure 12.1). In this model, known as the seven-eyed model of supervision, there are seven process areas to help focus the supervisor. We summarize these below:

1. The coachee/mentee – known as 'the client' in this model. Here, the supervisor helps the supervisee to focus on the client and to pay attention to what they bring. As Hawkins and Smith (2006: 162) put it, it 'is almost impossible to do quality supervision on a particular client until that client has – metaphorically speaking – entered the room'.

2. The interventions and strategies used by the supervisee when with the client – here, the supervisee is encouraged to focus on the interventions they have made with the client, in terms of tools, techniques, models and frameworks, and is invited to consider other options.

3. The relationship between the supervisee and the client – in this mode, the supervisee is encouraged to reflect on their relationship and invited to consider why the client has chosen to work with them and what they see the relationship as being like. This starts to reveal the transference and parallel processing issues that might be playing out in the relationship – Hawkins and Smith suggest that the interplay between modes 3 and 4 is important, for this reason. Also, the supervisor brings 'the relationship' as another stakeholder to the conversation, thus encouraging the supervisee to pay attention to the dynamic between themselves and the client.

4. The supervisee – with this 'eye', the supervisee is prompted to reflect on their own feelings and issues and how the client affects them. Key to this process is the supervisee's countertransference (see Chapter 7) – the supervisor plays an important role in helping the supervisee to become more self-aware and therefore enables them to make choices about how to respond to the client.

5. The relationship between the supervisor and the supervisee – the supervisor uses the supervisory relationship itself as data for shedding light on how the supervisee and the client might be relating to each other. In particular, the supervisor helps the supervisee to recognize parallel processing within the supervisory relationships, which mirrors the dynamic within the coaching/mentoring relationship with the client.

6. The supervisor – in this mode, the supervisor uses their own feelings and responses to the supervisee as data. In doing so, the supervisor is (a) offering feedback to the supervisee based on what they feel they are 'picking up' from the supervisee, so as to give additional perspective for the supervisee to explore, and (b) modelling a process that the supervisee may try with their clients.

7. The wider context in which the work happens – includes the social, cultural, political and economic worlds of influence, as well as professional codes and ethics, organizational requirements and constrictions and relationships with other organizations involved. Here, the supervisor is helping the supervisee to acknowledge that there are a number of wider contexts and stakeholders to consider.

This model shows that however experienced a coach or mentor may be, there is need for another individual to keep an eye (or seven!) on the factors that influence the coach/mentor's ability to help others.

Despite this, we feel it is also important for a coach, mentor or supervisor to have some understanding and awareness of pertinent organizational and sociological constructs in order to frame these 'eyes' appropriately.

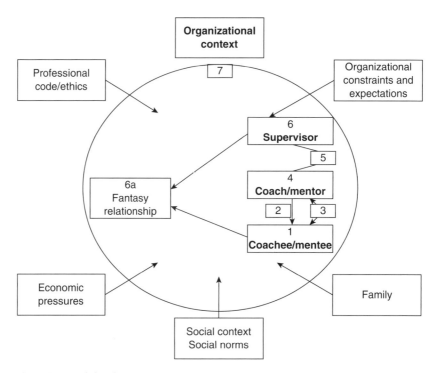

**Figure 12.1** Supervision in the organizational context

 ——— Case Study 12.1 ———————————————

### The supervisor's dilemma

A supervisor was working with a supervisee, using the seven-eyed approach. The supervisee was a practising independent coach with a background in social work (the seventh 'eye') and was very comfortable describing the client (the first 'eye') due to her prior professional training. The picture she painted of the client was one of a person who struggled to make decisions and take responsibility for her own choices in her life and work. Indeed, the supervisee reported that this client had been brought to coaching by her husband and he had even lingered at the start of the first session to ensure that she stayed the course! The client, in the first two or three sessions of the intervention, was exhibiting signs of developing a dependency relationship (the third 'eye') with the supervisee.

She would often press the supervisee for her advice and be reluctant to commit to even discussing her options without trying to discern what the supervisee thought. In supervision, the supervisee expressed some impatience with the client about this because she (the supervisee) felt she had spent a lot of time and effort contracting with the client about the coaching itself. She felt that it 'should be clear' to the client that the coaching was not about advice giving and developing a dependency relationship but about a deeper, more 'non-directive' approach where the coachee 'would find their own voice' (the second 'eye'). However, her experience of the client was the opposite, with the client seeming to prefer her coach's voice to her own.

At this point in the supervision, events took an interesting turn. The supervisee, noticing that she was feeling deeply frustrated (the fourth 'eye'), turned to the supervisor and said 'I'm really stuck. What do you think I should do?' At this point, the supervisor was faced with a dilemma. What they were noticing (the sixth 'eye') was that part of them wanted to give some advice to the supervisee in a desire to be helpful. Another part of them wanted to remind the supervisee that the focus of the work was about her and her work and was not about asking for advice from the supervisor. However, the supervisor recognized that these responses were data that could be used to help the supervisee with their coaching. Instead of advice giving or re-enforcing the psychological contract, the supervisor chose, instead, to use the supervisory relationship itself (the fifth 'eye') to examine the parallel process that was occurring. The supervisor said to the supervisee, 'I notice that our relationship could move in the same direction as yours with your client.'

## Questions from the Case

1. How do you think the conversation could proceed from here?
2. How might the supervisee use this observation in her own practice?
3. What else do you notice in this case study?

---

## THE MERRICK AND STOKES (2003) MODEL

This part of the chapter is adapted from an article by Merrick and Stokes (2003). In this article, they draw on their experience of designing and developing mentoring schemes to offer a framework for mentor development. Like Hawkins and Smith's (2006: 139) framework, this connects supervision needs with various developmental stages for the mentor. Hawkins and Shohet's (2006) work is primarily written for those working in the helping professions, whereas Merrick and Stokes (2003) write from a mentoring practitioner perspective, with a scheme design audience in mind.

Merrick and Stokes's (2003) categories for mentor development are:

- novice mentor
- developing mentor
- reflective mentor
- reflexive mentor.

We consider these in relation to mentor development and the implications for supervision.

## Novice mentor

A novice mentor is someone who may be new to mentoring, with little or no experience of mentoring in practice. This does not mean that they are untrained or unskilled, but that they have relatively little experience as a mentor of participating in a live, dynamic human mentoring process. They may have been mentored themselves or used mentoring skills in their work but may not have thought of themselves as a mentor before. As a result, such a mentor may have development needs that are different and distinct from more experienced mentors. For instance, they will need to become familiar with the protocols, aims and objectives of mentoring within their particular scheme. They will therefore need help and support in defining or refining their approach so that it is consistent with their scheme. Clearly, they will also need help in gaining access to the various existing theories and models of mentoring.

## Implications for supervision

At the novice mentor stage, a supervisor needs to ensure that the mentoring is operating congruently with the aims of the scheme. This closely resembles Hawkins and Shohet's (2006) management/normative function of supervision.

This is a quality assurance or auditing function and it has two main purposes:

- To check the mentor's ability as a mentor, i.e. that they are using the key skills of acceptance, empathy and congruence with their mentee.

- To bestow what Feltham (1995) calls the 'aura of professionalism' in order to ensure scheme credibility in the eyes of its sponsors.

Within organizational schemes, where supervisors may be organizational members, this affords the supervisor the opportunity to intervene to avoid any damage to the mentee as well as to the reputation of the programme. This intervention is likely to be indirect, by helping the mentor to rectify or repair any damage done. It may also be direct, where the supervisor may need to intervene personally – this is where the role of supervisor and of scheme organizer may be conflated. This conflation can create difficulties and a conflict of interests (see Megginson and Stokes, 2004, for a discussion of this).

## Developing mentor

In one sense, all mentors could be developing and continuing to learn. However, in this context, the developing mentor is someone who has some experience of mentoring 'under their belt' and understands the 'rules' within their particular context. They can employ a well-known mentoring model or process (e.g. Kram, 1983) that they can use within a mentoring conversation and they will have an awareness of some of the skills and behaviours required by an effective mentor. However, this knowledge and repertoire of behaviours is basic and their comfort zone as a mentor is still fairly limited and confined to a small repertoire of behaviours.

## Implications for supervision

At this stage, the developing mentor needs to start to identify other ways of mentoring to expand their effectiveness as a mentor. The supervisor may therefore need to pay more attention to supporting the mentor in their process development and in recognizing the dynamics within a mentoring relationship. This closely resembles what Hawkins and Shohet (2006) refer to as the educative/formative supervision role. The supervisor will need to model some of the behaviours involved to help the mentor acquire these skills and may indeed coach them specifically in these areas where appropriate.

At this stage, the supervisor needs to support the mentor to identify a mentoring process that is effective for them. The supervisor needs to help the mentor to understand the different phases and stages of the process and the application of the necessary skills.

Gaining an awareness of both the boundaries of the relationship and the skills needed is particularly important for the developing mentor. Mentors who are able to participate in a comprehensive programme of mentor training may have gained much of this knowledge on the programme, but not necessarily had the time for practice. They may be in the situation of practising their skills in their real-life mentoring relationship. Alternatively, perhaps, they may have received minimal training to become a mentor initially. The supervisor needs to explore these development needs with their supervisee and help them to identify ways of fulfilling them.

The meetings may be part of a course of prearranged meetings and the supervisor is looking for a level of development, which might be recorded formally.

## Reflective mentor

The reflective mentor is someone who has a fair amount of experience as a mentor and has successfully extended their repertoire of skills beyond that of the developing mentor.

They are probably aware of most of the different approaches to mentoring theory and practice. They may have developed an awareness of context and their own identity as a mentor within the mentoring community. They now have both the experience of mentoring and of supervision so they can critically reflect on their own practice to develop their skills and understanding of different mentoring approaches. They may draw insights from other mentors, their supervisor and other helping professions.

This process may have begun within the developing mentor stage but at this stage it becomes central. It is distinct from the developing stage in that the reflective mentor would have had the chance to reflect on some of their experience as a mentor through the lens of their supervisory discussions. Hence, the reflective mentor is someone who has begun to take some responsibility for thinking about and directing their own development as a mentor. They may also have started to incorporate ideas developed within supervision and elsewhere into their mentoring practice.

## Implications for supervision

One of the important aspects of effective supervision for the reflective mentor is that the supervisor is able to demonstrate empathic attention and insightful reflection to the mentor.

Cox (2002: 141) writes: 'What I want from my supervisor is intelligent listening, experienced reflection, realistic mirroring, perceptive confrontation and a sense of personal warmth and humour.' This development function is a combination of Hawkins and Shohet's (2006) role of educative/formative support. It is through reflecting on and exploring the supervisee's work that the supervisor focuses on developing the skills, understanding and ability of the mentor they are supporting. Therefore, there are two changes in focus here. First, the supervisor is focusing more on the mentee and the 'work' of the mentor, while at the same time encouraging the mentor to begin to recognize how the mentor's own experiences (including those as a mentor/supervisee) are beginning to impact on their mentoring work. Second, the supervisor is supporting the mentor to develop their own internal, critically reflexive capacity.

## Reflexive mentor

The reflexive mentor is someone with considerable experience as a mentor and who may also be a mentor supervisor. They have developed sufficient self-awareness, with the help of their supervisor, to reflect critically on their own practice and to identify areas for their own development, as well as being more competent in detecting and using their own feelings within mentoring conversations to inform their practice. They are, however, astute enough to recognize that there is a need to continue with their development and to understand the dangers that lie in complacency and a rigid approach. In this sense, the reflexive mentor needs supervision to assure the quality of their helping skills and to prevent blind spots or damage being done through arrogant or careless interventions.

## Implications for supervision

For the effective supervision of a reflexive mentor, the supervisor would need to be a highly competent, flexible and experienced mentor themselves, as the range of supervision required might range from very gentle support when a problem occurs, as a 'spot mentoring' transaction, to adopting a strong critical position in order to challenge the potentially complacent supervisee. As a result, the frequency of supervision may differ, depending on the needs of the supervisee. For instance, Feltham (1995) refers to a highly experienced psychotherapist, Arnold Lazarus, who does not use regular supervision:

> I probably ask for help or input from others mainly when I run into barriers or obstacles or when I feel out of my depth. If things are running along smoothly, why bother, but if there are some problems that make you feel lost or bewildered, or when you feel that you are doing OK, but could do better, why not bring it to the attention of somebody else, and discuss the issues? (Dryden, 1991: 81)

 **Reflective Questions**

- How closely do you see the framework fitting with where you are as a coach/mentor?
- What would you say were your particular needs as a supervisee?

# DISCUSSION

As suggested above, the models presented offer two different approaches to the idea of supervision. Hawkins and Shohet's (2006) approach has its roots in models of psychotherapy and counselling and presents the supervisory process as a complex and sophisticated one. Merrick and Stokes's (2003) approach draws on Hawkins and Shohet's previous iterations of their model but seeks to develop supervision against four archetypes of mentors, with different support needs due to their different stages of development. Hawkins and Shohet's model is particularly helpful in illuminating the supervisory process for the supervisor, in that it gives a conceptual framework to guide supervisory practice. Merrick and Stokes's (2003) model, reminiscent of situational leadership models, may be more useful to the supervisee and to the scheme organizer in understanding what sort of support needs (and indeed what sort of supervisor) might be helpful at certain points in the mentor or coach's development.

We have not yet explored in any depth the appropriateness of the term 'supervision' in the context of mentors and coaches. Hawkins and Shohet (2006) acknowledge that many discourses inform the word supervision, for example psychotherapy, counselling, education, social work and management.

Earlier in this chapter, we commented on Bluckert's (2006) observation of the dearth of supervision discourse prior to 2000. It is almost as if, as coaching and mentoring moved towards professionalization, there came with this a need to delineate clear channels of progression and development for coaches and mentors. Furthermore, within this profession, more experienced coaches and mentors needed to differentiate themselves from less experienced coaches and mentors and to create a role for themselves as senior members of such a profession. Unfortunately, this meant that there was a lack of a framework and no language to achieve this, thus leaving a gap in the coaching and mentoring discourse. It seemed in the earlier parts of the decade as if this gap in the discourse had been filled by the already established discourse and practices of psychotherapy and counselling. However, with edited books written by Bachkirova et al. (2011) and Passmore (2011) on supervision, we are starting to see coaches and coaching discourse developing to fill this space. Also, de Haan (2012) has drawn our attention to the role of supervisor as nurse (taking care of the supervisee), developer (working with a supervisee to develop new strategies and techniques) and gatekeeper (helping maintain professional standards and ethical codes). We believe that these discourses provide a useful way of understanding and working with coaches, mentors and their development.

However, Garvey (2011) argues that much of this discourse is derived from a sloganizing statement made in 2000 in an article by Morris and Tarpley in *Fortune* where the expression 'Wild West of coaching' was used. There then followed an article in the *Harvard Business Review* by Sherman and Freas called 'The Wild West of Executive Coaching', published in 2004 to reinforce this view. Garvey (2011) argues that this slogan has been the driving force behind the whole professionalization agenda (see also Chapter 15) and that this has led to power bases being established by professional groupings, not only to join people together but to keep the 'wild' people out! This is actually a very serious point. There is a risk. When a discourse becomes dominant within a social group, its members may cease to challenge or question it, and this can blind those members to alternative perspectives. Bertrand Russell (2009: 204), the philosopher, wrote, 'The stupid are cocksure and the intelligent are full of doubt' and 'Everything is vague to a degree you do not realize till you have tried to make it precise' (Russell, 1998: 38). The professionalization discourse seems to be moving down the 'make it precise route' relentlessly and is intolerant of the complexity of coaching in particular.

There is a possible explanation for this found in sociological thinking. Shearing (2001) argues that globalization has also brought us 'neofeudalism' where power is vested in the few and wielded over the many. The power comes from a centralization of wealth in the hands of a few. Garvey (2014) argues that this has created a new and rather unsavoury leadership model – the powerful and greedy model of leadership; consider the recent example of the collapse of the retail giant British Home Stores where its former owner, Sir Philip Green, was accused of representing the 'unacceptable face of capitalism' and overseeing the 'systematic plunder' of a company (Guardian online, 2016). Lasch (1995) suggests that in the global economy these new elites have abdicated fundamental social or political responsibility, that they have dubious loyalties and temporary commitment to the highest bidder. These leaders control the dominant discourse in their influence on governments and social and economic policy. They threaten to 'leave' the country if government doesn't pander to them and they call for deregulation and freedom at the same time as imposing greater regulation of those they control (Saul, 1997).

In the workplace, the controlling and neofeudalistic discourse seeps through into the increasing employment of normative frameworks or rules and surveillance in the form of appraisal systems, performance management systems, 360-degree feedback, the use of psychometrics, target setting, zero-hours contracting and performance-related pay – 'scientific' method applied to organizational life has become a dominant preoccupation of neofeudalistic managers. The theory of surveillance is straightforward. As Foucault (1979: 202–3) stated:

> He who is subjected to a field of visibility, and who knows it, assumes responsibility for the constraints of power; he makes them play spontaneously upon himself; he inscribes in himself the power relation in which he simultaneously plays both roles; he becomes the principle of his own subjection.

It could therefore be argued that supervision may be an attempt by the professional associations for coaching and, in the case of the EMCC, mentoring, to extract compliance or normalization from the membership to reassure the purchasers of coaching and strengthen the position of the association in the marketplace.

Despite these arguments, Ridler (2016), in the sixth report, notes that 88% of those surveyed believe that supervision is a 'fundamental requirement for any professional executive coach' (p. 50). However, 72% of those surveyed believe in group rather than individual supervision (32%), and one-third of those surveyed believe that 'A coach's individual accreditation with a professional body reassures me they are in regular supervision' (p. 50). It seems that despite the seemingly strong desire to have some form of supervision for coaches, there is little consensus on the form it should take. The problem with 'supervision' as a term is that, like coachee and mentee, it is passive. This militates against the learner as active participant in a learning dialogue at the same time as maximizing the power of the supervisor in relation to the supervisee. It plays down the possibility that the supervisor is learning as much as, *if not more than*, the supervisee and gives privilege to the all-seeing eye of the supervisor, particularly in Hawkins and Shohet's (2006) model. We can see how the normalizing of supervision via such mechanisms as coaching and mentoring professional bodies (see Chapter 13) and by other professional bodies such as the Chartered Institute of Personnel and Development (CIPD) in the UK (see Hawkins and Schwenk's (2006) work on this) has almost given a moral authority to those who are being supervised. In less than a decade, we appear to have gone from a place where supervision was hardly mentioned to a place where those who do not have supervision are deemed unprofessional.

Given that we have used the work of Foucault and touched on discourse analysis already (Chapter 7), it is tempting to draw power-related parallels again here. Gutting (2005: 72) argues that Foucault was critical of the modern psychiatric profession's rejection of the mad on moral grounds. He suggests that Foucault saw madness as a human alternative to normality, or even a meaningful challenge to what was reasonable or normal, and there was a 'conceptual exclusion of the mad from the human world'. Are we seeing the beginning of a similar totalizing discourse in coaching and mentoring, where those who are not supervised are deemed 'unfit to practise' and morally inferior to those who are 'responsible' enough to be supervised on their practice?

Hawkins and Schwenk's (2006) CIPD-commissioned research suggested that supervision practice lagged behind supervision rhetoric. Despite over 80% of respondents saying that supervision was important, the following quotation is surprising (Hawkins and Schwenk, 2006: 1): 'A striking revelation, though, is that far fewer (less than half) of all coaches actually do have coaching supervision and less than a quarter of organizations that use coaches provide any form of supervision for them.'

What does this say about supervision at that time? Hawkins and Schwenk's (2006) study was only one small-scale study commissioned by a professional body and it therefore cannot claim to represent the whole coaching and mentoring community. Nevertheless, it seemed to provide some support for the argument for the disciplinary power existing within the coaching and mentoring community where members have a clear sense of what 'ought' to be done. However, what is not clear is why there is a disparity between espoused theory and theory in use (Argryris and Schön, 1996) in the supervision discourse. Looking at the later work done by Stern and Stout-Rostron (2013), there does not seem to have been the anticipated upsurge in research activity in this area. The authors examined journal articles published between 2008 and 2012 and included those that were English-language, peer-reviewed articles that focused on coaching research. The research needed to be based on primary data. Using that set of criteria, there were only five peer-reviewed journal articles published on supervision in this period, which may suggest that not as much supervision is happening as was anticipated. However, de Haan (2016) finds in his small study that coaches tend towards one hour of supervision for every 35 coaching sessions and that supervisees are reasonably satisfied with their supervision. Despite this, a small number expressed concerns about trust, particularly around commercial sensitivities, suggesting that there is a potential power issue in the supervisory relationship. Interestingly, de Haan noted that there was little difference between those taking individual supervision and those taking group supervision in terms of trust and satisfaction. He concludes by arguing that 'Another factor that may play a big role here is that many coaches pay themselves or apply for budget to pay their supervisors, so that ordinary market forces play a role in making the supervision safer and dependable for them' (p. 3). Is this capitalism controlling the market, perhaps?

We acknowledge that supervision may be on the increase, particularly group supervision (see Mann, 2020). But we still maintain the view that there is a lack of understanding about what supervision is and how it applies to coaching and, particularly, mentoring (see Merrick and

Stokes, 2021). We also maintain that critical reflection is central to a coach/mentor's development and that this may be achieved in various ways which do not look like supervision, as articulated by the Psy Expert (Western, 2012) discourse and professional associations who have employed this discourse in their models. In our experience, coaches and mentors use many mechanisms to reflect on their practice in order to gain new insights and to improve their skills. These include:

- academic courses
- short courses
- action learning sets and Open Space events
- scheme gatherings and get-togethers
- action research or participating in evaluation exercises
- group supervision.

We are not suggesting that all or even any of these are necessarily equivalent to one-to-one supervision or equal in terms of depth and breadth of coverage. However, we are suggesting that it may be premature to suggest that people are not engaging in reflection on their practice simply because they say they are not in one-to-one supervision. Indeed, the books written by Passmore (2011), de Haan (2012), Lucas (2020) and Bachkirova et al. (2021) suggest that there are many different modes of supervision in coaching and mentoring that are already well established or emerging that mirror the brands of coaching referred to in Chapter 3. Nevertheless, there still does not seem to be the empirical data available to suggest how prevalent these practices are and how far they extend beyond their principal proponents.

Kennett (2006b) offered an alternative discourse in her unpublished Master's thesis. She questioned whether supervision is an appropriate term to use and ponders whether 'reflective practice' (Schön, 1991), with its emphasis on developing professional practice and reflection in action, is a better model. In a similar vein, Harlow's (2013) analysis of social work, coaching and supervision suggests (although using different terms) that this ability to reflect on professional practice is quite important for social work supervision (this is explored in the activity below). Others, like Wild (2001), have preferred to use terms like 'coaching the coaches' or 'meta-mentor' to suggest that there is no substantive difference between coaching a client or mentoring a mentor. Another part of the discourse that seems to get subdued by the dominant discourse of supervision is the idea that a mentee or a coachee is skilled in the process (see Chapter 8 for an account of the skilled coachee). This idea has important implications for coaching and mentoring development programmes in general.

## CONCLUSIONS

We will conclude this chapter by articulating our own position on supervision and the development of those involved in coaching and mentoring.

As coaching and mentoring has now become more commonplace and an accepted part of organizational life (and of wider society), it is natural that those involved in it as clients, practitioners and purchasers want to see the quality of what is being provided increase. One way of doing this is to pay more attention to developing the skills of coaches and mentors via properly designed coaching and mentoring programmes. Like Bluckert (2006), we believe that coaching and mentoring development programmes need to raise awareness, in coaches and mentors, of their own impact, and developing psychological and organizational mindedness are key parts of that. Like Bluckert (2006), we have come across plenty of coach-managers who do not understand enough about the organizational context and plenty of psychologically trained coaches and mentors who do not have sufficient self-awareness, as well as the other way around. Therefore, we do not believe it is necessary to be either a psychologist or a former CEO to work with a senior executive; both of these backgrounds – either together or separately – may be helpful in working with such a person but do not guarantee success.

We firmly believe that engaging in a rigorous, challenging and critically reflective process regularly with the support of skilled colleagues is helpful and necessary to develop reflexivity in coaches and mentors. This process could be paid one-to-one supervision in the way that Hawkins and Shohet (2006) describe it, or support could be gained by a skilful integration and use of a variety of different means of challenge and support from a range of mechanisms. Also, we believe that such support and challenge should be extended and encompass all those involved in a coaching and mentoring intervention and not just designated 'supervisors'. Of course, this is not always possible given the usual constraints on time, money and people.

A good coach or mentor is a critically reflective one. We do not believe that it is helpful to have an unquestioning, uncritical dominant discourse that only legitimates one-to-one psychologically driven supervision. However, we do believe, as Gibb and Hill (2006) cited earlier, that it is preferable to have challenge and disagreement around what is appropriate support and development for coaches and mentors.

 ## Future Direction

In the previous editions of our book, we predicted that the concept of supervision would come under increased scrutiny. While this has happened in terms of an increased intellectual interest in supervision, we have not seen such strong evidence of the expected increase in coaching and mentoring supervision in practice. This may be for three reasons.

First, as we have pointed out, while coaches and mentors may well have their own informal processes of supervision, these tend not to register as formal supervision processes and hence do not get counted in the same way. This is supported by Mann (2020), which reports that only 47% of respondents were confident that all their coaches were in supervision.

Second, there does still seem to be a relative paucity of primary data collection regarding supervision processes which may indicate that, while most people see the need for supervision, they are choosing not to engage in it. Merrick and Stokes (2021) argued, in relation to coaching, that this may be because of some conflation between coaches getting coached themselves and getting supervision. Also a relative lack of engagement in practical supervision over the last few years may be due, at least in part, to the difficult financial climate that is being faced by many across Europe at the moment, not least in the UK, because of COVID-19. Hence, coaches may not be getting formal supervision because they cannot afford to.

Third, while the professional bodies strive for a unifying and simplified model of supervision which is punitively applied to membership, practitioners recognize the need for a continuous development approach to their work. The practitioners live with and work with a complex

*(Continued)*

network of learning experiences where supervision may be just one – and perhaps as it is currently positioned, not a very good one – source of learning.

In his book on relational coaching, de Haan (2008b) raises some interesting questions about supervision. In particular, he asks whether formal supervision is substantially different in quality or effectiveness when we compare it with informal support. As we have discussed in this chapter, there are already those who question the usefulness of the term supervision, given its strong associations with management and control and its links with psychotherapy. As more becomes known about what effective support for coaches and mentors looks like, we predict that there will be an increase in demand for group supervision processes, such as action learning sets, which are likely to be cheap (with shared costs) and which expose coaches and mentors to a wide range of perspectives and other avenues for support. We also predict that there will be a significant growth in team coaching supervision, concomitant with the rise in team coaching activity itself. Currently, the team coaching supervision market, in the UK at least, seems restricted to established players in coaching supervision, e.g. David Clutterbuck, Peter Hawkins and Alison Hodge. However, as these markets mature, we expect to see growth here in both as those who have long since worked with executive teams as consultants see an opportunity to brand their work more distinctly and, in turn, existing coach supervisors see this as an opportunity.

 Activity

As a consultant, one of us was invited to work with a large local authority based in the middle of the UK. The authority wanted to encourage its social workers, working in children's services in particular, to support each other in their mutual personal development. Central government funding for a project was successfully bid for and a number of initiatives involving social workers from the authority as well as those from neighbouring authorities were set up. One of these strands was action learning sets. These were positioned as ways of supporting the individual helpers to be more effective in assisting the young people they were working with. In essence, this was group supervision and was based heavily on coaching and mentoring principles and techniques, although it was never named as such. The initiative was intended to complement other practices in the project such as social work peer supervision of cases and other training/communication events between psychologist and social workers. However, when running the first of these sets, the facilitator (one of us) noticed that some of the group were using the session as social work case supervision, while others were using it, as intended, to allow space for group support of individual development and support issues. This led to a protracted discussion at the end of the set as to the purpose of the intervention and how useful it would be to the participants. The tension for the facilitator was that one of the core principles of the process was that individuals could use it to address their own issues rather than working on things that others wanted them to work on. On the other hand, those who had chosen to use their slot to ask for help on their cases were, by doing so, avoiding much of a focus on themselves and their own development. Hence, by challenging the avoidance of individual issues, the facilitator/supervisor could be perceived as dictating to the individuals what they should and should not bring to the process.

**Questions**

1. If you had been in that position, how might you have dealt with this dilemma?
2. Consider how the dilemma in this case influences how you see group and individual supervision. Where would you draw the boundaries?

    i. What support are you currently getting for your coaching and mentoring practice?
    ii. To what extent does that support enable you to be both psychologically and organizationally minded?
    iii. What power dynamics are present within your current mode of coaching/mentoring support?

 **Further Reading**

For a practical yet theoretically informed guide to supervision, look at: Clutterbuck, D., Whitaker, C. and Lucas, M. (2016) *Coaching Supervision: A Practical Guide for Supervisees*. Oxon: Routledge.

For an approach which integrates coaching, mentoring and supervision, look at: Brockbank, A. and McGill, I. (2012) *Facilitating Reflective Learning: Coaching, Mentoring and Supervision*. London: Kogan Page.

# 13

# COACHING AND MENTORING AND DIVERSITY

## CHAPTER OVERVIEW

This chapter takes a critical perspective on the issue of diversity and its relationship to coaching and mentoring. Diversity presents perhaps the biggest challenge to humankind; it is a complex subject, one that, in an organizational context, can be dealt with in various ways. We attempt to explore these variations through the lenses of 'tolerance' and 'acceptance'. Coaching and mentoring offer an opportunity for individuals to explore the concepts of tolerance and acceptance and thus move forward to a new diverse future.

# INTRODUCTION

The term 'diversity' has many meanings; for example, on strategic, policy or philosophical levels it may relate to:

- multicultural philosophies
- political agendas
- business agendas.

## Multicultural philosophies

The notion of multiculturalism is an ideology based on the assumption of inclusiveness regardless of the diverse cultural and religious backgrounds of people in any specific society. Within an organizational setting, multiculturalism may be seen as a 'proactive and systematic process' (Dass and Parker, 1996: 384).

## Political agendas

Diversity, as a topic, could relate to a political agenda where policies are aimed at developing tolerance of diversity in terms of race, religion, age and sexual orientation. Governments of all persuasions around the world take different views on these issues but many create policies aimed at addressing what might be seen as diversity in political agendas. In turn, organizations participate in policy making in relation to diversity issues.

Political and economic agendas created by governments may contribute to the creation or development of either a tolerant or an intolerant society. In very recent times we have seen the rise in activity around diversity through movements like 'Me Too' and 'Black Lives Matter'.

The 'Me Too' movement started as a result of the gross misogyny found mainly in Hollywood, but the movement has grown to support victims of sexual abuse. At the heart of the movement is the call for more developed educational work on identity and self-worth.

The 'Black Lives Matter' (BLM) movement started in 2013 but gained huge momentum following the killing of George Floyd by a police officer in the United States in 2020. Parker et al. (2020) estimate that between 15 and 26 million people participated in the US protests which followed. In June 2020 the Pew Research Center, an independent think tank in the US, stated that the overall approval ratings of BLM had increased from 2018, and that by June 2020, the majority of Americans from all backgrounds supported BLM (Parker et al., 2020). This indicates a mass change in social attitudes.

Particularly at times of economic challenge, social attitudes towards 'difference' may take on stronger and more polarized positions which may isolate, ostracize or discriminate. Some politicians may capitalize on such feelings. The media, through the language it employs in its reporting, is not immune. A current example of this attitude in the UK is associated with Brexit. In 2019, Robert Booth of *The Guardian* newspaper reported that incidents of racial abuse had increased by 13% since the Brexit vote, and he argues that the two are linked. Additionally, there appeared to be some within UK society who saw the vote to leave the EU as an affirmation of their views on the UK's immigration policy as being a threat to their way of life and employment prospects, and that the leave vote had given these disturbing acts of aggression and abuse some legitimacy. This has been followed through by the current UK government with the introduction of new, stringent immigration rules and, even more recently, it appears, according to the popular press at least, that there is a migrant crisis.

## Business agendas

Diversity could also link to broad business agendas where the business tactic is to encourage a diversity of employees to better serve a heterogeneous customer base.

On a more individual level, diversity could relate to:

- race or cultural difference
- nationality or regional difference
- gender
- sexual orientation
- age or marital status
- political viewpoints

- religious views or ethnicity
- disability as well as health issues
- socio-economic difference and family structures
- values.

Clearly, there are many diverse positions on the subject of diversity! In an organizational context, the issue of diversity raises some dilemmas. A recent survey (Churchill, 2020) noted that people from different ethnic groups are far more likely to experience discrimination in all aspects of the workplace than their white counterparts. Often, this takes the form of 'occasional or persistent microaggressions during their career' (see, for example, https://www.theguardian.com/law/2020/sep/24/investigation-launched-after-black-barrister-mistaken-for-defendant-three-times-in-a-day). The Churchill (2020) article concludes that coaching and mentoring are vital in bringing about the necessary changes in the organisational narratives on diversity.

Ashley and Empson (2016), in their exploration of diversity within three accounting firms, articulate the arguments for and against seeing diversity as a source of competitive advantage for organizations. Interestingly, they offer a typology of cases that are made for diversity initiatives – the business case, the moral case, the client service and the fairness case – which sometimes compete and contradict each other. They conclude that the client service model – where it is important to be as flexible and available to clients as possible – is the narrative that tends to dominate, at least in the accountancy world. They therefore suggest that the argument that having a diverse and flexible workforce means more business (the business case) is significantly flawed. This raises interesting questions about the impact of coaching and mentoring, which we will explore below.

## METHODOLOGY

First, we discuss the meaning of diversity and examine current philosophies and practices found in organizations. We then present a new case study which looks at the issue of generational diversity and discuss this in relation to an edited version of an article that was published in the trade magazine, *Coaching at Work*. This is discussed critically. This chapter links to many of the themes already established throughout this book and we signal these in the text. We conclude the chapter by raising some challenging questions.

## CURRENT APPROACHES

Despite being published 25 years ago, Dass and Parker (1996) remains a key text when considering diversity in an organizational context. Organizational policies still tend to be formed and enacted through the practices of human resource management (HR), and Dass and Parker's observations remain relevant today. Diversity is an important issue and Dass and Parker (1996) suggest that organizations tend to take three main approaches to diversity:

- emergent and episodic
- programmatic
- strategic multiculturalist.

### Emergent and episodic

Organizations may develop an emergent and episodic approach to diversity. This is often a senior management-led process to identify unmet or unfulfilled needs or problems with the organization. At other times, incidents occur or examples arise from other levels within the organization that require action.

An organization adopting this approach may engage trainers to facilitate diversity training aimed at sensitizing organizational members towards better communication and awareness of difference. Training is often employed in organizational contexts to tackle such challenges. The advantages of training initiatives are:

Many people can be 'put through' the training.

The administrative processes can monitor and check attendance.

The administrative process can show statistics and numbers to confirm that 'something has been done'.

However, tackling diversity issues is about knowledge, skills and attitudes. Training can deal with knowledge and skills but attitudes are harder to reach and therefore training may not actually tackle the issues at the heart of the incident, leaving the possibility that it may reoccur. An alternative may be action learning.

Action learning sets tend to focus on and surface common concerns and resolve problems. While this approach can have a positive impact, it may also generate false and unresolved hopes by raising expectations which later cannot be met. Alternatively, it may be used as a precursor to more developed and prolonged diversity initiatives. An example of such an episodic initiative is the research and mentorship programme for future HIV vaccine scientists (Sopher et al., 2015). An intervention was set up in the USA by the National Institute of Health to encourage African Americans and Hispanic medical students to research in the field using a research mentoring support system. The study reported increases in knowledge and skills and increased interest in vaccine research. While the intervention appeared to be successful in relation to these particular groups, and there are plans to continue it, it seems limited to this particular issue, as opposed to addressing the wider inequity issues in the system.

## Programmatic

Some organizational recruitment approaches, in the pursuit of fairness, may attempt to neutralize difference by standardizing and attempting to anonymize recruitment and selection processes. An example of this would be anonymized application forms or, in the case of the classical music industry where there was a bias towards recruiting men as orchestral players, 'blind' auditions. Interestingly, Thomas (2020) argues that even with 'blind' auditions, bias can still be present. He noted that by asking candidates to remove their shoes, there was an increase in recruiting female orchestral players by 50%. The assessors were influenced by the sound of the candidate's footsteps! Thomas (2020) also notes the increased use of artificial intelligence systems in recruitment but cautions against their use. As was seen in the 2020 school examinations process in the UK where an algorithm was used to determine students' grades, the process was overturned because approximately 40% of students were downgraded on the basis of which school they went to and that students from poor areas were affected the most while those from wealthy areas achieved the most. The algorithm had built-in bias (BBC News, 2020).

Other organizations may take a more affirmative approach by positively highlighting, nurturing and valuing difference. The programmatic approach is sometimes developed from the episodic approach to create an organizational development approach to diversity. Dobbin and Kalev (2016), in their article in the *Harvard Business Review*, claim to have examined three decades' worth of data from 800 US organizations. They argue that a large number of diversity programmes fail because they rely on models and approaches that were prevalent in the 1960s – strong controls on obvious biases in recruitment and selection processes. These traditional approaches seem to fit with Dass and Parker's (1996) programmed classification in that they are implemented to deal with a litigation problem or a company image issue via the standardization of such processes. Interestingly, they argue that mentoring programmes make significant differences in terms of positively affecting measures such as racial diversity. Mentoring and coaching have the potential at least to tackle the attitudinal issues raised earlier in this chapter because they are focused on the individual.

## Strategic multiculturalist

The third level, according to Dass and Parker (1996), is a more strategic approach based on the positive philosophy of multiculturalism. This approach seeks social integration and cohesion for long-term strategic progression. Dass and Parker (1996: 385) believe that this approach makes it more likely that honest expression of difference 'can lead to a synthesis of the conflicting perspectives to take advantage of the similarities as well as the differences within organizations'.

They also argue that this approach is more holistic and balanced and represents a more realistic position on the complexities of diversity.

While it cannot be the case that the multicultural approach is the 'one best way', the other approaches listed above can lead to difficulties. For example, the more affirmative approaches outlined can be switched 'on' or 'off' as the circumstances allow. With these approaches, there is always the potential for lip-service policies supported by the assumption that more education and training is the way forward. Neither policies nor education and training necessarily alter the subtle ways in which people can be intolerant or find difference unacceptable.

McDonald and Westphal's (2013) study on the mentoring of women and minority directors is interesting in terms of this subtlety. They examined 1,305 responses to a questionnaire on how they experienced being a first-time director and hypothesized that woman and ethnic minority first-time directors would have fewer company directorships than incumbents and, critically, would receive less informal mentoring from those (predominantly white male) incumbents than other first-time directors. They refer to an aspect of mentoring that they call participation process mentoring and to the social norms of, for example, the appropriate protocols for raising concerns at board meetings. Without this informal mentoring, it would be difficult for first-time directors to know that the norm is to raise concerns separately with the CEO first before raising them publicly – to do otherwise might be considered to be too controlling. However, on the face of it, it would be difficult to see any obvious barriers to being in what McDonald and Westphal (2013: 1170) call the 'inner circle' of corporate boards. This lack of visibility also makes it challenging to move toward Dass and Parker's (1996) category of strategic multiculturalism as a result.

 **Reflective Questions** ————————————————

- What is your experience of diversity initiatives that are informed by coaching and mentoring principles?
- Which of the above categories would you say these experiences fall into?

## LANGUAGE

Language, spoken and written, is also a vehicle of culture (see Bruner, 1985, 1990). In relation to diversity, the concept of discourse is important because language or the discourses it creates help shape society. As Layder (1994: 97) states, 'Discourses are expressions of power relations and reflect the practices and the positions that are tied to them.' Dominant discourses from the media, from leaders and from politicians shape societal perceptions and may create an environment of either tolerance or intolerance. For example, both in the UK and the US, politicians and the news media are adept at using language to create an impression about the so called 'migrant crisis'. This language is often inflammatory, aggressive and dehumanizing. As the The *Guardian Observer editorial* (2020) maintains:

After reading the latest crop of ideas leaked to the press last week, one would be forgiven for thinking that Britain is a country overwhelmed by people dishonestly trying to bypass normal migration routes by seeking asylum, compelling the government to discourage people from coming to Britain by any means at all.

The editorial goes on to provide the facts and figures, sourced from the Home Office itself, of the current situation in the UK, which show that this impression is totally false and that there is no crisis!

However, individuals from different cultures with a shared language may still misunderstand each other because meaning is constructed in relation to cultural filters. For example, if a British person is asked by a Swiss-German-speaking person speaking English, 'Did I upset you?', the British person may reply, 'I was a little taken aback.' The Swiss-German person may then say, quite understandably, 'What?' The British person actually means, 'Yes, you did upset me', but their cultural conditioning of politeness would inhibit such a direct response. However, the Swiss-German would, according to his or her culture, expect a direct answer of 'Yes' or 'No', and is confused by the obscure British response. Although there is a small risk of conflict in this example, it does illustrate the potential for greater misunderstanding in other situations. It is not the actual words that matter, it is the cultural filter that may alter the meaning, and this example may lead to a stereotype of 'British people are not straightforward and Swiss-German people are rude'. Clearly, this is not the case.

The above are important issues and relate to the now familiar concept of mindset raised in Chapters 1, 2, 7, 9 and 11. At times, particularly where there are economic pressures, intolerance or prejudice are not only related to outward signs of difference, such as obvious disability, gender or skin colour, but may also appear as a political or conceptual issue. Differences in the way people think, influenced by their political position, educational background or financial position, can develop particular mindsets towards 'the other'.

## THE CHALLENGE OF MINDSET

Three philosophies which do not lend themselves to a diversity mindset are:

- power and control over the many by the few (neofeudalism; see Chapter 12)
- Newtonian concepts of cause-and-effect methodologies for improving efficiency and effectiveness
- Tayloristic 'one best way' thinking.

Garvey and Williamson (2002: 194) go further with their views, written shortly after 9/11, when they state: 'The old frameworks for thinking about the global order of our lives, its political fracture lines, religious and ideological diversity and its sustainability in environmental terms, are all shown to be inadequate.' Clearly, 9/11 was a horrific act, but the events which followed it can hardly be viewed as a change of such mindsets but rather as an aggressive restatement of old approaches based on the lack of understanding of difference and 'West is best' thinking. More recently, we find deep societal divisions in many countries of the world including in the Middle East, Asia, the

USA and the UK, where ideological differences have created intense and, at times, violent factionalism. The concept of diversity is truly challenging humankind. We can conclude, from such views, that the arguably natural human instinct of the intolerance of difference (see Back, 2004; Bhavnani et al., 2005) seems to be a major challenge across all sectors of global society.

There are two issues here. The first is that intolerance does not imply that the opposite concept – tolerance – is any less problematic. What a dominant group may see as normal, a minority group may see as an aberration worthy of punishment, or vice versa. Some may see the concept of 'toleration' as an acceptance or as 'putting up with' an unacceptable custom or behaviour. Such a position could be seen as moral relativism and, as such, as having dubious connotations. It is also difficult to separate tolerance from power. A dominant group may have more choice to tolerate than a minority group. The minority may simply have to 'endure', 'suffer in silence' or 'put up with' a dominant group's perspective.

Garvey and Alred (2001: 526), in using the term tolerance, suggest that it has at least two meanings:

> One is about 'putting up with'. Tolerance in this sense implies that a person views situations as simplistically tolerable or intolerable so that the very perception of a situation becomes part of what makes it more or less tolerable. This, we believe, chips away at the personal qualities and abilities that determine optimal performance.

The second meaning put forward by Garvey and Alred (2001) is 'closer to its etymological root [and means] "to sustain", to keep going and remain effective in prevailing conditions'. The second quote offers a more positive perspective and involves aspects of the Rogerian concept of 'positive regard' for difference. A positive alternative to positive regard may be found in the concepts of 'civility' or 'pluralism'. These ideas include the notion of 'acceptance'.

The second issue is that 'instinct' is not underpinned by knowledge and therefore there is no understanding in an instinct. In essence, we seem to be returning to the issue of the objective versus the subjective, as raised in Chapter 2. The ideas outlined above are deeply problematic because they involve both the rational (objective) and the emotive (subjective) aspects of the human brain. Acceptance or tolerance, or any other concept in the context of diversity, is a blend of the rational and the emotive. Many organizations attempt to 'manage' diversity and lever it for strategic or social benefit and this is a completely rational choice – it makes sense and is supported through a dominant discourse of 'diversity is a good thing'. However, making sense, as Bruner (1990) tells us in Chapters 1, 6 and 9, is a construction based on individual and societal narratives, mindsets and discourses. People have within them narrative lines about themselves and about others, mindsets and discourses. These influence behaviour and, by exploring an individual's narrative, attitudes which create mindsets or discourses which shape behaviour, understanding, tolerance and acceptance become possible.

As Edwards and Usher (2000: 41) point out:

> Through narratives, selves and worlds are simultaneously and interactively made. The narrator is positioned in relation to events and other selves, and an identity conferred through this. Positioning oneself and being positioned in certain discourses, telling stories and being 'told' by stories, becomes therefore the basis for personal identity. Narratives are unique to individuals, in the sense that each tells their own story, yet at the same time culturally located and therefore trans-individual – we are told by stories.

In diversity, there are no easy ways forward, but in the context of learning and development, diversity is an essential characteristic of the creative process. It is not about 'putting up' with each other but more about creating genuine tolerance, acceptance and understanding of difference, about living with it as normal rather than defining others by their differences and as outsiders.

So, these things can become the province of coaching and mentoring. Mentoring and coaching dialogue offers the potential to explore dominant narratives, mindsets and discourses and the potential to develop new meanings and understandings by exploring the emotive as well as the rational. Passmore et al.'s (2013) edited book on diversity in coaching, as well as Clutterbuck et al.'s (2012) on successful diversity mentoring programmes, contain a range of examples of programmes set up to realize this aim.

The following case study from the USA provides insight into a common issue found in organizations, that is, the question of generational differences.

 Case Study 13.1

### Talking about Generations

Linda, in her mid-40s, was a newly promoted Chief Marketing Officer of a US-headquartered global public firm. She requested an executive coach to help her transition into her new role, build relationships with global leadership, and set short and long-term priorities.

Linda was viewed by others as a confident leader who was able to control a room and champion her ideas. She was a visionary with a clear direction of how the company should be perceived globally, impressively delivered a message and had a savvy business mind. When she was passionate about an idea or initiative, she went all in with a level of professionalism and dignity that few had observed before.

But 360-degree feedback interviews also suggested Linda lacked empathy and understanding of the different motivations and working styles of the marketing team. Her team were perceived as being so heavily overloaded they were on the point of burnout. She was criticized for her lack of support and understanding of the challenges the team were facing.

Marketing is traditionally a young function, but Linda expressed high levels of frustration with her 'millennial' employees who she perceived to lack resilience, excellence, drive, and conveyed a high level of entitlement. Feedback interviews appeared to support Linda's initial assessment of her young team by questioning whether she had the right people: 'There's sometimes little accountability and deflecting' ... 'millennials work differently' or, 'when I worked at my prior company this is how we did it. That might be true but it's not how we do it here.'

At first, Linda's priority for coaching was to learn how to 'manage' the millennials on her team. However, in early coaching sessions she recognized that challenges could be career-stage- and life-stage-related rather than generational and decided that instead of trying to 'fix' her millennial team members, she would set two alternative objectives. First, she heightened the quality of her conversations by creating space for others to talk and asking open-ended questions. She also increased the role and ownership of the marketing leadership team in designing agenda and interactions with each other and rewarded quality interactions between team members.

Linda recognized many of the marketing leaders were still acquiring fundamental leadership skills within the team and with Partners, so she experimented with a more genuine leadership identity. She allowed herself to be vulnerable by telling the story of her leadership journey, shared her full 360-degree feedback report with her marketing leadership team and discussed her values and her childhood, which had been exceptionally challenging.

Furthermore, Linda actively rewarded a 'growth mindset' to show that she valued learning more than mastery. She invested in professional coaches for team members and encouraged openness and trust, so they were able to demonstrate vulnerability and confidently ask for help from others when it was needed.

After six months, building on overwhelmingly positive feedback, she provided visibility into high-level organizational priorities and actively created opportunities for her team with senior stakeholders. After two years, Linda and her team designed and oversaw a global rebrand of the company and Linda was promoted to Partner. She understood there was more work to do, which was frustrating, but recognizing that her team were at a different stage of the same development journey helped maintain her confidence in them.

Lianne Lyne<br>
Owner & Executive Coach<br>
PLP Coaching, LLC, USA

## DISCUSSION OF CASE

Case study 13.1 is a good example of a current theme found in executive coaching – generational differences. It either manifests as the executive, as in this case, having difficulties with their team or, at times, it may be the executive feeling fearful of being overtaken by another generation of up-and-coming people. In the context of the marketing function, this view is quite prevalent. There is also a lot of attention given to generational issues in the coaching press (see, for example, *Coaching at Work*, Volume 14, Issues 1, 2 and 3, and Volume 15, Issue 1).

In this case, Linda has an issue with the millennials. She has developed a view of who they are in her team and how they behave. She has exercised a judgement. How far this judgement is based on her own perceptions or the prevalence of such debates in the media is hard to determine. The central issue here is that unless Linda could 'reframe' her negative judgement or intolerance, the problem would just get bigger. Her coach enabled Linda to do just that and, by engaging differently with her team, she was able to make substantial progress in her leadership. This seems to be based on the idea that one cannot expect others to change unless we are able to change as well – a very established management idea!

We will now examine the wider issues behind the intolerance of different generations, in this case the so-called millennials.

The popular media discourse on millennials is, in some ways, overwhelming. A recent search using the term 'millennial UK' got 19.6 million hits! A general pattern found in this material is that millennials have the following characteristics:

- different work ethic
- lazy
- self-involved
- politically apathetic narcissists

- can't function without a smartphone
- live in perpetual adolescence
- not committed.

Millennials are also described as:

- creative
- flexible
- open-minded

- possessing a sense of social responsibility
- concerned for the environment.

We wonder if the negative judgements really are the case, or if it is simply one generation complaining about another, as has been done since time immemorial.

Within the business context, we find a range of similar themes about millennials presented in the media (e.g. Alsop, 2008; Stein, 2013; Asghar, 2014; Sinek, 2017). For example, millennials are described as:

- more confident
- teachable
- more pampered
- risk-averse
- in need of constant feedback and praise
- dress badly
- can't keep to time
- need clear goals and instructions

- have outlandish expectations
- feel entitled and superior
- hate long hours
- expect flexible work routines
- are disloyal
- expect immediate access to the senior people
- are tech savvy.

In some quarters, millennials are branded as the 'me, me' generation. In these business media outlets, Baby Boomers (the previous generation) are blamed for this because they, apparently, lavished unwarranted praise on their children and built their offspring's egos beyond realistic expectations. The business discourse is that millennials are hard to manage and, in terms of coaching, they need special treatment.

In HR circles, we find much advice on how to manage these 'difficult people' by accommodating them through investing in training, development and career growth activity. The HR press (see, for example, Gurchiek, 2017; Morel, 2019) suggests that millennials need help to understand how they contribute to the company's mission and leaders need to make their work 'meaningful'. Also, organizations should provide millennials with more paid leave and create flexible working arrangements. We wonder if these suggestions just represent 'good management practice' and are not something unique to any particular group?

The discourse within the coaching media on millennials draws on the discourses outlined above and it is often presented as the 'problem' of millennials. There is research on generational difference, but neither sociology nor psychology can agree a definition of generational difference. There is also no agreed timeframe for millennials. Strauss and Howe (1991) offer the widest age range – an individual born between 1982 and 2004. In the US in 2016, this category accounted for 71 million people.

We wonder if it is really possible that such a huge number of people share the same traits. It could be analogous with stating that all people from, say, Liverpool or certain ethnic or religious groups are the same. This makes this perception a possible discrimination issue, which is supported by the research philosophy of consensus (see Chapter 2): the idea that because many people say something, it must be true! The discourse about millennials is a very powerful one and adopted by many for a variety of reasons.

Historically, research on generational difference has two main perspectives:

- social forces
- cohort.

In the social forces perspective, Mannheim (1952) argues that a generation is a social group defined by birth dates that share events and experiences that influence their life and behaviour. He suggests that attitudes are shaped within generations and that generational difference is a force for social change.

Joshi et al. (2011) state that each generation, when faced with the norms of 'acceptable behaviour' imposed by previous generations, must either choose to accept or defy these norms. Young people, Mannheim (1952) claims, are more willing to accept 'new' ideas and are able to use their 'new' perspectives as a force for social change.

In the cohort view of generations, Ryder (1965: 845) defines a cohort as a group of individuals 'who experience the same event within the same time interval'. His research offers an alternative to the social force argument. He agrees that there are boundaries between generations, drawn according to birth years, and that birth cohorts may share similar experiences and events in their lives through time. However, Ryder (1965) states that the concept of 'generation' is a theoretical convenience category, that it is based on generalized assumptions and that there is no evidence that an event shared within a generation leads to certain attitudes or behaviours. This perspective would align with an underpinning assumption of humanist coaching and mentoring, which is that individuals may experience the same events but will interpret them differently.

In the current research on generations, Campbell et al. (2017) looked at values and attitudes over time in work and found some differences between generations but also found evidence that generational boundaries are 'fuzzy; social constructs. They concluded that a cohort view of generational difference is an unsophisticated indicator.

Ryder's (1965) criticisms are also reflected in current research. With data mainly drawn from surveys which are essentially 'broad stroke' research instruments – easy to do with little in-depth analysis – it is inevitable that we end up with generalized categories that say little about specifics and contexts in (see Chapter 1 on purpose and context in coaching and mentoring).

With regard to the 'tech savvy' view of millennials, a recent PhD study (Crabbe, 2018: 27) cites 11 pieces of research that state that age is not a factor in technology anxiety. She also found that 25% of first-year business students in her study suffered from technology anxiety – so much for the tech savvy argument!

These obvious problems within generational research have led researchers to a more subtle approach. Baltes (1987) offered the idea of a lifespan developmental perspective. He suggested that human aging is best understood as a complex process that takes into account the influences of biology and sociocultural factors across time. Life span research looks for linkages across disciplines and examines development across multiple levels. It takes into account the variability of human experience and the variations of interpretation of those experiences. It considers the universal potential for human growth and development – whatever the age of the individual (Levinson et al., 1978; Sheehy, 2006). Life span research seeks to understand developmental influences that may affect an individual's motives, values and attitudes at work.

Rudolph and Zacher (2017) suggest that life span research needs to be focused on the individual and not treated as shared phenomena that everyone catches from each other! They recommend that practitioners recognize aging as an ongoing developmental process – people's lives are dynamic and all people learn. Practitioners need to be cautious about creating policies and practices to put people in generational boxes.

Coaching and mentoring are for the individual, their hopes and fears, wants and needs, and it is our position here that generation is another diversity issue. People are not the same by virtue of a birthdate, any more than they are the same by virtue of country of origin, religion or sexual orientation. That road leads to discrimination and moves us away from tolerance and acceptance of difference.

Our argument is that it is through learning that social challenges are addressed. Therefore, understanding provides the basis for tolerance and acceptance. This position is, to some extent, justifiable and is the core assumption made by those who support 'learning solutions'. If learning is necessary for people to develop tolerance and acceptance, coaching and mentoring could provide help and support for what is an individual's strongly held position. We could therefore consider coaching and mentoring arrangements in organizational settings as offering co-mentoring or co-coaching (see Chapter 5). This would mean that both parties in the co-relationship need to learn and develop in the way Linda did in Case 13.1. It is our view that there is a need to focus on re-balancing power, or addressing these injustices of perception through developing critical thinking but there is a long road ahead because the educational and communication challenges this raises are considerable.

Ultimately, we argue that the one-to-one approach in the diversity context is a good thing because it considers the individual, and therefore potentially it reaches greater depth and has more impact through the development of critical thought. As in other contexts, the key is the relationship and its intent. As we have emphasized throughout this volume, it is important to understand how the political, social and organizational context can have a significant impact on how coaching and mentoring initiatives are enacted and, ultimately, on how successful they are.

 **Future Direction**

Overall, given the current tendency towards religious, social, cultural, generational and political polarization of difference in modern society, we believe that diversity is a major challenge to humanity but one which should be embraced. De Bono (1992) offers insight into polarization with his concepts of rock logic and water logic. Rock logic positions beliefs as right or wrong and therefore options are severely limited in this two-way system. Water logic is about flow and possibility: it is about where this might take us and therefore offers multiple possibilities. A key principle of coaching and mentoring is the generation of many options to work with, and they therefore offer scope to develop multi-layered perspectives on respect, tolerance and acceptance.

Without intending to overstate it, mentoring and coaching may offer a serious way forward for humanity and provide an alternative to the human tendency to simplify and polarize. While, as we have argued here, there are limits to what can be achieved via mentoring and coaching initiatives, the processes at least have the potential to open up dialogues on the important values of respect, tolerance and acceptance.

 Activity

Higher Education is a rapidly changing environment. The changes in fee structures and restrictions on international recruitment have both had an impact. Within this context, many universities are seeking to develop and enhance their research profiles. This includes seeking ways to encourage academic staff to become research active, to publish and attract research funds. Set against this, particularly in the so-called post-1992 universities, there are increasing pressures on teaching hours and assessment. One institution with an excellent reputation for teaching decided that the best way to achieve an increase in research activity was to introduce a mentoring programme for academic staff. Senior staff members with strong research profiles were identified as potential mentors. A key issue for the university, however, was that, of those staff who were research active, a disproportionately small number of them were women (15%), even though women constituted 56% of the employees. Furthermore, while a large number of the staff on fractional contracts were women, an even smaller percentage of those on such academic contracts were research active (7%). An exploratory qualitative research project, conducted in one of the faculties, suggested that part-time women academics found that the working culture of the university was not conducive to those who had young families having teaching and management commitments as well as aspirations to do research. For many in this situation, the research time was sacrificed to keep up with other demands.

Imagine that as a coaching and mentoring consultant, you are tasked with designing and implementing a mentoring scheme within this university:

- How will you deal with the challenges discussed above?
- What would be an appropriate measure of success for this scheme?
- What do you expect to be the impact of this scheme?

 Questions

- What is your organization's or your personal approach to diversity?
- How might coaching and mentoring offer realistic opportunities for a new order of things?
- How might you operationalize coaching and mentoring for diversity?

 **Further Reading**

Garvey, B. (2019) 'Generalising generations', *Coaching at Work*, 15(1): 50-53.

Kollen, T. (2016) 'Lessening the difference is more: The relationship between diversity management and the perceived organizational climate for gay men and lesbians', *International Journal of Human Resource Management*, 27(17): 1967-96. This research article puts forward the view that mentoring schemes that target LGBT workers add to the notion that they are different, which militates against a positive organizational climate for these workers.

Pelham, G. (2016) *The Coaching Relationship in Practice*. London: SAGE. This volume makes some strong references to diversity issues that might affect the coaching relationship, which may be useful for readers particularly interested in this area to examine.

Ragins, B.R. (1997) 'Diversified mentoring relationships in organizations: A power perspective', *Academy of Management Review*, 22(2): 482-521. Read this seminal article on diversity for an understanding of the roots of recent discussions on mentoring and diversity.

Garvey, B. (2013) 'Coaching people through life transitions', in J. Passmore (ed.) *Diversity in Coaching*. London: Kogan Page. Read this for case studies of working with individuals who are going through age transitions.

# 14

# A QUESTION OF ETHICS IN COACHING AND MENTORING

## CHAPTER OVERVIEW

In this chapter, we explore the question of ethics in coaching and mentoring. In doing so, we seek to uncover some of the dilemmas, challenges and questions that ethical practice raises for coaching and mentoring practitioners as well as examining some key conceptual frameworks for understanding and interpreting ethical practice. At the end of the chapter, we draw some conclusions for the future.

## INTRODUCTION

As we will argue in Chapter 15, there has been a considerable increase in efforts to regulate the behaviour of various stakeholders within coaching and mentoring relationships, with the rise of professional bodies and professional standards (the main issues and challenges in relation to professional bodies will be addressed in Chapter 15). With this, there has been a commensurate increase in the number of codes of ethical behaviour that are available via coaching and mentoring professional bodies. While, as Iordanou, Hawley and Iordanou (2017: 3) point out, some coaches and mentors 'rely primarily on the codes of ethics of the professional membership bodies that they have joined', other writers, such as Fatien Diochon and Nizet (2015), have called into question the merits of using ethical codes as vehicles for resolving ethical dilemmas that coaches and mentors face in their day-to-day practice. They have gone on to develop a metaphor of ethics as a fabric which knits together emotions and reflexivity (Fatien Diochon and Nizet, 2019). Some writers, such as Corrie and Lane (2015), have sought to develop a framework from which to understand such ethical dilemmas. Our intent, in this chapter, is to take a critical approach to the question of ethics by exploring some of the research and literature mentioned, and to seek to locate the place of ethics and ethical behaviour within the broader context of coaching and mentoring theory and practice. Following Fatien Diochon and Nizet (2015), we shall consider this from intrapersonal (micro), organizational (meso) and social (macro) contexts. Prior to this, however, we will begin by considering the principal characteristics of ethical theory as they relate to coaching and mentoring.

## METHODOLOGY

First, we present a brief discussion on ethical theories and then we employ these in our examination of ethics in coaching and mentoring. In order to do this, we make use of the micro, meso and macro framework outlined above (Fatien Diochon and Nizet, 2015) to explore the issues of ethical practice and how they impact on coaching.

## TYPES OF ETHICAL THEORIES

Passmore et al. (2011: 147) suggest that there are three main types of ethical action that are pertinent to coaching:

*Consequentialist or teleological* – actions themselves are ethically neutral and it is their consequences that matter in terms of right or wrong and in terms of the greatest good for the greatest number of people.

*Dutiful or de-ontological* – some actions are intrinsically good and some actions are intrinsically bad. Good ones might include telling the truth, being just and keeping promises.

*Pluralist* – balancing the above perspectives, for instance if keeping a promise would harm others, what is the most important consideration?

It is possible to interpret Passmore et al.'s (2011) typology as a straight choice between three broad alternatives – a focus on outcomes or methods or a balance of the two. These discourses do resonate, to some extent, with Western's (2012) discourses on coaching. For example, the consequentialist (or utilitarian) position seems to fit with the Managerial discourse with its focus on pragmatism, outcomes, roles and goals. The de-ontological position seems to have more connection with the Soul Guide discourse which emphasizes core values and personal experience. However, as Iordanou and colleagues (2017) suggest, the question of ethics is more sophisticated and complicated, with a more recent rise in other ethical approaches, such as virtue ethics (Hursthouse, 1999), ethics of care (Koggel and Orme, 2010) and ethics of power and structure (Beckett and Maynard, 2013). Each of these approaches has, at its core, a theory as to what should be the key focus for ethical action, some aspects of which may compete with each other. In this sense, we may be moving towards a series of narratives regarding ethical behaviour in which, following Foucault (1980), no one can be privileged above another to form a regime of truth. In this sense, there may be an emerging parallel between the increasing range of ethical theories and the range of models and perspectives on coaching itself (see Chapter 5). However, our intention in this chapter is not to conduct a literature review of ethical theories and models per se, but rather to seek to critically examine the place of such theories within coaching and mentoring theory and practice.

## MICRO ETHICAL ISSUES – INTRAPERSONAL

Iordanou et al. (2017) initially locate their debates about ethical theory at the level of the individual, followed by their interpersonal connection with another person, such as their coachee or mentee. Drawing on the work of David Hume, Michel Foucault and others, they make a useful distinction between values and ethics. They characterize values as a relatively unchanging set of principles about what is important to us as individuals, whereas they view ethics as being related to our activity, behaviour and conduct. Hence, for them, ethics 'can be seen as the practical application of values' (Iordanou et al., 2017: 16).

Their principal approach in examining ethics and values within coaching is to explore them through a series of scenarios and examples which raise questions and ethical dilemmas. For example, they raise an intrapersonal dilemma for a coach who is faced with how to deal with a coachee's alcohol problem and point to the importance of contracting and establishing boundaries within coaching relationships (Iordanou et al., 2017: 112). As we argue in Chapter 15, this is where professional bodies such as the International Coach Federation (ICF) and the European Mentoring and Coaching Council (EMCC) have sought to develop ethical codes of conduct which are intended to help guide coaches who face such dilemmas.

However, Fatien Diochon and Nizet's (2015) research into the utility of ethical codes and their use in informing intrapersonal coaching practice suggest that this can be challenged. They conducted critical incident interviews with 27 experienced French coaches where they were asked to reflect on situations in which they found it difficult to act due to what they saw as an ethical dilemma. They analysed the results in terms of whether the ethical code provided by their relevant coaching professional body was helpful. In all but one of the cases, the coaches were not satisfied with the code in terms of helping them to resolve their intrapersonal dilemma, for one of the following reasons:

1. The code is not relevant - either it does not cover all the issues or it is not legitimate as a reference for their dilemma.
2. The code has shortcomings - it is not self-sufficient, simplistic, rigid, cognitive, or opposed to economic rationality.
3. The code is an obstacle to the ethics of the coach - it is not like them, it does not allow the coach to have a say, it does not prevent the coach from being manipulated.

However, they do not call for an abandonment of ethical codes but for their amendment to include questions and illustrative case studies in order to enable coaches and mentors to educate themselves.

 **Reflective Questions**

- Do you use ethical codes to inform your practice?
- What do you consider to be their place in coaching and mentoring practice?

In order to explore these issues further, we put forward the following intrapersonal dilemma for consideration in Case Study 14.1.

 **Case Study 14.1**

An experienced male mentor is working in a paid relationship with a younger female mentee, helping her to think through her career options, following a breakdown in her personal relationship. The work has proceeded well, with a seemingly good personal rapport between the two parties. At the end of the third meeting - a particularly intense session with a strong emotional component - the mentee says to the mentor: 'I wish I could find someone like you in my life. You seem so caring and understanding and I always feel so good when I'm with you.' Almost immediately, she apologizes for this comment and says that she never meant to say anything 'like that' to him. The mentor is conscious of being flattered by the comment and of having friendly feelings towards her but is concerned now about what this means for their relationship going forward. What should he do?

# DISCUSSION OF CASE

This case study constitutes a dilemma for the mentor in that it is an intrapersonal and interpersonal one – concerned principally with the relationship and feelings of the two people involved. Some key questions can be raised:

1. How should the mentor work with the mentee now?
2. Should the mentor continue with the relationship?
3. To what extent is it possible to use the situation to support the mentee?
4. What lessons might be taken from this situation?

The answers to these questions do depend on the values of the person answering them. One possible avenue is to ignore or play down the comment and seek to continue with the relationship as though the comment had never been made. For some, such a response would be unethical in de-ontological terms (see above) in that this would be to purposefully deny the feelings of the mentee and their impact, in order to maintain this paid relationship and, perhaps, to perpetuate the positive dysfunctional transference (McAuley, 2003) at the expense of the mentee's well-being. If we consult the literature on coaching and mentoring on such dilemmas, a typical suggestion, as offered by Iordanou et al. (2017), would be to reflect on the contracting processes and reflect on whether boundaries have been appropriately set up and managed within the relationship. Alternatively, following de Haan (2008b), another route is to refer the mentee to someone else. This course of action, however, would probably require the mentor and the mentee to have a conversation about these expressed feelings which may embarrass and damage the mentee emotionally, particularly given that her past challenges have resulted, in part, from a breakdown in her previous relationship. This case also potentially raises a tension within Iordanou and colleagues' (2017) distinction between values and ethics. The mentor's personal values might tell him that he should operate in a way that is caring of others, particularly when they are in a fragile state – a dutiful approach to personal values. On the other hand, he may equally feel that by seeking to take action in relation to this dilemma, by engaging in 'good' actions, he, inadvertently, violates those values by withdrawing from the relationship and leaving the mentee vulnerable. Of course, there are other courses of action that the mentor might choose to follow, i.e. taking this to supervision, using his own countertransference to help the mentee understand what might be going on for them, and so on. However, our purpose is not to advocate for one position over another but, rather, to seek to shed light on how an interaction between a practice dilemma and ethical theories may work.

Corrie and Lane (2015) approach such intrapersonal ethical dilemmas from a supervision perspective. In doing so, they draw on the work of Carroll and Shaw (2013), who put forward an ethical framework that can be used to consider intrapersonal ethical issues (as well as macro and meso issues, discussed later in this chapter). It has six components, as paraphrased by Corrie and Lane (2015), which are:

1. Ethical sensitivity – awareness of self, of harm of consequences, of impact of behaviour of intention.
2. Ethical discernment – reflection, emotional awareness, problem-solving process, ethical decisions.

3. Ethical implementation - what blocks me/ what supports me, how to implement decisions.
4. Ethical conversation - defending the decision, going public, connecting to principles.
5. Ethical peace - living with the decision, support networks, crisis of limits, learning from the process, letting go.

6. Ethical growth and development of character - utilizing learning to enrich moral self-knowledge, extending ethical understanding, becoming more ethically attuned and competent.

 **Reflective Questions**

- To what extent do you recognize these ethical components when thinking about your own practice?
- Where do you feel you need to develop as a practitioner?

The framework above, while not explicitly referencing a particular ethical approach, has the benefit of helping individual coaches and mentors by giving them content areas to focus on. It has the advantage of not simply raising awareness of the ethical dimensions of coaching and mentoring dilemmas (ethical sensitivity and discernment) but also the internal and external structures that need to be put in place (ethical implementation and conversation) to enable action external to the relationship, and also attending to issues of coach/mentor development (ethical peace and growth). Writing for cognitive-behavioural therapy supervisors, Corrie and Lane (2015) argue that Carroll and Shaw's (2013) framework might then be used by supervisors to work with their supervisees to help them to develop their 'moral compass' in any of the six component areas. It is therefore possible to see how this might be a useful framework for supervision in coaching and mentoring (see Chapter 12 for a discussion of supervision).

Fatien Diochon (2012: 308) uses a Christian metaphor of the seven deadly sins to identify ethical traps that coaches might fall into. These are:

1. Greed - to rush to coaching without appropriate training.
2. Sloth - to make the minimum effort required.
3. Gluttony - to be attracted by what appears to be a lucrative market.
4. Envy - to be jealous of clients or colleagues.
5. Pride - to consider oneself as a new guru.
6. Lust - to seduce by wrong arguments/to lie.
7. Wrath - to show too much emotion and overpass the boundaries of the role.

In Carroll and Shaw's (2013) terms, these ethical traps might be used to enable ethical growth (component 6) in individual coaches and mentors but also to bring in the organizational context. Thus far, we have focused mainly on the micro (intrapersonal) level of ethics by looking at the dilemmas facing the individual and how they might go about dealing with them. In the next section, we will move on to look at the organizational issues.

# THE MESO CONTEXT: ORGANIZATIONAL CONTEXT AND ETHICS

As we have argued many times in this book, the context in which mentoring and coaching work takes place is critical to understanding it. This is particularly true when we are considering the organizational context. Looking at the question of ethics in this context means that we not only need to attend to the values and ethics of individual participants within the coaching and mentoring relationship but also to the positions of other stakeholders in that system such as:

- managers of coaches/mentors
- managers of coachees/mentees
- the Human Resources department
- senior managers who are sponsoring coaching and mentoring interventions

- other employees not directly involved in coaching and mentoring, who might be affected by it.

In Chapter 3, we critically examined the concept of organization culture and the idea of creating a coaching culture. The impact that organizational norms and values have on ethical behaviour in coaching and mentoring is significant. In Chapter 7, we explored how the voice of the organization can constitute a dominant discourse within that organization, where powerful stakeholders can seek to determine what is seen as appropriate or acceptable within the organization; in essence, cultural and power dynamics combine to have a significant impact on the behaviour. As in the previous section, we will use a case study (14.2) to explore how some of these issues might play out in an organizational context.

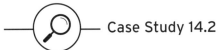 Case Study 14.2

An external executive coach is recruited to work with eight middle managers in a medium-sized professional services organization. The initiative is led by the HR manager who explains to the coach that she will be working with these managers on a one-to-one basis to assist them in 'making a significant change' in their working practices. It is his view that these managers need help in moving away from a more directive managerial style to one that is more collegial and enabling of others to take ownership and responsibility for their work. The chief executive has been persuaded to financially support the intervention by the HR manager, who tells the coach that he had to strongly advocate for the funds as the chief executive was initially unclear about what benefit the coaching would have for the business. The coach assisted in this advocacy by explaining her approach to coaching and, based on her experience, how such benefits have been accrued in previous places where she has worked. In doing so, the coach was clear in stating her belief that, in order for the coaching to be effective, there would need to be clear boundaries in terms of confidentiality and that, principally, the content of the conversation needed to remain between her and the coachees. This was accepted before the coach formally started on her assignments with the coachees. Initially, all seem to be working well, with good levels of openness and rapport between the coach and the coachees. However, after a couple of months, the coach began to notice coachees appearing more guarded in coaching conversations, with some postponing/cancelling pre-arranged coaching sessions.

*(Continued)*

Around the same time, the HR manager arranged to meet with the coach and explained that the chief executive was now 'anxious to see results' after all the investment that had been put in and wanted to know what progress was being made. It was then apparent that the chief executive had approached a number of the coachees individually to ask them to disclose what they had been doing in the coaching sessions. Seemingly unsatisfied with their responses, he had tasked the HR manager with getting 'progress updates' on each of the coachees from the coach. The HR manager explains that he is concerned that, if he is unable to provide these updates, the future of the coaching initiative would be in jeopardy as well as the HR manager's own reputation and position within the organization. What should the coach do?

## DISCUSSION ON CASE

Clearly, in addition to the intrapersonal dynamics at play in all coaching and mentoring relationships, we now have some additional stakeholder relationships to consider. The chief advocate and sponsor for the intervention appears to have taken a political risk by proposing the intervention and is now deflecting that risk onto the executive coach. The message being given to the coach is that the responsibility for the HR manager's future and the coachees' well-being is being placed on her and that she has to decide whether to find a way of giving some evidence of progress or else seek to withdraw from the contract with the resultant loss of client income. In Carroll and Shaw's (2013) terms, this constitutes making a decision and communicating this through 'ethical conversation' but also being able to live with the decision that is made ('ethical peace').

If the coach decides to disclose some information to the HR manager, does this constitute the sin of greed in Fatien Diochon's (2012) terms (see above), i.e. wanting to operate in a lucrative market? Or does the answer to this question depend on the degree of disclosure? If the coach was to feed back on 'general themes' that have come out of the coaching that the chief executive needs to think about, while anonymizing individual issues/contributions, would this be ethical, in utilitarian terms, i.e. the greatest good for the greatest number? The coach is being put in a difficult position in relation, once again, to a tension between personal values and ethics, i.e. 'I respect the confidentiality boundaries agreed with my coachees and I do not renege on these' versus a perceived responsibility to the coaching programme, to the HR manager and to the claims the coach made to the chief executive about the benefits of coaching itself. Furthermore, relationships with the coachees have already been damaged, as shown by the withdrawal of some of the coachees following the intervention of the chief executive.

According to a study by Coutu and Kauffman (2009) some years ago, 70% of those coaches surveyed disclosed progress reports to the organization, either through HR or to the line-management sponsor. However, this was contracted from the start rather than during the programme.

Recently, one of us (Stokes) was in a meeting within our institution about a leadership development programme for a corporate client. The discussion was about how the coaching component of the programme would work and involved two coaching practitioners and the business development manager (BDM) for the academic institution. The BDM had met with the chief executive of the business, who wanted the managers of the businesses he had acquired to work more effectively as a team. One of the coaches raised the issue of disclosure of 'themes' from the coaching being disclosed to the chief executive in order to help the business move forwards. The BDM felt that this was a good idea but also felt that some of the coachees were likely to be resistant to the idea of coaching and might possibly act defensively (see Chapter 8 for a discussion of skilled coachee behaviour) in order to protect themselves. Hence, it was suggested by one of the coaches that the coachees should be advised that themes would be fed back but that it would be anonymized and general, rather than disclosing details that would enable individual comments to be identified. However, the other coach raised the question as to whether flagging up possible disclosure would, in fact, 'frighten the horses' and militate against a successful coaching relationship. It was decided that it was important that coachees were told about this but that this would be downplayed by the coaches, so as to avoid this placing additional stress on the coachees (see Chapter 4 for a discussion of the impact of evaluation on coachees). To what extent might this be seen as an example of what Carroll and Shaw (2013) call ethical sensitivity? Or could it be argued that, within the meeting, the participants have colluded in abdicating their ethical responsibility to the coachees by seeking to distract the coachees from the political dangers inherent in disclosing things to their coaches? As Carroll and Shaw (2013: 243) argue, problems can occur because there is a difference between intentions and actions:

> It is all too easy to justify or tell moral narrative from the perspective of our intentions. Of course, our intentions are always 'good'. It is difficult for us to do deeds with bad intentions. Even when we intend bad actions, e.g. 'I will kill him, I will spread rumours about her and destroy her good name, I fully intend to embezzle money', we have a neighbouring intention of doing them for good reasons, e.g. 'I will kill him because he deserves it for what he did to me, I will spread rumours because she needs to be taken down a peg or two, I will embezzle this money because money will give me access to the good life I am missing'.

Hence, this concept of neighbouring intention might be used as a way of explaining the outcome of the above meeting, i.e. 'it is OK to downplay the political risk to the coachees because it will enable them to experience the coaching which will be good for them'. However, that choice of narrative serves to silence any other narrative, such as 'we need to downplay the political risk to the coachees or else they may choose to withdraw from the leadership programme and we will lose the income'.

The possibility of other discourses impinging on ethical decision making is something we will explore in the next section, where we examine ethics from a macro perspective, the societal aspect of ethics.

## THE MACRO PERSPECTIVE – SOCIETAL CONSTRUCTS

One of the areas we will examine in some detail is the impact of professional bodies, competences and standards in coaching and mentoring (see Chapter 15). In this chapter, our remit is to consider them – and other stakeholders – as promulgators of ethical practice. As we have already argued in this chapter, one of the principal impacts that professional bodies have is through their development and establishment of ethical codes of conduct that members of the organizations are expected to follow and use as a touchstone for their own actions and responses.

Another impact is the sense in which they might tap into what Fatien Diochon and Nizet (2015: 16) refer to as 'big collective causes', a phrase which also connects with Iordanou et al.'s (2017) definition of values, referred to earlier. Fatien Diochon and Nizet (2015) choose examples of big causes such as environmental sustainability, the emancipation of the oppressed and the advancement of human knowledge as those things that might inform the ethical practice of those involved in coaching and mentoring activity. These might also include the idea of self-actualization (Maslow, 1943) or, moving to less academic concepts, notions of meritocracy represented by, in the US context, 'the American Dream', or in the UK, 'the classless society'.

As we argue in Chapter 8, such prevailing discourses can have a powerful effect on behaviour by legitimizing certain kinds of behaviour and 'criminalizing' others. Examples of this can be seen in sport where, at the last Olympics in Rio de Janeiro, Brazil, Russian athletes were allowed to compete only when individual sporting associations allowed them to. However, there were several examples of Russian athletes – those who were cleared to compete – being heckled by the crowd as they received their medals, such was the furore over the disadvantage suffered by clean athletes when competing against those who had enhanced their performance through the use of illegal drugs. Furthermore, the British cyclist Lizzie Armitstead (now Deignan) broke down in tears in a BBC interview on the eve of her Olympic road race final as she felt that people would consider her a cheat whatever she did, despite being cleared to compete following missing previous drug tests. The dominant ethical discourse here was one of classifying athletes as either 'clean' or 'tainted', irrespective of whether the athlete had permission to compete/been acquitted of any such allegations. This discourse appeared, therefore, to transcend the intrapersonal and organizational ethical processes involved.

This dominant societal discourse can be seen in other areas. In relation to therapy, Rose (1999: 217) argues that 'over less than fifty years the territory of the psyche has been opened up for exploration, cultivation and regulation in many ways and along many channels'.

He argues that what writers such as Lasch (1980) describe as the culture of narcissism and Sennett (1998) as the corrosion of character has led to a situation where 'the links that once bound each person into the chain of all members of the community have been severed' and that 'the possibility has emerged of everyone living a truly private life' (Rose, 1999: 220).

Rose suggests that, given what he sees as a decline in community, individuals have turned inwards and use mechanisms such as therapy to regulate themselves and their emotions rather than seeing a function for the community in doing so. However, rather than arguing that there should be a return to an older, more traditional sense of society and community, Rose instead points to what he calls 'the fabrication of the autonomous self' as the key issue to be addressed (1999: 221). He suggests that modern institutions and professions construe individuals as the focus for their exercise of expert power (French and Raven, 1962). He describes the sense of self thus:

> The self does not pre-exist the forms of its social recognition; it is a heterogeneous and shifting resultant of the social expectations targeted upon it, the social duties accorded it, the norms accorded to which it is spoken about and about which it learns to account for itself in thought and speech. (Rose, 1999: 222)

Hence, he is arguing that society's norms serve to influence the self but in a way that encourages the individual, via the notion of an autonomous self-sufficient identity, to take personal responsibility for self-regulation and self-discipline:

The political subject is now less a social citizen with powers and obligations deriving from member-ship of a collective body, than an individual whose citizenship is to be manifested through the free exercise of personal choice among a variety of marketed options. (Rose, 1999: 230)

Rose argues that, as a result of the loss of community, therapeutic professions, i.e. psychology, psychiatry, psychotherapy, have developed to 'restore to individuals the capacity to function as autonomous beings in the contractual society of the self' (Rose, 1999: 231) when they are unable to function as an autonomous, private self. Building on Rose's (1999) work, Western (2012: 97) argues that the rise in the demand for coaching can be seen as a new expertise that can be used to 'satiate the alienated employees, lonely leaders at the top and managers struggling with increasingly complex work that demanded their cognition and attention'.

  Rose (1999) suggests that, as the choice to consume such services is made by the individual, this is construed by some as being an autonomous choice. Bauman (2005: 35) makes a simi-lar point when he discusses what he calls 'the vocation of the consumer' in relation to modern society. In this sense, there appears to be no obvious evidence of a power play on the part of individuals or groups, as individuals are choosing to purchase coaching and mentoring services and there is no sign of coercion. However, as Lukes (2005: 27) points out, the exercise of power need not result in conflict for it to be a power play:

To put the matter sharply, A may exercise power over B by getting him to do what he does not want to do, but he also exercises power over him by influencing, shaping or determining his very wants. Indeed, is it not the supreme exercise of power to get another or others to have the desires you want them to have – that is, to secure their compliance by controlling their thoughts and desires?

Jerome Bruner (1979: 132) refers to this influence as cultural control and draws a similar conclusion:

Once we have determined how men shall perceive and structure the world with which they have commerce, we can then safely leave their actions to them – in the sense that, if they believe them-selves to be standing before a precipice, they will not step over it unless they intend suicide.

In other words, we are suggesting that, in addition to the cultural norms that we explored in the previous section, ethical behaviour and practice are also influenced by societal norms, which, according to some of the above commentators, constitute a form of social control. To explore how this works, let us examine a coaching and mentoring dilemma through this lens (Case Study 14.3).

 **Case Study 14.3**

A large independent coaching organization is approached by a large international bank to work with a significant number of its senior executives in the wake of a significant change process, following the recent world financial crisis. The team managing the contract for the coaching firm is aware that the bank has been in the news recently, following allegations of a large payoff to the chief executive in the midst of poor financial performance overall and

*(Continued)*

multiple redundancies across a range of countries and locations. However, those in HR in the bank managing the contract have argued that this has been misrepresented and that the coachees are, in any event, not involved in this. Nevertheless, as the contract begins, a number of the coaches begin to report that some of their coachees appear to be engaging in behaviours that they (the coaches) are not comfortable with, i.e. seeking help in thinking through how to exit the organization with their share options intact; using the coaching relationship as a quasi-confessional space for offloading about 'things they've had to do' to customers and employees in order to maintain their own position. While these disclosures, in the main, fall short of disclosing criminal activity, they, for some of the coaches, raise conflicts, not only in terms of their personal values, but also for their commitment to ethical codes of practice within their professional coaching bodies. In addition, those in the coaching organization, despite the significant income stream that the work is generating, are concerned about the reputational risk that working for the bank is generating and are reluctant to advertise the bank as a client. What should the coaching organization do?

## DISCUSSION ON CASE

Case Study 14.3 raises an example of where societal norms around those deemed culpable, in some sense, for the financial crisis are impacting on the coaching contract and on relationships with individual clients. The coaching protagonists in the case seem to be experiencing cognitive dissonance (Festinger, 1957) towards their role in working for the bank and with these particular coachees. As in the previous two cases, there are the intrapersonal and organizational issues to look at, but, in addition to this, we now have a dominant societal discourse around banking and the conduct of bankers to consider. While it may not be unreasonable on the part of the individual coachees to seek to use coaching to offload and to safeguard their own future, these societal 'shoulds' are serving to dominate the usual coaching norm of seeking to focus on the individual client. In addition, there is a 'tug' on the professional bodies' norms which emphasize the importance of contracting, boundary management and non-collusion with clients as being ethical practice on the part of affiliated coaches. One way of seeking to answer the question of what to do is, of course, to use frameworks such as that of Carroll and Shaw (2013) in order to identify a touchstone for action; in this case, engaging in ethical conversation where a decision is made, defended and lived with might be the area to work on in pursuit of what they refer to as ethical maturity. However, as Boje (2008: 161), in his book on storytelling in organizations, argues, 'organisations are selectively attentive to societal discourses'. In other words, those working in organizations are used to focusing on certain aspects of what they do at the expense of others – to support this claim, Boje gives the example of advertising campaigns. A similar claim can surely be made about individuals – we are not necessarily compelled or bound to one particular view of societal 'reality' but can choose to privilege some views and silence others. Hence, how the decision is made, which is then defended, is worth examining further and is probably why many of those writing on ethics in coaching and mentoring are keen to emphasize ethical education as a means of establishing ethical maturity (Carroll and Shaw, 2013). In the final section of this chapter, we will draw together the various elements discussed in the chapter and examine what this means for coaching and mentoring and ethics in the future. Before doing that, we will explore the current context of COVID-19 and make connections between the various levels in light of this issue.

## A NOTE ON COVID-19

As we have mentioned a number of times, we are, at the time of writing this fourth edition, in the midst of the COVID-19 pandemic. At this point, in the UK, we are entering a second wave of infections. The current data suggests that the majority of new infections are being identified in the relatively young age groups (under 30), a group who are least likely to be symptomatic or to die from the virus. The messaging from the UK government does have overtones of a moral imperative, i.e. if we all behave responsibly then we will prevail over the virus.

However, there is also a countervailing discourse which points to a high overall recovery rate and the need to balance risk of exponential increase in the rate of infection against the long-term damage to individuals and to the economy of lockdown and restrictions on social interaction. In this sense, COVID-19 is presenting us with a classic macro ethical dilemma that permeates into most areas of society, including coaching and mentoring.

In this case, we have a 'pull' from individual liberty and longer term wellbeing on the one hand, set against a responsibility on one not to act in ways that put others at risk, i.e. the necessity of washing hands, social distancing and self-isolation if exposed or infected. There is a sense that the former drivers for individual liberty (at a societal level) are currently prevailing over the latter moral expectations – current estimates are that only two in five people who are expected to self-isolate are actually doing so and there has been a significant increase in the level of fines as a reaction to this. This tension could also be applied to the meso context in coaching and mentoring, as we have seen above, but specifically in relation to which counts for more – the wellbeing of the individual or the wellbeing of the organization?

Again, we see a parallel with this in the macro context, with current discussions taking place about the possible continuation of the UK government's furlough scheme for protecting the jobs and salaries of UK workers. On the one hand, the existence of the scheme thus far has protected the rights of individuals to continue to survive economically but this has also protected organizations in terms of salary costs. The scheme was extended to the end of September 2021.

The Chancellor of the Exchequer in the UK is required to balance the short-term macroeconomic cost of supporting individuals and business against the long-term damage to the economy if these individuals are not supported.

In the next chapter we will further explore the impact of competencies and the role that professional bodies like the EMCC and ICF play in this. However, from a macro-ethical perspective, we must ask the question of where the moral authority of the professional bodies comes from.

In Chapter 2, we introduced the idea of the consensus theory of truth as a basis for knowledge claims about coaching and mentoring. It is often the case that membership organizations, like professional bodies, use consensus truth claims to support action, often by surveying members. Of course, as we argued earlier, consensus truth claims can be challenged on the basis of power.

To what extent are members sufficiently informed and free to make appropriate judgements about, in our case, ethical coaching and mentoring practice? If they are not sufficiently well informed or feel compelled to act or vote in a certain way, then clearly this detracts from the moral authority to act claimed by the professional body.

A similar argument, of course, can be extended to local and national governance. Local and national politicians are making judgements about local and national restrictions in the face of COVID-19, borrowing their authority to do so from their democratically elected status. However, in the UK we know that questions have been raised as to the extent to which the voting public were fully informed when voting for Brexit and for the current Conservative government making such decisions. Whilst an in-depth discussion of modern democracy is beyond the scope of this text, we feel it is reasonable to ask the question as to whether it is always the case that elected bodies or indeed membership organizations act in the best interests of their individual members. Furthermore, we feel it is also reasonable to ask how these tensions apply at an interpersonal level between coach and client, where the coach may be providing a paid service (in some cases) to a client. In the current economic context, how likely is the coach to refer the client to a fellow coach – a competitor – even if they feel that coach would be better for the client? In this scenario, the economic drive to maintain a coaching business versus the moral imperative to act in the best interests of the client might be brought into sharp relief, we suggest. These tensions are likely to have a significant impact on coaching and mentoring activity and behaviour, going forward, not least in how such activity is conducted.

 **Reflective Questions**

- What role does power play in considerations of ethics?
- What are the limits of personal responsibility for ethical issues that manifest themselves at a societal level?
- How powerful a role does context play in these considerations?

## CONCLUSIONS

In this chapter, we have examined ethical questions about coaching and mentoring from the intrapersonal, organizational and societal perspectives. In doing so, we have raised questions about the role of professional bodies, ethical codes and ethical standards – these questions will be explored further in the next chapter. However, we have also raised broader philosophical questions about how ethical decisions get made and how these ethical practices relate to values. As we suggested at the start of the chapter, our aim here was not to provide a comprehensive review of ethical theories – that could be the subject of a whole new book. Instead, we sought, using case study examples, to bring to life some of the ethical dilemmas that coaches and mentors face, and then tried to make sense of them using selected theories and perspectives from the coaching ethics literature.

While the micro, meso and macro structure is a helpful lens through which to look at different aspects of coaching and mentoring, we, perhaps inevitably, found that all the ethical dilemmas have aspects of the intrapersonal, organizational and societal running through them at some level. Ultimately, it is artificial to argue that a particular dilemma is solely intrapersonal and it is more useful to try and understand the organizational and societal aspects of it as well.

While we found Carroll and Shaw's (2013) ethical framework useful, the concept of ethical maturity can be challenged as it can imply an ultimate destination, where, implicitly, the individual coach or mentor might 'rest easy' because they have reached the end – we do not believe that this is possible and that such an ethical journey is likely to be ongoing and never-ending. In fairness to Carroll and Shaw (2013: 350), they are very clear that this is not what they are claiming: 'We recognise that ethical maturity is an ideal to be pursued rather than an end-point to be achieved.'

However, as they have acknowledged, there is a difference between intent and actions, and this does not prevent others from seeing it so. Nevertheless, we agree with their emphasis on helper education, as do Iordanou et al. (2017). Like the latter, we conclude that it is better to place our emphasis 'not on solving ethical issues but, rather, on creating those conditions and conversations that will bring them to the surface' (Iordanou et al., 2017: 186).

 ## Future Direction

We predict that, while there will be repeated calls for increased standards and regulation in coaching and mentoring, the most likely route for a journey towards increasing ethical maturity will be through coaching training courses. There will always be those who train coaches (in particular) who wish to focus exclusively on the technical/rational skills of the coach or mentor and will see other elements such as ethics and power relations as being superfluous. However, we see these elements becoming increasingly central to coach and mentor education, such that they will become an expected part of the education process and will run through the skills-based components of coaching training in credible programmes. As we will examine in the next chapter, the increased complexity of what it means to be an ethical coaching and mentoring practitioner raises significant challenges for those working in professional bodies and on standards and competences for coaches and mentors.

 ## Activity

Consider the following YouTube clip on ethical codes based on the International Coach Federation's code of ethics: https://www.youtube.com/watch?v=G_3kGAUrgRc

1. How easy is it to subscribe to these codes?
2. To what extent should the context of the coaching/mentoring process be taken into account when considering what is ethical?

**Questions**

- Overall, how would you sum up the role of ethical theories and frameworks in the coaching and mentoring world?
- To what extent do we need ethical codes to guide our actions?
- How should the coaching and mentoring professions ensure compliance with ethical standards (if at all)?

 **Further Reading**

For a debate about the different ethical codes of professional bodies, see Chapter 30 by Diane Brennan and Leni Wildflower in E. Cox, T. Bachkirova, and D. Clutterbuck (eds) (2014) *The Complete Handbook of Coaching*, 2nd edition. London: SAGE.

This book offers a broad perspective on ethical maturity in the helping professions: Carroll, M. and Shaw, E. (2013) *Ethical Maturity in the Helping Professions: Making Difficult Life and Work Decisions*. London: Jessica Kingsley.

For a comprehensive overview of ethics in coaching practice, read: Iordanou, I., Hawley, R. and Iordanou, C. (2017) *Values and Ethics in Coaching*. London: SAGE.

For a superb macro-level analysis of ethical issues at a societal level, look at: Sennett, R. (1998) *The Corrosion of Character: The Personal Consequences of Work in the New Capitalism*. New York: W.W. Norton.

# 15

# COMPETENCIES, STANDARDS AND PROFESSIONALIZATION

## CHAPTER OVERVIEW

In this chapter, we look at the debates around competencies, standards and the professionalization of coaching and mentoring. Rather than adopting a position on these issues, we raise many questions and present a comprehensive list of the extensive opposing arguments.

## INTRODUCTION

It is our view that the issues of competency, standards and professionalization in coaching and mentoring present a conundrum and indeed contradictory positions. Standards, for example, seem to be a basis for a higher and higher proportion of qualifications and curricula throughout the Western world. These standards are increasingly based on competencies or learning outcomes, and this approach seems to have become a dominant discourse that is rarely challenged. As discussed in Chapter 6, this is an example of linear thinking about learning and, as discussed in Chapter 11, it also relates to goal assumptions applied in the context of learning and development.

The consequence of these discourses, as we have discussed in relation to other discourses, is that they have become so loud and so embedded in professional associations, universities and other providers' minds that alternatives become marginalized or, worse, ignored and discounted and risk becoming wiped out by those who have the loudest voices. This presents a paradoxical problem for coaching and mentoring practice. In the literature on coaching and mentoring, humanism, individualism, variety, difference and complexity are celebrated as core values, and yet the discourse of professionalization, standards and competencies appears to seek the opposite!

## METHODOLOGY

Overall, this chapter addresses three main questions:

> Can and should competencies be used as a basis for describing the role of coach and mentor?
>
> Can and should standards be built upon these competencies?
>
> Can and should a professional accreditation be established on the basis of these standards?

To address these questions, we start with a discussion on the issue of competency. We then explore the pros and cons of the competency-based view and repeat this process for standards and professionalization.

This chapter offers more questions and activities than in other chapters. This is because this area of coaching and mentoring remains unresolved and therefore offers scope for critical debate. We conclude by exploring an alternative perspective.

## COMPETENCIES

On competencies we ask, 'what, in their turn, are the competencies based upon?' In some cases, it seems as if the basis is what providers currently do; but we could ask, 'what are these existing providers' competencies based on?' This line of questioning takes us into the Discworld created by the late novelist Terry Pratchett. Featured in most of his 26 books, the Discworld is an imaginary location which consists of a flat disc sitting on top of four huge elephants which are in turn standing on the back of an enormous turtle as it slowly swims through space. One of his characters believes that the turtle sits on another turtle which sits on another turtle and so on. With competencies, it's perhaps from here on down just turtles all the way!

Competencies emerged from the systematic training model of the 1960s. Systematic training identified skills and knowledge (and later, attitudes) as a basis for building curricula. In the 1970s, there was a move to replace these curriculum-based units of analysis with a work-based unit, the competence. This described something that an individual in a job was able to do. At that time in history it seemed a significant step forward, and we would agree that competencies do have a number of advantages. Before considering their dark side, we outline these below. Looking at the positive side of these issues, we make the case for competencies being based on research – illustrating this point by employing the now changed EMCC work in this area.

## Arguments for a competency basis

### Regulates the Wild West of executive development

As raised in Chapter 12, coaching has been described as the Wild West of executive development (Sherman and Freas, 2004). It is depicted as being populated by quacks and charlatans making unlikely claims based upon dubious methods inadequately researched (see Chapter 2). We found in the early 1990s that corporate purchasers of coaching were crying out for something to show them who were the sound coaches and who the fly-by-nights, among the dozens who were approaching each organization every week and offering their wares.

### Grounds understanding of the role of practitioners

Willis's (2005) research for the EMCC was perhaps the most thorough study of mentoring and coaching competencies undertaken anywhere. She developed her long list of over 900 competencies for mentors and coaches from the curricula of organizations that had produced detailed specifications to train coaches and mentors. This approach has the advantage of grounding the framework in practice but, as discussed above and in Chapter 12, there is a risk that the dominant discourse of current practice has the disadvantage of not allowing for innovation and new emerging perspectives.

### Creates a framework of comparison

By bringing together differing frameworks on competencies, researchers have enabled the profession to see commonalities and contrasts between various approaches. For example, the ICF's competency, C 5, is in part about active listening, and the EMCC's Competence Category 'Enabling Insight and learning' also considers listening as important. This also contributes to developing a typology of roles such as executive mentor or career coach (see Chapter 5). In addition, they have created a template that individuals can use in planning their professional development.

### Validation by the field

Both the EMCC's and the ICF's framework was distributed to members and other leaders in the field who were asked to indicate which competencies they saw as core to their practice, which related to a particular approach or clientele they addressed, and which were not relevant to their practice. In this way, patterns of competencies emerged that were doubly grounded in existing practice – first, from the competencies list that had been developed from existing curricula and second, from the survey of experienced practitioners. As discussed in Chapter 2, this approach is based on a consensus view of truth. Whilst this is a reasonable approach, it could also become a process by which a sense of 'group think' emerges where there is little room for a divergent viewpoint. We discuss this point a little later in this chapter.

## Ease of assessment

Competence frameworks are often written with key areas and graded descriptors for each key area. For example, the EMCC has eight categories with four 'levels'. This approach enables an assessor to use the check list to assess the competency that is demonstrated or the evidence that has been produced to show that the candidate for assessment meets a particular standard. This introduces a degree of objectivity into the process.

## Arguments against a competency basis

### Atomistic

The practice of any reasonably high-level skill is conducted and experienced as an integrated whole. We illustrate this point with terms in the EMCC's competency framework (www. EMCCouncil.org) which might apply to one action by a coach or mentor. The coach or mentor, when they reflect back to their client what has just been said, may be showing 'empathy', and they could also be said to be demonstrating 'listening', 'feedback', perhaps 'assessment', 'learning theory', 'supporting independence', 'ensuring understanding', 'active listening', 'building and maintaining the relationship' and many other items from the detailed list of competencies. To break down what a coach or mentor is doing and to specify it in unambiguous terms could be flying in the face of the dynamic complexities of practice as experienced by both helper and helped. It also suggests that there is a critical path or blueprint to be followed when a conversation is audited against these competences and this makes developing computer-based coaching and mentoring with technical systems and robotics more easily possible. Could this be an own goal for the professional bodies? (see https://www.youtube.com/watch?v=ejczMs6b1Q4)

### Monoculture – Group think

There is a question for the profession of whether a standardization of coaching or mentoring practice is a good thing or not, or if it achieves what it sets out to achieve. Coachees and mentees are hugely varied in what they can do and what they want, and standardizing the offering is not necessarily a desirable feature for those seeking help. Mentees and coaches come to the mentor or coach for a variety of purposes in a range of contexts (see Stokes et al., 2020). Further, if this is the case, coaching and mentoring are complex activities (Nadeem and Garvey, 2020) that do not lend themselves to an atomistic or reductionist approach, and biologists remind us of the inherent instability of monocultures.

## Tick-box assessment

The counter argument to the 'ease of assessment' point made above is that the assessment process can become a 'tick-box' exercise which gives the impression of objectivity, but it could also be an example of 'misplaced concreteness' (see Chapter 1) and the managerialist discourse (Western, 2017) in action. It may be possible for an individual to enact the competency but lack authenticity. It is akin to the alleged objectivity of manager-led performance ratings or objective driven evaluation (see Chapter 4).

## Mere competence

Another concern about competencies is that they create a frame of mind where professionals seek simply to do a 'good enough' job, rather than to create their own kind of excellence. Coaching and mentoring are therefore not viewed as ongoing developmental opportunities for the coach or mentor. Achieving the highest level on a competency framework may mean that the coach or mentor feels that they have arrived at the destination and that there is no need for further development or reflection on their own practice.

## Deficiency model

Competencies and standards can lead to a 'training gap' orientation, focusing coaching or mentoring on what the client lacks. This seems a pity motivationally and it misses all kinds of opportunities. Fairbairns (1991), an early critic of the gap mentality, argued that in organizations where 'we have little idea about what is coming next, maybe we should stop looking at training needs analysis to help us to decide what training and development programmes to run' (1991: 45). Solutions-focused (Berg and Szabó, 2005), humanistic and appreciative inquiry approaches offer a reminder that the deficiency model is only one perspective on coaching.

## Competencies degrade in the context of high anxiety and low resource case

A shrewd observer of mentoring, Ed Rosen, made the observation to us that when professionals are highly anxious – perhaps because of detailed surveillance, and under strong resource pressure, then the delivery of competencies can degrade. The professional is tempted merely to deliver what has been specified, even if it does not meet the emerging and dynamic requirements of the situation. Alternatively, as Garvey (2012) found, competencies may be deliberately abandoned as irrelevant in a crisis, and he points out that, in mentoring, Kram (1983), Beech and Brockbank (1999) and Clutterbuck (2004) argue that mentoring takes people beyond the immediately obvious. Alred and Garvey (2000: 268) suggest that mentoring can go beyond competencies and skills 'to promote balanced growth'.

In contrast to the idea of competencies, Richard Oliver's purposive drift offers another perspective (Oliver, 2006). He suggests coaches be clear about purpose, and open about what might turn up on the way: we should pay attention to making it up as you go along. Machine thinking and the claims made for it are a 'reassuring fiction'. 'We are smarter than we think, even though we may be more ignorant than we know' (2006: 20) and 'Our life work consists of identifying, maintaining, extending and amplifying our states of well-being' (2006: 23). In essence, Oliver believes that a sense of well-being is our compass point. Purposive drift is a relationship between values, competencies and contexts. Focusing on your context and your interactions with it tells you both what you value and the competencies that you can bring to bear on it (2006: 25–9).

## Conclusions

There are arguments for and against competencies. The arguments for are about regulating a perceived chaotic market and understanding what it is that coaches and mentors are purported to do. The arguments against are grounded in the contrast between the ambiguous and complex nature of the world and the need for embedded control and certainty which the competency suggests. Competencies are part of the Managerialist discourse (Western, 2017).

A great irony is that the taming of the 'Wild West of coaching' has created a proliferation of professional associations, all with their own positions on these things; in effect, they have created a 'Wild West' of professional bodies! There is a further problem, however, that the self-styled 'Wild West' of professional bodies are now accrediting themselves, and this is often justified by the 'consensus' argument. The ICF, for example, declares that their new set of competencies is based on the response of 1,300 coaches (https://coachfederation.org/core-competencies) and they declare this as 'The Gold Standard'. The ICF's own survey of 2016 suggests that there are 53,300 professional coaches worldwide. If this is the case, the sample used to create the current competency framework represents approximately 2.4% of the coaching industry as identified by the ICF. Even more starkly, the business-related social media site LinkedIn estimate, by using their worldwide membership, that in 2019 there were 586,292 coaches worldwide. If this is the case, the ICF sample is approximately 0.22% of the total population (Venkatesh, 2019). As researchers, it is important to ask key questions about this sample.

How was the sample selected?

What does it represent in terms of age and gender?

What does it represent in terms of the contexts of practice?

What does it represent in terms of the purpose of the coaching or mentoring?

How far does the analysis of the findings break down in relation to these questions?

Our view is that some kind of assessment framework has become necessary. However, the form that it is currently taking may not match with the complexities of the role of coach or mentor, nor does it take into account the coachee or the mentee (see Chapter 8). One issue for us is the use of the word 'training' to describe the developmental activity. We think that this assumes a linear process, often hierarchical in levels or stages (Garvey, 2016). This does not consider the complexities of the processes of mentoring and coaching. A central argument here is that coaching and mentoring are complex activities. Therefore, a repertoire approach (see Chapter 12), underpinned by research, learning theories and enacted with critical reflection, is a serious alternative. It is here that educational institutions come to the fore.

## STANDARDS

On standards, we ask the questions: Do you accredit the programme or the individuals or both? Are standards possible in coaching and mentoring?

This field is not an occupation with an overall model of theory or of practice. Comparison can be made with occupations like 'Transactional Analysis therapist', which have strong unifying theory behind them; or accountancy, which has national and international practices that dictate how it should be conducted. In contrast to this position, there are many ways of delivering coaching and mentoring.

 **Reflective Questions**

- How much desire is there to standardize practice?
- Are those who purport to be interested in setting standards driven to further the profession and to improve the service to users or are they seeking personal advantage in an ambiguous marketplace?
- Is the development of standards in mentoring and coaching likely to lead to a pass or fail mentality, or is it likely to contribute to open-ended development?

There is a parallel with the World Boxing Federation which raises further questions: Are we seeking to create a unified belt in order to win the inter-professional competition for influence, to regulate out deviants or to improve standards?

Megginson et al. (2006) argue that there is a significant risk that the standard becomes the de facto maximum that training providers will aspire to and thus it becomes questionable if standards do indeed raise standards! A related issue is whether the requirement in some standards' frameworks for 'flying hours' (or number of hours of practice) as a criterion are another example of 'misplaced concreteness' (see Chapter 1). This approach has been pioneered by the International Coach Federation. A requirement for a number of coaching hours for particular grades of membership has also been adopted by the EMCC and by the Association for Coaching. For us it is a question of the quality of critical reflection that makes up those hours. This is rather like someone saying 'I have 30 years' experience' when what they might mean is they have had the same uncritical experience for 30 years!

If you decide to follow the standards route, then a pragmatic question is: Do you accredit the programme or the individuals or both? The EMCC has followed the route of both accrediting programmes and individuals in the UK, and increasingly in other European countries coach and mentor training providers are seeking accreditation. The International Coach Federation (ICF) is now going down this route as well.

## ARGUMENTS FOR A STANDARDS APPROACH

### Time of sponsors in dealing with bids

One of the ways that the need for standards emerged within EMCC conferences and other gatherings was in sponsors from large organizations complaining about the time they had to spend in dealing with unsolicited bids for work from coaches. It was as if aspiring coaches were going away on a weekend course and then stopping off at a service station on the motorway, going to a machine and printing off a business card claiming that they were a business coach. A perception arose that something had to be done – and the professional associations saw accreditation as the way to go.

### Creating an efficient market for coaching services

In an ambiguous market, there are greater transaction costs if product quality is hard to verify. These greater costs are borne in part by sponsors, who have to create bespoke processes to verify the quality of suppliers. However, the transaction costs also impinge on the suppliers.

First, the overall size of the market may reduce by marginal purchasers deciding that the game is not worth the candle and opting out.

Second, the ambiguity creates costs for sellers of services because they may have to spend unremunerated time on bespoke selection processes (beauty parades) in order to obtain work. Reducing ambiguity makes the market work more efficiently – sponsors can ask: Do you have ICF accreditation, or does your training as a coach receive the EMCC quality standard? And this could be all they need to ask because the profession has created standards for itself that are acceptable to the sponsors.

### Customers can judge standards easily

There are of course inherent ambiguities in answering the question: What is quality in coaching provision? However, for some purchasers getting a guarantee that a supplier is an accredited professional may be all the assurance they need. The Association for Professional Executive Coaching and Supervision (APECS) seeks to take the simplification process further by encouraging purchasers to become members and to allow the association to do the selecting of coaches for them.

## Arguments against a standards approach

On the other hand, there are arguments against standards. These are arguments of principle rather than of practice, so the debate about the usefulness of standards can be seen as a tussle between pragmatists, who want order and to get on with the job, and theorists, who see the apparent rationality of standards as being spurious and as kowtowing to unacknowledged and unattainable needs for certainty. There is clearly a conflict of discourses here!

## Creating problems in the market for coaching services

A new market has been created by the professional bodies, and that includes the accreditation market, the supervision market and now the team coaching market. The accreditation market has become highly successful with an ever-increasing supply of training providers in the marketplace. Arguably at least, this has created an oversupply of accredited coaches. The implications of this are yet to play out. The supervision market is still developing but, as mentioned in Chapter 5, there are now team coaching supervision specialist courses as well as accreditations in supervision offered by some universities and professional bodies. The team coaching seems to be developing at a pace. The reasons for this are varied and may include cost efficiency – coaching an individual is expensive, and doing it with a team may spread the cost. It will take time to access this development.

## Illusion of control – Misplaced concreteness

Many feel that if there are variable standards and opacity of performance in an occupation, then setting standards will resolve this problem. Critics of this view argue that standards related to mentor or coach training or alleged coach performance miss the point. Standards, to influence the improvement of coaching, need to attend to the relationship between the coach or mentor and their client. It is between our noses rather than between the coach's ears that the standard is established, and this raises the issue of authenticity in relationships. Pre-specified standards have the potential to create a coaching or mentoring relationship 'by numbers', thus unravelling core attributes of empathy and trust.

In practice, standards are located in an even wider forum than this – the context also dictates whether the experience is judged as being 'up to standard'. A mentor and mentee may both agree that the relationship was transformative and energizing for the mentee, but if the organization sponsor thinks it didn't meet the scheme agenda, or if the mentee's boss thinks that it didn't address their staff member's needs as the boss perceived them, then it may be judged as a failed intervention. And what about the mentee's colleagues or staff? Or the mentee's customers? Or the HR department? Or the government body funding the scheme? These are all important issues which, in our view, can only be addressed within the specific context of application because the boundaries that we put round the relationship – who is inside and who is outside – will influence, perhaps markedly, how any one-to-one relationship is perceived (see Colley, 2003; Stokes et al., 2020)

## Credentializing the passable

It is often said that 'what's measurable gets measured'. When people enquire about a course from a training provider or an education establishment they often ask: but can you be sure that it will make me a better coach? Providers, to deal with such enquiries, focus on particular competencies or curriculum that seems to them to satisfy their potential clients. What they offer is a set of abilities, and they say that in order to pass you have to demonstrate that you have these. But what about maverick coaches who want to use their own view of what helps? Or principled mentors who lodge their interventions in a view about what a just society might be like?

Providers of training have to be fair to all, so they are drawn into ensuring that there is a common template against which all will be measured. And then there is the question of marginally passable people. As external examiners and in our own institution we experience difficult cases where a course member's performance has been marginal – just about good enough to pass the course, but no more. Would you want to be coached or mentored by such a candidate? Probably not, but the credentializing process means that such people will inevitably be out there. No one wants to be operated upon by a brain surgeon who got 1% over the pass/fail boundary, but lots of patients are operated on by just such people, and the same principle follows for qualified coaches.

## Lack of coherence to coaching and mentoring as activities

We have made the point that many professional associations are held together by an extensive shared body of knowledge. In spite of the attempts by associations such as the EMCC and ICF, it is still the case that there is a huge range of ways of coaching and mentoring in all sectors of society (see Chapter 1). As this is the case, it makes setting standards more problematic than it would be for a more established profession. As pointed out in Chapter 1, both the literature and the marketplace are populated by people who see the practices of others as deeply flawed. For example: 'Don't go to a gestalt coach, they mess with your head'; 'If you go for a business coach who isn't solutions focused you'll spend all your time looking at problems'; 'Don't go to a mentor at all; they'll just dish out gratuitous advice.' This positioning is perhaps an inevitable consequence of the commodification of coaching and mentoring first raised in Chapter 1.

## A note on 360-degree feedback

A very helpful short article on 360-degree feedback (Goodge and Coomber, 2007) argues that coaches using 360-degree feedback should focus on performance rather than on the data. This accords with our own experience of using these tools. A crucial step is to identify the big goal, instead of getting bogged down in the minutiae. While working on this goal, Goodge and Coomber (2007) suggest that the coach helps the client to find 10 options for action, especially attending to change processes, use of time, delegation, meetings, structures, jobs, relationships and information systems, and not just books, courses or learning from others. This is strong advice, as 360-degree feedback tends to be an HR intervention and therefore HR remedies are often recommended.

Goodge and Coomber (2007) redirect our attention to learning and action in and through work itself, and away from the standards that lie behind most feedback frameworks. Additionally, the emergence of the self-mentoring model (Carr, 2012) outlined in Chapter 5 may provide an alternative way forward where the power of change is firmly placed in the hands of the mentee.

Such models as these would not require standards and accreditation because individuals genuinely hold their own development in their own hands.

## Conclusions

Standards are a pervasive part of organizational life. They can do much less than is often claimed for them. Nonetheless, for many, they are a necessary part of developing an emerging profession of coaching or of quality assuring the social movement of mentoring. In their somewhat different ways, all the major coaching and mentoring associations are advocating the use of quality assurance and standards. The main resistance against this trend comes from experienced and successful coaches and executive mentors who either see their competitive advantage and uniqueness in the marketplace eroded by such measures or feel that what is proposed does not reflect the reality of how experienced coaches and mentors actually work.

# PROFESSIONALIZATION

On professionalization, we ask how much professionalization is needed and appropriate in the field of coaching and mentoring, and the requirements for a profession that serves its customers. Is professionalization a convenient rationale by the proto-profession of coaching to help to raise prices, by restricting supply? Or does it regulate the 'dog eat shark' approach of commercialism? What happens to an occupation when it makes the journey from an unregulated group of practices to a unified profession? Will the insiders move closer to the centre while the outsiders are pushed further out? The latter point is offered as a critique of communities of practice in Chapter 9.

In coaching and mentoring we are dealing with a thoroughly amorphous cluster of interests and foci. The population varies according to:

Client group – the differences could not be wider: some executive coaches deal with the most senior levels in global companies; some social mentors deal with the most disadvantaged, demoralized and deskilled in our communities.

Level of skill – some line managers operating as coaches do so after a day or even less of training; some executive coaching organizations argue that to be a coach you need to first be qualified as a psychologist and then do extensive training after that.

Basis for helping skill – some executive coaches and small business mentors seem to think that having been in a senior position and having trod the same path as their clients, that is all they need to function well; other executive coaches argue that therapeutic skills of a high order are needed. Even among this latter group there are many sharp differences – some feel that existential therapy is the answer, others adhere to transactional analysis, others gestalt therapy; the list is endless.

We explore how much professionalization is needed or appropriate in the field of coaching and mentoring, and the requirements for a profession that serves its customers. What are the arguments for and against professionalization?

## Arguments for professionalization

### Emerging profession

Professionalization can be seen as a natural process that is followed by a huge range of occupations as part of their evolution. A body of knowledge is identified, it is codified (Blackler, 1995) and one or more membership organizations seek to defend the code and define the field. There are ancient professions – medicine, church, law – newer professions – accountancy, surveying, architecture – and proto-professions – coaching and mentoring, IT, facilities managers. According to this view, professionalization is a natural process and different occupations will flow along this course in a natural and somehow inevitable way.

### Control of poor performers and unethical practitioners

Every membership body concerned with coaching and mentoring has a code of ethics and an ethics committee to oversee it. This interest in ethics seems to be unfeigned. The EMCC ethics committee at a formative stage conducted a survey of members and found a remarkably high degree of interest in and use of the ethical standards among members. When offering external coaching or mentoring, sponsors are pleased to know that those selling their services are bound by a professional code. It is very unlikely that the purchaser will need to invoke the code – and the sanctions that its upholders can apply are limited in proto-professions. Nonetheless, sponsors report that it is good to know that it is there (see Chapter 14 for a discussion on ethics).

### Reduce burden of assessment of potential coaches

As discussed above under the heading 'Standards', there are money and time costs of not having standards, and professional membership acts as a useful first filter in assessing which coach or mentor a purchaser will use.

### Enables committed professionals to differentiate themselves in the market

Any rigorous process of entry to a professional body, if it does nothing else, at least separates those committed to the profession from casual or dilettante practitioners. And some years of study and reflection on professional practice is highly likely to create some improvement in performance in an overwhelming majority of cases, even if it can offer no guarantee in every individual so accredited.

Carried by a public-spirited and non-doctrinaire body, it can prevent partisan advocates of one particular approach from dominating the scene

In recent years, our experience of EMCC has led us to the conclusion that without associations like this the coaching profession could have been hijacked by people with a self-interested axe to grind. Psychologists would have been more tempted to claim that you have to be a psychologist to coach; retired executives would have had a louder voice calling for the T-shirt test (that you have to have been there to help others); and alumni of a particular school of coach training might have had a disproportionate traction on the market.

## Arguments against professionalization

### Focus on where the big bucks are rather than areas of greatest social need

It is surely no coincidence that the biggest interest in the multiplicity of associations involved in professionalizing coaching has clustered round executive coaching. There is an old joke that the answer to the question, 'What's the difference between a life coach and an executive coach?' is '£300 an hour'. In some quarters of central London the fee for executive coaching may change the punchline to as much as '£1,000 per hour'. By encouraging the development of a profession we might unwittingly marginalize those who work in unfashionable or badly funded areas, and this would be undesirable. It is also clear, as raised in Chapter 5, that there is an increasing interest in the notion of internal coaches within organizations, and how far the issue of professionalization is even relevant to this growing group is yet to be resolved.

### Self-interest of providers

More generally, professionalization can be seen as serving the self-interest of their members and not focusing on the good of the wider community of customers, clients, purchasers and society at large. So, while professions may not do much harm, they attend to doing 'good' primarily for their members and only secondarily for others if this helps them to maintain their mandate from society.

### Professionals are a conspiracy against the laity

George Bernard Shaw called all professions an organized conspiracy against the laity. This is the strongest case against professions in general: that they actively do harm to others by protecting the incompetent, defending the indefensible and preserving the mystery of the occupation from the prying eyes of outsiders who might question the taken-for-granted beliefs or dominant discourses of practitioners. A particular target of this attack on professions is the practice of members of the profession serving as judge and jury of behaviour in the profession. Cases of professional misconduct are handled universally by members of the profession themselves, and those outside the charmed circle may feel that their experience of the profession is given short shrift in the process.

## Ethical codes

As discussed in the above, professional associations claim that their ethical frameworks reassure potential clients or sponsors, ensure quality control, standards, accountability and protection. These are bold claims. However, there are complex arguments surrounding ethical behaviour and we wonder whether it is possible to deliver on these promises. So, what is ethics?

Ethics is a moral philosophy in which complex issues of good and evil, right and wrong, justice and injustice are considered. However, one person's right may be another person's wrong! Most professional associations create normative, prescriptive and often punitive ethical frameworks, which means that members who sign up to them will inevitably be either right or wrong, and this can mean that genuine ethical dilemmas could be swept under the carpet. For example, 'When is it OK to break confidentiality?' Normative certainty for complex questions such as this is a recipe for problems. Further, these codes offer 'protection from harm' without considering the potential benefits of actions that a code might deem as unethical. Ethical thinking (rather than codes) weighs up benefit versus harm on a case-by-case basis.

Additionally, ethics are socially defined and, as such, they are often created in a period of time to satisfy particular prevailing conditions. A set of rules created by one group of people to guide another at another time in the future may not remain contextually relevant. Therefore, it is ethically dubious to develop universal codes for future and unknowable situations because ethics are dynamic. For example, as already mentioned in this and previous chapters, an often-cited force behind the call for ethical frameworks is the 'Wild West' of coaching slogan. This could be construed as a controlling mechanism of 'frighten the horses and build a corral to pen them in!' Further, these codes are often justified in terms of 'it's what our members want', but the members are reflecting the same discourse that gives rise to the codes – better inside the proverbial tent etc., etc.! The sad result is paternal authority where the rights of individuals are side-lined 'under the guise of business ethics' (Schwartz, 2000: 175).

A further point is the often unacknowledged assumption behind ethical codes that individuals are 'rational purposive actors who act in accordance with their intentions and understand the implications of their actions' (De Cremer et al., 2010: S2). This leads to the conclusion that misdemeanours happen because of a few 'bad apples' or a few 'rogues'. Of course, this makes blame and punishment easier to dish out! More seriously, embedded in these codes are assumptions that an individual is able to balance an ethical dilemma consciously and thus avoid ethical misdemeanours. What of the coach or mentor who is working with their executive whose agenda is an improved performance involving taking huge risks with the organization's resources? The prize is personal gain for the executive and earning potential for the colluding coach but a possible threat to the organization's existence. Ethics here takes on a wider consideration than just the learner's agenda! Codes assume that ethics are clear and obvious when set in the context of 'real' practice (see Chapter 14).

Finally, so-called 'good' people do 'bad' things and may not even know! Tenbrunsel and Messick (2004: 224) suggest that 'individuals do not "see" the moral components of an ethical decision, not because they are morally uneducated, but because psychological processes fade the "ethics" from an ethical dilemma'. A classic case of the infinite human capacity to reframe and reinterpret, justify and post hoc rationalize – the very things that we as coaches work on with our clients! So, as coaches and mentors we know that people are not rational, have a marvellous capacity for making unsubstantiated assumptions and for self-delusion and yet we subscribe to ethical frameworks that assume that people are the opposite!

## Conclusions

Professions are seen as a pervasive feature of contemporary life, and so, it could be argued, coaching and mentoring need to get in on the game with everyone else. The case for this is supported by an austere vision for professions as the disinterested guardians of standards in public life. Standing against this argument for professions is the perspective that they operate largely on an agenda of self-interest. Reflecting on our own involvement with the coaching and mentoring profession, we see both these motives at work. Professionalization provides more education work for universities; it creates a climate where more people are likely to seek paid coaches and mentors. At the same time, we find ourselves impelled by a sense that we owe it to our clients and to the wider society to ensure that people who are licensed to coach and mentor abide by the highest professional standards and ethical codes and yet …

 **Case Study 15.1**

### The Redundant Manager

An individual with ten years' experience as a middle manager in large organizations has come to the point where they are threatened by the likelihood of redundancy in a year's time. They decide to set up as an independent self-employed coach.

### Case Questions

1. What would you advise them to do in preparation for making this transition?
2. How much attention do you think that they should pay to competencies, standards and professionalization?
3. Which professional body or associations do you think they should join and why?

 **Activity**

Access the EMCC's and the ICF's competency frameworks: https://www.emccglobal.org/wp-content/uploads/2018/10/EMCC-competences-framework-v2-EN.pdf; https://coachfederation.org/core-competencies.

*(Continued)*

## Questions

Compare and contrast these frameworks and consider:

- How far do these consider the purpose of the coaching or mentoring?
- How far do they consider the influences of the context in which the coaching and mentoring may occur?
- How far are the coachee's or mentee's requirements considered?
- How far are the commissioning organization's needs considered?
- How far are cultural issues taken into account?
- How easily are these assessed? How would you go about assessing them?

## CONCLUSIONS

To return to the three main questions we raised at the start of the chapter:

- Can and should competencies be used as a basis for describing the role of coach and mentor?
- Can and should standards be built upon these competencies?
- Can and should a professional accreditation be established on the basis of these standards?

This chapter, while focusing on standards, competencies and professionalization, has as an underlying theme: the question of social order and how it is maintained in communities of practice and in organizations availing themselves of the communities' services.

Taking the first question: yes, competencies can be used as a way of describing the role of a coach or mentor. The question of 'should they be?' is debatable with no clear answer.

To take the second question: standards could be built on a competency framework but, again, the question of 'should they be?' is still debatable.

The third question raises some conflicting issues. We conclude that there are strong pressures to bring order to mentoring and coaching communities, but perhaps this is driven by the dominant concept of the rational pragmatic manager first raised in Chapter 1. While there is nothing wrong with this concept, several hundred years of research into learning and development also point to alternative ways of interacting with the world. The risk of the rational pragmatic dominating is the risk inherent in Tayloristic 'one best way' practices which may be fine in a stable world but, as discussed in Chapter 13, diversity is a big challenge to humankind and a diversity-informed perspective embraces different and alternative views.

There are also persuasive arguments against a competency-based approach. These are based on both libertarian values and the search for innovation and impact from coaching and mentoring and a diversity mindset where difference is to be celebrated. The alternative is the logic of 'turtles all the way down' or the dominance of one powerbase (see Chapter 7) over another. In the end the current state is based on 'you pays your money and you take your choice': but is paying your money, one way or the other, a sophisticated and all-embracing position fit for the 21st century? Perhaps not!

## The Future Direction

While professional associations persist with the aim of normative and controlling models of competence, standards and ethical codes, there will always be a 'turtles' problem because there is no consensus as to what is right or wrong within coaching or mentoring – nor is there likely to be. In this situation, the legitimacy of universal ethical codes must continue to be questioned (see Chapter 16).

An alternative for professional associations is to aim to 'maximize benefit' and seek to enable members to 'do the right thing' through educational debate and collective continuing professional development. In this way the professionalization issues can be put into the open and discussed rather than become mired in the doubt that simple certainty creates. This is a much tougher task than writing standards and codes but one that recognizes the dynamic, individualistic and societal influences of competence, standards and ethics.

By way of an example, The British Association for Counselling and Psychotherapy (BACP) attempt to offer just this. In their publication *Guidance for Ethical Decision Making: A Suggested Model for Practitioners* (Gabriel and Casemore, 2010), they offer a 10-point checklist to assist the ethical decision-making process:

1. Stop, think and identify the situation or problem
2. Construct a description
3. Whose problem is it?
4. Review in terms of the Ethical Framework
5. Consider moral principles and values
6. Identify the support that is available
7. Identify courses of action
8. Select course of action
9. Evaluate the outcome (with the use of supervision where appropriate)
10. Regularly check the personal impact of these events. (2010: 2)

This checklist is preceded by a series of questions, for example:

What if... my client decides they want to commit suicide and refuses to give me permission to break confidence?

What if... my client wants me to hug her/him?

What if... my client wants to know details of my personal life?

What if... my clients live in the same small town as me and we find ourselves sharing social and recreational facilities?

What if... I want to become friends with one of my clients? (2010: 2)

This document offers a dynamic, developmental approach which is neither prescriptive nor punitive. It recognizes that ethical questions are dynamic, contextual and often in the moment.

*(Continued)*

We see pressure for competencies, standards and professionalization growing in the future, thanks to the combined interests of suppliers, purchasers, educators and regulators. We dream of a world where people have a more nuanced approach than this and negotiate their wishes between each other as free and responsible citizens. In a recent email post by Susan David (co-author of *Beyond Goals: Effective Strategies for Coaching and Mentoring*) she writes of:

> ...our tendency to look at one another as caricatures rather than the complex creatures we are. *Instead of seeing the whole person, it's easy to define one another by a single action* [...] it can be helpful to remember that the person you disagree so vehemently with is the same uncle who taught you to cast a fishing line or the same cousin who kept your middle school confidences. You don't have to see eye-to-eye or even condone your relatives' views to recognize each other's humanity. (Susan David, *Emotional Agility Newsletter*, 03/11/20: https://www.susandavid.com/)

At our university the number of people wanting to come on our competency-grounded, EMCC-standard-approved, professional Master's course is increasing year by year. This suggests that this approach is dominant. On the other hand, in recent years we have met a growing trickle of people coming to us and saying, 'Is there any way of studying this subject in a coaching way, where I negotiate the curriculum to meet my idiosyncratic needs, and where I do only what will be useful to my practice in my context?' We are developing ways to encourage and work with this trickle of people. Will the trickle become a flood? We hope so, but we are not holding our breath.

---

 ### Activity (based on email correspondence with ICF members, June 2015)

There appear to be dissenting factions within the coaching business. This seems to revolve around those who are for supervision and those who are against.

Those coaches who are for coaching supervision stake their claim with the use of a particular language. For example: 'marketing niche', 'lucrative', 'revenue opportunities', 'enormous sales volume' as well as 'manifold markets' that would be created if coaching supervision was made a compulsory requirement for, for example, ICF-accredited coaches. These new revenue streams would come from two main sources: further training fees to train to be a supervisor and fees from coaches supervising each other for fees. It appears that there are no 'quality' or 'safety' concerns here, just blatant business development without concern for the development of the profession. Some on the *for* side, particularly coaching psychologists, argue that it is essential to have supervision training because only trained people could spot the parallel process.

Those against mandatory coaching supervision are not totally against supervision, indeed many see it as a good idea, but this group would prefer choice as to the form it takes and see supervision as a CPD issue. The ICF already has a membership requirement of 40 hours of 'approved' ICF training and development every three years to maintain accreditation. This group also argues that they regularly participate in peer-to-peer consultation, have a strong network of 'critical friends' and engage in 'coach consultation'.

Consider this viewpoint: 'Supervision proponents seem to want no questioning or critique; indeed, I think they do want blind compliance. I can totally see the 'darker side' vulnerabilities, both the serious abuses and more subtle misuses of power.'

## Questions

- What discourses can you identify in this case example?
- What might be these 'darker sides'?
- How might these tensions be resolved?

 **Questions**

- For coaches and mentors, from where do you draw your professional credibility?
- What do purchasers say about the process and effects of working with you?
- What do the people you work with and their customers say about the effects of the coaching or mentoring?
- For sponsors of coaching in organizations, one of the big questions is: is it better to use proprietary selection processes for external coaches or go for some industry standard?
- Is the extra work involved in coming up with your own standards worth the benefits of customization?
- In one case in the public service in the UK, a department of state (the Department of Work and Pensions) has used the same list of external coaches as another public body (the National Health Service Institute) – for you to do this, would it be avoiding reinventing the wheel or is it sub-optimizing on being clear about what you are looking for in external providers?
- For those seeking to regulate the activity, a core question is: do you go it alone or seek wider co-ordination across a number of associations? (The latter path is more difficult but potentially has more rewards for participants and users alike.)
- Another question is: do you focus upon regulating out by keeping those less fit to practise at a disadvantage in the market?
- Or do you attempt to improve standards with a focus upon increasing the average effectiveness of practitioners?

 **Further Reading**

For some fresh air in discussions about coaching, have a look at: Du Toit, D. (2014) *Making Sense of Coaching*. London: SAGE.

For some debate relevant to the discussions in this chapter, read: Gray, D.E., Garvey, B. and Lane, D.A. (2016) *A Critical Introduction to Coaching and Mentoring*. London: SAGE.

For a discussion on assessment and accreditation see: Garvey B. (2016) 'Issues of assessment and accreditation of coaches', in T. Bachkirova, G. Spence and D. Drake (eds) *The SAGE Handbook of Coaching*. London: SAGE, pp 682–697.

# PART 4

## TOWARDS A THEORY OF COACHING AND MENTORING

# 16

# PERSPECTIVES ON COACHING AND MENTORING FROM AROUND THE GLOBE

## CHAPTER OVERVIEW

This chapter is different from previous chapters as it acts as a critical springboard into the final chapter where we refine our developing theories of coaching and mentoring.

This chapter offers views on the state of play in coaching and mentoring practice from a variety of international perspectives. The discussion begins with a presentation of nine case studies provided by colleagues from nine different international locations. These have been reviewed for this fourth edition. Some of these include references to the continent to which they belong, for example South America and Africa, while at the same time being anchored in a particular country. To our knowledge, this is the first attempt to do this and, apart from survey data (see Bresser, 2009, 2013; ICF, 2016; Sherpa Coaching, 2016; see also Coaching Survey at www.coaching-surveys.com), little else is published on the subject of globalization in coaching and mentoring. Each case is analysed and the various themes identified are explored by considering how far practices are converging, diverging or crossverging (see the Introduction for an explanation of these terms) in the various locations represented here. We consider how far these trends are influenced by the specific cultural settings and how far they are products of globalization and possible neofeudalistic (see Chapter 12) tendencies of the professional associations. The cases are not presented as research or research findings but rather as illustrative examples from practitioners and academics working in various international locations. However, from a narrative research point of view, we believe that these are 'authentic' descriptions and therefore have some legitimacy.

## INTRODUCTION

In Chapter 12, we introduce the idea that, according to Clifford Shearing (2001), globalization has brought with it neofeudalism. This is, in essence, power over the many by the few. Bauer (2014) states: 'Neofeudalism replaces a broadly prosperous middle with a highly stratified society, in which a tiny elite lords it over a vast mass of the struggling poor.'

The neofeudalistic discourse finds its way into the workplace – particularly in Human Resource Management discourses – where:

> firms are increasingly pressured to develop coherent global strategies, resulting in the coordinated internationalization of HR at all levels. To effectively meet this challenge, firms seek to lower costs by identifying best economic practices in general business operations, and in human resource management (HRM) in particular, and standardizing these practices across their global operational units. (Paik et al., 2011: 648)

Paik et al. (2011) go on to argue that the limitations of this approach are not appropriately explored. For example, little account is taken of local differences in management practices, the political climate, religious and social differences, attitudes and values, the stage of technical development and the workforce demographics. They comment: 'All of these factors may bedevil a convergence perspective and support a divergence perspective, where managing HR on international and global scales becomes more challenging and complex than within one fairly homogeneous domestic context' (2011: 648).

We use the term 'convergence' here to mean the idea that practices in different countries and contexts are becoming similar to each other. In contrast, we use the term 'divergence' to refer to the idea that practices are becoming more different from each other across different countries and contexts.

This brings us to the practices of coaching and mentoring. With the rise of professional associations for coaching and, to some extent, mentoring, we speculate as to how far their role is a neofeudalistic one which advocates 'convergence' to international standards. There is a paucity of literature within coaching and mentoring on this topic and we therefore draw on research on cultural practices in management and employment within globalized businesses as 'proxy' literature.

A study by Frenkel and Peetz (1998) suggested that cultural factors tend to limit convergence, despite there often being a convergence of management and employment practices. They concluded that the impact of globalization is dependent on factors related to the specific and individual contexts of practice. Frenkel and Kuruvilla (2002) argue that while there is some convergence of employment practices across countries, there are counter pressures for a more divergent approach caused by localized practices on income protection and what constitutes harmonious relationships. Katz and Darbishire (2000) argue that there is both a convergence of global HR practices globally and a greater localized divergence of practices within individual countries. This is a curious position and suggests that, while neofeudalistic tendencies abide in globalized companies, local practices tend to alter or moderate these. This tendency can result in what Paik et al. (2011) call 'crossvergence', where a compromise position is reached which contains elements of both convergent and divergent pressures. Parboteeah et al. (2009), for example, show that all major religions promote values such as supporting one another, providing help and developing respect, which can translate into positive behaviours and outcomes at work. Further, Jackson (2002) noted that a crossvergence approach within a place such as Hong Kong created a successful hybrid management system. Crossvergence theory suggests that as different cultures interact with each other, cultural hybrids develop and the effects of strong instrumentalist approaches, as promoted by the USA, Australia and other English speaking countries, tend to weaken. Similarly, humanistic cultures, as found in the East and Asia, become hardened by instrumentalism.

With the rise of professional associations for coaching and, to some extent, mentoring, we speculate as to how far their role is a neofeudalistic one and, therefore, in taking an international perspective on coaching and mentoring practices, we consider how far standardization (convergence), as specified by professional bodies like, for example, the ICF, is the norm and how far there is localized or culturally sensitive variation (divergence or crossvergence).

## METHODOLOGY

In this chapter, we have collected case examples of coaching and mentoring practice from the USA, Africa, Saudi Arabia, Hong Kong, Russia, Australia, South America, the Czech Republic and Sri Lanka. We present these narratives or personal commentaries, written by academic practitioners located within these places, and then discuss the cases by considering how far practices are converging in line with a normalizing view and how far practices are divergent, reflecting local and cultural attitudes. In requesting these commentaries, we did not want to ask the contributors to work to a template but rather to express their own views. This is in keeping with the principles of narrative research, where providing a template would, in some ways, be us working to our agenda. In this way, these narratives are authentic and provided in 'good faith'. We do not seek to 'prove' anything with these narratives but to start a train of thought and a debate. This work may develop in the future.

We consider the question of how far professional bodies could simply be following the same patterns as the neofeudalistic tendencies of globalized business where freedom of activity is for the few and oppression through legislation and regulation is for the many. Thus, we are moving away from the dominant discourse of psychology in coaching and mentoring towards a sociological and economic perspective by taking into account localized social practices in relation to coaching and mentoring.

The ICF, for example, claims that membership represents 'the highest quality of professional coaching. We are committed to helping you be the best coach you can be by connecting you with opportunities for network-building and continuous growth. Succeed in your coaching career by connecting with outstanding business development and professional growth opportunities, the local and global ICF coaching communities, and cutting-edge research' (https://coachingfederation.org/join-icf).

In addition, it offers individual and programme accreditation, an extensive list of competencies arranged in a hierarchical and progressive table (in five different languages), bylaws, a code of conduct, a code of ethics and a recommendation that coaches receive regular supervision by a trained supervisor. The ICF also claims that its position on CPD is aligned with the Chartered Institute of Personnel and Development (CIPD), the Association for Coaching (AC) and the European Mentoring and Coaching Council (EMCC), a heavyweight of power indeed!

We employ the above paragraph in our thinking about the cases.

## Reflective Questions

- In relation to coaching and mentoring, how far is convergence appropriate and necessary across the world?
- In relation to coaching and mentoring, how far is convergence possible and desirable?
- In relation to coaching and mentoring, how far is divergence manageable and appropriate?
- Within the discourse of professional coaching and mentoring bodies, what are the implications of divergence, convergence and crossvergence?

We thank our contributors for their efforts here and acknowledge their important contributions to the discussions.

## Case Study 16.1

### The state of play of coaching and mentoring in Australia by Paul Lawrence

Most organizations in Australia use coaches and mentors, though few yet integrate coaching or mentoring into their business strategies. In most cases external coaches and mentors are deployed on an ad-hoc basis or as part of standalone schemes, usually part of individual development offerings. Many organizations are seeking to build their internal capacity for coaching and mentoring, offering internal skills development programs to leaders inside the organization.

There remains a lack of consensus as to the difference between coaching and mentoring. The prevalent view is still that coaching is best defined as helping someone to help themselves, whilst mentoring is advising someone what to do, based on the wisdom and experience of the mentor. For example, from the website of the Australian Human Resources Institute (AHRI):

> To be a mentor - by definition an experienced and trusted adviser – you need to have at least four years' HR experience. Being a mentor means you have the HR experience and skills that you can pass on to someone with less experience.

The Australia Council for the Arts, *Guide to Mentoring*, on the other hand, differentiates between coaching and mentoring as follows:

> Coaching is a training relationship with some aspects of mentoring. A coach will help a person to solve specific problems and may set specific tasks or homework for the person to do between sessions. There is generally less 'sharing' by the coach of personal experiences; the relationship is not as peer-based and is more focused on particular issues rather than overall personal development. The mentor helps the mentee to see the big picture. As part of this process, the mentor helps the mentee to identify themes and patterns in their past behaviour, and potentially limiting or unproductive beliefs. (www.australiacouncil.gov.au/workspace/uploads/files/_aca_guide-to-mentoring_2016_f-584f4208ee372.pdf)

This lack of alignment as to the nature of coaching and mentoring shows up across the board, as HR professionals without a specialist background in coaching or mentoring seek guidance from different external parties in creating their internal frameworks.

There is little visible activity yet when it comes to professionalizing mentoring or attempting to establish common competency frameworks or processes for accreditation. All three of the big global coaching/mentoring associations are now present in Australia. The International Coaching Federation (ICF) has been established for more than 10 years and has approximately 1,200 members. The Association for Coaching (AC) established a New South Wales presence late in 2018, followed by the emergence of active hubs in Victoria, Queensland, Australian Capital Territory and South Australia in 2019/2020. The European Mentoring and Coaching Council (EMCC) hosted its inaugural Asia Pacific conference in 2019 but as of yet there is little local activity in Australia.

The importance of coaching supervision is now more widely recognized. Research suggests that supervision had made only modest inroads into the local profession as recently as 2014. The growth of supervision since may be linked to the offering of coach supervision training locally, first by the Coaching Supervision Academy and more recently by Oxford Brookes University, and by the continuing advocacy for supervision by academic institutions. The arrival of the AC into Australia means that there is now also present a global coaching association that is an unequivocal advocate for coaching supervision.

## SUMMARY OF MAIN POINTS

In Australia, coaching and mentoring activity seems widespread. It appears that the ICF is a dominant body, although the AC seems to be gaining traction. Supervision appears to be developing but its uptake is sporadic; however, the AC's approach to supervision is informed by 'psychological mindedness' (Bluckert, 2006) and currently follows a CPD route. Paul Bluckert suggests that supervision training is important and developing. Paul argues that there is a 'lack of consensus' about the similarities and differences between coaching and mentoring and this has led to HR professionals seeking external help to create internal frameworks. The presence of three main professional bodies suggests that these may be the providers of 'help'. The fairly recent presence of the EMCC in Australia suggests that this may be the source of information on mentoring.

---

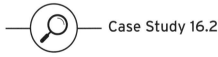 Case Study 16.2

### The state of coaching and mentoring in the USA by Dawn Chanland

Coaching and mentoring are two popularly used practices in the United States as tools to enhance employee development and performance. With regard to mentoring, Americans in their formative years are acculturated informally and through primary education on the value of having a mentor as a way to grow their skills and knowledge and to advance in their careers. Later, universities and onboarding and leadership development programs formally educate employees on the wide array of professional and personal relationships that can offer

*(Continued)*

mentoring functions and encourage people to seek out their own 'board of advisors' (Shen et al. 2015). In the workplace, formal mentoring programs are widely used in medium- and large-sized organizations to pair more seasoned professionals with junior ones for the purpose of growth and development. Over 70% of Fortune 500 companies provide them in some structured format (Johnson et al., 2020). Reverse mentoring programs and team and group mentoring are also used to a lesser degree as organizations to enable protégés to gain exposure to multiple individuals with varied skills, as well as partner senior and junior employees to support generational understanding and the transmission of both parties' skills and knowledge (Murphy, 2012; Chopra et al., 2020).

While the success of formal programs in the United States varies across organizations, human resources professionals and executive sponsors of programs generally encourage volunteerism on the part of mentors, input into the matching process, and include some form of training for the paired dyads at the onset of the program, all of which have been shown to enhance mentoring program effectiveness (e.g. Egan and Song, 2008). Although recognized as of value, relatively few programs require senior mentors to sponsor their protégés to advance them to the next level. This is a current challenge and consideration among some executives and human resources professionals as organizations seek to provide workplaces that are inclusive and grow and value a diverse employee base. In particular, there is increasing awareness that women and minorities need sponsorship support and equal access to formal and informal mentorship in order for diversity and inclusion goals to be reached, and more importantly, to nurture a strong workplace and culture. Reflecting this growing awareness, there are more calls in corporate America for white men to ally with women and marginalized colleagues to support and advance them (e.g., Melaku et al., 2020).

The term 'coach' in the United States is used in a number of ways, most commonly referring to someone who provides guidance to enhance an employee's performance. Coaching as a practice usually involves one of two mechanisms: high-potential and other leadership development program participants are asked to coach each other or more commonly provided with an 'executive coach' (usually an externally hired coach) to support them during the program; managers are being trained to become better coaches of their teams and direct reports.

Some have aptly noted the 'Wild West' of executive coaching (Sherman and Freas, 2004) in which the lack of universally accepted standards that guide coaches' experience and knowledge base makes it difficult to choose externally hired coaches and ensure coaching is effective. Countering this challenge, however, is the International Coach Federation, a global organization committed to educate coaches through skill development – i.e. culminating in coaching certification – and ethical conduct codes (ICF, 2020). Aspiring coaches who secure one of the ICF credentials tout them as a means to legitimize their coaching abilities and thus gain contracts with companies with budgets that support their hire.

More US organizations are formally educating managers on how to be coaches of their employees for the purpose of employee performance, retention, and organizational and job satisfaction. Varied approaches prevail at this point, as some organizations emphasize that their managers should be able to provide direction and constructive feedback to their direct reports, while others, consistent with the ICF approach, guide their managers to ask powerful questions of their employees and allow those employees to lead coaching conversations. A key cultural challenge to managerial coaching is the US emphasis on immediate productivity, which prevents managers from spending the time needed to coach their teams in favor of immediate outcomes either requested by senior leaders or assumed to be more valued. Time will tell as to whether managerial coaching continues to grow within US workplaces.

## SUMMARY OF MAIN POINTS

Mentoring is associated with development in the USA and coaching more with immediate employee performance.

Both are common practices yet formal mentoring programs are more pervasive alongside employees' understanding of the need to cultivate their own boards of advisors.

The ICF, which offers certifications, a coaching code of conduct, and competencies, has helped nurture accountability and capability within the coaching field.

The United States has yet to fully harness mentoring and coaching as vehicles to support all employees, focusing on high-potentials and middle managers rather than a full swath of employees, including women and marginalized groups.

---

 Case Study 16.3

### Coaching in South America – a 'glocal' practice? By Pauline Fatien Diochon

*NB: The term 'glocal' in this context means a combination of both generic and specific local features in perhaps a more crossvergent way.*

Coaching in South America reflects the state of affairs of the global industry: a burgeoning and diversified discipline, with strong local characteristics. Despite homogenization forces (such as the growing presence of international coaching training schools and associations), each region, if not country, in South America (La Plata countries, Brazil, Andean countries, countries at the Caribbean Sea) presents specificities in terms of the growth of coaching, its acceptance as a business tool, and types of practices (Bresser, 2013).

Overall, coaching is expanding in South America, and coaching seems adopted as a business tool in Argentina, Brazil, Colombia and Perú. According to a 2020 ICF Coaching Global study, in 2019, there are about 11,000 coaching practitioners (+323% compared to 2012), 65% being female coaches (against 70% in the global coaching population), generating an average annual income of $20,900 US dollars (against $47,100 globally), which amounts to $191 million of revenues for the region (+107% increase, largely over the +21% growth rate worldwide).

**Table 16.1** Number of coaches and annual income worldwide

| | Number of coach practitioners (female share) | Average annual revenue/ income from coaching | Total annual revenue from coaching for the region (million) | % of change in revenue rate; # of coach practitioners for the region (2012-19) |
|---|---|---|---|---|
| South America | 11,000 (65%) | $20,900 | $191 | +161%; +323% |
| North America | 23,300 (75%) | $62,500 | $1296 | +83%; +47% |
| Global | 71,000 (70%) | $47,100 | $2849 | +43%; +49% |

*Source*: Summarized from 2020 ICF and PwC Global Coaching Study.

*(Continued)*

This recourse and expansion, as well as the nature of coaching, seem to be shaped by local characteristics, such as cultural, social, economic, political and historical factors. First, access to coaching seems conditioned by its financial availability, which potentially correlates its use to economic wealth. In this matter, the emergence of online coaching, with lower fees and more affordable apps and programs, might be a way to democratize the access to the practice. Second, a limited exposition to coaching, and familiarity with its principles, for social or cultural reasons, can increase the reluctance to engage in this introspective practice (Shoukry, 2016) sustained by a formal dialogue with an external third party. In high power distance cultures (such as Venezuela), directivity and a knowing position from the helping figure would be expected, which can contradict some ground principles of most coaching approaches.

Still, the practice benefits in some areas from an expanding culture of self-growth (like Argentina, Colombia) and a favourable economic context. This can translate, mostly in international and large national organizations, into the development of a strong coaching culture where managerial coaching is blooming, since, in 2019, 2,900 leaders and managers (including HR and Talent Development Managers) applied coaching skills and approaches in their workplace (ICF, 2020).

In terms of approaches, Bresser (2009) interestingly points out that in many countries (e.g. Argentina, Brazil, Chile, Perú), there are national coaching schools and associations, which suggest a more local shape and development of coaching, even if international coaching associations are also present (such as the ICF having chapters in most countries in South America). But attention to social and historical factors can again explain some specificities; practices such as ontological, spiritual coaching, or peace coaching contrast with more goal- and performance-oriented approaches that seem to prevail in the USA especially.

Overall, the social engagement of coaches is noticeable; South American coaches seem to demonstrate, more than in any other part of the world, a strong commitment to local charitable missions.

To conclude, prospects look very interesting for coaching and mentoring in South America. While mentoring is starting to get attention, internal coaching has room for development. External coaching is generally on its way to professionalization, with not only a noticeable effort to educate coaches, but also a larger set of stakeholders (such as the paying organization); supervision is a domain that still requires further attention, as it seems only widespread in Venezuela. But, as importantly, the development of coaching and mentoring in South America, with a combination of both generic and specific local features, which is called 'glocal' in the title of this text, is probably an inspiring invitation to focus on the social-cultural-political contexts of the practice and its evolution; it raises awareness of the self-improvement paradigm (see Wildflower, 2013) that has shaped this phenomenon and calls for increased recognition of the interdependence of individual, organizational and social changes (Shoukry, 2016), in an effort to support the empowerment of individuals within organizational and national emancipatory contexts (Fatien Diochon and Lovelace, 2015; Louis and Fatien Diochon, 2018; Shoukry and Cox, 2018).

The author would like to thank all the coaches that were interviewed when writing this text.

## SUMMARY OF MAIN POINTS

Coaching in South America, from this case study, appears to be increasing and fast developing in both social and commercial contexts. While there is the presence of professional bodies like the ICF, there is also evidence that more local concerns in relation to coaching activity are also present. Supervision is in its infancy. It is interesting to note the charitable orientation of coaching in South America as opposed to a commercial orientation. This may indicate that coaching and mentoring activity is part of a movement for social change. It is also interesting to note the interest in non-mainstream approaches which may indicate a movement away from the larger professional bodies. Time will tell.

 Case Study 16.4

## Coaching and mentoring in the Czech Republic by Roman Chudoba

Coaching is a still-growing industry. For businesses and the general public, coaching seems to be now even a more standard term; however, still with a vast range of meanings, understanding and experiences. There is easy access to a full offer of individual coaching services and coaching education except for the academic level. Team coaching and a systemic approach to organizational development start to be mentioned, though very seldomly practised. There is a growing acceptance and expectation that a coach may need at least a course and some certificate.

The number of coaches produced by coaching schools is increasing. However, the demand from businesses seems to have stagnated or even decreased, so it is hard for the newly established coaches to find business opportunities.

Also, the current development associated with coronavirus in the Czech Republic mainly leads to a reduction in the budget for development and education. This can be expected further to reduce the demand for external coaching and mentoring services. It could be said that supply far exceeds demand. One of the critical factors of this situation may be rooted in that coaching is provided mainly on an individual level with a focus on individuals, and organizations do not see adequate cost/benefit justification.

During recent years mentoring and use of mentors has grown faster than coaching. Mentoring has still a widely shared understanding of having someone senior and more experienced to teach you something you need to perform at work or in life, and that it is based on advice provisioning. It is now more common that you may have access to a mentor at your workplace, and this possibility is rather welcome and appreciated. Other approaches to mentoring are quite rare. We can notice a growing number of mentoring programs being provided internally, on a cross-company basis or by different agencies, mainly on a volunteer free-of-charge basis. The training of mentors is still considered unnecessary, and the same is even more true for the mentees.

Coaching and mentoring is still looking for a way to academia. There is no university accredited program at a graduate or postgraduate level. Thanks to international collaboration through research organized by EMCC or surveys by ICF, interested individuals are involved in these projects. A few universities offer coaching/mentoring as a one or two-semester optional course.

Coaching and mentoring are predominantly used as performance development approaches or tools in businesses and organizations focusing on individuals. Life coaching is widely offered with blurred boundaries with therapy or counselling. Sport coaching has a more substantial presence with its dedicated quarterly magazine and accent on mental capacity development. Coaching or mentoring support is becoming broadly available in aid and charity industries. There are many uses of the term coaching and mentoring in such cases where consultancy or advisory approaches are the reality. Professional coaches usually refer to education with a

*(Continued)*

psychological, psychotherapeutic or therapeutic background which suggests limited ability for work at a systemic organizational level.

The professionalization agenda is still well behind business development. Until 2018 there were three professional associations: EMCC, ICF and CAKO (Czech Association of Coaches) offering the full professional offerings for its members. In 2019 CAKO joined EMCC recognizing the potential of international outreach and quality of standards. There are some other associations which represent rather concrete coaching or mentoring approaches/methods and which promote the business interests of its members. Still, the two international associations have around 200 members out of an estimated 4,000 coaches/mentors in the Czech Republic. There are about 90 accredited coaches within these associations. Accreditation is used mostly for business promotion purposes rather than a quality assurance tool, and the need for professionalization is not strongly recognized by either a majority of coach practitioners or by businesses and organizations. However, unlike in previous years, there is a growing interest in professional accreditation, especially among beginning coaches.

The previously created shared platform for ethics (EPPOK), which used to organize three workshops on this subject a year, has come to an end. ICF decided to take its own way after CAKO joined EMCC. In general, it could be said that ethics does not enjoy focused attention. Anecdotally expressed, the vast majority of coaches, mentors, and organizations feel more ethical than average. We can attribute a particular share to the current political and social development of the Czech Republic, when some ethical nuances in coaching and mentoring may fall below the discernment threshold compared to the number and size of ethical dilemmas in the society.

Supervision for coaches is in its very natal phase. Occasionally it is provided for those who have completed some coaching training in the form of follow-up. The need for supervising mentors is not understood. If supervision is offered, it is provided and delivered on a psychotherapeutic/therapeutic basis. Specific supervision for coaches is still to be introduced and is in need of further development.

## SUMMARY OF MAIN POINTS

Coaching and mentoring are still developing and growing as business activities within the Czech Republic. It appears, from this case example, that there are many different approaches and two main professional bodies in operation in the Czech Republic. The dominant focus is on individuals and their individual performance. Coach training appears to be on the increase, although there are few recognized educational institutions engaging in the activity. Internal coaching or, perhaps, mentoring activity seems to be increasing as costs are creating pressures on businesses. Supervision is in its early stages and not fully understood.

---

 **Case Study 16.5**

### Coaching and mentoring in The Russian Federation and other eastern countries by Boris Tkachenko

The practice of mentoring in entrepreneurship started in Russia in 2008 with the Youth Business Russia programme (YBR) being implemented by the International Business Leadership Forum (IBLF), Russia. The YBR managers explored the international experience of Youth Business International (www.youthbusiness.org) mentoring in entrepreneurship in at least four countries around the world. Boris Tkachenko, CEO of Youth Business Russia, completed the training on international mentoring methodology in August 2008, provided by John Cull during a YBI/Accenture joint seminar. Thereafter, YBI methodology was translated and tailored for use in Russia.

The word 'mentorstvo' or 'mentoring' has a preaching connotation in the Russian language, so, within YBR, the term 'nastavnichestvo' is used to describe mentoring. 'Nastavnichestvo' comes from Soviet times when a young employee who was starting his/her career at a manufacturing or scientific enterprise was supervised by an expert who introduced them to practical work in the profession.

Within YBR, training seminars for mentors and mentees were developed and tested and now a common approach is developing in other regions of Russia. There is regular consultation among mentoring coordinators in the various regions and the training is regularly reviewed and developed.

After having gained experience in mentoring through the regional programmes, IBLF Russia and YBR have extended their activities to support mentoring for young entrepreneurs in Serbia, Mongolia, Kyrgyzstan, Uzbekistan and Armenia.

YBR actively seeks to learn and to develop its mentoring work and has interacted with many international leaders in the field to this end, often via webinars given by such experts as David Clutterbuck, John Sunderland Wright, Bob Garvey and Catherine Mossop.

Continuing to promote mentoring for young entrepreneurs, IBLF Russia/YBR was the first to introduce mentoring methodology in the framework of a pilot project for budding entrepreneurs, together with the Centre for Entrepreneurship, in 2010–11 in Moscow. At the beginning of 2016, IBLF established the Mentoring Institute as a social business, for systemic activity on mentoring promotion, further development of methodology and implementation of partner projects in various areas, including mentoring projects for business and educational institutions. In 2017–18 The Mentoring Institute provided methodological and expert support in the launch and implementation of the online mentoring component in the 'Business Class' programme of Google and the Sberbank.

During the coronavirus pandemic in 2020, Youth Business International launched a new global initiative SOS MENTORING (see Chapter 10) to provide additional support entrepreneurs in the countries of presence, leveraging the expertise of mentors. Youth Business Russia and the Mentoring Institute took part in development of this new initiative and are actively promoting it into the Russian speaking YBI programmes. To this end, YBR led a series of webinars for more than 200 mentors from six countries; the webinars were conducted in May–June 2020.

YBR faced skepticism on the part of entrepreneurs at the beginning of the promotion of mentoring. Later, as pioneers in mentoring, YBR understood the necessity of pilot projects. The most challenging task in the beginning was to find the first mentors. The next important step was to show the cases and offer mentors and mentees to talk about their experiences and involve others. With the help of YBR and MI, mentoring in Russia has become a trend. Unfortunately, part of our success has been replicated by others who have sadly developed, in our view, unethical and unprofessional approaches with the sole purpose of creating commercial opportunities. YBR and the MI constantly work to maintain high quality, professional and ethical mentoring, which is based on research and international experience.

In every case of implementing mentoring, the systemic project approach is important, with all stages – search and selection of mentors and mentees, training of mentors and mentees, matching using a special methodology, conducting first meetings of pairs under supervision,

*(Continued)*

monitoring pairs, assessing the performance of each pair at the end and the project as a whole. A system of support for running projects / mentors / mentees is required – holding Mentoring Clubs for all project participants, conducting training to improve the skills of mentors. It is necessary to constantly promote mentoring through events, websites and social networks.

Next steps: YBR and MI are now in the process of creating a Russian-speaking movement of business mentors on the basis of the website www.mentorship.su and channel in Telegram for mentors' communication and improving their mentoring skills online; there is an integration of the Russian-speaking movement of business mentors into the YBI Global Movement of business mentors.

## Coaching

Coaching started in Russia in the early 1990s and was fully based on European technologies. The first coaches studied in Europe and western trainers were invited to Russia. Coaching was very popular in the 1990s and noughties until the 2008 recession. During these years, the breed of Russian coaches with their own programmes matured. Coaching can generally be divided into two types: one psychotherapy oriented and the other not related to psychotherapy. In recent years, the demand for coaching has dropped due to the economic downturn and the subsequent decreased ability to pay in the private sectors. Trying to overcome this situation, coaches have combined into several associations (competing with each other), based on international or domestic connections, and have organized training for members and conferences for promotion of their services for the corporate sector.

## SUMMARY OF MAIN POINTS

Coaching has been established in Russia since the 1990s, whereas mentoring is more recent. Coaching has been either therapy based or performance based. The economy in Russia has led to a downturn in coaching activity and various groups have set up to try to counter this, but these are now competing with each other. Mentoring has developed in The Russian Federation mainly in relation to youth entrepreneurship but there is growing interest in educational settings. The development of mentors has, so far at least, been based on good international practice and not on any one approach as promoted by professional associations; however, YBI invites various country members to establish a consistent approach to mentor training while respecting local and cultural variations. In line with YBI's approach, the organizers of mentoring in the youth business setting in Russia are open to and willing to learn from good practice from wherever it comes, and to adapt this to suit the Russian context. Mentoring, through YBI, has expanded into other eastern countries.

---

 Case Study 16.6

### Coaching and mentoring in Hong Kong by Pansy Lam

Coaching was 'imported' from the West into Hong Kong more than two decades ago and has been used mostly in the corporate setting. To many people, coaching is still a relatively new kind of people intervention and it is often misunderstood to be an equivalent to mentoring or counselling.

Most of the professional coaches have been trained in local training schools in English, which is the second language of most people in Hong Kong, who are mainly (98%) of Chinese ethnic origin. This is a unique group of Chinese people who have been highly influenced by western customs and traditions due to 155 years of British rule. However, they are also very Chinese in their thoughts and behaviours due to their original Chinese heritage. This includes Confucianism as an underpinning philosophy.

I conducted (Lam, 2016) a mixed methods research study into culture and coaching within Hong Kong with a focus group and a 62-person survey. Its purpose was to explore three things:

1.   Whether Chinese culture prevails in Hong Kong
2.   Whether Confucianism is the dominant value in Hong Kong
3.   Views regarding whether coaching is compatible with the unique culture of Hong Kong.

In summary, the findings suggested that Hong Kong people accept coaching as an open discussion for both parties to share issues and concerns freely at an equal status level. Confucianism does not appear to have a high impact on Hong Kong people's acceptance of the western technique of coaching. Despite their Confucian views on respecting seniors and following advice from wiser people, Hongkongers do not see the coach as a senior. They understand the role of the coach as a facilitator of learning and someone who helps draw out their potential. The idea of the future orientation of coaching is acceptable to most Hongkongers. They do not see coaching as the solution to issues and problems, but rather see it as being about helping clients see the future clearly, as they set objectives after evaluating their various options with the coach. They do not tend to expect the coach to provide answers to their questions or give them any advice.

Another qualitative research was conducted in 2016 (Lam, 2019) to investigate the perception of coaching in eight Asian countries/territories, Hong Kong being one of them. The research aimed to collect opinions on:

•   how can coaching methods rooted in the western approach be applied in the context of other cultures;
•   identifying unique indigenous cultural characteristics as well as challenges associated with coach-client relationships in the Asian Confucian context.

One of the significant findings is about the term 'coaching' in Chinese (a language with a lot of similarities in many Sinosphere countries/territories). The 'misperception' of coaching to many Chinese participants comes from the translation of the word 'coaching', which is made up of two characters 教練'. The first character '教' (gaau3) means someone who teaches, trains or instructs and the second character '練' (lin6) means practises or drills. It gives people the idea that the coach provides training, gives instruction and new knowledge as well as drills the client. This people-helping professional is expected to be an expert like a professional trainer, a specialist or a consultant. Due to this terminology issue, the role of the coach and the function of coaching might have been overtly misinterpreted. Human resource professionals have yet to be educated when purchasing and implementing coaching for people development as many have always been referring coaching to mentoring and/or counselling for star performers and/or under-performers.

K.T. Lai, a veteran human resource professional and ex-president of the Hong Kong Institute of Human Resource Management, together with his group of coaching colleagues, recommended

*(Continued)*

a more insightful translation of the term 'coaching' as '啓悟'. This proposed translation combines two characters, the first '啓' (kai2), means exploring and understanding the self; stimulating thinking, as well as enlightening. The second character '悟' (ng6) means revelation, the realization of the truth. These two Chinese characters encompass 'inspiring' and 'enlightening', which may be more appropriate functions of a coach.

It is imperative that the Chinese term 'coaching' needs re-defining and officializing by professional coaching associations for more impactful development of coaching, especially in the area of executive coaching in Hong Kong and in other Sinosphere territories.

## SUMMARY OF MAIN POINTS

Coaching has always been seen as a people intervention 'imported' from the West as most coach trainings are conducted in English. Hong Kong Chinese seem able to live with the tensions between an individual's status in society and the role of a coach. A coach is viewed as a facilitator of learning and Hong Kong people seem comfortable with the idea that a coachee is able to come to their own conclusions.

The Chinese translation of the term 'coaching' has recently raised concerns from veteran coaches and human resource professionals. The term 'coaching' in Chinese leads to misperception of the role and functions of a coach. This could be clarified and rectified if a new Chinese terminology could be recommended to reflect the genuine nature of coaching and the role of the coach.

---

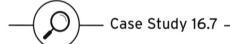 **Case Study 16.7**

### The state of coaching and mentoring in Saudi Arabia by Iftikhar Nadeem

Though Saudi Arabia's Vision 2030 is aiming to diversify its sources of national income by reducing its dependence on oil revenue, the contribution of petro dollars remains far and wide. The rapid development of non-oil sectors is giving rise to deployment of new methods of talent management in these sectors as well as government organizations. Coaching and mentoring have been recognized as an increasingly popular interventions for leadership development, career advancement, skills development, and performance improvement, particularly in large corporations. Unlike coaching, mentoring has older roots in the Kingdom. Large organizations such as Saudi Aramco have adopted mentoring as an important development method for its engineers and other professional staff for over half a century now. However, in recent years, coaching is being observed as a more popular learning method than mentoring in many local organizations. Some learning and development managers are considering coaching as a substitute of training and/or as an essential component of leadership development for middle and senior managers. Most organizations are hiring internal coaches on a full-time basis whereas executive coaches focusing on senior executives are largely contracted as external coaches. According to a recent survey by a business school, the main reason behind external coaching engagements is confidentiality needs of senior leaders.

Coaching and mentoring in Saudi Arabia is influenced by its culture. Gender, tribalism and religion play important roles in coaching conversations rather than mentoring. In the traditionally male-dominated tribal society, men may be a bit resistant to coaching; however, feminine consciousness is rising. In corporate Saudi Arabia, English is generally acceptable or sometimes the preferred language in coaching and mentoring engagements. However, speaking Arabic is definitely an advantage for a coach because it also helps to understand the Saudi culture. A coach may be more effective if he/she focuses on coachees and makes extra efforts to meet them where they are while being sensitive to their values and behaviors, which are often conditioned by religion, tribal values as well as a strict legal position (although this is changing rather rapidly).

Coach education remains one of the under-addressed aspects of coaching and mentoring practices in the Kingdom of Saudi Arabia. No university in the Kingdom has started a coach education program so far. There is no Accredited Coach Training Program (ACTP) on the ground. Most coaches have completed their coach training in neighboring Dubai or in the USA and Europe. However, some training organizations have started offering Accredited Coach Specific Training Hours (ACSTH) that leads to becoming a coach credentialed by the International Coach Federation (ICF). According to the latest data available from ICF, currently, there are 42 ICF credentialed coaches in Saudi Arabia. About half of these coaches are Saudis whereas 29% represent female coaches, which is a lower percentage than most countries. The lower female representation could be due to lower female participation in the business sector in the past, which is set to change rapidly in the years to come.

## SUMMARY OF MAIN POINTS

Saudi Arabia is a country that is attempting to change its culture. This is driven by a need to make the country less dependent on oil revenues and this means changing the economic and cultural model. However, cultural differences in leadership and power dominate coaching practice in Saudi Arabia. This is in relation to gender, although there are some noticeable changes here. Since our last edition, there have been a few changes in coaching. Credentializing has come on to the agenda and the ICF has a small presence here and some small steps towards coach education have been taken. The arrangements for supervision seem scant. Interestingly, coaches are employed as internal coaches in some organizations.

---

 **Case Study 16.8** ───────────────────

### Coaching and mentoring in Uganda – an update by Theo Groot (with thanks to Norah Bwaya)

Over the last five years the coaching field in Uganda has undergone quite some change and interesting developments are taking place. To a large extent these changes are due to external factors: an international coach training company that entered the market some five years ago and the growing demand for coaching services from mainly big international corporations like the oil industry and the banking sector. Although the field is still in a state of flux, a few trends can be recognized.

*(Continued)*

### Creation of ICF chapter

A few years back an international coach training institute from Singapore, The Coach Masters Academy, entered the market and began a strong campaign for business. This coincided with a higher demand for training of mainly internal coaches. More and more international companies, e.g. the oil companies, were looking to have internal coaches mostly to improve staff performance and bring staff to international levels. International clients are familiar with coaching and generally require them to be accredited. Where in the past most clients would simply require the coach to have successfully completed an accredited training, these days accreditation is the norm. Hence in October 2019 the Uganda chapter of the International Coach Federation (ICF) was officially created with the minimum of 25 accredited coaches, almost all graduates from the above-mentioned coach training institute. Although still early, it seems that the creation of the Uganda ICF chapter is becoming the single most important factor that is driving coaching in the country.

### The coach

The profile of a coach is also changing. The average age has come down and many professional coaches are now in their 30s. Many have started or still work as internal coaches within a company that has often contributed to their training cost. Few can make a living as an independent coach, but many manage to diversify their income sources through a combination of part-time employment and delivering other consulting or training services. Competition is stiff and more and more clients request for coaches to be part of an established firm; there is less appetite for freelance coaches. The price per hour has increased accordingly. Gender and ethnicity still play a role. A senior and very experienced female coach in her late 50s described the trouble she had to be selected as a coach for an international institution; she clearly felt that as an African she had to negotiate additional hurdles. She also mentioned an African CEO of an international company in Uganda who preferred a 'white' coach, even when she had better qualifications and more experience.

### Coach demand

Clients seeking coaching services are mainly large international businesses where coaching is an integral part of their HR. Within the corporate world in Uganda coaching services seem to be used in two main different situations. Most of the coaching is performance related; employees have at times difficulty keeping up with the high international standards. Coaching has to provide results in terms of improved performance and within a restricted timespan of a couple of months. A second type of coach demand is to prepare promising employees for executive positions. This focus on coaching for performance seems to be driven by growing competition and demanding stakeholders who are constantly pushing for higher levels of efficiency and results. Ugandan executives are now, more than ever before, operating at a global level.

### Coaching style

It is interesting to see how over the years the approach to coaching has moved towards a more what you could call 'American' perception of coaching, undoubtedly influenced by the methodology of the above-mentioned training institute on the one hand and the clear expectations of the main clients. Where coaching is used in supporting promising staff members to grow into senior executive positions, a very challenging executive style of coaching is expected. On the other hand, in the case of performance improvement the coachees tend to push the coach toward a very directive and advice-giving role. Here we clearly see the impact of the general education whereby people are not encouraged to think for themselves and to be problem-solvers.

## The undercurrent

It is interesting to see how the discourse on coaching has rather dramatically changed over a relatively short period of time. Mainstream coaching is now clearly geared towards performance coaching on the one hand and executive coaching on the other. Focus is on short-term with measurable outputs. Years back coaching had a much broader scope and focused more on life coaching and a longer-term supportive approach. This is still the case in what we could now call the undercurrent in coaching land in Uganda. Clients here are mainly local and international NGOs who see coaching as an important method in the overall development of key staff members. Perhaps one could say that it's the mentoring aspect that dominates here. For other local organizations without external funding coaching remains too expensive and many keep focusing on trainings whereby more people are reached for the same amount of money. This is a pity because coaching can make a different contribution.

## Future developments

Although the mainstream discourse about coaching has changed a lot over the years, as has the coaching method, coaching in Uganda is almost exclusively restricted to face-to-face meetings. Virtual coaching is hardly happening. Partially this is due to the culture whereby being in one's physical presence is appreciated. It is unclear to what extent the current COVID pandemic will push for changes here; more coaches have taken up e-coaching and both coaches and coachees are discovering that virtual coaching can be as effective as face-to-face and is definitely more cost effective. Team coaching too is hardly taking place. Elsewhere this is becoming an increasingly popular approach and Ugandan companies and organizations could benefit a lot.

Finally, there is hope that coaching will be recognized as a profession through an act of parliament which would give the professional coach a legal status and stimulate a national register of coaches.

## SUMMARY OF MAIN POINTS

Coaching has clearly changed in Uganda since the last edition. It seems that training has entered the agenda and the marketplace is dominated by an American approach brought in by a Singapore-based organization. There is also a growing ICF presence in Uganda. Similar to Saudi Arabia, Uganda appears to be having a cultural change influenced by a changing economy. However, there still seem to be some cultural barriers for women and a preference for 'white' coaches – perhaps influenced by the American model of performance coaching highlighted in this case. Developmental mentoring appears to be something that NGOs tend to use.

 Case Study 16.9

### Coaching and Mentoring in Sri Lanka by Duminda Rajasinghe

Coaching and mentoring are relatively new concepts in practice, especially for learning and development in the Sri Lankan context. For many years, Coaching and Mentoring (C&M) were taught at introductory level in business management qualifications, particularly in Human Resource Management (HRM). Evidence suggests that coaching and mentoring are seen through psychological lenses with life coaching being one of the popular terms. In Sri Lanka, for many, coaching reminds people of cricket, the most popular sport in the country. However, coaching is becoming diversified into many different fields and in the business context it has become a new trend.

There is an increasing number of self-proclaimed coaches. However, the understanding of C&M and the abilities of many of these coaches or mentors are contestable. Certification and accreditation are becoming a popular discourse in SL, and to cater to this demand, there is the presence of some international authorities such as the 'International Coaching Federation' and the 'International Authority for Professional Coaching and Mentoring', though these groups have low numbers of members. The organizations that claim to offer accredited training from these professional bodies mainly focus on developmental coaching in business organizations. However, the Institute of Mental Health (SL) provides training to become certified life and relationship coaches. There are few other educational and training institutes that conduct coaching services and most of them are relatively new initiatives.

The education system in the country is largely linear, structured and hierarchical. The guaranteed free education up to secondary level and competitive merit-based selection criteria for free university enrolment appear to influence learners to focus on their grades rather than their learning and development. This can have a significant influence on accepting the potentials of non-linear, flexible and inclusive approaches of learning and development. The power dominant culture encourages individuals to follow advice and guidance from seniors (e.g. age, position). Therefore, engaging in a critical reflective dialogue, questioning and self-directed learning can be challenging exercises for many individuals. These may have influenced the relative lack of popularity of coaching and mentoring over other learning and developmental interventions.

On the positive side, within the university system, there is a very popular term called 'Kuppiya', where a voluntarily chosen individual supports other individuals or a group of peers for their learning and development. 'Kuppiya' in the Sinhala language can mean a small lamp; perhaps the term is used in the context of lighting someone's understanding. This depicts some interesting insights of informal peer learning that have been practiced for decades. Similarly, many organizations facilitate buddying or shadowing systems and, traditionally, most trades in SL were taught through informal, one-to-one or small group-based open curriculum approaches. The majority of the population claims to practice Buddhism, which promotes actions/behaviours based on questioning and understanding (see 'Kalama Sutta'). Therefore, there is a good social structure and some cultural support despite the above-mentioned challenges to promoting coaching and mentoring in SL. It is possible that the country already practises coaching and mentoring but nobody calls those practices coaching and mentoring!

Acceptance, inclusivity and conversational learning that coaching endorses can be a remedy for many challenges within the country. Therefore, the individuals and professional institutes that provide coaching and mentoring services should be playing an active role to promote coaching and mentoring practices. For this, encouraging research and providing access to current knowledge of C&M are vital for the country.

## SUMMARY OF MAIN POINTS

Coaching and mentoring are under development in Sri Lanka. There is a presence of some professional bodies but credentialization seems to be low on people's agendas to date. Coaching and mentoring's development may be hampered by the inherent hierarchy in the culture, but it is interesting that there are cultural resonances associated with Buddhism that relate to coaching and mentoring. It is also interesting to note the association that business coaching has with sport. How far these three elements will influence the development of coaching and mentoring remains to be seen.

---

# ANALYSIS AND DISCUSSION

From these accounts, we can see a number of common themes. In industrialized continents – represented by accounts from Australia and the USA, in particular – there appear to be stronger elements of convergence in practice. These elements include the establishment of professional bodies, distinctions between coaching and mentoring as activity labels and an accompanying qualification infrastructure for coach training, in particular. As in the UK, the coaching label in the USA and Australia seems to be the one more readily associated with paid activity, but there are signs in all three countries that mentoring as a label is increasing in its pervasiveness in a range of sectors and for a range of purposes. In South America and in Europe, we can see variations in the acceptance and practice of coaching and mentoring, perhaps reflecting a more divergent perspective. For example, supervision appears prevalent in Venezuela but is not really attended to in other parts of South America. It is also interesting to note the use of coaching as a potential instrument for social change in some South American countries. We speculate that this social and charitable purpose may make coaching more resistant to neofeudalistic convergence than commercial forms.

In Europe, the Czech Republic example can be seen as a microcosm for the continent, in the sense that, in some ways, coaching is well established in terms of professional bodies, though there is less take-up within universities. A parallel can be drawn between the UK, France and Germany with their relatively numerous courses and accreditation mechanisms and that of Poland where, like the Czech Republic, there is widespread use of coaching as a business tool but less of a formal infrastructure for training and accreditation.

The Russian experience of mentoring, in particular, is interesting. Here, it is being very successfully employed within a youth entrepreneurship context. While there is some international agreement through YBI on the form of mentor training, there is also a need for local adaptation. It is further worth noting that there is growing interest in mentoring within educational social settings in Russia.

In Hong Kong, we see a sophisticated cultural awareness of coaching. Here, various cultural practices seem to be accepted and absorbed into coaching practice. This type of cultural awareness, with its acceptance and tolerance of diversity, is something to be admired and observed. The tendencies of industrialized countries to expect convergence in a globalized world appear to be handled differently here.

The Saudi experience is quite different to all the other cases. It is interesting to note that both coaching and mentoring are becoming activities of interest to Saudis; however the cultural practices there are clearly very powerful, and, whilst there is divergence from other countries represented here, Saudi appears to be changing and the US influence is beginning to appear through the ICF. Interestingly, mentoring has had a presence in corporations in Saudi Arabia for many years.

Turning to Uganda, coaching and mentoring seem to be in a more nascent position in terms of their professional development as compared with the more industrialized continents. Despite this, there is clear evidence in this account that there is some convergence towards the US/UK/Australian model. A key mechanism or driver for convergence appears to be the role of professional bodies, with the US-based International Coach Federation being particularly prevalent. It appears that ICF activity is increasing slightly. However, as our discussion in Chapter 3 on culture illustrates and in Chapter 15 where we discuss professionalization, there is a risk in making monocultural assumptions about groups, whether they be groups of individuals, organizations or, in this case, countries and continents.

Sri Lanka appears as the newest entrant to the coaching and mentoring world. Its beginnings seem to be within the education system as well as there being cultural influences of religion and sport in the potential development of coaching and mentoring here. The high-power distanced culture may be an inhibitor to the development of coaching and mentoring but, as is the case in Africa, this has the potential to change over time. Professional bodies, although present, have not made much impact on Sri Lanka. Perhaps this is a good thing?

## CONCLUSIONS

It appears that our case studies add support to Bresser (2009, 2013) in that coaching is present in many different parts of the world. They also suggest that mentoring is present, often as a voluntary activity, in many different countries. It further appears that industrialized countries are more accepting of a 'convergence' of practice, particularly in coaching and its professionalization agenda – the dominant body being the ICF.

It is interesting that some countries are willing to take a 'divergent' or 'crossvergent' perspective, as in the cases of Hong Kong, Russia, parts of South America and Sri Lanka.

While we do not claim that this chapter presents any definitive position, it is encouraging to us that diversity and crossvergence have a place in the world where neofeudalism dominates. It is particularly heartening to note the social and charitable direction of coaching in parts of South America because, for us, this is more akin to the social origins of coaching and mentoring (see Chapter 1). It is also clear from these illustrative cases that there are many influences on coaching and mentoring activity, for example:

- the economic context – present in all cases above
- the philosophical underpinning – highlighted particularly in the Ugandan, South American, Hong Kong and Sri Lankan cases
- technology – found in the Russian case
- the legal context – notably in the Saudi case

- the political climate – raised in the South American case
- sociological and cultural issues – found in all cases.

 ── **Future Direction** ──────────────────────

We have argued throughout this book that there are many more influences on coaching and mentoring activity than just psychology. The CIPD (2012c), for example, argues that the influence of psychology on coaching in particular is so pervasive that it is difficult to separate coaching from counselling. In Chapter 1, we indicate that the views taken within the coaching world on psychology differ from the mentoring world. In the mentoring context, psychology is often employed to develop theory and not to drive practice or the professionalization agenda. We argue in Chapter 12 that a sociological perspective is also necessary to engage in coaching and mentoring.

For the future, we wonder how far commercial coaching is sustainable, while at the same time we recognize that the use of internal coaching and mentoring is generally on the increase. We also note that the voluntary nature of mentoring is finding a new voice in different international contexts and that there is movement, in some locations, towards a social use of mentoring and coaching aimed at societal change and emancipation.

The globalized world is changing. Since the global financial crisis of 2008, there has been a general questioning of the ethics of business and its ability to really lift the majority of people in the world out of poverty. In the book *Them and Us*, Will Hutton (2011) argues that capitalism creates some 'unwelcome biases'. He goes on to argue that when a society is both fair and seen to be fair, trust is fostered, democracy works, and openness and reciprocity together create a successful and prosperous economy. Clearly, there are some strong resonances here with the espoused values of coaching and mentoring.

Professional bodies claim that their policies and rules reassure potential clients or sponsors and ensure quality control and, as discussed above, these practices come from the neofeudalistic convergence model. Many writers suggest that the roots of coaching and mentoring are in person-centred humanism (Parsloe and Leedham, 2009; Whitmore, 2009; Connor and Pokora, 2012; Western, 2012; Cox et al., 2014; Du Toit, 2014; Garvey et al., 2014), and we speculate that there is a paradox between this inclusive philosophy and the approaches taken by professional associations.

There are a few glimmers of a more divergent or crossvergent approach to coaching and mentoring beginning to emerge. These glimmers include the values espoused by Hutton (2011) and are in tune with the humanistic roots of coaching and mentoring. If these are the small seeds of social change happening in localized settings, then the future holds some optimism for humanity. How far the global pandemic will influence the future of coaching and mentoring, remains to be seen.

 Activity

The economy of Uganda in East Africa is unstable and volatile (The World Bank, 2016). Growth has slowed in relation to its neighbours, particularly Rwanda, Tanzania and Kenya. In this context, performance and productivity among the workforce become important considerations. With this in mind, executive coaching clearly has a role to play. However, what form should this take? The ICF, for example, has its perspective on executive coaching and has an expectation that any members adhere to the established standards but, what of the culture? In Uganda, the majority (84%) of the population is Christian, and 14% is Muslim. Older people are automatically considered to be wise and advice giving is expected. Men have a higher status than women and experience is measured in years served.

- If you were an ICF member working in Uganda, how would you consider developing executive coaching in Ugandan business?
- What would you need to take into account?
- How far is convergence appropriate and necessary?
- What consideration would you give to the ethics of the ICF approach to executive coaching, taking into account the Ugandan context?

 Questions

- Within the spheres of your coaching or mentoring practice, how far do you see divergence, crossvergence or convergence?
- If social change is on the agenda, what signs do you see that this is the case?
- What might professional bodies do to become more inclusive?

 Further Reading

For an account of a divergent perspective on ethics in coaching, see: Fatien Diochon, P. and Nizet, J. (2015) 'Ethical codes and executive coaches: One size does not fit all', *Journal of Applied Behavioural Science*, 51(2): 277-301.

For an interesting discussion of the inequalities in society and what might be done to address them, see: Hutton, W. (2011) *Them and Us: Changing Britain – Why we Need a Fairer Society*. London: Abacus Publications.

For a discussion on coaching for social change, see: Shoukry, H. (2016) 'Coaching for social change', in T. Bachkirova, G. Spence and D. Drake (eds), *The SAGE Handbook of Coaching*. London: SAGE, pp. 181-96.

# 17

# TOWARDS A META-THEORY OF COACHING AND MENTORING

## CHAPTER OVERVIEW

In this chapter, we will bring together the various threads and themes explored in the book so far and seek to develop a theory of coaching and mentoring which addresses the issues raised.

## INTRODUCTION

Throughout this book, we have sought to raise key questions across a range of themes related to coaching and mentoring, such as:

- the impact of different definitions of coaching and mentoring and what behaviours they refer to
- discourses on research and how coaching and mentoring activities can be evaluated
- coaching and mentoring schemes and cultures within organizations
- models, modes and perspectives on coaching and mentoring conversations
- power, expertise and skill in coaching and mentoring relationships
- discourses on the professionalization of coaching and mentoring: training, accreditation and supervision
- ethical dilemmas and moral challenges within coaching and mentoring.

Following Western (2012, 2017), we want to put forward a meta-theory of coaching and mentoring. Like him, we are not proposing this as a comprehensive theory of coaching and mentoring activity. Rather, we want to provide readers of this book with a heuristic, through which they can seek to explore and question their current understandings of coaching and mentoring and therefore conceive of new and different ways of engaging with their theory and practice. The heuristic will inevitably be partial and derived from the particular lenses through which we understand these practices. However, we hope we have been sufficiently transparent about those lenses and that our heuristic will be useful as an artefact through which readers can become clearer about the foundations of their own perspectives on coaching and mentoring. We also hope that it gives readers a framework within which they might begin to build on those foundations.

## METHODOLOGY

We will develop our heuristic by first engaging in a discussion about the conclusions we have drawn from the preceding chapters in this book. This will be integrative and will expand on the themes identified in the introduction. Following this, we will bring together those insights into a heuristic which will be represented in diagrammatic form which seeks to represent those key themes. We will then conclude the book by bringing together some key issues for the future of coaching and mentoring.

## THEMATIC DISCUSSION

### Definitions and behaviours in coaching and mentoring

In Chapter 1, we explored, in depth, the traditions and roots of coaching and mentoring as labels. Our essential conclusions were that, although the labels have different roots, they draw on the same narratives and skill sets. Following Stokes, Fatien Dichon and Otter (2020), we see them as being two sides of the same coin. As we have argued in several places throughout the text, particularly in Chapters 1, 5, 7 and 8, various stakeholders in coaching and mentoring have strong reasons for wanting to clearly define what they are doing. These reasons link to the need to evaluate the activity (see discussion below) but also to branding and to being distinctive about what the coach/mentor is doing. For example, for an independent executive coach, it may well be important to identify with a particular strand of discourse (Western, 2012, 2017) about what an executive coach does and position it as being different from other labels, for example mentoring, buddying. However, this may cause them to overstate the difference between coaching and mentoring per se, in terms of the skills used. Also, as a result of what we have called 'misplaced concreteness', the importance of the context in which the activity takes place can be downplayed, or even ignored. We find this abstraction of coaching and mentoring as universally distinct and different behaviours, irrespective of the context, hugely problematic. This is because it implies that, as practitioners, we would be able to go into any two (or more) organizations that have, say, mentoring programmes and see the 'same thing' happening. This map of coaching and mentoring does not describe the territory as we experience it. The sheer breadth of mentoring activity across a whole range of sectors, and different sizes of organizations with different agendas and purposes, means that you cannot rely on seeing the exact same thing when going into those organizations. However, we argue that the dimensions frameworks that we explored in Chapter 1 do give us a language and a set of parameters through which we can make sense of that context. It means we have a way of defining mentoring or coaching (or whatever label) in terms of the expected behaviours of the parties in those relationships. We have no problem with generating clear definitions of coaching and/or mentoring that are context-sensitive and specific, and indeed we encourage this in our work as practitioners. Hence, in terms of our heuristic, the role of context is critical.

## Discourses on coaching and mentoring research, design and evaluation

In Chapters 2 and 4, we examined the ways in which researchers and practitioners try to understand how/whether coaching and mentoring activities are working. We focused particularly on how different mindsets and orientations to what 'works' drive what is attended to in research, design and evaluation activities. Clearly, this resonates heavily with Western's (2012, 2017) four coaching discourses in terms of what is seen as important. It also connects with broader metaphors for organization and management (see, for example, Morgan, 2006) as well as philosophical questions around what evidence of something working can be trusted. We argued that the label 'coaching' in the scheme evaluation literature has tended to be associated with insider accounts that are more rooted in philosophical commitments to pragmatism, whereas the label 'mentoring' has more often been associated with a more academic discourse concerned with a more positivist tradition of research in the natural sciences. This split, between a more theoretical, critical orientation towards evaluating coaching and mentoring activity, on the one hand, and a more pragmatic stance, on the other, is also mirrored in the literature on coaching and mentoring scheme design. As we discussed in Chapter 4, there are those who write books and articles from a very practical perspective, with a practitioner audience in mind. This practical discourse is very focused on addressing the practical issues involved in getting coaching and mentoring programmes up and running, and often gives advice to the reader on key points to pay attention

to – for example, getting senior managers on board, communicating well with other stakeholders, clear criteria for matching, and robust training and support mechanisms for participants.
The more critical, academic literature tends to either raise questions about outcomes in terms of
evidence of the approach working, or questions around power and impact; in other words, it has
a more 'negative' critical stance than the much more 'positive' stance taken by those writers who
are invested in the intervention and believe in its power. Hence, if our heuristic is to be useful in
terms of stimulating different thoughts and ideas in those who engage with it, then accounting for
both of these different mindsets is important. One way of doing that is to recognize the contribution that different base disciplines play in drawing our attention to different aspects of a coaching
and mentoring activity, in the same way that Morgan (2006) does with organizational theory and
Mintzberg et al. (1998) do in the field of strategic management. Examples of base disciplines
include philosophy, sociology and psychology with their relatively long theoretical and practical
traditions. In addition, we have newer disciplines which are, arguably, drawn from combinations
of these, such as economics or psychotherapy and, in turn, applied disciplines which have their
roots in these, such as change management or human resource management. We see coaching and mentoring as being in this third category and our heuristic needs to acknowledge these
roots, or antecedents, in order to be useful as a vehicle for critical discussion and debate.

## Coaching and mentoring schemes and cultures within organizations

In Chapter 3, we focused on how coaching and mentoring activities are implemented within an
organizational context, usually as part of a scheme or initiative to embed coaching and mentoring
principles within the culture of an organization. As well as addressing the practical issues as to
how this might be done, we also raised a series of philosophical issues about the idea of creating
a coaching or mentoring culture within an organization. To articulate this further, we introduced an
additional set of dimensions: change versus stability; deficit versus appreciative inquiry; problem
versus solution; internal versus external; performance versus whole life; manager versus master coach; performance versus whole-life focus; roll-out versus creep-in. These were different
to the dimensions raised in Chapter 1, as they, instead, served to articulate some philosophical
choices that key stakeholders in organizations have when engaging with coaching and mentoring schemes. Each of these choices will have a different impact and the choices that are made
depend on what key stakeholders see as the ultimate goal or purpose of the coaching and mentoring activity that is introduced. Again, this brings to the fore the issue of organizational mindset.
We argue that the position that is taken relates directly to the assumptions that are made about
what organizations are there to do and how they should work. As per our critical discussion on
organizational culture in Chapter 3, this inevitably is based on a value judgement about what
these organizational goals should be and there may well be different and contrasting positions
within the organization about those goals. In Chapter 11, we critically examined this notion of
goals within coaching and mentoring. In particular, we explored the question of whose agendas
are being addressed when moving towards these goals. Our argument was that, sometimes, an
unreflective but very strong commitment to a particular set of goals can militate against effective
organizational performance, with the coaching and mentoring intervention having a magnifying
effect on the pervasiveness of the message. This can have the worrying effect of suppressing

any alternative voices or perspectives within the organizational context, which might be dissenting in relation to the goal(s).

As we argued in Chapter 13, tolerance and acceptance of difference is often a core value within coaching and mentoring interventions. The unitary assumptions (Fox, 1974) that can come with some of the more practically orientated processes towards creating a coaching culture can raise a tension between the cultural predisposition for everyone to be of the same mind, on the one hand, and the importance of tolerating difference on the other. In terms of our heuristic on coaching and mentoring, it seems critical that we acknowledge, in some way, the existence of these different perspectives. These differences do not just exist within organizations. As we argue in Chapter 16, differences in the ways that coaching and mentoring are understood and enacted are present between countries and, indeed, between different continents across the world. Of course, there are also similarities and common patterns to recognize. These patterns of difference and similarity do not just describe that which is done but also that which 'should' be done. In Chapter 14, we raised the ethical question of whether organizational coaching and mentoring interventions always encourage those engaged in them to act in their own self-interest, not just in an organizational context but also in a societal context. Ethical values are, as we argued, also a matter of choice, and different perspectives need to be embedded in our heuristic.

## Models, modes and perspectives on coaching and mentoring conversations

In Chapter 6, we explored the nature of a non-linear conversation at the level of the different questions and interventions that can be made within that conversation, whereas in Chapter 5 we had explored the different brands and models of coaching. Within these different brands, there are embedded different orientations towards coaching and mentoring activity. Our dilemma in developing a heuristic of coaching and mentoring is that the brands that make up the coaching and mentoring landscape vary significantly in their make-up and core assumptions. For example, gestalt coaching has an emphasis on working with the here and now and is relatively light in terms of tools and techniques, whereas cognitive behavioural coaching (CBC) has a range of models and tools to inform its practice. Despite these sometimes quite stark differences, however, we argue, in Chapter 6 that there is, nevertheless, something distinctive about non-linear, one-to-one developmental conversations which enables us to group these seemingly disparate approaches together. We argue that there is something in the very nature of such conversations which is qualitatively different to other forms of learning. Even though we recognize, in Chapter 10, that new technology has had a significant impact on the mode by which we engage with coaching and mentoring activity, the essential principles that we first raised in Chapter 1, which bring together coaching and mentoring, seem to pervade. In Chapter 9, we raise the importance of the social and cultural dimensions of coaching and mentoring in particular. As with all the chapters, the social context in which coaching and mentoring are located is critical. However, we draw readers' attention to some broader changes in that context, such as the pace of change and degree of uncertainty. These generic factors, coming from a range of social, technical and political contexts, need to have their place in a heuristic about coaching and mentoring activity.

## Power, expertise and skill in coaching and mentoring relationships

Power has been a dominant theme throughout this text. We have particularly focused on power in Chapters 7 and 8, but the power of discourse has been examined, drawing on Western's (2012, 2017) and that of others, in the majority of the chapters. It is our contention that the issue of power is one that has been relatively underplayed within coaching and mentoring discourse. This is perhaps due to the pervasiveness of the celebrated self (Western, 2012, 2017) within coaching and mentoring discourse. By this, we mean that discourses on power are often drawn from a more critical academic discourse which, by their very nature, challenge the more 'positive' perceptions of coaching and mentoring that tend to dominate insider accounts of coaching, in particular, as we argued in Chapter 2.

In Chapter 8, we asserted that the dominant discourse in coaching is one that tends to privilege the skills of the coach while remaining almost silent on the skills that the coachee brings to the relationship. Hence, the bulk of the responsibility for making the relationship work is given to the coach or mentor, whereas, as we discuss in Chapters 6 and 9, in particular, the relationship is key to the effectiveness of the conversation. How, then, does it make sense not to account for the possibility that the coachee/mentee has a part to play in that skilful 'dance' between the protagonists in the relationship? As we will argue in the following section, the professionalization of coaching and mentoring activity has had a significant effect in terms of influencing what participants 'should' do. However, we note that, as we are discussing power here, we see a tension in the field between an espoused agenda of emancipation within coaching and mentoring, as we argued in Chapters 1 and 7, and the professionalization and standardization of an increasing culture of compliance with professional standards and ethics (see Chapters 14 and 15). The seemingly rational discourse on 'being professional' seems to us to be masking a more political discourse about power and roles within the coaching and mentoring relationship. As Western (2017: 57) argues, 'any meta-theory has to open up these questions'. In opening them up, it is important, as we have argued above, to be able to identify where such questions come from: do the questions emerge from considering the issue through a different discipline lens, from taking account of the specific contextual issues, or from a combination of both?

## Discourses on the professionalization of coaching and mentoring: training, accreditation and supervision

In Chapter 16, we examined accounts from a range of countries and continents across the world. Our reason for doing so was to examine the extent to which practice in those different locales was either becoming similar to each other (converging), more different from each other (diverging), or showing evidence of a hybrid set of practices (crossvergence) constituting a blend of different practices (Paik et al., 2011). Our conclusion was that, while there is some evidence of both convergence and divergence within coaching and mentoring practice, a key dynamic we are seeing is one of crossvergence. We see this as an interesting development in the context of the rise in the 'grip' that professional bodies, such as the ICF and the EMCC, have across the world. For us, it raises again the question of a dominant, totalizing discourse about standards and professionalization. In Chapter 15, we took a critical but balanced view of the role that competences play in coaching and mentoring. Our concern is that by seeking to standardize practice for, on the face of it, good and noble reasons of wishing to improve quality, this can serve to militate against a diversity of practice. As we have argued above, the different contexts in which coaching and mentoring take place are vital in determining to what extent certain approaches or practices can be effective. Furthermore, as we also argue above, tolerance of difference is important. As professional bodies seek to expand their influence and dominance, we see evidence of this being accepted in some areas of the world with, as Paik et al. (2011) argue, a degree of imitation of best practice, often based on North American or European constructs. However, in some contexts, such as in Uganda, the processes of coaching and mentoring are construed differently, with the context militating against the dominance of professional bodies' discourse, as we argue in Chapter 16. In a similar way to the debate on competences, we argued in Chapter 12 that supervision as a process has a number of benefits in terms of helping participants in coaching and mentoring relationships to be more effective in helping others. Here, we argued strongly for supervision as a developmental process. However, we also acknowledged that there is a power dimension involved for those who supervise, potentially giving them what we refer to as the moral authority over those who they supervise. Rather, as we argue in Chapter 8 in relation to the skilled coachee, we might also make a strong case for the skilled supervisee and see supervision as a collaborative partnership, with learning on both sides, not just on the part of the supervisee.

## Coaching and mentoring meta-theory: A heuristic

In the preceding sections of this chapter, we have sought to summarize our conclusions from the various chapters and draw out lessons for coaching and mentoring theory and practice. Inevitably, it is not possible to capture all of the richness and complexity of this within a simple diagram. However, what we offer, in Figure 17.1, is a basic mental map of the territory we have covered so that the reader can seek to locate their experience of that world within it. Western (2017: 58) offers us a model which gives us a way of 'scrutinising the theories of coaching practice'. As we have repeatedly argued, his focus on discourses of coaching is incredibly helpful in acknowledging the issue of mindset and perspective. We have tried to build on his work by acknowledging (see Figure 17.1) the base disciplines, or antecedents, of coaching and mentoring: sociology, psychology and philosophy. As we also argued earlier on in this chapter, we recognize that, of course, coaching and mentoring can also trace their roots to other disciplines, such as psychotherapy, counselling, economics or organizational theory. However, we feel that each of these secondary disciplines has its roots in these three main discipline areas. For each of these base disciplines, we argue that each contributes a distinctive set of lenses or perspectives on coaching and mentoring activity. For instance, sociology as a discipline area draws our attention to dynamics within societies and cultures and, in particular, to how certain discourses around what 'should' be done become normalized. Psychology, with its traditional emphasis on the individual's motivations, behaviours and approaches to learning, helps us to understand how different mindsets and perspectives influence what is done and understood within one-to-one developmental relationships. Philosophy brings with it a critical understanding of the nature of evidence of success as well as a consideration of what 'should' be done from a moral philosophy standpoint. In addition, however, we recognize that the relationship between coaching/mentoring and these disciplines is two-way

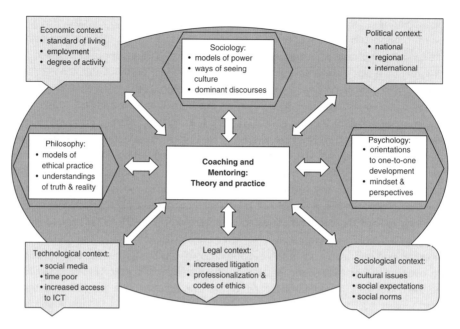

**Figure 17.1**  A meta-theory of coaching and mentoring

and iterative. Discourses developed from practice can and do influence those base disciplines, in turn. Hence, we are proposing a dialectical relationship between these disciplines and coaching and mentoring, where both construct and are constructed by those disciplines. For example, how power dynamics are enacted within a coaching and mentoring scheme can also be used to speak to more general sociological discourses about how societal cultures are understood, as well as to sociological discourses on, say, the emancipation of dominant forms of social control being used to understand the creation of a coaching culture.

In a similar way, we also propose that coaching and mentoring theory and practice both construct and are constructed by their contexts. For example, as we have shown in Chapter 16, the social context has a significant impact on how coaching and mentoring are enacted within, for example, Sri Lanka and Saudi Arabia, placing significant cultural limits on the activity. On the other hand, in Hong Kong, we can see glimpses of how coaching and mentoring may be modifying the social context in terms of being able to reconcile tensions between different dominant discourses. Similarly, notions of legal contracts of employment have influenced contracting within coaching and mentoring relationships, even where no payment is made, and these often pervade the coaching and mentoring discourse. However, we can also see that terms like 'psychological contract' (Rousseau, 1989), which are more common in the coaching and mentoring discourse, have influenced the legal context regarding what are understood to be reasonable expectations within the workplace. In addition, as we argue in Chapter 10, the increased use of communicative technologies, for example Zoom, Skype, FaceTime and apps such as BetterPoints, has impacted on the way coaching and mentoring are conducted. Arguably, however, the need to develop and sustain rich personal relations across boundaries of space and time, to accrue the benefits of coaching and mentoring, has also influenced the direction of the technological context. Of course, as we shall argue below, the COVID-19 pandemic has had a significant impact on the use of communicative technologies for coaching and mentoring purposes. Finally, in terms of the political context from a UK perspective at least, we can see that Brexit (the UK's withdrawal from the European Union) is already having an impact on cross-cultural coaching and mentoring relationships and schemes, but that coaching and mentoring discourses may have the potential to influence the political arena as well.

It is also clear from the preceding discussion that coaching and mentoring theory and practice can act as a mediating artefact through which the base disciplines of sociology, psychology and philosophy impact on the political, economic, sociological, technological and legal contexts. This, therefore, brings into play all six of the themes explored in this chapter. Definitional issues of differences in the language and purpose of coaching and mentoring are influenced by these disciplines and contexts and, in turn, contribute to their impact and how they are enacted. Consequently, the impact of coaching and mentoring activities in terms of whether they are effective or not depends by what criteria they are evaluated, which again is drawn from context and discipline. Choices that are made by key stakeholders about what 'should' happen are again influenced by these two factors. And so on.

In summary, we argue that coaching and mentoring theory and practice need to be understood as a discourse which has a number of mutually constituting and interdependent variables. Like Western (2017), we understand coaching and mentoring to be multifaceted and as having the potential to be seen in quite different ways, depending on the mindset through which the activity is viewed. This makes it complex and difficult to get hold of in a comprehensive way but, as we have argued, it was not our intent to be a definitive some sort of 'last word' on coaching and mentoring. Rather, we hope that our analyses and heuristic open up further the debates on coaching and mentoring and give readers of this book a language and set of concepts through which they might engage with the area. Below, we will spell out what we think this means for coaching and mentoring in the future.

## COVID-19: A Postscript

One final theme deserves special attention before we move on to talk about the future. Throughout this text, we have made reference to the specific and unprecedented context of the coronavirus pandemic. At the time of writing this chapter, we were at the peak of the so-called 'second wave' of this in 2021 and in the middle of a third national lockdown in the UK. Whilst there are clearly many challenging aspects of this pandemic, being forced to be socially distant from other people and to remain at home has forced us to reframe and reconsider what we construe as coaching and mentoring activity. For us as teachers on coaching and mentoring courses in a higher education context, it has forced us to teach, coach, mentor and supervise online and consider what protocols need to be developed in order to do this. This, of course, is paralleled by the context that our course participants face in their own practice. Hence, delivering courses in this way has its own content validity as it enables people to develop their practice for, and within, this new virtual context. Online delivery and work has, of course, developed its own argot – who has not experienced the delight of being told 'You're on mute' when on a Zoom call? It has also enabled legitimate parallel conversations to be conducted on the Chat function on Zoom, which would have been considered rude in face-to-face meetings and educational contexts. This has opened up new countervailing discourses within work meetings which speak to the earlier points we make about culture and power, in particular. In our desire to 'get back to the old normal', it would pay us not to forget some of these lessons that being in this context has taught us.

 Reflective Questions

- Using the heuristic, what particular contextual factors and discipline areas impact on how you work with coaching and mentoring activities?
- What are the tensions and challenges for you as you engage with these?
- How might prevailing national and international contexts be incorporated in your thinking?

 Future Direction

As in the previous edition, we have spelt out, at the end of each chapter, what we see as the future direction for that particular aspect of coaching and mentoring discourse. As we have said before, it is that much more challenging now that we have reached the end of the book and want to conclude our analysis in some way! Clearly, we cannot make claim here to have any sort of definitive answer on the way forward for all coaching and mentoring activity. Inevitably, ours is a partial view, though we have tried to honour different perspectives as we have gone through. What we do predict is that there will, through the different branches of discourse that Western (2017) describes, always be a pull towards being definite about what coaching and mentoring mean and how they should be. As Fillery-Travis and Collins (2017) argue, the ultimate future of the activity rests in the hands of its practitioners. However, as we have argued throughout, practitioners, who very much include ourselves, are influenced by a range of factors. Perhaps, therefore, we should recognize the importance of a continuing conversation about coaching and mentoring, rather than seeking closure or definitive answers to what it is or is not. To paraphrase Iordanou, Hawley and Iordanou (2017: 186), perhaps our focus needs, instead, to be on creating the conditions and conversations that will continue to enable us to construct and then re-construct what coaching and mentoring look like in the future.

However, it does seem important to recognize the importance of future thinking itself at this juncture. We will do that here by considering the implications of two recently published texts: *The Good Ancestor* (Krznaric, 2021) and *The 100-Year Life* (Gratton and Scott, 2020). In the former, Krznaric (2021) points to the current discourse around climate change and sustainable living. In doing so, he argues powerfully for a more long-distance vision of the future to avoid leaving a damaging legacy for future generations:

> The moment has come, especially for those living in wealthy nations, to recognise that we have colonised the future. We treat the future like a distant colonial outpost devoid of people, where we can freely dump ecological degradation, technological risk and nuclear waste, and which we can plunder as we please. (Krznaric, 2021: 7)

He expands on his thesis by extolling the virtues of thinking not just one or two decades in the future but 100+ years into the future. Adopting this thinking involves imagining this more distant future, caring about it and planning for it. It seems to us that those of us working in coaching and mentoring have already bought into the idea of developing capacity in others and leaving a legacy in terms of future generations. Knznaric (2021: 12) invites us to think long term in six main ways, which we have summarized below, and made connections to coaching and mentoring for each:

1.  Deep-Time Humility – recognizing that human activity is a very brief period in cosmic time terms; in coaching and mentoring terms, adopting such a position can militate against personal narcissism and egocentric thinking.
2.  Legacy Mindset – to be remembered well by posterity; in coaching and mentoring terms recognizing the impact we can have on future generations through our impact on those we work with in the present.
3.  Intergenerational justice – considering the seventh generation ahead; in coaching and mentoring terms, recognizing the role that our interventions can play in advocating for the voices of distant future generations who cannot otherwise have a voice in the present.
4.  Cathedral thinking – plan projects beyond a human lifetime; in coaching and mentoring terms, recognizing the longitudinal nature of our interventions by building a critical mass of helping interventions, systems and organizations that can outlive us, the developers of them.
5.  Holistic thinking – envision multiple pathways for civilization; recognizing the critical importance of coaching and mentoring space as the place to scenario plan different possible future pathways.
6.  Transcendent goal – strive for one-planet thriving; in coaching and mentoring terms, helping ourselves and our clients in recognizing the interdependent context and environment in which we live and action to sustain this.

We argue that when thinking about the future of coaching and mentoring, the temporal context that Kznaric (2021) offers gives us an important additional lens through which to consider this future. This is also the case for Gratton and Scott's (2020) work on the 100-year life. Whilst they approach the future from a very different perspective, some of the implications of their work are similar to those of Kznaric (2021). Gratton and Scott's (2020) work focuses on the fact that for all nations, but particularly richer ones, life expectancy has increased steadily for years. A child born in 1997 now stands a 50% chance of reaching 102 or 103 years of age. They argue that the traditional model of a three-stage life of full-time education followed by a period of work and then complete retirement is no longer sustainable for Generation Z or millennials, given the possibility of a much longer life, not least in financial terms. Rather, Gratton and Scott (2020) argue that it will be increasingly important for people of all ages to focus on developing their intangible assets – relationships, networks and, most crucially, their

*(Continued)*

continual learning and development. This has interesting implications for those of us who work in coaching and mentoring. We will need to, more than ever, recognize that our learning and development stages (see Garvey, 2016) will no longer be locked into our chronological ages. Whilst we are already seeing an increase in the age range of those engaging in coaching and mentoring activity as clients, we predict that the pace of this change will increase due to the dynamics discussed above. Hence, we expect that the current trend towards retirement coaching will become normalized into mainstream coaching and mentoring activity as more and more people live longer – and better – and remain economically and organizationally active into their 80s and 90s. This is likely to remain true even despite the current pandemic and future challenges that may emerge. Amongst other things, this will make for an increasing client base for coaches and mentors! Ultimately, though, it will require us to take a longer-term view of the future and of people development in general.

 **Questions**

- What are the key lessons that you have learnt from reading this edition of *Coaching and Mentoring: Theory and Practice*?
- What are the next steps that you will take in your effort to further engage with this area of work?

# BIBLIOGRAPHY

AHRI (Australian HR Institute (n.d.) Mentoring program FAQs, at, https://www.ahri.com.au/continuing-professional-development/ahri-mentoring-program/faqs/ (accessed 17 June 2021).

Allen, T.D. and Eby, L.T. (eds) (2007) *Blackwell Handbook of Mentoring: A Multiple Perspectives Approach*. Oxford: Blackwell.

Allen, T.D. and O'Brien, K.E. (2006) 'Formal mentoring programs and organizational attraction', *Human Resource Development Quarterly*, *17*(1): 43–58.

Allen, T.D., Eby, L.T. and Lentz, E. (2006a) 'The relationship between formal mentoring program characteristics and perceived program effectiveness', *Personnel Psychology*, 59: 125–53.

Allen, T.D., Eby, L.T. and Lentz, E. (2006b) 'Mentorship behaviors and mentorship quality associated with formal mentoring programs: Closing the gap between research and practice', *Journal of Applied Psychology*, *91*(3): 567–78.

Alred, G. and Garvey, B. (2019) *The Mentoring Pocket Book, 4th edition*. Alresford, Hants: Management Pocket Books.

Alred, G. and Garvey, B. (2000) 'Learning to produce knowledge: The contribution of mentoring', *Mentoring and Tutoring*, *8*(3): 261–72.

Alred, G., Garvey, B. and Smith, R. (1997) *The Mentoring Pocket Book*. Alresford, Hants: Management Pocket Books.

Alred, G., Garvey, B. and Smith, R. (1998) 'Pas de deux: learning in conversations', *Career Development International*, *3*(7): 308–14.

Alred, G., Garvey, B. and Smith, R. (2006) *The Mentoring Pocket Book*, 2nd edition. Alresford, Hants: Management Pocket Books.

Alsop, R. (2008) 'The "trophy kids" go to work', *Wall Street Journal*, at https://www.wsj.com/articles/SB122455219391652725 (accessed 31 March 2021).

Anderson, D. and Anderson, M. (2005) *Coaching that Counts*. New York: Elsevier.

Anderson, E.M. and Lucasse Shannon, A. (1995 [1988]) 'Toward a conceptualisation of mentoring', in T. Kerry and A.S. Shelton Mayes (eds), *Issues in Mentoring*. London: Routledge.

Appelbaum, S.H., Ritchie, S. and Shapiro, B. (1994) 'Mentoring revisited: An organizational behaviour construct', *International Journal of Career Management*, *6*(3): 3–10.

Argyris, C. (1977) 'Double loop learning', *Harvard Business Review*, Sept.–Oct.: 115–25, in J. Bowerman and G. Collins (1999) 'The coaching network: A program for individual and organizational development', *Journal of Workplace Learning: Employee Counselling Today*, *11*(8): 291–7.

Argyris, C. (1986) 'Skilled incompetence', *Harvard Business Review*, Sept.–Oct.: 74–9, in J. Bowerman and G. Collins (1999) 'The coaching network: A program for individual and organizational development', *Journal of Workplace Learning: Employee Counselling Today*, *11*(8): 291–7.

Argyris, C. and Schön, D. (1996) *Organizational Learning II*. London: Addison Wesley.

Arnaud, G. (2003) 'A coach or a couch? A Lacanian perspective on executive coaching and consulting', *Human Relations*, *56*(9): 1131–54.

Asghar, R. (2014) 'Millennials are the true entrepreneur generation', *Forbes*, at https://www.forbes.com/sites/robasghar/2014/11/11/study-millennials-are-the-true-entrepreneur-generation/#abd501173dc4 (accessed 31 March 2021).

Ashley, L. and Empson, L. (2016) 'Convenient fictions and inconvenient truths: Dilemmas of diversity at three leading accountancy firms', *Critical Perspectives on Accounting*, 35: 76–87.

Auxier, J.N., Roberts, S., Laing, L. Finch, L., Tung, S. and Hung, L. (2020) 'An appreciative inquiry into older adults' pain in long term care facilities: A pain education initiative', *International Practice Development Journal*, 10(1): 1–17.

Bachkirova, T. (2011) *Developmental Coaching: Working with the Self*. Maidenhead: Open University Press.

Bachkirova, T., Jackson, P. and Clutterbuck, D. (eds) (2011) *Coaching and Mentoring Supervision: Theory and Practice*. London: McGraw-Hill.

Bachkirova, T., Jackson, P. and Clutterbuck, D. (2021) *Coaching and Mentoring Supervision: Theory and Practice*, (2nd Ed), Maidenhead, UK, Open University Press.

Bachkirova, T., Jackson, P., Hennig, C. and Moral, M. (2020) Supervision in coaching: Systematic literature review. *International Coaching Psychology Review*, 15(2), 31–53.

Back, L. (2004) 'Ivory towers? The academy and racism', in L. Law, D. Phillips and L. Turney (eds), *Institutional Racism in Higher Education*. Stoke on Trent: Trentham Books, pp. 1–6.

Bandura, A. (1997) *Self-efficacy: The Exercise of Control*. New York: Freeman.

Bandura, A. and Locke, E.A. (2003) 'Negative self-efficacy and goal effects revisited', *Journal of Applied Psychology*, 88(1): 87–99.

Bacq, S., Geoghegan, W., Josefy, M., Stevenson, R. and Williams, T.A. (2020) 'The COVID-19 Virtual Idea Blitz: Marshaling social entrepreneurship to rapidly respond to urgent grand challenges', *Business Horizons*, 63: 705–23.

Baltes, P. B. (1987) 'Theoretical propositions of life-span developmental psychology: On the dynamics between growth and decline', *Developmental Psychology*, 23 (5): 611–626.

Barnett, B. (1995) 'Developing reflection and expertise: Can mentors make the difference?', *Journal of Educational Administration*, 33(5): 45–59.

Barnett, R. (1994) *The Limits of Competence*. Milton Keynes: Open University Press/SRHE.

Barnett, R. (2000) 'Working knowledge', in J. Garrick and C. Rhodes (eds), *Research and Knowledge at Work*. London: Routledge, pp. 15–32.

Barrett, R. (2002) 'Mentor supervision and development: Exploration of lived experience', *Career Development International*, 7(5): 279–83.

Bauer, F. (2014) 'The New Feudalism: It's not too late to stop it from undermining our liberal republic', *National Review*, 9 July, at www.nationalreview.com/article/382266/new-feudalism-fred-bauer (accessed 3 November 2016).

Bauman, Z. (1989) *Modernity and the Holocaust*. Cambridge: Polity.

Bauman, Z. (2005) *Work, Consumerism and the New Poor*, 2nd edition. Maidenhead: Open University Press.

BBC News (2020) Coronavirus: The story of the big U-turn of the summer, 13 September. Available at: https://www.bbc.co.uk/news/education-54103612 (accessed 17 June 2021).

Bear, S. (2018) 'Enhancing learning for participants in workplace mentoring programmes', *International Journal of Evidence Based Coaching & Mentoring*, 16(1), 35–46. https://doi-org.hallam.idm.oclc.org/10.24384/000462.

Beckett, C. and Maynard, A. (2013) *Values and Ethics in Social Work*, 2nd edition. London: SAGE.

Beckford, A. (2013) 'Mentoring yourself to success: Thoughts from educator Marsha Carr', *The Invisible Mentor*, at http://theinvisiblementor.com/mentoring-yourself-to-success-thoughts-educator-marsha-carr (accessed May 2020).

Beech, N. and Brockbank, A. (1999) 'Power/knowledge and psychological dynamics in mentoring', *Management Learning*, 30(1): 7–25.

Beisser, A.R. (1970) 'The paradoxical theory of change', in J. Fagan and I.L. Shepherd (eds), *Gestalt Therapy Now*. New York: Harper Row, pp. 77–80.

Ben-Hador, B. (2016) 'Coaching executives as tacit performance evaluation: A multiple case study', *Journal of Management Development*, 35(1): 75–88.

Berg, I.K. and Szabó, P. (2005) *Brief Coaching for Lasting Solutions*. New York: W.W. Norton.

Berger, P.L. and Luckmann, T. (1966) *The Social Construction of Reality*. New York: Anchor Books.

Berglas, S. (2002) 'The very real dangers of executive coaching', *Harvard Business Review*, 80(6): 86–92.

Berne, E. (1964) *Games People Play: The Psychology of Human Relationships*. Harmondsworth: Penguin.

Berne, E. (1968) *Games People Play*. London: Penguin.

Bernstein, B. (1971) 'On the classification and framing of educational knowledge', in M.F.D. Young (ed.), *Knowledge and Control: New Directions for the Sociology of Education*. London: Open University, Collier–Macmillan, pp. 47–69.

Bettis, R.A. and Prahalad, C.K. (1995) 'The dominant logic: Retrospective and extension', *Strategic Management Journal*, 16: 5–14.

Bhaskar, R. (1975) *A Realist Theory of Science*, London: Routledge.

Bhavnani, R., Mirza, H.S. and Meetoo, V. (2005) *Tackling the Roots of Racism: Lessons for Success*. Bristol: Policy Press.

Bimrose, J. and Hearne, L (2012) 'Resilience and career adaptability: Qualitative studies of adult career counseling', *Journal of Vocational Behavior*, 81(3): 338–44.

Biswas-Diener, R. and Dean, B. (2007) *Positive Psychology Coaching: Putting the Science of Happiness to Work for Your Clients*. Hoboken, NJ: John Wiley.

Blackler, F. (1995) *Knowledge, Knowledge Work and Organizations: An Overview and Interpretation*. London: SAGE.

Blattner, J. (2005) 'Coaching: The successful adventure of a downwardly mobile executive', *Consulting Psychology Journal: Practice and Research*, 57(1): 3–13.

Blitvich, J.D., McElroy, G.K. and Blanksby, B.A. (2000) 'Risk reduction in spinal cord injury: Teaching safe diving skills', *Journal of Science and Medicine and Sport*, 3(2): 120–31.

Bluckert, P. (2005) 'Critical factors in executive coaching: The coaching relationship', *Industrial and Commercial Training*, 37(7): 336–40.

Bluckert, P. (2006) *Psychological Dimensions of Executive Coaching*. Maidenhead: Open University Press.

Bluckert, P. (2010) 'Gestalt approaches to coaching', in E. Cox, T. Bachkirova and D. Clutterbuck (eds), *The Complete Handbook of Coaching*. London: SAGE, pp. 80–94.

Boje, D.M. (2008) *Storytelling Organizations*. London: SAGE.

Bond, N. and Hargreaves, A. (2014) *The Power of Teacher Leaders: Their Roles, Influences, and Impact*. New York: Kappa Delta Phi in partnership with Routledge/Taylor & Francis Group.

Bono, J.E., Purvanova, R.K., Towler, A.J. and Peterson, D.B. (2009) 'A survey of executive coaching practices', *Personnel Psychology*, 62: 361–404.

Booth, R. (2019) 'Racism rising since Brexit vote, nationwide study reveals', *Guardian Newspaper*, 20 May.

Bowerman, J. and Collins, G. (1999) 'The coaching network: A program for individual and organizational development', *Journal of Workplace Learning: Employee Counselling Today*, 11(8): 291–7.

Bozeman, B. and Feeney, M.K. (2007) 'Towards a useful theory of mentoring: A conceptual analysis and critique', *Administration and Society*, 39(6): 719–39, at http://aas.sagepub.com/content/39/6/719 (accessed 7 September 2015).

Bozer, G., Sarros, J.C. and Santora, J.C. (2013) 'The role of coachee characteristics in executive coaching for effective sustainability', *Journal of Management Development*, *32*(3): 277–94.

Bozionelos, N. and Bozionelos, G. (2010) 'Mentoring received by protégés: Its relation to personality and mental ability in the Anglo-Saxon organizational environment', *The International Journal of Human Resource Management*, *21*(4): 509–29.

Bozionelos, N. and Wang, L. (2006) 'The relationship of mentoring and network resources with career success in the Chinese organizational environment', *International Journal of Human Resource Management*, *17*(9): 1531–46.

Brantley, E. (2010) *Coaching the Inner Leader: Transpersonal Executive Coaching for Breakthrough Results*. Saarbrucken, Germany: Lambert Academic Publishing (LAP).

Bresser, F. (2009) 'Global Coaching Survey', Bresser Consulting and Associates, at www.frank-bresser-consulting.com (accessed 1 October 2013).

Bresser, F. (2013) *Coaching across the Globe: Benchmark Results of the Bresser Consulting Global Coaching Survey with a supplementary update highlighting the latest coaching developments to 2013*. Norderstedt, Germany: Books on Demand.

Bridges, W. (2003) *Managing Transitions: Making the Most of Change*. Cambridge: Perseus Books.

Broad, M.L. and Newstrom, J.W. (1992) *Transfer of Training: Action-packed Strategies to Ensure High Payoff from Training Investments*. Reading, MA: Addison-Wesley.

Brock, V. (2011) 'The secret history of coaching: What you know and what you don't know about how coaching got here and where coaching is going in the future', *The International Journal of Mentoring and Coaching*, *9*(1): 46–66.

Brockbank, A. and McGill, I. (2006) *Facilitating Reflective Learning through Mentoring and Coaching*. London: Kogan Page.

Brockbank, A. and McGill, I. (2012) *Facilitating Reflective Learning: Coaching, Mentoring and Supervision*. London: Kogan Page.

Brocki, J.M. and Wearden, A.J. (2006) A critical evaluation of the use of interpretative phenomenological analysis (IPA) in health psychology. *Psychology & Health*, *21*(1): 87–108.

Brockmeier, J., and Carbaugh, D. (Eds.). (2001). *Studies in narrative and identity: Studies in autobiography, self and culture*. John Benjamins Publishing Company.

Brounstein, M. (2000) *Coaching and Mentoring for Dummies*. Newtonville, MA: IDG.

Bruner, J. (1979) *On Knowing: Essays for the Left Hand*. London: Belknap Press.

Bruner, J. (1985) 'Vygotsky: A historical and conceptual perspective', in J.V. Wertsch (ed.), *Culture, Communication and Cognition: Vygotskian Perspectives*. Cambridge: Cambridge University Press, pp. 21–34.

Bruner, J. (1990) *Acts of Meaning*. Cambridge, MA: Harvard University Press.

Brunner, R. (1998) 'Psychoanalysis and coaching', *Journal of Management Psychology*, *13*(7): 515–17.

Burke, R.J., Bristor, J.M. and Rothstein, M.G. (1995) 'The role of interpersonal networks in women's and men's career development', *International Journal of Career Management*, *7*(3): 25–32.

Burkeman, O. (2012) *The Antidote: Happiness for People Who Can't Stand Positive Thinking*. Edinburgh: Canongate.

Burrell, G. and Morgan, G. (1979) *Sociological Paradigms and Organizational Analysis*. London: Heinemann.

Butler, J. (1990) *Gender Trouble: Feminism and the Subversion of Identity*, New York: Routledge.

Byrne, C. (2005) 'Getting to know me! Not getting results? Carmen Byrne explains how a lack of self-awareness can hold you back', *MW Coach*, April: 21.

Byron, Lord (1821) *The Curse of Minerva: A Poem*, 5th edition. Paris: Galignani.

Byron, Lord (1829) *Childe Harold's Pilgrimage*. Brussels: Du Jardin-Sailly Brothers.

Byron, Lord (1843) *The Works of Lord Byron in Four Volumes*, ed. T. Moore. Philadelphia, PA: Carey and Hart, Volume *III*, p. 187.

Campbell, S., Twenge, J. & Campbell, W. K. (2017) 'Fuzzy But Useful Constructs: Making Sense of the Differences Between Generations', *Work, Aging and Retirement*, *3*(2): 130–139.

Caplan, J. (2003) *Coaching for the Future: How Smart Companies Use Coaching and Mentoring*. London: CIPD.

Caraccioli, L.A. (1760) *The True Mentor, or, an Essay on the Education of Young People in Fashion*. London: J. Coote at the Kings Arms in Paternoster Row.

Carden, A.D. (1990) 'Mentoring and adult career development: The evolution of a theory', *The Counselling Psychologist*, *18*(2): 275–99.

Cardinal, D., Hayward, J. and Jones, G. (2011) *Rene Descartes: The meditations*. London, Hodder Murray.

Carr, D., Boerner, K. & Moorman, S. (2020) 'Bereavement in the time of coronavirus: Unprecedented challenges demand novel interventions', *Journal of Aging & Social Policy*, *3*(4–5): 425–431. DOI: 10.1080/08959420.2020.1764320.

Carr, M. (2011) *The Invisible Teacher: A Self-Mentoring™ Sustainability Manual*. Wilmington, NC: UNCW Center for Teaching Excellence.

Carr, M. (2012) *The Invisible Leader: A Self-Mentoring™ Sustainability Model for University Faculty*. Wilmington, NC: UNCW Center for Teaching Excellence. http://digital.ncdcr.gov/cdm/ref/collection/p249901coll22/id/714398 (accessed May 2020)

Carr, M. (2014) 'The tale of two studies: Using self-mentoring™ to build teacher leader confidence', *International Journal for Cross-Disciplinary Subjects in Education (IJCDSE)*, *5*(3).

Carr, M., Pastor, D. and Levesque, P. (2015) 'Learning to lead: Higher education faculty explore self-mentoring', *International Journal of Evidenced Based Coaching and Mentoring*, *13*(2).

Carroll, M. and Gilbert, M. (2008) *Becoming an Executive Coachee: Creating Learning Partnerships*. London: Vulkani Publishing.

Carroll, M. and Shaw, E. (2013) *Ethical Maturity in the Helping Professions: Making Difficult Life and Work Decisions*. London: Jessica Kingsley.

Carter, A. (2001) Executive coaching: Inspiring performance at work. *Institute of Employment Studies Report* 379, at www.employment-studies.co.uk/pubs/summary.php?id=379 (accessed April 2013).

Caruso, R.E. (1996) 'Who does mentoring?' Paper presented at the Third European Mentoring Conference, London, 7–8 November (www.emccouncil.org).

Caulkin, S. (2006) 'Friedman's unethical rot made wrongs into a right', *Observer, Business and Media*, 2 December.

Cavanagh, M., Grant, A.M. and Kemp, T. (eds) (2011) *Evidence-Based Coaching*. Bowen Hills, QLD: Australian Academic Press.

CBI (2015) 'The Path Ahead: CBI/Accenture Employment Trends Survey', at http://news.cbi.org.uk/news/job-creation-up-but-skills-shortages-rising-labour-costs-start-to-bite-cbi-accenture-survey/the-path-ahead (accessed 10 May 2016).

Chadwick-Coule, T. and Garvey, B. (2009) *London Deanery Mentoring Service: A Formative and Developmental Evaluation of Working Practices and Outcomes*. An Evaluation Report by the Coaching and Mentoring Research Unit. Sheffield: Sheffield Hallam University.

Chandler, D.E. and Kram, K.E. (2005) 'Applying an adult development perspective to developmental networks', *Career Developmental International*, Special Edition on Mentoring, *10*(6/7): 548–66.

Chang, J., Baek, P. and Kim, T. (2020) 'Women's developmental networks and career satisfaction: Developmental functions as a mediator', *Journal of Career Development*. https://doi.org/10.1177/0894845319900005.

Chanland, D.E. and Murphy, W.M. (2018) 'Propelling diverse leaders to the top: A developmental network approach', *Human Resource Management, 57*: 111–126. https://doi.org/10.1002/hrm.21842.

Chao, G.T. (2009) 'Formal mentoring: Lessons learned from past practice', *Professional Psychology, Research and Practice, 40*(3): 314–20.

Chesterfield, P.D.S. (1838) *The Works of Lord Chesterfield, including Letters to his Son to which is prefixed an original life of the author*. First complete American edition. New York: Harper and Brothers, p. 331.

Choi, A.M.K, Moon, J.E., Steinecke, A. and Prescott, J.E. (2019) 'Developing a culture of mentorship to strengthen academic medical centers', *Academic Medicine, 94*(5): 630–33.

Chopra, V., Dimick, J.B. and Saint, S. (2020) 'Making mentorship a team effort', *Harvard Business Review*, March.

Choy, C.K. and Hean, L.L. (1998) 'Learning relationships at work: A Singapore concept of mentoring', *Asia Pacific Journal of Education, 18*(2): 64–73.

Churchill, F. (2020) 'Ethnic minority HRs subject to racism and barriers to progression, poll finds', *People Management*, at https://www.peoplemanagement.co.uk/news/articles/ethnic-minority-hrs-subject-to-racism-and-barriers-to-progression#gref (accessed 28 August 2020).

CIPD (2007a) 'Managing change: The role of the psychological contract', at www.cipd.co.uk (accessed 17 July 2007).

CIPD (2007b) 'Annual Survey Report: Learning and development', April, at www.cipd.co.uk/surveys (accessed 2 January 2013).

CIPD (2007c) 'Survey Report: The changing HR function', September, at www.cipd.co.uk/surveys (accessed 2 January 2013).

CIPD (2012a) 'A barometer of HR trends and prospects 2013', at www.cipd.co.uk/hr-resources/survey-reports/cipd-surveys-overview-hr-trends-prospects-2012.aspx (accessed 2 January 2013).

CIPD (2012b) 'Annual Survey Report: Learning and talent survey', at www.cipd.co.uk/research/_learning-talent-development (accessed 12 December 2012).

CIPD (2012c) *Coaching and Mentoring Factsheet*. Wimbledon: CIPD.

CIPD (2015a) 'Learning and Development Survey', at www.cipd.co.uk/learninganddevelopmentsurvey2015.pdf (accessed 30 May 2016).

CIPD (2015b) 'Resourcing and Talent Planning Survey', at www.cipd.co.uk/binaries/resourcing-talent-planning_2015.pdf (accessed 10 May 2016).

CIPD (2020a) 'Learning and Skills at Work: Mind the gap', at www.cipd.co.uk/Images/learning-skills-work-report-1_tcm18-79434.pdf (accessed 21 June 2021).

CIPD (2020b) 'Resourcing and Talent Planning Survey', at www.cipd.co.uk/Images/resourcing-and-talent-planning-2020_tcm18-85530.pd (accessed 21 June 2021).

Clawson, J.G. (1996) 'Mentoring in the information age', *Leadership and Organization Development Journal, 17*(3): 6–15.

Clegg, S. (1989) *Frameworks of Power*. London: SAGE.

Clegg, S. and Haugaard, M. (eds) (2012) *Power and Organizations*. London: SAGE.

Clutterbuck, D. (1992) *Everyone Needs a Mentor*. London: IPM.

Clutterbuck, D. (1998) *Learning Alliances: Tapping into Talent*. London: CIPD.

Clutterbuck, D. (2002) 'Building and sustaining the diversity–mentoring relationship', in D. Clutterbuck and B.R. Ragins (eds), *Mentoring and Diversity: An International Perspective*. Oxford: Butterworth-Heinemann, pp. 87–113.

Clutterbuck, D. (2003) 'The problem with research in mentoring', *The International Journal of Mentoring and Coaching*, *1*(1).

Clutterbuck, D. (2004) *Everyone Needs a Mentor*, 4th edition. London: CIPD.

Clutterbuck, D. (2007a) *Coaching the Team at Work*. London: Nicholas Brealey.

Clutterbuck, D. (2007b) 'An international perspective on mentoring', in B.R. Ragins and K.E. Kram (eds), *Handbook on Mentoring at Work: Theory, Research and Practice*. London: SAGE, pp. 633–56.

Clutterbuck, D., & Hodge, A., (2017) Team Coaching Supervision Survey, at https://alisonhodge. com/wp-content/uploads/2020/03/team-coaching-supervision-survey-2017.pdf (accessed 21 June 2021).

Clutterbuck, D. and Hussain, Z. (eds) (2009) *Virtual Coach, Virtual Mentor*. London: Information Age Publishing.

Clutterbuck, D. and Megginson, D. (1995) *Mentoring in Action*. London: Kogan Page.

Clutterbuck, D. and Megginson, D. (1999) *Mentoring Executives and Directors*. Oxford: Butterworth-Heinemann.

Clutterbuck, D. and Megginson, D. (2005a) *Techniques for Coaching and Mentoring*. London: Butterworth-Heinemann.

Clutterbuck, D. and Megginson, D. (2005b) *Making Coaching Work: Creating a Coaching Culture*. London: CIPD.

Clutterbuck, D.A., Kochan, F.K., Lunsford, L.G., Smith, B., Dominguez, N. and Haddock-Millar, J. (eds) (2017) *The SAGE Handbook of Mentoring*. London: SAGE.

Clutterbuck D., Megginson, D. and Bajer, A. (2016) *Building and Sustaining a Coaching Culture*. London, CIPD.

Clutterbuck, D., Poulsen, K.M. and Kochan, F. (2012) *Developing Successful Diversity Mentoring Programmes: An International Casebook*. Maidenhead: Open University Press/McGraw-Hill Education.

Clutterbuck, D., Whitaker, C. and Lucas, M. (2016) *Coaching Supervision: A Practical Guide for Supervisees*. Oxon: Routledge.

Colley, H. (2002) 'A "rough guide" to the history of mentoring from a Marxist feminist perspective', *Journal of Education for Teaching*, *28*(3): 247–63.

Colley, H. (2003) *Mentoring for Social Inclusion: A Critical Approach to Nurturing Mentoring Relationships*. London: RoutledgeFalmer.

Collins, J. (2001) *Good to Great: Why Some Companies Make the Leap and Others Don't*. London: Random House.

Collins, P. (1994) 'Mentoring moving on: A network in development', *Education and Training*, *36*(5): 16–19.

Connor, M. (1994) *Counsellor Training: An Integrated Approach*. London: Kogan Page.

Connor, M. and Pokora, J. (2012) *Coaching and Mentoring at Work: Developing Effective Practice*. Maidenhead: McGraw-Hill.

Cooperrider, D. (1995) *Appreciative Enquiry: An Emerging Direction for Organization Development*. Champaign, IL: Stipes.

Corrie, S. and Lane, D. (2015) *CBT Supervision*. London: SAGE.

Coultas, C.W. and Salas, E. (2015) 'Identity construction in coaching: Schemas, information processing and goal commitment', *Consulting Psychology Journal: Practice and Research*, *67*(4): 298–325.

Coutu, D. and Kauffman, C. (2009) 'What can coaches do for you?', *Harvard Business Review*, Research Report, January: 1–8, at www.teammassiveresults.com/tl_files/files/Free%20Stuff/ What%20Can%20Coaches%20do%20for%20you.pdf (accessed May 2013).

Cox, E., Bachkirova, T. and Clutterbuck, D. (eds) (2014) *The Complete Handbook of Coaching*, 2nd edition. London: SAGE.

Cox, M. (2002) 'Reflections', in D. Feasey (ed.), *Good Practice in Supervision with Psychotherapists and Counsellors: The Relational Approach*. London: Whurr.

Crabbe, S.J. (2018) *Computer anxiety: The development of tools to measure severity and type, and offer appropriate mitigation strategies*, Unpublished PhD research, University of Newcastle, https://theses.ncl.ac.uk/jspui/bitstream/10443/4382/1/Crabbe%20S%202018.pdf (accessed 05 October 2020).

Cranwell-Ward, J., Bossons, P. and Gover, S. (2004) *Mentoring: A Henley Review of Best Practice*. Basingstoke: Palgrave Macmillan.

Creswell, J. (2012) *Qualitative Inquiry and Research Design: Choosing among Five Approaches*. Thousand Oaks, CA: SAGE.

Cross, R. and Parker, A. (2004) *The Hidden Power of Social Networks*. Boston, MA: Harvard Business School Press.

Csikszentmihalyi, M. (2002) *Flow: The Classic Work on How to Achieve Happiness*. London: Rider.

Daloz, L.A. (1986) *Effective Teaching and Mentoring*. San Francisco, CA: Jossey-Bass.

Daloz, L.A. (1999) *Mentor: Guiding the Journey of Adult Learners*, 2nd edition. San Francisco, CA: Jossey-Bass.

Darwin, J. (2010) Kuhn vs. Popper vs. Lakatos vs. Feyerabend: Contested Terrain or Fruitful Collaboration? *Philosophy of Management*, 9, 39–57 https://doi.org/10.5840/pom20109117

Dass, P. and Parker, B. (1996) 'Diversity: A strategic issue', in E.E. Kossek and S.A. Lobel (eds), *Managing Diversity: Human Resource Strategies for Transforming the Workplace*. Oxford: Blackwell, pp. 365–91.

David, S. (2020) *Emotional Agility Newsletter,* 3 November. Available at: https://www.susandavid.com/ (accessed 17 June 2021).

David, S., Clutterbuck, D. and Megginson, D. (2016) *Beyond Goals: Effective Strategies for Coaching and Mentoring*. London: Routledge.

de Bono, E. (1992) *I'm Right and You're Wrong: From this to the New Renaissance – From Rock Logic to Water Logic*. London: Penguin Books.

de Botton, A. (2006) *The Architecture of Happiness*. London: Penguin Books.

de Botton, A. (2014) *The News: A User's Manual*. London: Penguin Books.

de Cremer, D., van Dick, R., Tenbrunsel, A., Pillutla, M. and Murnighan, J.K. (2010) 'Understanding ethical behaviour and decision making in management: A behavioural business ethics approach', Special Issue, *British Journal of Management*, *22*: S1–S4.

de Haan, E. (2008a) 'I doubt therefore I coach: Critical moments in coaching practice', *Consulting Psychology Journal: Practice and Research*, 60(1): 91–105.

de Haan, E. (2008b) *Relational Coaching: Journeys towards Mastering One-to-One Learning*. Chichester: John Wiley.

de Haan, E. (2012) *Supervision in Action: A Relational Approach to Coaching and Consulting Supervision*. Maidenhead: Open University Press/McGraw-Hill Education.

de Haan, E. (2016) *Trust and Safety in Coaching Supervision*. Ashridge Centre for Coaching Research Report, at www.ashridge.org.uk/getmedia/d30289b7-0508-4c7a-a313-5b1d7aae9124/Trust-and-Safety-in-Coaching-Supervision-Research-Report-Apr-2016.pdf (accessed 1 August 2016).

de Haan, E. and Burger, Y. (2005) *Coaching with Colleagues: An Action Guide for One-to-One Learning*. Basingstoke: Palgrave Macmillan.

de Janasz, S.C., Sullivan, S.E. and Whiting, V. (2003) 'Mentor networks and career success: Lessons for turbulent times', *Academy of Management Executive*, *17*(4): 78–91.

de Vries, K. and Miller, B. (1984) *The Neurotic Organization*. New York: Jossey-Bass.

Deloitte Survey (2020) https://www2.deloitte.com/uk/en/pages/consulting/articles/working-during-lockdown-impact-of-covid-19-on-productivity-and-wellbeing.html (accessed 14 October 2020).

Devins, D. and Gold, J. (2000) 'Cracking the tough nuts: Mentoring and coaching the managers of small firms', *Career Development International*, *5*(4): 250–5.

Dey, P. and Steyaert, C. (2014) 'Rethinking the space of ethics in social entrepreneurship: Power, subjectivity, and practices of concrete freedom', *Journal of Business Ethics*, *133*(4): 627–41.

Dirsmith, M., Helan, J. and Covaleski, M. (1997) 'Structure and agency in an institutionalised setting: The application and social transformation of control in the Big Six', *Accounting, Organizations and Society*, *22*(1): 1–27.

Dobbin, F. and Kalev, A. (2016) 'Why diversity programs fail and what works better', *Harvard Business Review*, July–Aug.: 52–60.

Dobrow, S.R. and Higgins, M.C. (2005) 'Developmental networks and professional identity: A longitudinal study', Special Issue on Mentoring, *Career Development International*, *10*(6/7): 567–87.

Downey, M. (1999) *Effective Coaching: Lessons from the Coach's Coach*. London: Orion Business.

Downey, M. (2003) *Effective Coaching: Lessons from the Coach's Coach*, 2nd edition. Mason, OH: Texere.

Downey, M. (2014) *Effective Modern Coaching: The Principles and Art of Successful Business Coaching*. London: LID Publishing.

Drake, D. (2010) 'Narrative approaches', in E., Cox, T. Bachkirova and D. Clutterbuck (eds), *The Complete Handbook of Coaching*. London: SAGE, pp. 120–31.

Drake, D. and Pritchard, J. (2016) 'Coaching for organizational development', in E. Cox, T. Bachkirova and D. Clutterbuck (eds), *The Complete Handbook of Coaching*. London: SAGE, pp. 159–175.

Driver, M. (2011) *Coaching Positively: Lessons for Coaches from Positive Psychology*. Buckingham: Open University Press.

Drucker, P.F. (1955) *The Practice of Management*. Oxford: Heinemann.

Drucker, P.F. (1993) *Post-capitalist Society*. New York: HarperCollins.

Dryden, W. (1991) *A Dialogue with Arnold Lazarus: It Depends*. Buckingham: Open University Press.

du Gay, P. (1996) *Consumption and Identity at Work*. London: SAGE.

Du Toit, A. (2006) 'The management of change in local government using a coaching approach', *International Journal of Mentoring and Coaching*, *IV*(2): 45–57.

Du Toit, A. (2014) *Making Sense of Coaching*. London: SAGE.

Ebrahimi, M. and Cameron, R. (2012) *Internal Coaching and Coaching Culture*. Perth, Australia: Australian and New Zealand Academy of Management Conference.

Eby, L.T. and Lockwood, A. (2005) 'Protégés' and mentors' reactions to participating in formal mentoring programs: A qualitative investigation, *Journal of Vocational Behavior*, 67 441–458.

Edwards, R. and Usher, R. (2000) 'Research on work, research at work: Postmodern perspectives', in J. Garrick and C. Rhodes (eds), *Research and Knowledge at Work*. London: Routledge, pp. 32–50.

Egan, G. (1993) 'The shadow side', *Management Today*, September: 33–8.

Egan, G. (2014) *The Skilled Helper: A Client Centred Approach*, 10th edition. Andover, Hants: Cengage Learning EMEA.

Egan, T.M. and Song, Z. (2008) 'Are facilitated mentoring programs beneficial? A randomized experimental field study', *Journal of Vocational Behavior*, *72*(3): 351–362.

Ehrenreich, B. (2009) *Smile or Die: How Positive Thinking Fooled America and the World*. London: Granta.

Ekstrand, C., Jamal, A., Ngyuen, R., Kudryk, A. and Mendez, I. (2018) 'Immersive and interactive Virtual Reality to improve learning and retention of neuroanatomy in medical students: A randomized controlled study', *CMAJ Open*, *6*(1): 103–109.

Ellen, B. (2020a) 'We homeworkers have been rumbled. Our tribe is under threat', *Observer*, 8 August.

Ellen, B. (2020b) 'Relationships, advice, careers... so much of life is lost when you work from home', *Observer*, 29 August.

Ellinger, A.D. and Bostrom, R.P. (1999) 'Managerial coaching behaviours in learning organizations', *Journal of Management Development*, *18*(9): 752–71.

Ellinger, A.E., Ellinger, A.D. and Keller, S.B. (2005) 'Supervisory coaching in a logistics context', *International Journal of Physical Distribution and Logistics Management*, *35*(9): 620–36.

Ellul, D.B. and Wond, T. (2020) 'The role and impact of executive coaching in the Maltese public sector', *International Journal of Public Leadership*, *16*(2): 145–73.

Ely, K., Boyce, L.A., Nelson, J.K., Zaccaro, S.J., Hernez-Broome, G. and Whyman, W. (2010) 'Evaluating leadership coaching: A review and integrated framework', *The Leadership Quarterly*, *21*: 585–99.

Ely, R.J. and Thomas, D.A. (2020) 'Getting serious about diversity: Enough already with the business case', *Harvard Business Review*, *98*(6): 114–22.

Engstrom, T.E.J. (2005) *Individual determinants of mentoring success*. Doctoral dissertation. Northumbria University, Newcastle, UK.

Ensher, E.A., Heun, C. and Blanchard, A. (2003) 'Online mentoring and computer-mediated communication: New directions in research', *Journal of Vocational Behaviour*, *63*(2): 264–88.

Erikson, E. (1950) *Childhood and Society*. Harmondsworth: Penguin Books.

Erikson, E. (1995) *Childhood and Society*. London: Vintage.

Evers, W.J.G., Brouwers, A. and Tomic, W. (2006) 'A quasi-experimental study on management effectiveness', *Consulting Psychology Journal: Practice and Research*, *58*(3): 174–82.

Fairbairns, J. (1991) 'Plugging the gap in training needs analysis', *People Management*, February: 43–5.

Fatien Diochon, P. (2012) 'Ethical challenges in business coaching', in P. O'Sullivan, M. Smith and M. Esposito (eds), *Business Ethics: A Critical Approach – Integrating Ethics across the Business World*. London: Routledge.

Fatien Diochon, P. and Lovelace, K. (2015) 'The coaching continuum: Power dynamics in the change process', *International Journal of Work Innovation*, *1*(3): 305–22.

Fatien Diochon, P. and Nizet, J. (2015) 'Ethical codes and executive coaches: One size does not fit all', *Journal of Applied Behavioural Science*, *51*(2): 277–301.

Fatien Diochon, P. and Nizet, J. (2019) 'Ethics as a fabric: An emotional reflexive sensemaking process', *Business Ethics Quarterly*, *29*(4): 461–89.

Fatien Diochon, P., Otter, K., Stokes, P. and Van Hove, L. (2019) 'Let's sculpt it: Experiencing the role of organizational context in coaching', *Management Teaching Review*, March. DOI: 10.1177/2379298119833692.

Feasey, D. (2002) *Good Practice in Supervision with Psychotherapists and Counsellors: The Relational Approach*. London: Whurr.

Feehily J (2018) 'Exploring the lived experience of internal coaches', *International Journal of Evidence Based Coaching and Mentoring*, Special Issue *12*: 73–84.

Feltham, C. (1995) *What is Counselling?* London: SAGE.

Fendt, J. and Sachs, W. (2008) 'Grounded theory method in management research: Users' perspectives', *Organizational Research Methods, 11*(3): 430–55.

Fénelon, F.S. de la M. (1808) *The Adventures of Telemachus, Vols 1 and 2*, translated by J. Hawkesworth. London: Union Printing Office, St John's Square.

Fénelon, F.S. de la M. (1835) *Oeuvres de Fénelon*, Vol. *III*, in P. Riley (1994) *Fénelon – Telemachus*. Cambridge: Cambridge University Press.

Festinger, L. (1957) *A Theory of Cognitive Dissonance*. Stanford: Stanford University Press.

Filipczak B. (1998) 'The executive coach: Helper or healer?', *Training Magazine, 35*, 30–37.

Fillery-Travis, A. and Collins, R. (2017) 'Discipline, profession and industry: How our choices shape our future', in T. Bachkirova, G. Spence and D. Drake (eds), *The SAGE Handbook of Coaching*. London: SAGE, pp. 729–40.

Fine, L. and Pullins, E.B. (1998) 'Peer mentoring in the industrial sales force: An exploratory investigation of men and women in developmental relationships', *Journal of Personal Selling and Sales Management, XVIII*(4): 89–103.

Flaherty, J. (1999) *Coaching: Evoking Excellence in Others*. Boston, MA: Butterworth-Heinemann.

Flores, F. (1999) 'The world according to Flores', *Fast Company*, January: 144–51.

Foucault, M. (1979) *Discipline and Punish: The Birth of the Prison*. London: Penguin.

Foucault, M. (1980) 'Truth and power', in *M. Foucault: Power/Knowledge – Selected Interviews and Other Writings 1972–1977*, ed. C. Gordon. Hemel Hempstead: Harvester Wheatsheaf.

Fox, A. (1974) *Beyond Contract*. London: Faber and Faber.

Fox, A. and Stevenson, L. (2006) 'Exploring the effectiveness of peer mentoring of accounting and finance students in higher education', *Accounting Education: An International Journal, 15*(2): 189–202.

Fracaro, K. (2006) 'Mentoring for career guidance', *Supervision, 67*(6): 13–16.

Francis, R. (2013) *Report of the Mid-Staffordshire NHS Foundation Trust Public Inquiry*. London: The Stationery Office.

Freire, T. (2013) 'Positive psychology approaches', in J. Passmore, D.B. Peterson and T. Freire (eds), *The Wiley-Blackwell Handbook of the Psychology of Coaching and Mentoring*. Chichester: John Wiley, pp. 426–42.

French, Jr, J.R.P. and Raven, B. (1962) 'The bases of social power', in C. Dorwin (ed.), *Group Dynamics: Research and Theory*. Evanston, IL: Peterson, pp. 607–23.

Frenkel, S. and Kuruvilla, S. (2002) 'Logics of action, globalization, and changing employment relations in China, India, Malaysia, and the Philippines', *Industrial and Labor Relations Review, 3*: 387–412.

Frenkel, S. and Peetz, D. (1998) 'Globalization and industrial relations in East Asia: A three-country comparison', *Industrial Relations, 3*: 282–310.

Frisch, M.H. (2001) 'The emerging role of the internal coach', *Consulting Psychology Journal: Practice and Research, 53*(4): 240–50.

Gabriel, L. and Casemore, R. (2010) *Guidance for Ethical Decision Making: A Suggested Model for Practitioners*. Lutterworth, UK: British Association of Counselling and Psychotherapy (BACP).

Gallwey, T. (1997a [1974]) *The Inner Game of Tennis*. New York: Random House.

Gallwey, T. (1997b) *The Inner Game of Work: Overcoming Mental Obstacles for Maximum Performance*. New York: Random House.

Garvey, B. (1994a) 'A dose of mentoring', *Education and Training, 36*(4): 18–26.

Garvey, B. (1994b) 'Ancient Greece, MBAs, the Health Service and Georg', *Education and Training, 36*(2): 18–26.

Garvey, B. (1995a) 'Healthy signs for mentoring', *Education and Training*, 37(5): 12–19.

Garvey, B. (1995b) 'Let the actions match the words', in D. Clutterbuck and D. Megginson (eds) *Mentoring in Action*. London: Kogan Page, pp. 111–23.

Garvey, B. (2004) 'Call a rose by any other name and perhaps it's a bramble?', *Development and Learning in Organizations*, 18(2): 6–8.

Garvey, B. (2006) *'Let me tell you a story'*, *International Journal of Mentoring and Coaching*, 4(1), at: www.emccouncil.org/uk/journal.htm (accessed 21 June 2021).

Garvey, B. (2011) *A Very Short, Slightly Interesting and Reasonably Cheap Book on Coaching and Mentoring*. London: SAGE.

Garvey, B. (2012) 'Mentoring for leadership development: A case study of executive mentoring during the banking crisis', *The International Journal of Mentoring and Coaching*, X(1): 56–76.

Garvey, B. (2013) 'Coaching people through life transitions', in J. Passmore (ed.) *Diversity in Coaching*. London: Kogan Page.

Garvey, B. (2014) 'Neofeudalism and surveillance in coaching supervision and mentoring?', *e-Organisations & People*, 21(4): 41–7.

Garvey, B. (2016) 'Issues of assessment and accreditation of coaches', in T. Bachkirova, G. Spence and D. Drake (eds), *The SAGE Handbook of Coaching*. London: SAGE, pp. 682–97.

Garvey, B. (2017) 'Philosophical origins of mentoring: the critical narrative analysis', in D. Clutterbuck, A. McClelland, F. Kochan, L. Lunsford and B. Smith (eds), *The SAGE Handbook of Mentoring*. London: SAGE.

Garvey, B. (2019a) 'Generalising generations', *Coaching at Work*, 15(1): 50–53.

Garvey, B. (2019b) 'How far is culture change through coaching and mentoring possible?', in R. Hamlin, A. Ellinger and J. Jones (eds), *Evidence Based Initiatives for Organizational Change and Development*, IGI Global Premier Reference Source Book. Hershey, PA: IGI Global.

Garvey, B. and Alred, G. (2000) 'Educating mentors', *Mentoring and Tutoring*, 8(2): 113–26.

Garvey, B. and Alred, G. (2001) 'Mentoring and the tolerance of complexity', *Futures*, 33(6): 519–30.

Garvey, B. and Galloway, K. (2002) 'Mentoring in the Halifax, a small beginning in a large organization', *Career Development International*, 7(5): 271–9.

Garvey, B. and Garrett-Harris, R. (2005) *The Benefits of Mentoring: A Literature Review*. Report for East Mentors Forum, Mentoring and Coaching Research Unit. Sheffield: Sheffield Hallam University.

Garvey, B. and Langridge, K. (2006) *The Pupil Mentoring Pocketbook*. Alresford, Hants: Teachers' Pocketbooks.

Garvey, B. and Megginson, D. (2004) 'Odysseus, Telemachus and Mentor: Stumbling into, searching for and signposting the road to desire', *International Journal of Mentoring and Coaching*, 2(1): 16–40.

Garvey, B. and Williamson, B. (2002) *Beyond Knowledge Management: Dialogue, Creativity and the Corporate Curriculum*. Harlow: Pearson Education.

Garvey, B., Alred, G. and Smith, R. (1996) 'First person mentoring', *Career Development International*, 5(1): 10–14.

Garvey, B., Stokes, P. and Megginson, D. (2014) *Coaching and Mentoring: Theory and Practice*, 2nd edition. London: SAGE.

Garvey, B. Stokes, P. and Megginson, D. (2018) *Coaching and Mentoring theory and practice*, 3rd Edition. London: SAGE

Garvey, R. and Westlander, G. (2013) 'Training mentors: Behaviors which bring positive outcomes in mentoring', in J. Passmore, D.B. Peterson and T. Freire (eds), *The Wiley-Blackwell Handbook of the Psychology of Coaching and Mentoring*. Chichester: John Wiley, pp. 243–65.

Geertz, C. (1974) *Myth, Symbol and Culture*. New York: W.W. Norton.

Geissler, H., Hasenberin, M., Kanatouri, S. and Wegener, R. (2014) 'E-Coaching – Concept and Empirical Findings of a Virtual Coaching Programme', *International Journal of Evidence Based Coaching and Mentoring*, 12(2): 165–187.

Ghods, N. and Boyce, C. (2013) 'Virtual coaching and mentoring', in J. Passmore, D.B. Peterson, and T. Freire (eds), *The Psychology of Coaching and Mentoring*. Chichester: John Wiley & Sons, pp. 501–24.

Gibb, S. and Hill, P. (2006) 'From trail-blazing individualism to a social construction community: Modelling knowledge construction in coaching', *International Journal of Mentoring and Coaching*, 4(2): 58–77.

Gibb, S. and Megginson, D. (1993) 'Inside corporate mentoring schemes: A new agenda of concerns', *Personnel Review*, 22(1): 40–54.

Giglio, L., Diamante, T. and Urban, J. (1998) 'Coaching a leader: Leveraging change at the top', *Journal of Management Development*, 17(2): 93–105.

Gill, J. and Johnson, P. (1997) *Research Methods for Managers*. London: Paul Chapman.

Gill, J., Johnson, P. and Clark, M. (2010) *Research Methods for Managers*, 4th edition. London: SAGE.

Gladwell, M. (2002) *The Tipping Point: How Little Things Can Make a Big Difference*. London: Abacus.

Godshalk, V.M. and Sosik, J.J. (2000) 'Does mentor-protégé agreement on mentor leadership behavior influence the quality of a mentoring relationship?', *Group and Organization Management*, 25(3): 291–317.

Godshalk, V.M. and Sosik, J.J. (2003) 'Aiming for career success: The role of learning goal orientation in mentoring relationships', *Journal of Vocational Behavior*, 63(3): 417–37.

Golding, W. (1964) *The Spire*. London: Faber and Faber.

Goldman, L. (1984) 'Warning: The Socratic method can be dangerous', *Educational Leadership*, 42(1): 57–62.

Goldsmith, M. (2005) 'Coaching leaders and behavioural coaching', in H. Morgan, P. Hawkins and M. Goldsmith (eds), *The Art and Practice of Leadership Coaching*. Hoboken, NJ: Wiley, pp. 56–60.

Goldsmith, M. (2006) 'Where the work of executive coaching lies', *Consulting to Management*, 17(2): 15–17.

Goleman, D. (1996) *Emotional Intelligence*. London: Bloomsbury.

Goleman, D. (1998) *Working with Emotional Intelligence*. London: Bloomsbury.

Goodge, P. and Coomber, J. (2007) 'How to … get 360-degree coaching right', *People Management*, 3(May): 44–5.

Gosling, J. and Mintzberg, H. (2003) 'The five minds of a manager', *Harvard Business Review*, 81(11): 54–5.

Grant, A.M. (2003) 'The impact of life coaching on goal attainment, metacognition and mental health', *Sports Behaviour and Personality*, 31(3): 253–64.

Grant, A.M. (2006a) 'An integrative goal-focused approach to executive coaching', in D. Stober and A.M. Grant (eds), *Evidence Based Coaching Handbook*. New York: Wiley, pp. 153–92.

Grant, A.M. (2006b) 'Solution focused coaching', in J. Passmore (ed.), *Excellence in Coaching*. London: Kogan Page, pp. 73–90.

Grant, A.M. (2007) 'Enhancing coaching skills and emotional intelligence through training', *Industrial and Commercial Training*, 39(5): 257–66.

Grant, A.M. (2012) 'ROI is a poor measure of coaching success: Towards a more holistic approach using a well being and engagement framework', *Coaching: An International Journal of Theory, Research and Practice*, 5(2): 74–85.

Grant, A.M. (2020) An Integrated Model of Goal-Focussed Coaching: An Evidence-Based Framework for Teaching In: Passmore, J. and Tee, D. (2020) (eds) *Coaching Researched: A Coaching Psychology Reader for Practitioners and Researchers (BPS Textbooks in Psychology)*. London: John Wiley & Sons Ltd., Ch. 7: 113–139, Kindle Edition.

Grant, A.M. and Greene, J. (2001) *Coach Yourself: Make Real Changes in Your Life*. London: Pearson Momentum.

Grant, A.M. and Hartley, M. (2013) 'Developing the leader as coach: Insights, strategies and tips for embedding coaching skills in the workplace', *Coaching: An International Journal of Theory, Research and Practice*, 6(2): 102–15.

Grant, A.M., Franklin, J. and Langford, P. (2002) 'The self-reflection and insight scale: A new measure of private self-consciousness', *Social Behaviour and Personality*, 30(8): 821–36.

Graßmann, C., Schölmerich, F. and Schermuly, C.C. (2020) 'The relationship between working alliance and client outcomes in coaching: A meta-analysis', *Human Relations*, 73(1): 35–58.

Gratton, L. and Scott, A. (2020) *The 100-Year Life: Living and Working in an Age of Longevity*, 2nd edition. London: Bloomsbury.

Gray, D. (2006) 'Executive coaching: Towards a dynamic alliance of psychotherapy and transformative learning processes', *Management Learning*, 37(4): 475–97.

Gray, D. (2009) *Doing Research in the Real World*. London: SAGE.

Gray, D. and Jackson, P. (2011) 'Coaching supervision in the historical context of psychotherapeutic and counselling models: A meta model', in T. Bachkirova, P. Jackson and D. Clutterbuck (eds), *Coaching and Mentoring Supervision: Theory and Practice*. Maidenhead: Open University Press, pp. 15–28.

Gray, D.E., Garvey, B. and Lane, D.A. (2016) *A Critical Introduction to Coaching and Mentoring*. London: SAGE.

Gregory, J.B. and Levy, P.E. (2013) 'Behavioural coaching', in J. Passmore, D.B. Peterson and T. Freire (eds), *The Wiley-Blackwell Handbook of the Psychology of Coaching and Mentoring*. Chichester: John Wiley, pp. 298–318.

Grint, K. (2010) *Leadership: A Very Short Introduction*. Oxford: Oxford University Press.

Grodzki, L. and Allen, W. (2005) *The Business and Practice of Coaching: Finding Your Niche, Making Money and Attracting Ideal Clients*. London: Norton.

Groot, W. (1993) 'Het rendement van bedrijfsopleidingen' [The return of the company]', in J. Kessels (ed.), 'Opleidingen in arbeidsorganisaties: Het ambivalen-te perspectief van dekennisproduktiviteit' [Training in organisations: The ambivalent perspective of knowledge productivity], *Comenius*, 15(2): 179–93.

Guardian Online, The (2016) 'Philip Green accused of being evil as Frank Field escalates war of words', at www.theguardian.com/business/2016/jul/31/philip-green-accused-of-being-evil-as-frank-field-escalates-war-of-words (accessed 1 August 2016).

Guardian Observer editorial (2020) The Observer view on Britain's shameful treatment of asylum seekers, Sunday 4 October. Available at: https://www.theguardian.com/commentisfree/2020/oct/04/the-observer-view-on-britains-shameful-treatment-of-asylum-seekers (accessed 17 June 2021).

Gurchiek, K. (2017) 'Meeting millennial expectations can benefit your entire workforce', *Society for Human Resource Management (SHRM)*. https://www.shrm.org/resourcesandtools/hr-topics/pages/meeting-millennial-expectations-can-benefit-your-entire-workforce.aspx.

Gutting, G. (2005) *Foucault: A Very Short Introduction*. Oxford: Oxford University Press.

Habermas, J. (1974) *Theory and Practice*. London: Heinemann.

Hackman, R.J. and Wageman, R. (2005) 'A theory of team coaching', *Academy of Management Review*, 30(2): 269–87.

Hakro, A.N. and Matthew, P. (2020) 'Coaching and mentoring in higher education institutions: A case study in Oman', *International Journal of Mentoring and Coaching in Education*, 9(3): 307–322.

Hale, R. (2000) 'To match or mis-match? The dynamics of mentoring as a route to personal and organizational learning', *Career Development International*, 5(4/5): 223–34.

Hall, D.T., Otazo, K.L. and Hollenbeck, G.P. (1999) 'Behind closed doors: What really happens in executive coaching', *Organizational Dynamics*, Winter: 39–53.

Hallett, C. (1997) 'Learning through reflection in the community: The relevance of Schön's theories of coaching to nursing education', *International Journal of Nursing Studies*, 34(2): 103–10.

Hamburg, I. (2013) 'Facilitating Learning and Knowledge Transfer through Mentoring', 5th International Conference on Computer Supported Education, Aachen, Germany, 6–8 May, at www.csedu.org/?y=2013 (accessed 10 May 2016).

Hamilton, B.A. and Scandura, T.A. (2003) 'Implications for organizational learning and development in a wired world', *Organizational Dynamics*, 31(4): 388–402.

Hamlin, R., Ellinger, A., Jones, J. (eds) (2019) *Evidence Based Initiatives for Organizational Change and Development* (IGI Global Premier Reference Source Book). Hershey, PA: IGI Global.

Hansford, B. and Ehrich, L. (2006) 'The principleship: How significant is mentoring?', *Journal of Educational Administration*, 44(1): 36–52.

Hardingham, A. (2005) 'A job well done? The coach's dilemma', *People Management*, 11(8): 54.

Hardingham, A. (2006) 'The British eclectic model in practice', *International Journal of Mentoring and Coaching*, IV(1): 39–45.

Hardingham, A., Brearley, M., Moorhouse, A. and Venter, B. (2004) *The Coach's Coach: Personal Development for Personal Developers*. London: CIPD.

Hargrove, R. (1995) *Masterful Coaching: Extraordinary Results by Impacting People and the Way They Think and Act Together*. San Francisco, CA: Jossey-Bass/Pfeiffer.

Harlow, E. (2013) 'Coaching, supervision and the social work zeitgeist', *Social Work in Action*, 25(1): 61–70.

Harquail, C.V. and Blake, S.D. (1993) 'UnMasc-ing mentor and reclaiming Athena: Insights for mentoring in heterogeneous organizations'. Paper 8 in Standing Conference on Organizational Symbolism, Collbato, Barcelona, Spain. (Further information on access to paper at www.scos.org).

Harris, M. (1999) 'Look, it's a 1–0 psychologist … no, it's a trainer… no, it's an executive coach', *TIP*, 36(3): 1–5.

Harrison, F. (1887) *The Choice of Books, and Other Literary Pieces*. London: Macmillan.

Hatch, M.J. and Cunliffe, A.N. (2013) *Organization Theory: Modern, Symbolic and Postmodern Perspectives*, 3rd edition. Oxford: Oxford University Press.

Hatfield, I. (2015) *New Skills at Work: Self-employment in Europe*, JP Morgan Chase Co. London: Institute for Public Policy Research.

Hawkins, C. (2006) 'East of England (Harlow) e-Mentoring Pilot Project', in D. Megginson, D. Clutterbuck, B. Garvey, P. Stokes and R. Garrett-Harris (eds), *Mentoring in Action*, 2nd edition. London: Kogan Page, pp. 62–7.

Hawkins, P. (2012) *Creating a Coaching Culture*. Maidenhead: Open University Press.

Hawkins, P. and Schwenk, G. (2006) '*Coaching Supervision*'. Paper prepared for the CIPD Coaching Conference, London, September.

Hawkins, P. and Shohet, R. (2006) *Supervision in the Helping Professions*, 3rd edition. Maidenhead: Open University Press.

Hawkins, P. and Shohet, R. (2011) *Supervision in the Helping Professions*, 4th edition. Maidenhead: Open University Press.

Hawkins, P. and Smith, N. (2006) *Coaching, Mentoring and Organizational Consultancy: Supervision and Development*. Maidenhead: Open University Press.

Hayes, P. (2008) *NLP Coaching*. London: Open University Press.

Headlam-Wells, J., Gosland, J. and Craig, J. (2006) 'Beyond the organisation: The design and management of e-mentoring systems', *International Journal of Information Management, 26*: 272–85.

HEFCE (2011) *Consultation on Draft Panel Criteria and Working Methods, Higher Education Funding Council for England, Scottish Funding Council, Higher Education Funding Council for Wales, Department for Employment and Learning, Northern Ireland*, at www.ref.ac.uk/pubs/2011–03 (accessed January 2013).

Hemmestad, L.B., Jones, R.L. and Standal, Ø.F. (2010) 'Phronetic social science: A means of better researching and analysing coaching?', *Sport, Education and Society, 15*(4): 447–59.

Henochowicz, S. and Hetherington, D. (2006) 'Leadership coaching in health care', *Leadership and Organization Development Journal, 27*(3): 183–9.

Heo, W., Grable, J.E. and Rabbani, A.G. (2020) 'A test of the association between the initial surge in COVID-19 cases and subsequent changes in financial risk tolerance', *Review of Behavioral Finance*. E-pub ahead-of-print. https://doi-org.hallam.idm.oclc.org/10.1108/RBF-06–2020-0121.

Higgins, M.C. (2000) 'The more the merrier? Multiple developmental relationships and work satisfaction', *The Journal of Management Development, 19*(4): 277–96.

Higgins, M.C. and Kram, K.E. (2001) 'Reconceptualizing mentoring at work: A developmental network perspective', *Academy of Management Review, 26*(2): 264–88.

Higgins, M.C., Dobrow, S.R. and Roloff, K.S. (2007) *Resilience and Relationships: The Role of Developmental Support over Time*. Working Paper. Fordham University, at http://nrs.harvard.edu/urn-3:HUL.InstRepos:5372958 (accessed March 2013).

Higgins, M.C., Dobrow, S.R. and Roloff, K.S. (2010) 'Optimism and the boundaryless career: The role of developmental relationships', *Journal of Organizational Behavior, 72*(2): 207–24.

Hislop, D. (2005) *Knowledge Management in Organizations: A Critical Introduction*. Oxford: Oxford University Press.

Hoddinott, P., Lee, A.J. and Pill, R. (2006) 'Effectiveness of a breastfeeding peer coaching intervention in rural Scotland', *Birth, 33*(1): 27–36.

Hofstede, G. (1980) *Culture's Consequences: International Differences in Work-related Values*. Beverly Hills, CA: SAGE.

Hofstede, G. (2001) *Culture's Consequences: International Differences in Work-related Values*, 2nd edition. Thousand Oaks, CA: SAGE.

Hollembeak, J. and Amorose, A.J. (2005) 'Perceived coaching behaviours and college athletes' intrinsic motivation: A test of self-determination theory', *Journal of Applied Sports Psychology, 17*(1): 20–36.

Honoria (1793) *The Female Mentor or Select Conversations, Vols 1 and 2*. London: T. Cadell.

Honoria (1796) *The Female Mentor or Select Conversations, Vol. 3*. London: T. Cadell.

Houghton, J.D. and Neck, C.P. (2002) 'The revised self-leadership questionnaire: Testing a hierarchical factor structure for self-leadership', *Journal of Managerial Psychology, 17*: 672–91.

Huang, C.A. and Lynch, J. (1995) *Mentoring: The TAO of Giving and Receiving Wisdom*. New York: HarperCollins.

Hughes, J. (2003) A reflection on the art and practice of mentorship. *Institutional Investor plc*.

Hui, R.T., Sue-Chan, C. and Wood, R.E. (2013) 'The contrasting effects of coaching style on task performance: The mediating role of subjective task complexity and self-set goal', *Human Resource Development Quarterly, 24*(4): 429–58.

Humble, J.W. (1971) *Management by Objectives*. London: Management Publications/BIM.

Hunt, J.M. and Weintraub, J.R. (2002) *The Coaching Manager: Developing Top Talent in Business*. London: SAGE.

Hunt, J.M. and Weintraub, J.R. (2007) *The Coaching Organization: A Strategy for Developing Leaders*. Thousand Oaks, CA: SAGE.

Hurley, A.E. and Fagenson-Eland, E.A. (1996) 'Challenges in cross-gender mentoring relationships: Psychological intimacy, myths, rumours, innuendoes and sexual harassment', *Leadership and Organization Development Journal*, *17*(3): 42–9.

Hursthouse, R. (1999) *On Virtue Ethics*. Oxford: Oxford University Press.

Hutton, W. (2011) *Them and Us: Changing Britain – Why we Need a Fairer Society*. London: Abacus Publications.

Ibarra, H. and Lineback, K. (2005) 'What's your story?', *Harvard Business Review*, *83*(1): 64–71.

ICF (International Coach Federation) (2012) *2012 ICF Global Coaching Study*. www.coachfederation.de/files/2012globalcoachingstudy.pdf (accessed March 2013).

ICF (International Coach Federation) (2016) *2016 ICF Global Coaching Study*. www.coachfederation.org/files/filedownloads/2016ICFglobalcoachingstudy_executivesummary.pdf (accessed March 2016).

ICF (International Coach Federation) (2020) *2020 ICF Global Coaching Study: Executive Summary*. https://coachfederation.org/app/uploads/2020/09/FINAL_ICF_GCS2020_ExecutiveSummary.pdf (accessed 11 January 2021).

ILO (International Labour Organization) (2013) *Global Employment Trends: Recovering from a Second Jobs Dip*. Geneva: ILO.

ILO (International Labour Organization) (2019) *World Employment Social Outlook: Trends 201 6*. Geneva: ILO.

Inden, R. (1990) *Imagining India*. Oxford: Blackwell.

Iordanou, I., Hawley, R. and Iordanou, C. (2017) *Values and Ethics in Coaching*. London: SAGE.

Irwin, G., Hanton, S. and Kerwin, D. (2004) 'Reflective practice and the origins of elite coaching knowledge', *Reflective Practice*, *5*(3): 425–42.

Ives, Y. (2008) 'What is "coaching"? An exploration of conflicting paradigms', *International Journal of Evidence Based Coaching and Mentoring*, *6*(2): 100–13.

Jackson, B. and Parry, K. (2018) *A Very Short, Fairly Interesting and Reasonably Cheap Book about Studying Leadership*, 3rd edition. London: SAGE.

Jackson, N. and Carter, P. (2000) *Rethinking Organizational Behaviour*. Harlow: Pearson Education.

Jackson, P.Z. and McKergow, M. (2002) *The Solutions Focus: The Simple Way to Positive Change*. London: Nicholas Brealey.

Jackson, T. (2002) 'The management of people across cultures: Valuing people differently', *Human Resource Management*, *41*: 455–75.

Jacques, R. (1996) *Manufacturing the Employee: Management Knowledge From the 19th to 21st centuries*. London: SAGE.

Jamieson, D. (2013) 'Role models, mentors, and other heroes', *Relational Child Care & Youth Practice*, *26*(1): 43–7.

Jarvis, J., Lane, D. and Fillery-Travis, A. (2006) *The Case for Coaching: Making Evidence-Based Decisions on Coaching*. London: CIPD.

Jarvis, P. (1992) *Paradoxes of Learning: On Becoming an Individual in Society*. San Francisco, CA: Jossey-Bass.

Jessup, G. (1991) *Outcomes: NVQs and the Emerging Model of Education and Training*. Oxford: Falmer.

Johnson, B., Smith, D.G. and Haythornwaite, J. (2020) 'Why your mentorship program isn't working', *Harvard Business Review*.

Johnson, H.T. and Bröms, A. (2000) *Profit beyond Measure*. New York: Free Press.

Johnson, S.K., Geroy, G.D. and Griego, O.V. (1999) 'The mentoring model theory: Dimensions in mentoring protocols', *Career Development International*, *4*(7): 384–91.

Jones, G. and Gorrell, R. (2014) *How to Create a Coaching Culture*. London: Kogan Page.

Jones, R. and Wallace, M. (2005) 'Another bad day at the training ground: Coping with the ambiguity in the coaching context', *Sport, Education and Society*, 10(1): 119–34.

Jones, R., Rafferty, A. and Griffin, M. (2006) 'The executive coaching trend: Towards more flexible executives', *Leadership and Organization Development Journal*, 27(7): 583–95.

Jones, R.J., Woods, S.A. and Zhou, Y. (2019) 'The effects of coachee personality and goal orientation on performance improvement following coaching: A controlled field experiment', *Applied Psychology: An International Review*. DOI: 1111/apps.12218.

Joo, B. (2005) 'Executive coaching: A conceptual framework from an integrative review of practice and research', *Human Resource Development Review*, 4(4): 462–88.

Joo, B., Sushko, J. and McLean, G.N. (2012) 'Multiple faces of coaching: Manager-as-coach, executive coaching, and formal mentoring', *Organization Development Journal*, 30(1): 19–38.

Joseph, S. (2010) 'The person-centred approach to coaching', in E. Cox, T. Bachkirova and D. Clutterbuck (eds), *The Complete Handbook of Coaching*. London: SAGE, pp. 68–79.

Joshi, A., Dencker, J.C. and Franz, G. (2011) Generations in Organizations, *Research in Organizational Behavior*, 31: 177–205.

Jung, C. (1958) *Psyche and Symbol*. New York: Doubleday.

Kampa-Kokesch, S. and Anderson, M.Z. (2001) 'Executive coaching: A comprehensive review of the literature', *Consulting Psychology Journal: Practice and Research*, 53(4): 205–28.

Kanatouri, S. (2020) *The Digital Coach*. London: Routledge-EMCC Masters in Coaching and Mentoring.

Kanter, R. (1977) *Men and Women of the Corporation*. New York: Basic Books.

Katz, H. and Darbishire, O. (2000) *Converging Divergencies: Worldwide Changes in Employment Systems*. Ithaca, NY: ILR/Cornell University Press.

Kauffman, C., Boniwell, I. and Silberman, J. (2010) 'The positive psychology approach to coaching', in E. Cox, T. Bachkirova and D. Clutterbuck (eds), *The Complete Handbook of Coaching*. London: SAGE, pp. 158–71.

Kavannah, J. and Rich, M. (2018) *Truth Decay: An Initial Exploration of the Diminishing Role of Facts and Analysis in American Public Life*. Santa Monica, CA: RAND Corporation.

Kayes, D.C. (2006) *Destructive Goal Pursuit: The Mount Everest Disaster*. Basingstoke: Palgrave Macmillan.

Kegan, R. and Lahey, L.L. (2009) *Immunity to Change: How to Overcome It and Unlock the Potential in Yourself and Your Organization*. Boston, MA: Harvard Business Press.

Kellar, G.M., Jennings, B.E., Sink, H.L. and Mundy, R.A. (1995) 'Teaching transportation with an interactive method', *Journal of Business Logistics*, 16(1): 251–79.

Kennett, K. (2006a) 'Kate Kennett is e-mentored by David Clutterbuck', in D. Megginson, D. Clutterbuck, B. Garvey, P. Stokes and R. Garrett-Harris (eds), *Mentoring in Action*, 2nd edition. London: Kogan Page, pp. 216–20.

Kennett, K. (2006b) *Reflective practice groups for learning mentors: An alternative to supervision?* Unpublished Master's dissertation, Sheffield Hallam University, UK.

Kessels, J. (1995) 'Opleidingen in arbeidsorganisaties: Het ambivalen-te perspectief van dekennisproduktiviteit' [Training in organizations: The ambivalent perspective of knowledge productivity], *Comenius*, 15(2): 179–93.

Kessels, J. (1996) 'Knowledge productivity and the corporate curriculum', in J.F. Schreinemakers (ed.), *Knowledge Management: Organization, Competence and Methodology*. Wurzburg: Ergon Verlag, pp. 168–74.

Kessels, J. (2002) 'You cannot be smart against your will', in B. Garvey and B. Williamson (eds), *Beyond Knowledge Management: Dialogue, Creativity and the Corporate Curriculum*. Harlow: Pearson Education, pp. 47–52.

Kilburg, R.R. (2004) 'Trudging toward Dodoville: Conceptual approaches and case studies in executive coaching', *Consulting Psychology Journal*, 56(4): 203–13.

Kimball, B.A. (1986) *Orators and Philosophers: A History of the Idea of Liberal Education*. New York: Teachers College Press.

Kimsey-House, H., Kimsey-House, K., Sandahl, P. and Whitworth, L. (2011) *Coactive Coaching: Changing Business, Transforming Lives*. London: Nicholas Brealey.

King, P. and Eaton, J. (1999) 'Coaching for results', *Industrial and Commercial Training*, 31(4): 145–51.

Kirkpatrick, D.L. (1959) 'Techniques for evaluating training programmes', *Journal of the American Society of Training Directors*, 13: 3–26.

Klasen, N. and Clutterbuck, D. (2002) *Implementing Mentoring Schemes*. Oxford: Butterworth-Heinemann.

Knowles, M. (1980) *The Modern Practice of Adult Education: From Pedagogy to Andragogy*. Englewood Cliffs, NJ: Prentice Hall.

Knowles, M.S., Holton, E.F. III and Swanson, R.A. (1998) *The Adult Learner*. Houston, TX: Gulf.

Kochan, F.K. and Trimble, S.B. (2000) 'From mentoring to co-mentoring: Establishing collaborative relationships', *Theory into Practice*, 39(1): 20–8.

Koggel, C. and Orme, J. (2010) 'Editorial: Care ethics – new theories and applications', *Ethics & Social Welfare*, 4(2): 109–14.

Kolb, D.A. (1984) *Experiential Learning*. Englewood Cliffs, NJ: Prentice Hall.

Kollen, T. (2016) 'Lessening the difference is more: The relationship between diversity management and the perceived organizational climate for gay men and lesbians', *International Journal of Human Resource Management*, 27(17): 1967–96.

Koshksaray, A.A., Ardakani, A., Ghasemnaejad, N and Azbari, A.Q. (2020) 'The role of customer orientation coaching on employee's individual performance: A case of Tejarat bank in Iran', *International Journal of Islamic and Middle Eastern Finance and Management*, 13(3): 437–69.

Koukpaki, A.S.F. and Adams, K. (2020) 'Enhancing professional growth and the learning and development function through reflective practices: An autoethnographic narrative approach', *European Journal of Training & Development*, 44(8/9): 805–27. https://doi-org.hallam.idm.oclc.org/10.1108/EJTD-09-2019-0165.

Krackhardt, D. (1992) 'The strength of strong ties: The importance of philos in organizations', in N. Nohria and R.G. Eccles (eds), *Networks and Organizations: Structures, Form and Action*. Boston, MA: Harvard University Business School Press, pp. 216–39.

Krackhardt, D. and Stern, R.N. (1988) 'Informal networks and organizational crises: An experimental simulation', *Social Psychology Quarterly*, 51: 123–40.

Kram, K.E. (1980) *Mentoring processes at work: Developing relationships in managerial careers*. Unpublished doctoral dissertation, Yale University, USA.

Kram, K.E. (1983) 'Phases of the mentor relationship', *Academy of Management Journal*, 26(4): 608–25.

Kram, K.E. (1985a) *Mentoring at Work: Developmental Relationships in Organizational Life*. Glenview, IL: Scott, Foresman.

Kram, K.E. (1985b) 'Improving the mentoring process', *Training and Development Journal*, 39(4): 42–3.

Kram, K.E. and Hall, D.T. (1996) 'Mentoring in a context of diversity and turbulence', in E.E. Kossek and S.A. Lobel (eds), *Managing Diversity: Human Resource Strategies for Transforming the Workplace*. Cambridge, MA: Blackwell Business, pp. 108–36.

Kram, K.E. and Isabella, L.A. (1985) 'Mentoring alternatives: The role of peer relationships in career development', *Academy of Management Journal*, *28*(1): 110–32.

Krazmien, M. and Berger, F. (1997) 'The coaching paradox', *International Journal of Hospitality Management*, *16*(1): 3–10.

Kroger, R.O. and Wood, L.A. (1998) 'The turn of discourse in social psychology', *Canadian Psychology*, *39*(4): 266–79.

Krohn, D. (1998) 'Four indispensable features of Socratic dialogue', in R. Saran and B. Neisser (eds), *Enquiring Minds: Socratic Dialogue in Education*. Stoke on Trent: Trentham Books.

Krznaric, R. (2021) *The Good Ancestor: How to Think Long Term in a Short Term World*. London: Penguin Books.

Kuhn, T.S. (1970) *The Structure of Scientific Revolutions*. Chicago, IL: University of Chicago Press.

Kwon, W., Clarke, I. and Wodak, R. (2014) 'Micro-level discursive strategies for constructing shared views around strategic issues in team meetings', *Journal of Management Studies*, *52*(2): 265–90.

Lam, P. (2006) *Culture and distance learning in Hong Kong: A case study of an overseas distance learning programme offered to Chinese learners in Hong Kong*. Unpublished PhD thesis, University of Leicester, UK.

Lam, P. (2016) 'The impact of Chinese culture on coaching in Hong Kong', *International Journal of Evidence Based Coaching and Mentoring*, *14*(1): 57–73.

Lam, P. (2019) '*The perception of coaching in Asia.*' Paper presented in 'A Cut Above: Experience the Difference', Inaugural Conference, 17–18 January, European Mentoring and Coaching Council: Kuala Lumpur, Malaysia.

Lambert, L. (2003) 'Leadership redefined: An evocative context for teacher leadership', *School Leadership and Management*, *23*(4): 421–30.

Lankau, M.J. and Scandura, T.A. (2002) 'An investigation of personal learning in mentoring relationships: Content, antecedents, and consequences', *Academy of Management Journal*, *45*(4): 779–90.

Lantos, G. (1999) 'Motivating moral corporate behaviour', *Journal of Consumer Marketing*, *16*(3): 222–33.

Lasch, C., (1980) *The Culture of Narcissism: America Life in an Age of Diminished Expectations*, New York: W.W. Norton.

Lasch, C. (1995) *The Revolt of the Elites and Betrayal of Democracy*. New York: W.W. Norton.

Lattimore, R. (1965) *The Odyssey of Homer*. New York: Harper Perennial.

Lave, J. and Wenger, E. (1991) *Situated Learning: Legitimate Peripheral Participation*. Cambridge: Cambridge University Press.

Law, H. (2013) *The Psychology of Coaching, Mentoring and Learning*, 2nd edition. Oxford: John Wiley & Sons.

Lawrence, P. (2015) 'Building in a small Australian multinational organisation', *Coaching: An International Journal of Theory, Research and Practice*, *8*(1): 53–60.

Lawson, S. (2017) *Mentoring in specialist workforce development: A realist evaluation*. Unpublished PhD thesis, University of Leeds, UK.

Layder, D. (1994) *Understanding Social Theory*. London: SAGE.

Lazovsky, R. and Shimoni, A. (2007) 'The on-site mentor of counseling interns: Perceptions of ideal role and actual role performance', *Journal of Counseling and Development*, *85*(3): 303–16.

Lee, G. (2003) *Leadership Coaching: From Personal Insight to Organizational Performance*. London: CIPD.

Legge, K. (1995) *Human Resource Management: Rhetorics and Realities*. Basingstoke: Macmillan.

Levinson, D.J., Darrow, C.N., Klein, E.B., Levinson, M.H. and McKee, B. (1978) *The Seasons of a Man's Life*. New York: Knopf.

Li, J., Ghosh, R. and Nachmias, S. (2020) In a time of COVID-19 pandemic, stay healthy, connected, productive, and learning: Words from the editorial team of HRDI. *Human Resource Development International*, *23*(3): 199–207.

Lievegoed, B. (1993) *Phases: The Spiritual Rhythms of Adult Life*. Bristol: Rudolf Steiner Press.

Lines, D. and Robinson, G. (2006) 'Tough at the top', *International Journal of Mentoring and Coaching*, *IV*(1): 4–25.

Lloyd, B. and Rosinski, P. (2005) 'Coaching culture and leadership', *Team Performance Management*, *11*(3/4): 133–8.

Longenecker, C.O. and Neubert, M.J. (2005) 'The practices of effective managerial coaches', *Business Horizons*, *48*: 493–500.

Louis, D. and Fatien Diochon, P. (2014) 'Educating coaches to power dynamics: Managing multiple agendas within the triangular relationship', *Journal of Psychological Issues in Organisational Culture*, *5*(2): 31–47.

Louis, D. and Fatien Diochon, P. (2018) The coaching space: A production of power relationships in organizational settings. *Organization*, *25*(6): 710–731.

Lucas, M. (ed.) (2020) *101 Coaching Supervision Techniques, Approaches, Enquiries and Experiments*. London: Routledge.

Lukes, S. (2005) *Power: A Radical View*, 2nd edition. Basingstoke: Palgrave Macmillan.

Luthans, F. and Peterson, S.J. (2003) '360-degree feedback with systematic coaching: Empirical analysis suggests a winning combination', *Human Resource Management*, *42*(3): 243.

Lyons, P. and Bandura, R.P. (2020) 'Skills needs, integrative pedagogy and case-based instruction', *Journal of Workplace Learning 32*(7): 473–87.

Lyotard, J.-F. (1984) *The Postmodern Condition: A Report on Knowledge (Theory & History of Literature)*. Manchester: Manchester University Press.

MacLennan, N. (1995) *Coaching and Mentoring*. Farnborough: Gower Publishing.

Mann, C., (2020) Safety Net, Coaching at Work, 15(1) 33–35.

Mannheim, K. (1952) *The Problem of Generations*, in: Kecskemeti, P. (ed.), Karl Mannheim Essays, USA, Routledge.

Manz, C.C. and Neck, C.P. (2004) *Mastering Self-leadership: Empowering Yourself for Personal Excellence*. Upper Saddle River, NJ: Pearson/Prentice Hall.

Marshall, C. and Rossman, G.B. (2010). *Designing Qualitative Research*, 5th edition. Thousand Oaks, CA: SAGE.

Martin, J. (2001) *Organization Culture: Mapping the Terrain*. London: Sage.

Maslow, A.H. (1943) 'A theory of human motivation', *Psychological Review*, *50*: 370–96.

Matarazzo, K.L. and Finkelstein, L.M. (2015) 'Formal mentorships: Examining objective-setting, event participation and experience', *Journal of Managerial Psychology*, *30*(6): 675–91.

Mazhar, U. and Rehman, F. (2020) 'Manufacturing as a growth escalator in low and middle income countries', *Journal of Economics & Finance*, *44*(4): 790–809.

McAuley, J., Duberley, J. and Johnson, P. (2007) *Organizational Theory: Challenges and Perspectives*. Harlow: Pearson Education.

McAuley, M.J. (2003) 'Transference, countertransference and mentoring: The ghost in the process', *British Journal of Guidance and Counselling*, *31*: 11–24.

McCauley, C.D. and Hezlett, S.A. (2001) 'Individual development in the workplace', in N. Anderson, D. Ones, H.K. Sinangil and C. Viswesvaran (eds), *Handbook of Industrial, Work and Organizational Psychology*. London: SAGE, pp. 313–35.

McCauley, C.D., Moxley, R.S. and Van Velsor, E. (eds) (1998) *'What Leaders Read': Centre for Creative Leadership Handbook of Leadership Development*. San Francisco, CA: Jossey-Bass.

McComb, C. (2012) 'Developing coaching culture: Are your coaching relationships healthy?', *Industrial and Commercial Training*, *44*(4): 232–5.

McDonald, M.L. and Westphal, J.D. (2013) 'Access denied: Low mentoring of women and minority first-time directors and its negative effects on appointments to additional boards', *Academy of Management Journal*, *56*(4): 1169–98.

McElrath, M., Godat, L., Musson, J., Libow, J. and Graves, J. (2005) 'Improving supervisors' effectiveness: Mayo clinic finds answers through research', *Journal of Organizational Excellence*, Winter: 47–56.

McGovern, J., Lindemann, M., Vergara, M., Murphy, S., Barker, L. and Warrenfeltz, R. (2001) 'Maximizing the impact of executive coaching: Behavioral change, organizational outcomes, and return on investment', *The Manchester Review*, *6*(1): 1–9.

McGurk, J. (2012) *Coaching: The Evidence Base*. London: CIPD.

McIntosh, S. (2003) 'Work–life balance: How life coaching can help', *Business Information Review*, *20*(4): 181–9.

McKergow, M. and Clarke, J. (undated) 'Coaching with OSKAR: A solutions-focused approach to effective and sustainable change'. Available at: https://sfwork.com/pdf/Coaching%20 with%20OSKAR.pdf. (Accessed 14 September 2016).

McLeod, A. (2003) *Performance Coaching: A Handbook for Managers, HR Professionals and Coaches*. Bancyfelin, Carmarthen: Crown House.

McMahan, G. (2006) 'Doors of perception', *Coaching at Work*, *1*(6): 36–43.

Mecca, A.M. (2007) *Mentoring Works: California Programs Making a Difference*. California Mentoring Association, at www.californiamentorfoundation.org/scorecard (accessed May 2008).

Megginson, D. (1994) 'Planned and emergent learning: A framework and a method', *Executive Development*, *7*(6): 29–32.

Megginson, D. (1996) 'Planned and emergent learning: Consequences for development', *Management Learning*, *27*(4): 411–28. [Reprinted in C. Grey and E. Antonacopoulou (eds) (2004) *Essential Readings in Management Learning*. London: SAGE, pp. 91–106.]

Megginson, D. (2012) 'Who is setting the goalposts?', *Coaching at Work*, *7*(6): 57.

Megginson, D. and Boydell, T. (1979) *A Manager's Guide to Coaching*. London: BACIE.

Megginson, D. and Clutterbuck, D. (1995) *Mentoring in Action*. London: Kogan Page.

Megginson, D. and Clutterbuck, D. (2005a) *Techniques for Coaching and Mentoring*. Oxford: Butterworth-Heinemann.

Megginson, D. and Clutterbuck, D. (2005b) 'The meaning of success', *Training Magazine*, October: 19.

Megginson, D. and Clutterbuck, D. (2009) *Further Techniques for Coaching and Mentoring*. Oxford: Butterworth-Heinemann.

Megginson, D. and Stokes, P. (2004) 'Development and supervision for mentors', in D. Clutterbuck and G. Lane (eds), *The Situational Mentor: An International Review of Competences and Capabilities in Mentoring*. Aldershot: Gower, pp. 94–107.

Megginson, D., Clutterbuck, D., Garvey, B., Stokes, P. and Garrett-Harris, R. (2006) *Mentoring in Action*, 2nd edition. London: Kogan Page.

Megginson, D., Garrett-Harris, R. and Stokes, P. (2003a) *Business Link for London E-mentoring Scheme Conducted by Prevista.biz – for Small to Medium Enterprise (SME) Entrepreneurs/Managers*. Evaluation Report for Business Link London.

Megginson, D., Stokes, P. and Garrett-Harris, R. (2003b) *MentorsByNet – an E-mentoring Programme for Small to Medium Enterprise (SME) Entrepreneurs*. Evaluation Report on behalf of Business Link Surrey.

Meister, J.C. and Willyerd, K. (2010) 'Mentoring millennials', *Harvard Business Review*, 88(5): 68–72.

Melaku, T.M., Beeman, A., Smith, D.G. and Johnson, W.B. (2020) Be a better ally. *Harvard Business Review*, November - December https://hbr.org/2020/11/be-a-better-ally (accessed 21 June 20201).

Mental Health First Aid England (2020) Mental health statistics. Available at: https://mhfaengland.org/mhfa-centre/research-and-evaluation/mental-health-statistics/ (accessed 5 October 2020).

MENTOR (2013) *MENTOR's Mission*, at www.mentoring.org/about_mentor/mission (accessed May 2013).

Merrick, L. and Stokes, P. (2003) 'Mentor development and supervision: A passionate joint enquiry', *International Journal of Coaching and Mentoring* (e-journal), 1, at www.emccouncil.org.

Merrick, L. and Stokes, P. (2008) 'Unbreakable? Using mentoring to break the glass ceiling', *International Journal of Mentoring and Coaching* (e-journal), vi(2), at www.emccouncil.org.

Merrick, L. and Stokes, P. (2011) 'The Coach's Ego'. Paper presented at the European Mentoring & Coaching Council Conference, Paris, November 2011, https://www.emccglobal.org/conference/18th-annual-mentoring-and-coaching-conference/.

Merrick, L. and Stokes, P. (2021) 'Supervision in mentoring programmes', in T. Bachkirova, P. Jackson and D. Clutterbuck (eds) *Coaching and Mentoring Supervision: Theory & Practice*, 2nd edition. London: McGraw Hill, Ch. 27.

Meyerson, D. and Martin, J. (1987) 'Culture change: An integration of three different views', *Journal of Management Studies*, 24(6): 623–47.

Miller, A. (2002) *Mentoring Students and Young People: A Handbook of Effective Practice*. London: RoutledgeFalmer.

Mintzberg, H., Ahlstrand, B. and Lampel, J. (1998) *Strategy Safari: A Guided Tour through the Wilds of Strategic Management*. New York: Free Press.

Molloy, J.C. (2005) 'Developmental networks: literature review and future research', *Career Development International*, 10(6/7): 536–47.

Monaghan, J. and Lunt, N. (1992) 'Mentoring: Person, process, practice and problems', *British Journal of Educational Studies*, 40(3): 248–63.

Moran, M. (2014) *Identity and Capitalism*. London: SAGE.

Morel, D. (2019) 'How to engage your millennial workforce', *HR Magazine*, September, https://www.hrmagazine.co.uk/article-details/how-to-engage-your-millennial-workforce

Morgan, G. (1986) *Images of Organization*. Beverly Hills, CA: SAGE.

Morgan, G. (1993) *Imaginization: The Art of Creative Management*. Newbury Park, CA: SAGE.

Morgan, G. (2006) *Images of Organization*, 3rd edition. London: SAGE.

Morgan, H., Hawkins, P. and Goldsmith, M. (eds) (2005) *The Art and Practice of Leadership Coaching*. Hoboken, NJ: Wiley.

Morris, B. and Tarpley, N.A. (2000) 'So you're a player, do you need a coach?', *Fortune*, 141(4): 144–50.

Morrison, A., White, R., Velsor, E. and the Center for Creative Leadership (1994) *Breaking the Glass Ceiling: Can Women Reach the Top of America's Largest Corporations?* Reading, MA: Addison-Wesley.

Mukherjee, S (2012) 'Does coaching transform coaches? A case study of internal coaching', *International Journal of Evidence Based Coaching and Mentoring*, 10(2): 76–87.

Mulec, K. and Roth, J. (2005) 'Action, reflection, and learning: Coaching in order to enhance the performance of drug development project management teams', *R&D Management*, *35*(5): 483–91.

Mullen, C.A. (2007) 'Naturally occurring student-faculty mentoring relationships', in T.D. Allen and L.T. Eby (eds), *The Blackwell Handbook of Mentoring: A Multiple Perspectives Approach*. Oxford: Blackwell, pp. 119–38.

Murphy, W.M. (2011) 'From e-mentoring to blended mentoring: Increasing students' developmental initiation and mentors' satisfaction', *Academy of Management Learning and Education*, *10*(4): 604–22.

Murphy, W.M. (2012) 'Reverse mentoring at work: Fostering cross-generational learning and developing millennial leaders', *Human Resource Management*, *51*: 549–74.

Murray, E. (2004) 'Intuitive coaching: Summary', *Industrial and Commercial Training*, *36*(5): 203–6.

Nadeem, I. and Garvey, B. (2020) 'Learning experiences for academic deans: Implications for leadership coaching', *International Journal of Evidence Based Coaching and Mentoring*, *18*(2): 133–151.

Nadeem, I., Garvey, B. and Down, M. (2021) 'The adequacy of competency frameworks for coaching academic deans: A critical review', *International Journal of Evidence Based Coaching and Mentoring*.

Nakane, C. (1972) *Japanese Society*. Berkeley, CA: University of California Press.

Nankivell, C. and Shoolbred, M. (1997) 'Mentoring: A valuable tool for career development', *Librarian Career Development*, *5*(3): 98–104.

Natale, S.M. and Diamante, T. (2005) 'The five stages of executive coaching: Better process makes better practice', *Journal of Business Ethics*, *59*: 361–74.

Neck, C.P. and Houghton, J.D. (2006) 'Two decades of self-leadership theory and research', *Journal of Managerial Psychology*, *21*(4): 270–95.

Neff, T. and Citrin, J. (2005) *You're in Charge – Now What?* Bancyfelin, Carmarthen: Crown Business.

Neilson, T. and Eisenbach, R. (2003) 'Not all relationships are created equal: Critical actors of high-quality mentoring relationships', *International Journal of Mentoring and Coaching*, *1*(1).

Nelson, D.L. and Quick, J.C. (1985) 'Professional women: Are distress and disease inevitable?', *Academy of Management Review*, *10*(2): 206–18.

Niehoff, B.P. (2006) 'Personality predictors of participation as a mentor', *Career Development International*, *11*(4): 321–33.

Nielsen, A.E. and Nørreklit, H. (2009) 'A discourse analysis of the disciplinary power of management coaching', *Society and Business Review*, *4*(3): 202–14.

Nietzsche, F. (1974) *The Gay Science*. London: Vintage Books.

Nizet, J. and Fatien Diochon, P. (2012) 'Comprendre les ambiguïtés du coaching: L'apport du fonctionnalisme', *Gérer et Comprendre*, *1*(10): 24–33.

Noblit, G.W and Hare, R.D. (1988) *Meta-ethnography synthesizing qualitative studies*. Newbury Park, California: SAGE.

Noer, D.M., Leupold, C.R. and Valle, M. (2007) 'An analysis of Saudi Arabian and US coaching behaviours', *Journal of Managerial Issues*, *19*(2): 271–87.

Nonaka, I. (1991) 'The knowledge creating company', *Harvard Business Review*, Nov.–Dec.: 96–104.

Nonaka, I. (1996) 'The knowledge-creating company', in K. Starkey (ed.), *How Organisations Learn*. London: International Thompson Business Press, pp. 18–31.

Nonaka, I. and Horotaka, T. (1995) *The Knowledge-creating Company: How Japanese Companies Create the Dynamics of Innovation*. Oxford: Oxford University Press.

Northouse, P.G. (2019) *Leadership Theory and Practice*, 8th edition. London: SAGE.

O'Brien, J. (2020) *How Not to Be Wrong: The Art of Changing Your Mind*. London: Penguin.

O'Brien, K.E., Biga, A., Kessler, S.R. and Allen, T.D. (2010) 'A meta-analytic investigation of gender differences in mentoring', *Journal of Management*, 36(2): 537–54.

O'Neill, D.K. and Harris, J.B. (2004) 'Bridging the perspectives and developmental needs of all participants in curriculum-based telementoring programmes', *Journal of Research on Technology in Education*, 37(2): 111–28.

O'Neill, R.M. (2005) 'An examination of organizational predictors of mentoring functions', *Journal of Managerial Issues*, XVII(4): 439–60.

O'Sullivan, P., Smith, M. and Esposito, M. (2012) *Business Ethics: A Critical Approach – Integrating Ethics across the Business World*. London: Routledge.

Oliver, R. (2006) 'Purposive drift: Making it up as we go along', at http://changethis.com/manifesto/31.06.PurposiveDrift/pdf/31.06.PurposiveDrift.pdf (accessed 14 October 2013).

Olivero, G., Bane, K.D. and Kopelman, R.E. (1997) 'Executive coaching as a transfer of training tool: Effects on productivity in a public agency', *Public Personnel Management*, 26(4): 461–9.

Ordóñez, L.D., Schweitzer, M.E., Galinsky, A.E. and Bazerman, M.H. (2009) 'Goals gone wild: The systemic side effects of overprescribing goal setting', *Academy of Management Perspectives*, February: 6–16.

Owen, H. (1997) *Open Space Technology: A User's Guide*, 2nd edition. San Francisco, CA: Berrett-Koehler.

Oxford Reference Online (2006a) 'Mentor', at www.oxfordreference.com/search?q=mentor&searchBtn=Search&isQuickSearch=true (accessed 23 February 2006).

Oxford Reference Online (2006b) 'Coaching', at www.oxfordreference.com/search?q=coaching&searchBtn=Search&isQuickSearch=true (accessed 23 February 2006).

Oxford Reference Online (2006c) 'Protégé', at www.oxfordreference.com/search?q=protege&searchBtn=Search&isQuickSearch=true (accessed 23 February 2006).

Ozanne, J.L. and Saatcioglu, B. (2008) 'Participatory action research', *Journal of Consumer Research*, 5: 423–39.

Paik, Y., Chow, I.H. and Vance, C.M. (2011) 'Interaction effects of globalization and institutional forces on international HRM practice: Illuminating the convergence–divergence debate', *Thunderbird International Business Review*, 53(5): 647–59.

Palmer, S. and Williams, H. (2013) 'Cognitive Behavioral Approaches' in J. Passmore, D.B. Peterson and T. Freire (eds), *The Wiley-Blackwell Handbook of the Psychology of Coaching and Mentoring*. Chichester: John Wiley, pp. 319–338.

Parboteeah, K.P., Paik, Y. and Cullen, J. (2009) 'Religious groups and work values: A focus on Buddhism, Christianity, Hinduism, and Islam', *International Journal of Cross Cultural Management*, 9(1): 51–67.

Parise, M.R. and Forrett, M.L. (2008) 'Formal mentoring programs: The relationship of program design and support to mentors' perceptions of benefits and costs', *Journal of Vocational Behavior*, 72(2): 225–40.

Parker, K., Horowitz, J.M. and Anderson, M. (2020) 'Majorities across racial, ethnic groups express support for the Black Lives Matter movement', *Pew Research Center's Social & Demographic Trends Project*.

Parker-Wilkins, V. (2006) 'Business impact of executive coaching: Demonstrating monetary value', *Industrial and Commercial Training*, 38(3): 122–7.

Parliament.uk (2015) www.parliament.uk/business/publications/research/key-issues-parliament-2015/work/self-employment (accessed 3 March 2016).

Parsloe, E. (1992) *Coaching, Mentoring and Assessing*. London: Kogan Page.

Parsloe, E. and Leedham, M. (2009) *Coaching and Mentoring: Practical Conversations to Improve Learning*. London: Kogan Page.

Parsloe, E. and Wray, M. (2000) *Coaching and Mentoring: Practical Methods to Improve Learning*. London: Kogan Page.

Passmore, J. (2007) 'Coaching and mentoring: The role of experience and sector knowledge', *International Journal of Evidence based Coaching and Mentoring*. Special Issue 1: 10–16.

Passmore, J. (ed.) (2011) *Supervision in Coaching: Supervision, Ethics and Continuous Professional Development*. London: Kogan Page.

Passmore, J. and Fillery-Travis, A. (2011) 'A critical review of executive coaching research: A decade of progress and what's to come', *Coaching: An International Journal of Theory, Research and Practice*, 4(2): 70–88.

Passmore, J. and Tee, D. (2020) (eds) *Coaching Researched: A Coaching Psychology Reader for Practitioners and Researchers (BPS Textbooks in Psychology)*. London: John Wiley & Sons Ltd., Ch. 7: 113–139, Kindle Edition.

Passmore, J., Peterson, D.B. and Freire, T. (eds) (2013) *The Wiley-Blackwell Handbook of the Psychology of Coaching and Mentoring*. Chichester: John Wiley.

Pawson, R. and Tilley, N. (1997) *Realistic Evaluation*. London: SAGE.

Pearson, M. and Kayrooz, C. (2004) 'Enabling critical reflection on research supervisory practice', *International Journal for Academic Development*, 9(1): 99–116.

Peat, D.F. (1995) *Blackfoot Physics: A Journey into the Native American Universe*. London: Fourth Estate.

Pedler, M., Burgoyne, J. and Brook, C. (2005) 'What has action learning learned to become?', *Action Learning: Research and Practice*, 2(1): 49–68.

Pegg, M. (1999) 'The art of mentoring', *Industrial and Commercial Training*, 31(4): 136–41.

Pelham, G. (2016) *The Coaching Relationship in Practice*. London: SAGE.

Pemberton, C. (2006) *Coaching to Solutions: A Manager's Toolkit for Performance Delivery*. Oxford: Butterworth-Heinemann.

Perry, W.G. (1970) *Forms of Intellectual and Ethical Development in the College Years: A Scheme*. New York: Holt, Rinehart and Winston.

Peters, S. (2012) *The Chimp Paradox*. London: Ebury.

Peterson, D. and Hicks, M. (1999) 'Strategic coaching: Five ways to get most value', *HR Focus*, February: 57–8.

Petty, T., Good, A. and Putman, S. (2016) *Handbook of Research on Professional Development for Quality Teaching and Learning*. Hershey, PA: IGI Global.

Pfeffer, J. (1995) 'Producing sustainable competitive advantage through the effective management of people', *Academy of Management Executive*, 9(1): 55–69.

Pfeffer, J. (1997) *New Directions for Organization Theory: Problems and Prospects*. New York: Oxford University Press.

Phillips, A. (1995) *Terrors and Experts*. London: Faber.

Phillips, A. (2007) 'After Strachey', *London Review of Books*, 4 October: 36–8.

Phillips, R. (1996) 'Coaching for higher performance', *Employee Counselling Today*, 8(4): 29–32.

Pickstone, J.V. (2000) *Ways of Knowing: A New History of Science Technology and Medicine*. Manchester: Manchester University Press.

Plato (1989) *The Symposium*. Trans. A. Nehamas and P. Woodruff (HPC Classics Series). Indianapolis, IN: Hackett.

Plato (1997) *The Republic*. Trans J. Davies and D. Vaughan. London: Wordsworth Classics.

Plato (2004) *The Trial and Death of Socrates*. Trans. B. Jowett, intro. D. Taffel. New York: Barnes and Noble.

Platt, G. (2001) 'NLP – no longer plausible', *Training Journal*, May: 10–15.

Porter, M., Lorsh, J. and Nohria, N. (2004) 'Seven surprises for new CEOs', *Harvard Business Review*, *82*(10): 62–72.

Post, D. (2006) 'Important flight parameters in the shot put', *Track Coach*, *175*: 5601–2.

Potrac, P., Jones, R. and Armour, K. (2002) 'It's all about getting respect: The coaching behaviours of an expert English soccer coach', *Sport, Education and Society*, *7*(2): 183–202.

Pulijala, Y., Pears, M., Ma, M. and Peebles, D. (2018) 'Effectiveness of immersive virtual reality in surgical training – A randomized controlled trial', *Journal of Oral Maxillofacial Surgery*, *76*(5): 1065–72.

Ragins, B.R. (1997) 'Diversified mentoring relationships in organizations: A power perspective', *Academy of Management Review*, *22*(2): 482–521.

Ragins, B.R. (2012) 'Relational mentoring: A positive approach to mentoring at work', in K. Cameron and G. Spreitzer (eds) *The Handbook of Positive Organizational Scholarship*. New York: Oxford University Press, pp. 519–36.

Ragins, B.R. and Cotton, J.L. (1999) 'Mentor functions and outcomes: A comparison of men and women in formal and informal mentoring relationships', *Journal of Applied Psychology*, *84*: 529–50.

Ragins, B.R. and Kram, K.E. (eds) (2007) *The Handbook of Mentoring at Work: Theory, Research, and Practice*. Thousand Oaks, CA: SAGE.

Ragins, B.R. and Verbos, A. (2007) 'Positive relationships in action: Relational mentoring and mentoring schemas in the workplace', in J. Dutton and B.R. Ragins (eds) *Exploring Positive Relationships at Work: Building a Theoretical and Research Foundation*. Mahwah, NJ: Lawrence Erlbaum and Associates, pp. 91–116.

Rajasinghe, D.R. (2018) *Leadership development through executive coaching: An interpretative phenomenological analysis*. Unpublished PhD, University of Leeds, UK.

Ramaswami, A. and Dreher, G.F. (2010) 'Dynamics of mentoring relationships in India: A qualitative exploratory study', *Human Resource Management*, *49*(3): 501–30.

Reissman, C. K. (2008) *Narrative Methods for the Human Sciences*. California: SAGE.

Reissner, S.C. and Du Toit, A. (2011) 'Power and the tale: Coaching as storyselling', *Journal of Management Development*, *30*(3): 247–59.

Rettinger, S. (2011) 'Construction and display of competence and (professional) identity in coaching interactions', *Journal of Business Communication*, *28*(4): 426–45.

Revans, R.W. (1983) *ABC of Action Learning*. London: Lemos and Crane.

Reynolds, J., Caley, L. and Mason, R. (2002) *How Do People Learn?* London: CIPD.

Rhodes, J.E., Reddy, R. and Grossman, J.B. (2005) 'The protective influence of mentoring on adolescents' substance use: Direct and indirect pathways', *Applied Developmental Science*, *9*(1): 31–47.

Ridler and Co. (2011) *Ridler Report 2011: Trends in the Use of Executive Coaching*, at www.ridlerandco.com/ridler-report-2011-trends-in-the-use-of-executive-coaching.pdf (accessed 3 October 2013).

Ridler and Co. (2013) *Ridler Report 2013: Executive Coaching Rides Recession*, at www.ridlerandco.com/ridler-report-2013-executive-coaching-rides-recession.pdf (accessed 3 October 2013).

Ridler and Co. (2016) *Ridler Report 2016: Strategic Trends in the Use of Coaching*, at www.ridlerandco.com/ridler-report-2016-strategic-trends-in-the-use-of-coaching.pdf (accessed 1 October 2016).

Rigsby, J.T., Siegal, P.H. and Spiceland, J.D. (1998) 'Mentoring among management advisory services professionals: An adaptive mechanism to cope with rapid corporate change', *Managerial Auditing Journal*, *13*(2): 107–16.

Riley, P. (1994) *Fénelon – Telemachus*. Cambridge: Cambridge University Press.

Roberts, A. (1999) Homer's Mentor: Duties fulfilled or misconstrued. Available at: www.nickols. us/homers_mentor.pdf (accessed 9 October 2016).

Roberts, R.H. Sir (1887) *In the Shires*. Southampton: F.W. Waite and Co.

Robertson, L. (2005) 'The cost of missed opportunities', *Strategic Communication Management*, *9*(3): 5.

Robinson, J. (2005) 'GROWing service improvement within the NHS', *International Journal of Mentoring and Coaching*, *III*(1): 87–91.

Rogers, C.R. (1961) *A Therapist's View of Psychotherapy: On Becoming a Person*. London: Constable and Co.

Rogers, C.R. (1969) *Freedom to Learn*. Columbus, OH: Merrill.

Rogers, J. (2012) *Coaching Skills: A Handbook*, 2nd edition. Milton Keynes: Open University Press.

Rollag, K. (2007) 'Defining the term "new" in new employee research', *Journal of Occupational and Organizational Psychology*, *80*(1): 63–75.

Rorty, R. (1989) *Contingency, Irony and Solidarity*. Cambridge: Cambridge University Press.

Rose, N. (1999) *Governing the Soul: The Shaping of the Private Self*, 2nd edition. London: Free Association Books.

Rosinski, P. (2003) *Coaching across Cultures*. London: Nicholas Brealey.

Rousseau, D.M. (1989) 'Psychological and implied contracts in organizations', *Employee Responsibilities and Rights Journal*, *2*(2): 121–39.

Rousseau, D.M. (1995) *Psychological Contracts in Organizations: Understanding Written and Unwritten Agreements*. Newbury Park, CA: SAGE.

Rousseau, J.-J. (1762) *Emile*. Auckland: Floating Press.

Rowan, J. (2010) 'The transpersonal approach to coaching', in E. Cox, T. Bachkirova and D. Clutterbuck (eds), *The Complete Handbook of Coaching*. London: SAGE, pp. 146–57.

Rudolph, C. W., & Zacher, H. (2017) 'Considering Generations From a Lifespan Developmental Perspective', *Work, Aging and Retirement*, *3*(2): 113–129.

Ruona, W.E.A. and Lynham, S.A. (2004) 'A philosophical framework for thought and practice in human resource development', *Human Resource Development International*, *7*(2): 151–64.

Russell, B. (1998) *The Philosophy of Logical Atomism* (reprint). La Salle, IL: Open Court.

Russell, B. (2009) *Mortals and Others: American Essays 1931–1935* (reprint). Abingdon, UK: Routledge Classics.

Ryder, N. B. (1965) 'The cohort in the study of social change,' *American Sociological Review*, *30* (6): 843–861.

Salimbene, F., Buono, A.F., Van Steenberg Lafarge, V. and Nurick, A.J. (2005) 'Service-learning and management education: The Bentley experience', *Academy of Management Learning and Education*, *4*(3): 336–44.

Samier, E. (2000) 'Public administration mentorship: Conceptual and pragmatic considerations', *Journal of Educational Administration*, *38*(1): 83–101.

Saul, J.R. (1997) *The Unconscious Civilization*. London: Penguin.

Scandura, T. (1998) 'Dysfunctional mentoring relationships and outcomes', *Journal of Management*, *24*: 449–67.

Scandura, T., Tejeda, M., Werther, B. and Lankau, M. (1996) 'Perspectives on mentoring', *Leadership and Organization Development Journal*, *17*(3): 50–6.

Scarbrough, H., Swan, J. and Preston, J. (1999) *Knowledge Management: A Literature Review*. London: IPD.

Schein, E.H. (1985) *Organizational Culture and Leadership*. San Francisco, CA: Jossey-Bass.

Schön, D.A. (1987) *Educating the Reflective Practitioner: Towards a New Design for Teaching and Learning in the Profession*. San Francisco, CA: Jossey-Bass.

Schön, D.A (1991) *The Reflective Practitioner: How Professionals Think in Action*. Aldershot: Ashgate Arena.

Schostak, J.F. (2002) *Understanding, Designing and Conducting Qualitative Research in Education*. Buckingham: Open University Press.

Schwabenland, C. (2015) 'Discursive strategies for navigating the terrain between the sacred and the profane', *Culture and Organisation*, *21*(1): 59–97.

Schwartz, J.P., Thigpen, S.E. and Montgomery, J.K. (2006) 'Examination of parenting styles of processing emotions and differentiation of self', *Family Journal: Counselling and Therapy for Couples and Families*, *14*(1): 41–8.

Schwartz, M. (2000) 'Why ethical codes constitute an unconscious regression?', *Journal of Business Ethics*, *23*: 173–84.

Segerman-Peck, L. (1991) *Networking and Mentoring: A Woman's Guide*. London: Piatkus.

Seibert, S. (1999) 'The effectiveness of facilitated mentoring: A longitudinal quasi-experiment', *Journal of Vocational Behavior*, *54*: 483–502.

Self, T.T., Gordon S. and Jolly, P.M. (2019) Talent management: A Delphi study of assessing and developing GenZ hospitality leaders. *International Journal of Contemporary Hospitality Management*, *31*(10): 4126–4149. doi:10.1108/IJCHM-11-2018-0915.

Seligman, M. (2008) *Authentic Happiness*. London: Nicholas Brealey.

Seligman, M. (2011) *Flourish*. London: Nicholas Brealey.

Senge, P.M. (1992) *The Fifth Discipline*. Chatham: Century Business.

Sennett, R. (1998) *The Corrosion of Character: The Personal Consequences of Work in the New Capitalism*. New York: W.W. Norton.

Shaw, P. (2002) *Changing Conversations in Organizations: A Complexity Approach to Change*. London: Routledge.

Shearing, C. (2001) 'Punishment and the changing face of the governance', *Punishment & Society*, *3*(2): 203–20.

Sheehy, G. (1974) *Passages: Predictable Crises of Adult Life*. New York: E.P. Dutton.

Sheehy, G. (1996) *New Passages: Mapping Your Life across Time*. London: HarperCollins.

Sheehy, G. (2006) *Passages: Predictable Crises of Adult Life*, 2nd edition. New York: Ballantine Books.

Shen, Y., Cotton, R.D., and Kram, K.E. (2015) 'Assembling your personal board of advisors', *MIT Sloan Management Review*, *56*(3), at https://sloanreview.mit.edu/article/assembling-your-personal-board-of-advisors/ (accessed April 2021).

Sherman, S. and Freas, A. (2004) 'The Wild West of executive coaching', *Harvard Business Review*, *82*(11): 82–90.

Sherpa Coaching (2016) *Executive Coaching Survey, 11th Annual*. Cincinnati, OH: Sherpa Coaching.

Shoukry, H. (2016) 'Coaching for social change', in T. Bachkirova, G. Spence and D. Drake (eds), *The SAGE Handbook of Coaching*. London: SAGE, pp. 181–96.

Shoukry, H. and Cox, E. (2018) Coaching as a social process. *Management Learning*, *49*(4): 413–428. https://doi.org/10.1177/1350507618762600

Sieler, A. (2003) *Coaching to the Human Soul: Ontological Coaching and Deep Change*. Melbourne, Australia: Newfield.

Simmel, G. (1950) *The Sociology of Georg Simmel*, ed. K.H. Wolff. New York: Free Press.

Sinek, S. (2017) Millennials in the workforce: A generation of weakness, https://www.youtube.com/watch?v=QXWNChoIIuo

Smedley, F. (1866) *Frank Farleigh; or Scenes from the Life of a Private Pupil*. London: Virtue Brothers and Co.

Smith, I.M. and Brummel, B.J. (2013) 'Investigating the role of active ingredients in executive coaching', *Coaching: An International Journal of Theory, Research and Practice*, *6*(1): 57–71.

Smith, J.A., Flowers, P. and Larkin, M (2009) *Interpretative Phenomenological Analysis: Theory, Method and Research*, London: Sage.

Smith, P.B., Peterson, M.F. and Schwartz, S.H. (2002) 'Cultural values, sources of guidance and their relevance to managerial behavior: A 47-nation study', *Journal of Cross-Cultural Psychology*, *33*: 188–208.

Smither, J.W., London, M., Flautt, R., Vargas, Y. and Kucrie, I. (2003) 'Can working with an executive coach improve multisource feedback ratings over time? A quasi-experimental field study', *Personnel Psychology*, *56*(1): 23–44.

Society for Industrial and Organizational Psychology (2013) Workplace Topics: Introduction to coaching, at www.siop.org/Workplace/coaching/introduction.aspx (accessed 18 April 2013).

Sopher, C.J., Adamson, B.J.S., Andrasik, M.P., Flood, D.M., Wakefield, S.F., Stoff, D.M., et al. (2015) 'Enhancing diversity in the public health research workforce: The research and mentorship program for future HIV vaccine scientists', *American Journal of Public Health*, *105*(4): 823–30.

Sosik, J.J. and Godshalk, V.M. (2005) 'Examining gender similarity and mentor's supervisory status in mentoring relationships', *Mentoring and Tutoring*, *13*(1): 39–52.

South Yorkshire Police (SYP) (2016) South Yorkshire Police workforce monitoring reports, at www.southyorks.police.uk/content/equality-and-diversity (accessed 20 October 2016).

Sparrow, S. (2007) 'Model behaviour', *Training and Coaching Today*, April: 24–5.

Speizer, J.J. (1981) 'Role models, mentors and sponsors: The elusive concepts', *Journal of Women in Culture*, *6*(4): 692–712.

Spinelli, E. (2010) 'Existential coaching', in E. Cox, T. Bachkirova and D. Clutterbuck (eds), *The Complete Handbook of Coaching*. London: SAGE, pp. 94–106.

Spoth, J., Toman, S., Leitchman, R. and Allen, J. (2013) 'Narrative approaches', in J. Passmore, D.B. Peterson and T. Freire (eds), *The Wiley-Blackwell Handbook of the Psychology of Coaching and Mentoring*. Chichester: John Wiley, pp. 385–406.

Spreier, S.W., Fontaine, M.M. and Mallery, R.L. (2006) 'Leadership run amok', *Harvard Business Review*, *84*(6): 72–82.

St John-Brooks, K. (2013) *Internal Coaching: The Inside Story*. London: Karnac.

Stacey, R.D. (1995) 'The science of complexity: An alternative perspective for strategic change processes', *Strategic Management Journal*, *16*(4): 77–95.

Stake, R.E. (2004) 'Case studies', in N.K. Denzin and Y.S. Lincoln (eds), *Strategies of Qualitative Inquiry*. London: SAGE, pp. 88–109.

Starr, J. (2008) *The Coaching Manual: The Definitive Guide to the Process, Principles and Skills of Personal Coaching*. London: Pearson.

Starr, J. (2014) *The Mentoring Manual: A Step by Step Guide to Becoming a Better Mentor*. Harlow: Pearson Education.

Stein, J. (2013) 'Millennials: The me me me generation', *Time Magazine*, http://time.com/247/millennials-the-me-me-me-generation/

Stelter, R. (2013) 'Positive psychology approaches', in J. Passmore, D.B. Peterson and T. Freire (eds), *The Wiley-Blackwell Handbook of the Psychology of Coaching and Mentoring*. Chichester: John Wiley, pp. 426–42.

Stelter, R. (2019) *The Art of Coaching Dialogue: Towards Transformative Exchange*. Abingdon, Oxon: Routledge

Stern, L. and Stout-Rostron, S. (2013) 'What progress has been made in coaching research in relation to 16 ICRF focus areas from 2008 to 2012?', *Coaching: An International Journal of Theory, Research and Practice*, *6*(1): 72–96.

Stevens, J.A. and Kincaid, J. P. (2015) 'The relationship between presence and performance in virtual simulation training', *Open Journal of Modelling and Simulation*, *3*: 41–8.

Stokes, P. (2007) 'The Skilled Coachee.' Paper presented at the European Mentoring and Coaching Conference, Stockholm, October. Proceedings available at www.emcc.org.

Stokes, P., Fatien Diochon, P. and Otter, K. (2020) 'Two sides of the same coin? Coaching and mentoring and the agentic role of context', *Annals of the New York Academy of Sciences*, at: https://www.ncbi.nlm.nih.gov/pubmed/32083348

Stone, I.F. (1988) *The Trial of Socrates*. Boston, MA: Little, Brown.

Strauss, W. and Howe, N. (1991), *Generations: The History of America's Future, 1584 to 2069*, USA, Harper Perennial.

Style, C. and Boniwell, I. (2010) 'The effect of group based life coaching on happiness and wellbeing', *Groupwork*, *20*(3): 51–72.

Sy, T. and Côte, S. (2004) 'Emotional intelligence: A key ability to succeed in the matrix organization', *Journal of Management Development*, *23*(5): 437–55.

Tabbron, A., Macaulay, S. and Cook, S. (1997) 'Making mentoring work', *Training for Quality*, *5*(1): 6–9.

Tenbrunsel, A.E. and Messick, D.M. (2004) 'Ethical fading: The role of self-deception in unethical behavior', *Social Justice Research*, *17*: 223–36.

Tharenou, P. (2005) 'Does mentor support increase women's career advancement more than men's? The differential effects of career and psychosocial support', *Australian Journal of Management*, *30*(1): 77–109.

Thomas, D.A. and Gabarro, J.J. (1999) *Breaking Through: The Making of Minority Executives in Corporate America*. Boston, MA: Harvard Business School Press.

Thomas, E. L. (2020) Fast company, at https://www.fastcompany.com/90369924/the-effectiveness-of-blind-recruitment (accessed August 2020).

Tickle, L. (1993) 'The wish of Odysseus?', in D. MacIntyre, H. Hagger and M. Wilkin (eds), *Mentoring: Perspectives on School Based Teacher Education*. London: Kogan Page.

Tobias, L.L. (1996) 'Coaching executives', *Consulting Psychology Journal: Practice and Research*, *48*(2): 87–95.

Toffler, A. (1970) *Future Shock*. Oxford: The Bodley Head.

Torrance, E.P. (1984) *Mentor Relationships: How They Aid Creative Achievement, Endure, Change and Die*. Buffalo, NY: Bearly.

Townley, B. (1994) *Reframing Human Resource Management: Power, Ethics and the Subject at Work*. London: SAGE.

Townley, B. (2008) *Reason's Neglect*. Oxford: Oxford University Press.

Trevitt, C. (2005) 'Universities learning to learn? Inventing flexible (e)learning through first- and second-order action research', *Educational Action Research*, *13*(1): 57–83.

Tucker, R. (2005) 'Is coaching worth the money? Assessing the ROI of executive coaching', in H. Morgan, P. Hawkins and M. Goldsmith (eds), *The Art and Practice of Leadership Coaching*. Hoboken, NJ: Wiley, pp. 245–54.

Turban, D. and Dougherty, T. (1994) 'Role of protégé personality in receipt of mentoring and career success', *Academy of Management Journal*, *37*(3): 688–702.

Turner, B. and Chelladurai, P. (2005) 'Organizational and occupational commitment, intention to leave and perceived performance of intercollegiate coaches', *Journal of Sports Management*, *19*: 193–211.

Tyson, L. (2012) 'US jobs data reveals economy is bouncing back strongly from recession', *The Guardian Online*, 17 October, at www.guardian.co.uk/business/2012/oct/17/us-employment-data-recession-recovery (accessed 30 December 2012).

US Census Bureau (2005) *Fact Sheet for Race, Ethnic, Ancestry Group*, at http://factfinder.census.gov (accessed 1 May 2007).

Van Emmerik, H. (2008) 'Influences of individual-level and team-level support on job performance', *Career Development International*, *13*(7): 575–93.

Van Emmerik, H., Baugh, S.G. and Euwema, M.C. (2005) 'Who wants to be a mentor? An examination of attitudinal, instrumental, and social motivational components', *Career Development International*, *10*(4): 310–24.

Venkatesh, U. (2019) COACHING INDUSTRY - STATISTICS!!, LinkedIn, 11 September. Available at: https://www.linkedin.com/pulse/coaching-industry-statistics-umesh-venkatesh/ (accessed 20 November 2020).

Vermaak, H. and Weggeman, M. (1999) 'Conspiring fruitfully with professionals: New management roles for professional organizations', *Management Decision*, *37*(1): 29–44.

Von Krogh, G., Roos, J. and Slocum, K. (1994) 'An essay on corporate epistemology', *Strategic Management Journal*, *15*: 53–71.

Vygotsky, L.S. (1978) *Mind in Society: The Development of Higher Psychological Processes*. Cambridge, MA: Harvard University Press.

Wagstaff, C., Jeong, H., Nolan, M., Wilson, T., Tweedlie, J., Phillips, E., and Holland, F. (2014) The Accordion and the Deep Bowl of Spaghetti: Eight Researchers' Experiences of Using IPA as a Methodology. *Qualitative Report*, *19*(24): 1–15.

Wanberg, C.R., Welsh, L. and Hezlett, S. (2003) 'Mentoring: A review and directions for future research', in J. Martocchio and J. Ferris (eds), *Research in Personnel and Human Resources Management*, vol. *22*. Oxford: Elsevier Science, pp. 39–124.

Warr, P., Bird, M. and Rackham, N. (1978) *Evaluation of Management Training*. London: Gower.

Wasylyshyn, K.M. (2003) 'Executive coaching: An outcome study', *Consulting Psychology Journal: Practice and Research*, *55*(2): 94–106.

Watkins, M. (2005) *The First 90 Days*. Boston, MA: Harvard Business School Press.

Watts, R.E. and Pietrzak, D. (2000) 'Alderian encouragement and the therapeutic process of solution-focused brief therapy', *Journal of Counselling and Development*, Fall: 442–7.

Webster, F. (1980) *The New Photography: Responsibility in Visual Communication*. London: John Calder.

Weer, C.H., DiRenzo, M.S. and Shipper, F.M. (2016) 'A holistic view of employee coaching: longitudinal investigation of the impact of facilitative and pressure based coaching on team effectiveness', *Journal of Applied Behavioural Science*, *52*(2): 187–214.

Weick, K. (1995) *Sensemaking in Organizations*. London: SAGE.

Weisbord, M. and Janoff, S. (1995) *Future Search: An Action Guide to Finding Common Ground in Organizations and Communities*. San Francisco, CA: Berrett-Koehler.

Welman, P. and Bachkirova, T. (2010) 'Power in the coaching relationship', in S. Palmer and A. McDowall (eds), *The Coaching Relationship: Putting People First*. Hove: Routledge, pp. 139–58.

Wenson, J.E. (2010) 'PERSPECTIVES: After-coaching leadership skills and their impact on direct reports – recommendations for organizations', *Human Resource Development International*, *13*(5): 607–16.

Western, S. (2012) *Coaching and Mentoring: A Critical Text*. London: SAGE.

Western, S. (2017) 'The key discourses of coaching', in T. Bachkirova, G. Spence and D. Drake (eds), *The SAGE Handbook of Coaching*. London: SAGE, pp. 42–61.

Western, S. (2020) 'Covid-19 an intrusion of the real: The unconscious unleashes its truth', at https://www.academia.edu/42201252/Covid19_An_intrusion_of_the_Real_The_unconscious_unleashes_its_Truth

Whitehill, A.M. (1991) *Japanese Management: Tradition and Transition*. London: Routledge.

Whitmore, J. (2002) *Coaching for Performance: GROWing People, Performance and Purpose*, 3rd edition. London: Nicholas Brealey.

Whitmore, J. (2009) *Coaching for Performance: Growing Human Potential and Purpose*, 4th edition. London: Nicholas Brealey.

Whittington, J. (2020) *Systemic Coaching and Constellations: The Principles, Practices and Application for Individuals, Teams and Groups*, 3rd edition. London: Kogan Page.

Whitworth, L., Kimsey-House, H. and Sandhal, P. (1998) *Co-active Coaching: New Skills for Coaching People toward Success in Work and Life*. New York: Davies-Black.

Wiginton, J.G. and Cartwright, P.A. (2019) 'Evidence on the impacts of business coaching', *Journal of Management Development*, *39*(2): 163–80.

Wild, A. (2001) 'Coaching the coaches, to develop teams, to accelerate the pace of change', *Industrial and Commercial Training*, *33*(5): 161–6.

Wildflower, L. (2013) *The Hidden History of Coaching*. Maidenhead: McGraw-Hill.

Williams, H. and Palmer, S. (2020) 'Coaching during the COVID-19 pandemic: Application of the CLARITY solution-focused cognitive behavioral model', *International Journal of Coaching Psychology*, *1*(2): 1–11.

Williams, H., Edgerton, N. and Palmer, S. (2010) 'Cognitive behavioural coaching', in E. Cox, T. Bachkirova and D. Clutterbuck (eds), *The Complete Handbook of Coaching*. London: SAGE, pp. 37–53.

Willis, P. (2005) *European Mentoring and Coaching Council, Competency Research Project: Phase 2*, June. Watford: EMCC.

Wilson, C. (2004) 'Coaching and coach training in the workplace', *Industrial and Commercial Training*, *36*(3): 96–8.

Wilson, C. (2011) 'Developing a coaching culture', *Industrial and Commercial Training*, *43*(7), 407–14.

Wilson, J.A. and Elman, N.S. (1990) 'Organisational benefits of mentoring', *Academy of Management Executive*, *4*: 88–94.

Wong, S.C., Rasdi, R.M., Samah, B.A. and Wahat, N.W.A. (2017) 'Promoting protean career through employability culture and mentoring', *European Journal of Training and Development*, *41*(3): 277–302.

Wood, L.A. and Kroger, R.O. (2000) *Doing Discourse Analysis*. Thousand Oaks, CA: SAGE.

The World Bank (2016) Uganda Economic Update: Fact Sheet, 6 June. Available at: https://www.worldbank.org/en/country/uganda/brief/uganda-economic-update-fact-sheet-june-2016 (accessed 19 June 2021).

Yates, K. (2015a) 'Managing, tracking and evaluating coaching Part 1: Where are you now?', *Industrial and Commercial Training*, *47*(1): 36–41.

Yates, K. (2015b) 'Managing, tracking and evaluating coaching Part 2: Where could you be?', *Industrial and Commercial Training*, *47*(2): 95–8.

Young, A.M. and Perrewé, P.L. (2004) 'The role of expectations in the mentoring exchange: An analysis of mentor and protégé expectations in relation to perceived support', *Journal of Managerial Issues*, *XVI*(1): 103–26.

Youth Mentoring (2007) Home page, at www.youthmentoring.org (accessed 1 May 2008).

Zeus, P. and Skiffington, S. (2000) *The Complete Guide to Coaching at Work*. Sydney: McGraw-Hill.

Zeus, P. and Skiffington, S. (2002) *The Coaching at Work Toolkit*. Roseville, NSW: McGraw-Hill.

Zey, M.G. (1989) 'Building a successful formal mentor program', *Mentoring International*, *3*(1): 48–51.

Zhang, K., Chen, J., Suo, J., Chen, J., Liu, X. and Gao, L. (2017) '*Design and implementation of fire safety education system on campus based on virtual reality technology*', 2017 Federation Conference on Computer Science and Information Systems (Fed CSIS), Prague. Czech Republic.

Zimmerman, D.H. (1998) 'Identity, context and interaction', in C. Antaki and S. Widdicombe (eds), *Identities in Talk*. London: SAGE, pp. 87–106.

Žižek, S. (2008) *Violence*. London: Profile.

Zuboff, S. (1988) *In the Age of the Smart Machine: The Future of Work and Power*. New York: Basic Books.

# INDEX

Page numbers in *italics* refer to Figures and Tables.